FASCISM AND THE
MAFIA

Christopher Duggan

FASCISM AND THE MAFIA

Yale University Press
New Haven and London
1989

PHOTOGRAPHIC ACKNOWLEDGEMENTS

Pl. 1, Chatto and Windus, London. Pl. 2, Giorgio Forattini, La Repubblica. Pl. 3, Editore Capelli, Bologna. Pl. 4, Publifoto, Palermo. Pls. 5–7, 12, 20, Professor Giuseppe Tricoli. Pls. 8–10, 13–18, 21, Mondadori, Milan. Pl. 11, © 1971, Shenkman Pub Co, Inc, Vermont. Pl. 19, Fondazione Whitaker, Palermo. Jacket image, Foto Saporetti, Milan.

Map by Liz Bowles

Designed by Elaine Collins

Set in Linotron Bembo by Best-set Typesetter Ltd, Hong Kong

Printed and bound in Great Britain at The Bath Press, Avon

Library of Congress Cataloging-in-Publication Data

Duggan, Christopher
  Fascism and the Mafia/Christopher Duggan,
    p. cm.
  Bibliography: p.
  Includes index.
  ISBN 0-300-04372-4
  1. Mafia – Italy – Sicily – History.   2. Fascism – Italy – Sicily –
History.   3. Sicily – History – 1860–1945.   I. Title.
HV6453.I83M327   1989
364.1′06′0458–dc19

For Denis Mack Smith

CONTENTS

PART I

PART II

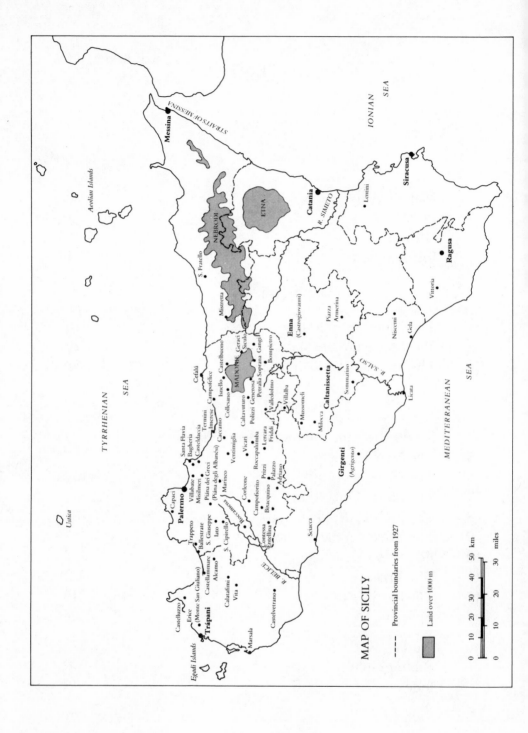

MAP OF SICILY

- - - Provincial boundaries from 1927

▨ Land over 1000 m

0 10 20 30 40 50 km

0   10   20   30 miles

IONIAN SEA

TYRRHENIAN SEA

MEDITERRANEAN SEA

STRAITS OF MESSINA

Messina

Siracusa

Catania

R. SIMETO

Ragusa

Lentini

Vittoria

ETNA

NEBRODI

MADONIE

Enna
(Castrogiovanni)

Piazza
Armerina

Niscemi

Gela

Licata

R. SALSO

Caltanissetta

Sommatino

Milocca

Mussomeli

Girgenti
(Agrigento)

Sciacca

Villalba

Valledolmo

Bompietro

Petralia Soprana Gangi

Polizzi Generosa

Friddi

Lercara

Prizzi

Adriano

Palazzo

Bisacquino

Campofiorito

Corleone

Roccapalumba

Vicari

Ventimiglia

Caccamo

Collesano

Castelbuono

Caltavuturo

Ianello

Geraci
Siculo

Mistretta

S. Fratello

Cefalù

Campofelice

Termini

Imerese

Casteldaccia

Bagheria

Santa Flavia

Palermo

Capaci

Villabate

Misilmeri

Piana degli Albanesi)

Piana dei Greci

S. Marmeo

Iato

S. Giuseppe

S. Cipirello

Contessa
Entellina

R. BELICE

Ballestrate

Trappeto

Castellammare

Alcamo

Vita

Calatafimi

(Monte San Giuliano)

Erice

Castelluzzo

Trapani

Egadi Islands

Marsala

Castelvetrano

Ustia

Aeolian Islands

R. SOSANNAR

PREFACE

This is a study, not of an organisation, but of an idea. Every serious writer on Sicily, beginning with Romualdo Bonfadini in 1876, has agreed that 'the mafia' was not a secret society, but a 'way of life' or an 'attitude of mind'. Nevertheless, belief in a large-scale criminal association has continued to this day. My aim in this book is to suggest why this should be. I have concentrated on the period between 1860 and 1945 as post-war developments deserve separate treatment. But, as I hope I make clear, I see no reason to suppose that anything significant has changed in the last forty years. The recent testimony of Tommaso Buscetta is less novel than has been alleged, and his account of Cosa Nostra should be seen against a background of more than a century of similar (if often less detailed) 'revelations'. I have said little about the situation in the United States, except when it seems to have impinged on the idea of the mafia in Italy. However, as I have suggested in the Introduction, belief in a Sicilian secret society was no less ill-founded here than on the other side of the Atlantic.

The book is divided into two parts. In the first, I try to explain how the idea of the mafia in Sicily developed after 1860. My approach has been to consider the problem from several different angles, as I feel that it was a combination of factors that generated belief in a criminal organisation. I begin with a discussion of the meaning and etymology of the word 'mafia', as a good deal of confusion has been caused by misuse and misunderstanding of this term. I also look briefly at how the idea of the Neapolitan *camorra* influenced perceptions of the mafia. I then consider how the concept of the mafia was used to explain the political and social unrest in the island after 1860. This is followed by a discussion of those character-istics of Sicilian society that seemed both enigmatic and unacceptable to the new liberal state, and that contributed to the idea of a criminal organisation. These characteristics included *omertà* and the belief in personal justice.

The second part of the book is a detailed study of the campaign conducted by the fascist government against the mafia between 1925 and 1929. This is the most famous operation of its kind, and in recent years it has been the subject of a good deal of nostalgic recollection by those who see the answer to Sicily's problems in resolute police action unhampered by political interference. My intention in this section is to illustrate some of the general observations made in the first part. I hope to show the extent of the gap between the official view of the mafia as a criminal organisation and the more complex reality. I also wish to illustrate how the idea of a secret association was exploited for political ends. In the Epilogue I discuss Sicily in the 1930s and during the Second World War, a period of the island's history that has received too little attention, given the extraordinary outburst of separatist feeling after the collapse of fascism.

This book began as a doctoral dissertation which was submitted in 1985. Most of the second part is a revised version of the thesis. The research was conducted over a period of several years, chiefly in Pavia (where the private papers of Cesare Mori are held), Rome, and Sicily. In the course of my work I have incurred debts to many individuals and institutions, and my gratitude to them is enormous. I should like to thank the Warden and Fellows of All Souls College, Oxford, and the President and Fellows of Wolfson College, for their support, both financial and academic. The Fondazione Einaudi in Turin generously gave me a scholarship in 1981–2 which permitted me to spend longer abroad than would otherwise have been possible. I am grateful to the assistants at the state archives in Pavia, Palermo, and Rome, for their considerable help.

My debts to individuals are legion, and many of the people I encountered in the course of my research have since become friends and colleagues. I am particularly grateful to Totò Benavoli, and to all those who made my stay at Pavia so enjoyable. In Palermo, Giovanna Fiume and Renata Zanca Pucci have been unstinting in their hospitality and kindness. Francesco Brancato, Marcello Cimino, Giuseppe Carlo Marino, Francesco Renda, Antonino Sorgi, Michele Pantaleone, Umberto Tusa, Massimo Ganci, and Giuseppe Tricoli are among those who generously agreed to answer my questions. Giuseppe Tricoli also gave me invaluable assistance with the illustrations. Danilo Dolci put me in touch with an old rural worker who remembered the Mori years vividly. Various inhabitants of Gangi helped me by recalling the siege of their town in 1926. Aristide Spanò kindly answered a number of questions concerning his father, and so too did Giovanni Cucco. I would like to thank Humaira Ahmed for her great patience and good humour in the preparation of the typescript, and Gillian Malpass of Yale University Press for her constant professionalism and hard work.

My greatest debt is to Denis Mack Smith, whose writings first aroused my interest in modern Italian history. His support, inspiration, and generosity have been unfailing over the years. No research student could have been better served by a supervisor, either as a guide or a model. As a small token of my gratitude, this book is dedicated to him.

GLOSSARY

abigeato	Animal-rustling, especially cattle.
agrari	Great landowners.
ammonizione	Form of surveillance by the police.
assissiano	Member of a dissident servicemen's association.
borg(h)ese	Wealthy peasant.
campiere	Field guard.
carabiniere	Military policeman.
confino	Forced residence, usually on a penal island or in a remote, mountainous region. Introduced by the fascist government to replace *domicilio coatto*.
cosca	Small group of criminals, consisting of a boss and his dependents.
domicilio coatto	Forced residence, usually on a penal island.
Fasci	Socialist-led movement of Sicilian workers in the 1890s.
fasci	Literally, 'bundles'; local organisations of fascists.
federale	Provincial leader of the fascist party.
feudo	Large estate (literally, fief).
(in) gabella	Form of agricultural lease, consisting of a fixed annual payment over a period of several years.
gabelloto	Leaseholder of a large estate.
giudice istruttore	Type of field guard, usually on small, intensively cultivated farms.
guardiano	Examining magistrate.
istruttoria	Preliminary investigation to determine if the accused should be sent to trial.

latifondo	Great estate.
latifondista	Owner of a great estate.
latitante	Man on the run from the police.
malvivenza	Criminality, usually of a petty kind.
manutengolo	Protector of criminals.
Mezzogiorno	Term commonly used for the south of Italy.
milite a cavallo	Form of mounted policeman.
Nationalists	Members of the right-wing Nationalist party, formed shortly before the First World War. Fused with the Fascist party in 1923.
omertà	Silence before the law.
picciotto	Young man, youngster.
podestà	Fascist equivalent of mayor.
popolari	Members of the Partito Popolare Italiano, a Catholic, left-of-centre party formed in 1919.
pretore	Local magistrate.
questore	Local chief of police.
retata	Large-scale police round-up.
soprastante	Form of field guard.
squadrismo	Term for the organised violence of the fascist 'squads'.

Note on spelling

In Italian, 'mafia' is generally spelt with a small 'm', and this is the form I have adopted throughout most of the book. However, when writers wished to stress the idea of a formal organisation, they often used a capital 'm'. In such cases I have adjusted the spelling of the word accordingly. In the nineteenth century (and occasionally in this century too), the word was sometimes written with two 'f's.

INTRODUCTION

Few subjects in the last century have had the power to attract more publicity, or generate greater excitement, than the mafia. The idea of a vast criminal organisation, with a strict hierarchy and an archaic code of honour, whose activities extend from its native Sicily to North America and beyond, has been a source of constant fascination. Over the years, however, fact has mingled with fiction, speculation with fantasy, to such a degree that any clear assessment of what the mafia is has become very difficult. The problem has been not so much a lack of evidence (police records, trial proceedings, government enquiries, and, in recent years, a spate of mafia autobiographies have provided plenty of material), but rather that the field is strewn with preconceptions that tend to determine the way the evidence is read.

Nowhere is this problem of preconceptions more apparent than in discussions of whether or not the mafia is a formal organisation. Since clear-cut evidence to prove the matter one way or the other has always been lacking, the arguments for and against have rested ultimately on assumptions about conspiracies. Though secret societies have unquestionably existed, the need to explain disorder has also led at times to ill-founded theories of causation. The 'proof' for these has been read into certain selected facts, and once the interpretation has been accepted, it has assumed a life and power of its own that are often hard to destroy.

Fascination with the mafia is everywhere in evidence: the novels, films, newspaper stories, and media documentaries on the subject have been innumerable. Moreover, the idea has enjoyed a remarkable capacity to transcend national barriers, and today there is talk of the organisation, not only in Sicily and the United States, but also in Canada, Australia, South America, and elsewhere. Many societies operate with the idea of an 'enemy within', and the notion of a powerful criminal conspiracy, whose values are diametrically opposed to those of the state, is tailor-made for this purpose. It transfers the blame for crime on to a group of identifiable outsiders and offers a

1

legitimate pretext for strong action. Above all, it provides hope of an effective solution; for if an organisation is to blame, all that needs to be done is to crush it.

It is often said that historians cannot prove a negative, and this is certainly true when it comes to conspiracies. According to a common line of argument, the mafia is by nature clandestine, and therefore no proof should be expected of its existence. Such logic is impeccable; but what needs to be explained is why the notion of a Sicilian secret society should have emerged at all, despite the lack of any evidence for its existence. Indeed, in Italy, talk of the mafia flourished although every serious observer admitted that no organisation as such existed. It is the gap between the popular conception and the reality that is so startling, and this disparity has been as great in the United States as in Sicily.

The idea of the mafia in the United States[1]

Belief in a national criminal conspiracy has nowhere been stronger, nor arguably more irrational, than in the United States. The idea of the mafia first took root there at the end of 1890, following the murder in mysterious circumstances of the New Orleans Chief of Police, David Hennessy. A wave of hysteria swept the country, fuelled by evident xenophobia, as well as by allegations that the mafia had been responsible for the killing. The newspapers were full of lurid stories about this deadly secret society, which was said to be infiltrating the United States through immigration channels. When those accused of the crime were acquitted, they were lynched by a mob led by a number of local politicians, who claimed that there had been a miscarriage of justice.

At the turn of the century, the idea of an Italian criminal society resurfaced in what was known as the 'Black Hand'. The evidence for this putative organisation came from a number of extortion letters, each of which was inscribed with symbols such as a black hand, a dagger, a skull, or a pierced heart. These were widely interpreted as emanating from a single source, and many people assumed that 'Black Hand' was just another name for 'the mafia'. Once again, there was a good deal of hysteria and xenophobia. In fact, as a detailed report of 1908 showed, the Black Hand was not a monolithic organisation, but a number of small and separate gangs exploiting popular fears in order to extract money. The culprits included immigrant mainland Italians as well as Sicilians.

In the United States during the inter-war years, talk of the mafia, or an equivalent organisation, declined. The main threat to law and order was now seen as coming from 'rackets' and 'racketeers', rather than from a national conspiracy. However, some writers have claimed that the mafia continued in this period under the name of the 'Unione Siciliana'. Their reasons for assuming this are unclear, for the Unione Siciliana was simply one of a number of mutual-aid organisations that had emerged in the 1890s to cater to the needs of immigrants. In the 1920s it became an important vote-gathering machine and was exploited for this purpose by such notorious characters as Al Capone. This may be part of the explanation for its later notoriety.

After the Second World War, the idea of an Italian criminal conspiracy returned with a vengeance. Much of this was owing to the Senate Hearings on Organized Crime, which were held in 1950–1 under the chairmanship of a well-meaning, if somewhat naïve, politician called Estes Kefauver. In his concluding report, he claimed that the mafia had finally been uncovered, but the evidence adduced did not bear this out. The Senate Hearings had unearthed a good deal of material about gambling, drugs and prostitution rackets, and their connection with politics. However, nowhere was it shown that these disparate activities were co-ordinated by a national organisation. Nevertheless, the idea of a great underworld conspiracy led by Sicilians was now widely accepted.

In the 1950s, belief in Kefauver's allegations was sustained by such episodes as the so-called 'Apalachin convention'. In November 1957, the New York police accidentally disturbed what seems to have been a house party at the home of Joseph Barbara. They interrogated a number of the guests and then released them without bringing charges. The idea quickly spread that this had been a major underworld meeting, though again the evidence was not forthcoming. One reason why the affair gained so much publicity was that it became a political football, with the Republican candidate for the state governorship proclaiming the need to tighten up on law and order. The Apalachin convention grew in importance, and in the 1960s it was commonly referred to as a meeting of the 'Mafia Grand Council'.

In the last twenty-five years, the principal evidence for the existence of an American mafia has come from 'supergrasses'. The first, and perhaps most important of these, was a minor underworld figure called Joseph Valachi, who in 1963 testified to the existence of an organisation called 'Cosa Nostra'. Valachi's statements make puzzling reading, not least because his grasp of English was rudimentary. It is often hard to see how the idea of a formal structure could have been extrapolated from his incoherent and often contradictory remarks. Indeed, there seems to have been some uncertainty as to whether the organisation he referred to was called 'Cosa Nostra', 'Causa Nostra' or 'Casa Nostra'.

Valachi was particularly imprecise when he dealt with the structure of Cosa Nostra. The impression given was of someone trying hard to impose a formal pattern on a set of random and unconnected experiences. He referred, for example, to something called a '*griemeson*', and added: 'That is sort of like in English would express it as a commission' (a term that has recently gained fresh currency with the evidence of the Sicilian supergrass, Tommaso Buscetta). Valachi claimed that the *griemeson* had been introduced in the 1930s by 'Lucky' Luciano to protect small-fry like himself against the depredations of the bosses. However, it does not appear to have had an official status, as Valachi called it by different names including a '*concerti*', a '*consigio*', and a '*consegio*'.

In discussing the hierarchy of Cosa Nostra, Valachi was similarly confusing, and perhaps also confused. He spoke of the ranks within the organisation variously as '*sottocapo*', '*caporegime*', '*consigliere*', and 'lieutenant'. (This latter word was commonly used by both police and criminals to refer to someone who merely executed orders.) However, he employed the terms in a manner that suggests he was describing a loose, rather than rigid, structure of power. This was borne out by what he had to say about orders. He claimed at one point that if a boss gave a command, everyone had to obey it. However, he later revealed that Frank Costello's 'law' to keep out of drug-trafficking was disobeyed by his subordinates, simply because it suited them to do so.

The precise character or purpose of Cosa Nostra did not emerge clearly from Valachi's testimony. He used the term 'family' to indicate a particular branch of the organisation (though he applied it also to Cosa Nostra as a whole); but far from being a tight-knit and coherent unit, the 'family' seems to have been remarkably informal. When asked if his 'family' ever assembled collectively, Valachi replied: 'Well...I am there 30 years, and they never met, not as a whole. But we have every Christmas a table, like a dinner, and my regime consists of 30.' Valachi claimed also that he had never received any financial gain from Cosa Nostra, as there was no division of spoils; it was a question of each man for himself. Indeed, he said at one point that all he ever got out of his own boss, Vito Genovese, was protection.

Valachi indicated that the New York branch of Cosa Nostra consisted of five 'families'. However, his statements were again contradictory. He clearly knew a great deal about Vito Genovese and his followers, but he seems merely to have generalised from this to other groups. Moreover, he claimed at one point that Genovese controlled not only his own 'family', but also 'the power of the Gambino family and the Lucchese family'. This does not suggest a well-defined division of power. Valachi was similarly unconvincing when he was asked about the Cosa Nostra 'families' outside New

York, and seems to have been unaware of which cities, if any, had them.

In the course of the televised hearings in which Valachi presented his evidence, police officers from various parts of the United States appeared with charts showing the structure of crime in their particular cities. The diversity of terms used, and the hierarchical variations, ought perhaps to have undermined the idea of a national conspiracy. Underworld leaders figured variously as the 'top man', the 'boss', and the 'big man'; and subordinates as 'section leaders', 'soldiers', and 'lieutenants'. In each case, it seems that the police were converting underworld slang and loose structures into something formal and rigid. Valachi probably did much the same. Even the name 'Cosa Nostra' (our business) may have been merely a common underworld euphemism for criminal activities.

When the authorities want to establish the reality of a criminal conspiracy, the questions put to a suspect assume a particular form. They become, in effect, leading questions. A magistrate sets out to find the structure of the organisation by asking who was in charge, how were the leaders chosen, and what was the hierarchy. If the witness is keen to collaborate, he has a vested interest in confirming his interrogators' suspicions, otherwise he risks being discarded as unhelpful. Worse still, he might find himself upstaged by opponents who could dictate to the police their own version of events. This is not to say that a man such as Valachi will be lying when he 'sings'; it is more that he will try to interpret his experiences in a certain key.

All social relations contain an inherent order and pattern. No activity, whether it is tax evasion or running a government, can dispense with organisation. Sometimes the structures are formally defined; often the arrangements are no more than *ad hoc*. In the case of the mafia, it is all too easy for fragments of experience to be interpreted as if they formed part of a greater and more sinister whole. This is so for the protagonists as well as for outside observers. In his autobiography, Nick Gentile claimed that the greatest American mafia boss in the early years of this century was a certain Totò D'Aquila.[2] He may genuinely have believed this, but nobody else seems to have shared his view. Gentile was no doubt converting his youthful impressions of a local New York 'fixer' into the language of mafia hierarchy. As the police have often found, each criminal has his own distinctive vision of underworld affairs.

In recent years, the testimony of Tommaso Buscetta and the Cosa Nostra trials in Palermo and New York have ensured that the idea of a criminal conspiracy is today as strong as ever. Buscetta was more articulate and consistent than Valachi; but whether the Sicilian organisation he described (which he also said was known as 'Cosa

Nostra') was indeed a formal one, is by no means certain. Like Valachi, he had a vested interest in providing the authorities with confirmation of their suspicions, and his collaboration has led to his own immunity and the prosecution of many of his enemies. What was particularly unclear from Buscetta's testimony was what the organisation existed for. At one point he confessed to the Palermo magistrates that when it came to 'business' activities (including drug-trafficking) each 'man of honour' was free to do whatever he wanted.[3] How organised, then, was 'organised crime'?

Conspiracy theories have an enduring fascination, not least because they derive more from fear and imagination than from empirical evidence. The moral kudos that attaches to those who denounce the mafia, as well as the emotiveness of the term, has ensured its ready application to different manifestations of criminality. The exposure of fraud among southern-Italian olive-oil producers has led to talk of the mafia infiltrating the European Community. The discovery of Sicilian drug-traffickers in Surrey led quickly to the idea that the mafia had extended its operations to England. Meanwhile, in Sicily, vendetta killings have continued as before (including in January 1988 that of a former mayor of Palermo), leaving the authorities trying to piece together a map of the 'new' mafia, after strong hopes that the police operations in recent years had finally destroyed the organisation.

Sicily: the historical background[4]

Sicily is the largest island in the Mediterranean, with an area of some 26,000 square kilometres. It has a narrow but fertile coastal plain, and an interior dominated by rolling uplands and mountains. It is separated at its north-eastern corner from mainland Italy by the Strait of Messina; in the west, the shortest distance to Tunisia is about 150 kilometres. This position half-way between Europe and Africa has determined the shape of much of the island's history. For centuries it was fought over by a succession of Mediterranean powers. Each invasion brought with it new laws, a new ruling class, and sometimes a new culture. No other region of comparable size can boast such a varied past; the vestiges of this diversity are evident today in the Greek temples, the Arab-Norman cathedrals, and the Spanish baroque palaces.

The first settlers in Sicily to have left much trace were the Greeks. They arrived on the island's eastern coast in the eighth and seventh centuries BC and established cities that were to become among the most important of the day. Indeed, it was Syracuse that in 413 BC defeated Athens and brought to an end its golden age. Tyrants such

Pl. 1. The landscape of Sicily's interior. *Latifondi* near Contessa Entellina in the centre-west of the island.

as Phalaris, Gelon, Dionysius, and Agathocles were renowned in the fifth and fourth centuries BC for their enormous wealth and power, and this reflected the fact that the island was at that time one of the most fertile areas in the Mediterranean, abounding in wheat, timber, fruit, vines, and olives, which were exported far afield to Africa and Europe.

During the Punic Wars in the third century BC, Sicily was conquered by Rome, and for the next six hundred years it remained a province of the Roman Empire. Its history in this period seems to have been uneventful, and almost the only episodes to have attracted the attention of historians were two slave revolts and Cicero's famous prosecution of the corrupt and rapacious governor of the island, Gaius Verres. The Romans valued Sicily chiefly for its wheat (Cato referred to the island in a much-quoted phrase as the 'granary of the republic'), and this was grown on huge estates, or *latifundia*, worked by slave labour. The pattern of economic production established at this time was to remain almost unchanged for the next two thousand years.

With the fall of the Roman Empire in the west, Sicily was conquered successively by the Vandals, the Goths, and, in 535 AD, by the Byzantines. The influence of each of these peoples is hard to assess, though the fact that the island was ruled from Constantinople for three centuries must have reinforced the predominantly Greek character of local culture. In the ninth century, it was the turn of the Arabs to invade, and for two hundred years Sicily was part of an Islamic empire that stretched from North Africa to Spain. Descriptions of the island in this period suggest a flourishing economy. Palermo became a great city, and visitors were impressed to find a population that included Greeks, Lombards, Slavs, Jews, Persians, and Tartars. According to one visitor, there were more mosques in Palermo than in any other town he had visited except Cordoba.

In the late eleventh century, an army of Norman mercenaries arrived in the island and, after two decades of intense fighting, took control from the Arabs. The kingdom they established was one of the most remarkable that Europe had ever seen. The administration was an extraordinary mixture of Arab and Byzantine elements, and its concept of royal authority derived from that of the eastern emperors in Constantinople, with the ruler claiming his authority directly from Christ. The king surrounded himself with eunuchs and a harem, and even his most powerful subjects were obliged to prostrate themselves ritually before him. The court became a great cultural centre, and there were notable achievements at this time in science and literature.

As long as Sicily was itself the centre of an empire, it continued to prosper. In the twelfth century, much of the African coast from Tripoli to Cape Bon was controlled by the Norman kings in Palermo, as was the southern part of the Italian mainland. The beginning of the island's decline in modern times can be dated from the thirteenth century, when a succession of new rulers from Germany, France, and, in particular, Spain, turned it into an outlying province of their dominions. Sicily was cut off from Africa and drawn definitively into the orbit of European civilisation, but its position on the southern edge of the continent meant that it was remote from the achievements of the Renaissance and the Reformation. More and more, the island became an economic and cultural backwater.

The discovery of the Americas in the sixteenth century dealt a further blow to Sicily's fortunes. Whilst the Mediterranean remained the hub of the European economy, the island could profit from its central location on trade routes. Now the axis of commerce shifted northwards; Sicily was left on the fringes of the capitalist world and scarcely felt the effect of the technological changes being introduced in France and Britain. The huge farms, known as *latifondi*, remained intact, even though the owners increasingly forsook the countryside for the allures of the capital. Insufficient effort was made either by the island's Spanish rulers in the sixteenth and seventeenth centuries, or by the Neapolitan Bourbons in the eighteenth century, to push through much-needed social and economic reforms.

One important consequence of Sicily's relegation to the periphery of the Spanish empire was that the local nobility became accustomed to governing the island themselves. The process in many northern states whereby the ruler gradually extended his authority over and against the barons was largely lacking in Sicily. This situation was aggravated by the fact that the island changed hands several times in the eighteenth century (Piedmont, 1713–20; Austria, 1720–34; Neapolitan Bourbons, 1734–1860). As a result, there was little chance of consistent administration, let alone reform. When a government did try to impose a degree of centralised control and curtail the worst excesses of feudal privilege, the barons raised a storm of protest and refused to co-operate.

The inability of the Bourbon regime to undermine the power of the aristocracy meant that feudal practices remained perhaps more deeply entrenched in Sicily than elsewhere in Europe. The barons had lordship over about three-quarters of all the island's towns, and their jurisdiction there was almost total. They were rarely answerable to the royal courts for offences they committed, including even murder. They kept their own retainers, who acted as personal bodyguards and militia. One important aspect of a nobleman's sense of power was his capacity to grant protection to a wanted man and save him from the clutches of the law. Though formally abolished in 1812, feudalism continued to operate in spirit, and often also in practice, ·well into the present century.

Among the factors that contributed to the untrammelled rule of the island's aristocracy was the absence of a strong middle class. One of the most important features of the Middle Ages in Sicily had been the failure of the cities to emerge as a separate political force. This may have been the result of a lesser degree of commercial activity than elsewhere in Italy; but equally important was the reluctance of absentee monarchs to foster an urban bourgeoisie as a counterweight to the aristocracy. Rulers found it simpler to appease the nobility. One consequence was that Sicily lacked an entrepreneurial mentality. This was particularly true in the west of the island, where the only major city was Palermo. The eastern seaboard had several large ports, whose commercial character was more pronounced than that of the capital.

A belief in the legitimacy of personal rule, a disdain of economic activity, and a near total disregard for the peasantry were among the hallmarks of the Sicilian aristocracy. What middle-class elements there were, particularly in the countryside (from the seventeenth century the landowners resorted to leasing their estates to ambitious middlemen known as '*gabelloti*', who grew rich through exploitative farming), absorbed many of the characteristics of the nobility. They resented government interference in local affairs, except when it suited them; they employed their own armed guards to defend the *latifondi*; and they turned frequently to private violence. Their attitude to the land was often as cavalier as that of the owners, partly because the leases on their estates were usually too short to warrant investment.

The main victims of this cruel world were the peasants. They constituted the vast mass of the island's population, but only intruded on to the stage of Sicilian history when their frustration boiled over into open revolt or revolution, as in 1773, 1820, 1837, and 1860. Though their attitudes are hard to document, mistrust seems to have lain at the heart of their outlook. The struggle to eke out a living on land that was growing increasingly exhausted consumed most of their energies. Competition for resources in a society where the law was partial, the nobility exploitative, and the state repressive, led to a heavy reliance on the virtue of self-sufficiency. A great premium came to be attached to personal strength, for the best guarantee of survival in this world was a capacity to use violence effectively.

Sicily had once been a region of great fertility, rich in woodland, sugar, and cotton, as well as wheat and citrus fruit. By the nineteenth century, all traces of this former prosperity had vanished. Deafforestation had led to widespread soil erosion. Landslides were common, rivers regularly overflowed their courses, and malaria was endemic. The harshness of life was mirrored in the grim individualism of much of the peasantry. In the rural communities men learnt to value independence, for, as one proverb put it, 'he who plays alone, never loses'. This attitude only added to the impoverishment of the land, for it militated against the co-operative endeavours that alone would have stemmed the tide of agricultural decay. The island seemed to be locked into a downward spiral of economic decline.

The dogged individualism of the peasants was reinforced by the ruthlessness of their social superiors. The landowners and the *gabelloti* exercised a personal rule underpinned by private violence. The idea of the law as an abstract force operating above singular interests failed to take hold in this environment. The state rarely intruded into the life of most Sicilians, and when it did, it was usually in the shape of the soldier or the tax-collector. For the great mass of the population, power was easily equated with repression and selfishness, and not with any concern for justice or the common good. Indeed, those who used their authority to further collective interests ran the risk of being mistrusted or despised. The altruist was easily written off as a fool who neglected the higher claims of family and friends.

In the absence of an effective legal system, the peasantry resorted instead, like the landowners and the *gabelloti*, to private justice. No self-respecting individual turned to the police if it could be avoided, for that would have meant co-operating with a body widely regarded as hateful. Indeed, one of the strongest terms of abuse in Sicily was (and often still is) the word '*sbirro*' (cop). Collaboration with the authorities could also be regarded as an admission of personal weakness, and in a society where so much importance was attached to physical courage, this provided an additional moral disincentive to denounce a man who had wronged another. A capacity to exact retribution oneself, through violence if necessary, was much admired.

The esteem for private force in Sicily reflected the fact that many peasants saw life as virtually a war of all against all. The impoverishment of the soil, and the absence of adequate irrigation, made survival a continual struggle. Furthermore, the competition for resources was intensified by the over-population of the countryside. In the early eighteenth century, the island had perhaps a million inhabitants; by the time of Italian unification in 1860, this figure may have doubled. The demographic pressure was a source of constant unrest, and in times of agricultural slump, tensions could easily flare into a *jacquerie* or even a revolution. Attempts by the government to improve the situation by promoting agricultural reform foundered on the indifference or outright hostility of the aristocracy.

The over-population of the countryside might have been solved by an increase in industrial activity. However, the island (and in particular its western provinces) remained steadfastly impervious to the spirit of modern enterprise. The absence of public trust militated against the formation of joint-stock companies, and the continuance of aristocratic values ensured that what capital there was went ultimately into the acquisition of land. The main entrepreneurs in Sicily in the eighteenth and nineteenth centuries were of foreign (especially English) extraction; even the highly successful Florio family (which had enormous wine and shipping interests) came originally from Calabria.

In 1860, as a result more of accident than design, Sicily became part of the new kingdom of Italy. Giuseppe Garibaldi landed at Marsala in the spring of that year with a handful of volunteers and used a local peasant insurrection as a base from which to launch his campaign to unify the peninsula. All classes among the islanders lent him their support, but few did so out of commitment to the idea of Italy. The peasants were motivated by a perennial desire for land and lower taxes; the middle classes, by hopes of greater local power. Many landowners turned to Garibaldi as the best guarantee of order in the countryside. They also calculated that the overthrow of the Bourbons might lead to a lessening of governmental interference and a guarantee of their privileges.

The centralised Italian state that emerged from the revolution of 1860 proved a grave disappointment to many Sicilians. Local hopes for a degree of autonomy were quickly dashed, and the island was now made subject to the alien constitution and laws of Piedmont. Taxation became more onerous than ever; military conscription was introduced, and was widely resented; and Garibaldi's promises of land reform were dropped. Furthermore, the northern officials who were posted to the island found it almost as incomprehensible as it was hard to govern. In particular, the respect that many Sicilians had for private violence struck them as incompatible with a modern liberal regime based on the rule of law.

Sicily was the most troublesome and disturbed region of the new kingdom. Other parts of the south of Italy were similarly poor and backward, and had a high incidence of violence; but no other area displayed such a flagrant disregard for the spirit of impartial administration. Attempts to implement the law broke down in the face of local non-co-operation; when people did agree to testify to the authorities, it was often only to bear false witness against their enemies. The state found itself isolated in this world of private justice. It looked for an explanation, and 'discovered' a secret society, led by men of violence, that tyrannised the unconsenting mass of the population. The idea of 'the mafia' was born.

PART I

1   THE CONCEPT OF 'MAFIA'

There is no clear-cut reference to 'mafia' prior to the spring of 1865. This does not mean that the term was unknown, or even uncommon before that date.[1] Dictionaries tended to report literary and, in particular, poetic words, and 'mafia' was clearly not one of these. The great Sicilian ethnographer, Giuseppe Pitré, said in a well-known essay of 1889 that the term was used in the first half of the nineteenth century by the inhabitants of the Borgo, a popular quarter of Palermo: 'And in the Borgo', he wrote, 'the word mafia, and its derivatives, meant, and still means, beauty, gracefulness, perfection, and general excellence.'[2]

The etymology of the word was hotly debated in the late nineteenth century.[3] The variety of suggestions offered reflected the degree to which the mafia had already become a political issue; for behind each derivation there lay a particular assumption about the nature of the phenomenon. Vincenzo Mortillaro, a supporter of the deposed Bourbon dynasty and an ardent Sicilian patriot, dismissed the word in his dictionary of 1876 as a Piedmontese neologism.[4] Cesare Lombroso, the northern criminologist, said, by contrast, that 'mafia' derived from the name of a group of tufa caves near Trapani, the 'mafie', where local delinquents used to hide.[5] Among the more fanciful late nineteenth-century theories were those that regarded the word as an acronym. One suggestion was that 'mafia' had been adopted by a group of patriots in 1282, at the time of the Sicilian Vespers (an insurrection against the French), and that it stood for *'Morte alla Francia Italia anela'* (Italy longs for the death of France). Alternatively (and equally absurdly), it was the name of a secret society headed by the nationalist conspirator, Giuseppe Mazzini, and signified: *'Mazzini autorizza furti, incendi, avvelenamenti'* (Mazzini authorises robberies, fires, and poisonings).[6]

None of these etymologies has any basis in fact. They are of interest only for what they reveal about the operation of fantasy; and fantasy, in the case of the mafia, was often coloured by political considerations. Those who felt that Sicily was defamed by the

15

emphasis on crime would point to the word's positive attributes and ascribe to it a remote and honourable ancestry. Some, for example, alleged that it derived from a Greek word for beauty, 'morphe';[7] and an American newspaper of the 1920s elaborated on the classical theme by saying that the mafia may have begun as a Greek philosophical society that numbered Pythagoras among its early members.[8] Today, claims are still made for the mafia's antiquity: the idea is attractive to those who regard it as noble organisation and an expression of something quintessentially Sicilian. Longevity can also sound sensational. A recent British television documentary began by announcing that the mafia had terrorised Sicily for 700 years.[9] This was presumably an unwitting endorsement of the Sicilian Vespers etymology.

Non-Sicilians, and northern Italians in particular, have often found less benevolent sources for the word 'mafia'. Roquefort, for example, in his *Glossaire de la Langue Romane*, suggested that it came from the old French 'maufe-maufais', a synonym, he said, for 'the devil'.[10] Cesareo's dictionary posited a derivation from the Arab word 'mahias', meaning bully or braggart.[11] Such etymologies can be little more than conjectural. However, the weight of opinion points to an Arabic root of some kind, though the often quoted view that the word comes from 'ma'afir', the name of a Saracen tribe that retreated into the western hinterland of Sicily in the face of the Norman invasion in the late eleventh century, is almost certainly fanciful.

Giuseppe Pitré was sure that before 1860 the words 'mafia' and 'mafioso' had no pejorative connotations. They indicated beauty, or superiority, and could be applied to objects of all kinds, as well as to people. A house, he said, could be described as 'mafiosa'; so too could brushes, kitchen utensils, or fruit. An attractive girl might be said to 'possess mafia'.[12] However, the beauty referred to was not, it seems vague or generic. It was beauty of a lush, even strident kind. When applied to a male, according to Pitré, 'mafioso' signified an awareness of manhood, self-confidence, and, by extension, fearlessness; but it never, he added, implied arrogance or any kind of brutality.

Pitré was a fervent Sicilian patriot. When he wrote about the mafia in the 1880s, he was eager to correct the severe abuse to which he felt the term had been subjected since 1860. This may have caused him to exaggerate. Nevertheless there is plenty of evidence to show that 'mafia' and 'mafioso' did have connotations of praise in ordinary Sicilian speech well into the present century. To dismiss these, as is often done, merely as the attempt by common criminals to give themselves an aura of respectability, might be useful for those fighting the mafia, but it risks distorting the truth. Even today there are Sicilians who will refer to 'good' *mafiosi*. The supergrass Tommaso

Buscetta was probably sincere when he claimed that real *mafiosi* were men of honour and ideals.[13]

After 1860, the words 'mafia' and '*mafioso*' gradually assumed sinister overtones. One factor in this was a popular dialect play called *I Mafiusi di la Vicaria*. This comedy, first performed in 1863, dealt with a group of criminals in the main Palermo prison. They spoke in colourful jargon, played cards, duelled with knives, and observed a rudimentary hierarchy.[14] The play is usually ascribed to Giuseppe Rizzotto, but much of it was the work of a school teacher called Gaspare Mosca, who mingled elements of the Neapolitan *camorra* with snatches of Palermitan slang. The idea of calling the criminals '*mafiosi*' apparently came about by chance. Mosca overheard someone shouting, '*chi vurrisi fari u mafiusu cu mia?*' ('So you want to get tough with me do you?').[15] The result, according to various writers, including Pitré, was disastrous. The word '*mafioso*' was now linked with criminals, and this connection was impressed on audiences up and down the country.[16]

Rizzotto's play was immensely popular. In the quarter century that followed the first production, there were 2,000 performances in Italy. Successful tours were made also of North and South America.[17] Audiences relished the play for its colour and realism as much as for its humour, and because Sicily aroused such curiosity and yet was so little known, the threshold of credibility was low. The influential French sociologist, Gabriel Tarde, said in his *La Philosophie Penale* that *mafiosi* had a traditional 'uniform' of a cap and silk tassel, and a corduroy suit. He seems to have derived this idea from a line in Rizzotto's play in which one of the characters tells his wife to bring such clothes to him in prison.[18] Tarde was not the only one to confuse standard articles of Sicilian peasant dress with criminality. Some mainland policeman made the same mistake, according to the sociologist Giuseppe Alongi (who was himself a policeman), and the consequences were embarrassing.[19]

Rizzotto's comedy helped popularise the idea that *mafiosi* were common criminals. Its depiction of prison rituals and hierarchy may have fostered belief in the mafia as a secret organisation. However, it was almost certainly less influential than Sicilians such as Pitré maintained; other factors of equal, if not greater, importance were also at work. Particularly significant in this regard was the body of lore that surrounded the Neapolitan *camorra*, the workings of which had already been extensively, if over-imaginatively, written about in the early 1860s.[20] The image of the *camorra* was to intrude on the idea of the mafia down to the 1890s, and probably later.

The *camorra* was regarded by the authorities as a sinister criminal organisation. It was said to have elaborate initiation ceremonies, a strict hierarchy, and well-defined spheres of control within Naples.

The lowest grade, according to the criminologist Cesare Lombroso, was the *picciotto di sgarro* (henchman). He had to demonstrate his courage by picking up a coin while bystanders tried to stab his hand with knives. Several years of probation were needed before a *picciotto* could become a *camorrista*, and promotion was marked with an oath sworn on crossed daggers. The organisation's income came primarily from tithes that were extracted from a variety of sources, including card-players, water-melon-sellers, and beggars. There was a strict but unwritten code of laws which forbade contact with the police and prescribed death for anyone who betrayed the society or who killed or robbed without the permission of the chiefs.[21]

Almost all commentators stressed the close links between the *camorra* and the prisons. The organisation was said to have originated among convicts, and even after 1860 it was commonly held to be most virulent in the Neapolitan gaols.[22] Such ideas strongly influenced mainland perceptions of the mafia. The authorities often claimed in the 1860s that the activities of bandits and draft-dodgers in Palermo province were being co-ordinated from the Vicaria prison. Marquis di Rudinì, the young mayor of Palermo and future Prime Minister, told an official inquiry in 1867 that the inmates of the Vicaria constituted 'a form of government' that controlled criminal operations throughout the province.[23] The liberal politician, Baron Favara, was more conspiratorial: the mafia, he told the same inquiry, had its headquarters (*centro*) in the Palermo prisons.[24]

The idea that the Vicaria lay at the root of much of the unrest in and around Palermo in the early years of unification was strengthened by two factors. In the first place the authorities never ceased to marvel at how well-informed about events in the outside world prisoners appeared to be,[25] and this amazement was all the greater because of the depth of their own ignorance. In the second place, during the great Palermo rising of 1866, the insurgents tried, as in all previous insurrections, to break into the Vicaria and release the inmates. Though this was tactically motivated (it was well known that prisoners, who had everything to fight for, made good revolutionaries), it was easy for the authorities to construe matters in less rational terms.

The extent of official paranoia at this time was evident in the question of what to do with the 357 prisoners whose papers had been lost or destroyed during the 1866 rising. The government was frightened of acquitting them, because it assumed that they must have been ringleaders, and it invoked exceptional procedures as a way of keeping them in custody. However, the Procurator General of Palermo told the Minister of Justice that this was quite unnecessary. Extraordinary measures, he claimed, should be enforced only when the situation demanded them. True, he said, the province of

Palermo was turbulent; but was there any 'causal connection between this abnormal state of affairs and the prisoners'? Moreover, why should it be assumed that these 357 men had been singled out by the insurgents? Was not chance a more likely factor in the destruction of their papers? There was no grounds, he concluded, for treating these prisoners differently from any others, and certainly none for supposing that the 40,000 rebels had been at the beck and call of 'wretches' who had spent the rising 'between the solid walls of a prison'.[26]

The idea that the mafia was centred in the gaols died hard. Cesare Lombroso declared in 1889 that the *mafioso*, like the *camorrista*, had his 'principal headquarters' (*sede principale*) there, 'just like nearly all organised criminals'. Indeed he said, the word 'mafia' was itself a product of the prisons.[27] According to a government report of 1884, the province of Girgenti had branches of the mafia 'almost everywhere': 'And they seem to emanate from the prison in Girgenti'.[28] The *pretore* (local magistrate) of Racalmuto was more specific. The only way to destroy the provincial mafia, he said, was to attack it at its source, namely Girgenti prison. Ninety per cent of those who were admitted, he claimed, left the gaol 'members of the mafia' (*associati alla mafia*).[29]

In the absence of firm evidence to the contrary, foreign observers tended to write of the mafia as if it was an extension of the *camorra*. Heckethorn's encyclopaedic guide to secret societies of 1897 informed its English readers that the mafia was 'another *camorra*'. Candidates, it said, were admitted after a trial by duel. There was a regular code of laws, secret signs, passwords, and other means of recognition; and, 'like the *camorra*', the organisation had representatives in every class of society.[30] The *Encyclopaedia Britannica* of 1911 claimed that the mafia was a secret society whose 'organisation and purpose much resemble those of the Camorra'. Like Heckethorn, the author of this article maintained that candidates were admitted after a trial by duel.

2 THE MAFIA AND THE STATE

Political unrest and the birth of the concept, 1860–1866

The development of the idea of the mafia as a criminal association cannot be separated from the problems that confronted the new Italian state after 1860. Many of these problems were compounded by ignorance. Few mainlanders had visited the island before unification; what tourists there had been in the first half of the nineteeth century came principally from northern Europe. Indeed, it was said that if a continental Italian ventured off the beaten track in Sicily, he was liable to be mistaken for an Englishman.[1] William Gladstone or Cardinal Newman could admire the island for its combination of the romantic and the classical; most northern Italians, however, were often more interested in exploring societies based on modern industry and liberalism – and in these the Kingdom of the Two Sicilies was sadly lacking.

The confrontation between northern Italian administrators and Sicilians after 1860 proved painful. In the first place, many islanders who supported unification had done so in the firm belief that Sicily would be accorded a considerable degree of autonomy within the new state. The imposition of rigid centralisation produced much resentment, particularly as enthusiasm for the Italian cause in Sicily had been to a large extent the result of the growing intrusiveness since the 1770s of the Bourbon administration in Naples. In the second place, the northern officials who arrived in the island after 1860 were soon disenchanted. They discovered a world of semi-feudalism, based on archaic notions of honour, in which blood feuds abounded, and liberalism was scarcely understood, let alone practised.

The first Lieutenant-General of Sicily, Cordero di Montezemolo, was appointed towards the end of 1860. He was Piedmontese and knew little about the island. His ignorance soon turned to disgust. 'I doubt very much,' he told the Prime Minister in January 1861, 'whether the character of the people in *Kabylia* is more ferocious than that of the Bedouins in this part of the island'.[2] Similar sentiments

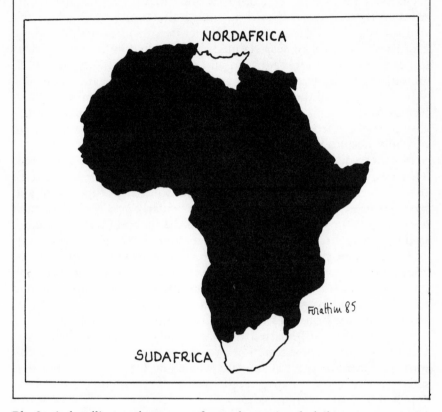

La mafia è tornata

NORDAFRICA

SUDAFRICA

Fonattim 85

Pl. 2. A headline and cartoon from the national daily newspaper, *La Repubblica*, after the killing of a policeman in Palermo, July 1985. The outline of Sicily has been drawn as part of North Africa.

were frequently to be found in official reports of the 1860s, and the feeling that Sicilians belonged more properly to Africa than Europe has persisted in some quarters to the present day.[3] In the last years of the nineteenth century this idea even gained intellectual respectability with the 'discovery', on the basis of skull measurements, of a pre-historic 'Mediterranean race' that had colonised southern Italy from Africa. Northern Italian officials found it hard to set aside deep-rooted feelings of superiority, and the more energetic of them were often accused by Sicilians of treating the island as a colony.

Northern views of Sicily were not helped by misconceptions of the island's wealth. Ignorance tinged with mythology had fostered belief in a garden paradise, rich in wheat, citrus fruit, and vines. When the stark reality emerged, many people found it tempting to blame Sicilians for squandering their patrimony. The islanders were accused of being lazy, self-centred, and corrupt. Some liberals attributed these faults to Bourbon maladministration, but others felt that the islanders suffered from a deeper personality problem. Many centuries of neglect, it was claimed, had resulted in 'hypertrophy of the ego', while all idealism, and any sense of collectivity, had been annihilated by more than 2,000 years of despotic rule and invasion.[4] 'The Sicilian', said the sociologist, Gaspare Nicotri, 'thinks and feels like an Arab, acts like a Greek, and views life like a Spaniard'.[5] It was easy to proceed from this position to a feeling that the islanders were not only despicable, but incorrigible.

Northern dislike and mistrust of Sicilians were soon reciprocated. There were complaints that the island was becoming 'Piedmontised', that Sicilians were being treated 'like so many conquered and bartered sheep'.[6] There was nothing particularly new in this. Almost every regime in Sicily, including that of the Piedmontese themselves in the early eighteenth century, had seen initial enthusiasm turn sour and recriminatory: expectations were perhaps too high and vague to admit of anything but disappointment. What made the situation particularly difficult after 1860 was that the new government aimed to create a modern nation-state. This was largely unprecedented, as attempts by the Bourbons to curtail local autonomies had never been much more than half-hearted and had usually ground to a halt in the face of baronial opposition. The process of trying to integrate Sicily into the fabric of the Italian state was to be long and painful, and references to the resistance faced by the government were usually couched in terms of the mafia.

As a recent Minister of the Interior implied, referring to Carlo Alberto Dalla Chiesa's appointment as prefect of Palermo in 1982, the basic problem in Sicily had always been how to inculcate 'the values of the state'.[7] Most observers thought the solution lay in a combination of force and reform. In practice, however, force prevailed, certainly in the years immediately after 1860. In part this was because repression was simpler; but there was also the fact that the new regime depended on the support of social groups who were opposed to fundamental changes in the island. One result of this was that for fifteen years after 1860, the government denied the existence of a social question in Sicily (and, indeed, in the south of Italy as a whole), despite a major insurrection, widespread banditry, and considerable support for the International Working Men's Association. The Sicilian problem was regarded primarily as one of law and order. Any other approach ran the risk of alienating the big land-owners, who dominated the island.

The repressive measures of the 1860s were in part occasioned by fear. The Bourbon government had been brought down in 1860 through a mixture of peasant discontent and external intervention. Might the same fate not overtake Italy? Insecurity soon began to degenerate into paranoia. Clerical and Bourbon conspiracies, many of them more imagined than real, were continually unearthed.[8] The upsurge in lawlessness after 1860 threatened to provide an ideal breeding ground for insurrection, and this, as much as any abstract concern for the rule of law, made firm measures seem essential. Conspirators had troubled waters to fish in, and if the government proved powerless to protect life and property, the danger was that the influential classes might turn and support the dissidents, as they had in 1860.

One important source of unrest in Sicily after 1860 was conscription. The island had been exempted from a military levy under the Bourbons. Garibaldi tried to introduce compulsory service in May 1860, shortly before his capture of Palermo, but he wisely allowed for sweeping exemptions when he saw how unpopular it was. The new Italian governments were less flexible. Conscription, it was felt, should simultaneously express and promote the fact of unity. More-over, as the Prime Minister told parliament in 1863, it was important to show the rest of Europe that the southern provinces were 'no less devoted than the other regions to the cause of Italy'. Liberty, he added, was incompatible with internal disparities of the law – a laudable, though some might have felt dangerously narrow, assertion.[9]

Opposition to conscription was partly the result of a more general hostility to united Italy. By 1861, many Sicilians were suffering the effects of higher taxation and unemployment, and there was disappointment at the government's failure to introduce land reform. Why should this alien state now claim the island's most able-bodied men? According to official figures, there were 4,897 draft-dodgers in Sicily in 1861, and nearly 3,000 deserters.[10] The support of Garibaldi (who was immensely popular in the island) for the national cause had initially helped mitigate dissatisfaction with the new regime; but when, in 1862, the government opened fire on Garibaldi at Aspromonte, in order to stop him leading an army (composed largely of Sicilians) on Rome, discontent flared into opposition. At Canicattì the local population dressed in mourning and for three days there were demonstrations against the government and even against the king.[11] Elsewhere in Sicily there were similar signs that the gap between people and state was growing.

The government responded to this situation by imposing a state of siege. Over 2,000 people, including women, were arrested in the province of Palermo alone, and summary executions took place at Alcamo, Racalmuto, and elsewhere.[12] Official reports spoke of widespread left-wing and Bourbonist conspiracies. The Minister of the Interior announced that Garibaldi's supporters were suborning soldiers in Sicily on 'a massive scale'.[13] It was certainly true that pro-paganda against the government was mounting. Demonstrations in favour of Garibaldi were banned, and anyone caught singing the 'Garibaldi Hymn' was liable to imprisonment.[14] As arbitrariness increased, so more and more people fled into the countryside to avoid arrest. The relatives of army deserters were liable to pro-secution for 'complicity' or for withholding information from the authorities, and this further increased the haemorrhage of fugitives to the hills. According to one writer in the 1860s, there were 34 *latitanti* (people in hiding) for every one draft-dodger.[15]

A vicious circle had been set in motion. The government tried to explain the situation, as well as to justify the severity of its response, by talking of conspiracy. In September 1861, the Palermo news-paper *Il Precursore* referred to a 'diabolical organisation' spreading across Sicily and this 'terrifying plot', it said, was the reason that people were failing to co-operate with the authorities.[16] The episode of the so-called '*Pugnalatori*' added to the general tension and insecurity. One night in October 1862, thirteen people were stabbed more or less simultaneously in different parts of Palermo. No motive was ever discovered for the attacks, and although the authorities tried to implicate both the Garibaldians and the Bourbonists, some observers felt that the government itself might have been involved.[17] The event certainly provided the pretext for a general disarmament in Sicily, and this, conveniently enough, on the eve of a fresh campaign against deserters and draft-dodgers.

Resistance to the new regime continued to mount in the island. In the summer of 1863, habeas corpus was suspended for the second time in a year, and the Piedmontese general, Giuseppe Govone, arrived in the island at the head of twenty battalions of soldiers to restore order. His campaign lasted from June till September, and became famous for its brutality. He made use of the '*legge* Pica', a law that had originally been introduced to deal with banditry on the mainland South, but which was now extended illegally to Sicily. This allowed for summary executions, military tribunals, and the imposition of *domicilio coatto* (forced residence) by a commission made up of a prefect and four local officials. As if this were not arbitrary enough, Govone issued instructions that anyone of military age, or 'with the face of an assassin', should be arrested.[18]

Govone's campaign led to the arrest of 4,000 draft-dodgers and

1,350 criminals. The operations were limited to the four western provinces, as these had been, for reasons that were not clear, the most troublesome in Sicily. It was not so much the extent of the campaign as its severity that caused an outcry. Towns were besieged and anyone caught leaving was liable to be shot. Water supplies were cut – a dangerous measure in mid-summer – and women and children were seized as hostages.[19] Two episodes caused particular outrage. One was that of a family in Petralia, burnt alive in their house after being wrongly suspected of harbouring wanted men. The other was the case of a deaf-mute, Antonio Cappello, who was arrested as a draft-dodger and badly tortured. The authorities had refused to believe that he was handicapped.[20]

Govone subsequently tried to justify his methods by appealing to exceptional circumstances. However, in a speech to parliament he unwisely let slip a reference to the 'barbarity' of Sicily. This caused enormous ill-feeling in the island. Nor were matters improved when the government promoted him to the rank of Lieutenant-General.[21] Garibaldi was incensed by the whole episode and resigned his seat as a deputy. To add insult to injury, it was later revealed that nearly half of the 16,225 entries in the Sicilian conscription lists had been wrong. They had apparently included many women, children, and deceased.[22] The government, however, remained tactlessly unrepentant, and even braved Sicilian wrath by trying to reappoint Govone to Palermo in 1864.[23]

The initial experience of unification engendered in Sicily a profound mistrust of the authorities that was to poison the island's relations with the new state. The fault was not entirely the government's. Sicily, and in particular its western provinces, had long been notoriously difficult to rule. This was partly because the local nobility had been uncooperative, but it was also the result of a deep-rooted belief in the supremacy of private over public justice. The mistake of Italian governments after 1860 was their assumption that Sicilians acted out of immorality, rather than according to an alternative, but no less coherent, system of values. This standpoint justified the use of exceptional measures, as well as the drastic campaigns that men such as Medici, Malusardi, and Mori were to conduct in the years to come. Each new operation was explained by saying that previous ones had failed to go far enough.

The government's use of force, and its repeated suspension of habeas corpus, troubled liberal consciences both at home and abroad. Books and articles started to appear in England in 1863 and 1864, condemning the actions of the Italian state. 'No savages in the most barbarous parts of Africa', said one, 'ever treated their prisoners with more summary violence than the Piedmontese troops have in Southern Italy.'[24] Govone's operations in Sicily aroused particular concern, and the parliamentary debate on his campaign of December 1863 was translated with a damning preface:

> The impartial English reader will probably find the admissions and apologies, necessary for the defence of the Government, more damaging than the attack of its assailants; and, following this train of thought, he may be tempted to ask, 'How is it that since the establishment of this new state of things in Southern Italy there have been only continual complaints and appeals against the tyranny of the Northern Government? – allegations worse than the worst that were ever made against the Bourbons'.[25]

These criticisms were bound to be galling to a state eager to show the outside world that it enjoyed the support of its people. Italian politicians were no doubt genuine in their belief that the unrest in Sicily was due to Bourbon or Garibaldian conspiracies (and such conspiracies certainly existed); but the scale of the disorders indicated that more fundamental factors were at work. The social and political problems, however, were hard to admit to, largely because they entailed responses that were unacceptable to the conservative élite. From 1864, it was the criminal aspects of the Sicilian question that were highlighted. After all, every government had the right to maintain public order, and even a liberal regime could be forgiven the use of exceptional measures when the enemy that opposed it was a criminal leviathan.

In April 1865, Count Filippo Gualterio was appointed prefect of Palermo. He had been born in Umbria but had spent the 1850s in political exile in Piedmont where he had developed a strong regard for the political methods and principles of Cavour. He was a man of authoritarian temperament, with a keen nose for conspiracies,[26] and his appointment to Sicily marked the beginning of yet another attempt to restore order. Persistent draft-dodging and mounting unemployment had produced widespread lawlessness, and the fear, as always, was that the unrest would precipitate a rebellion. The difficulty lay in justifying exceptional measures. The government was more wary of suspending habeas corpus than it had been at the time of Govone's appointment.

Gualterio knew little about Sicily; and as prefect he showed scant curiosity for the province, or indeed the city, that he had been sent to govern.[27] A day or two after his arrival in Palermo, he wrote a report to the Minister of the Interior on the general situation in the province. 'What is...certain', he said,

> is that not only are there criminals, but they are organised. The mafia exists. The very word suggests association. This association of criminals is a large and long-standing sore, and when it shows

its head it is a sign that someone is manipulating it. The difficulty lies in establishing who this is . . . . Every party made the mistake of using it; and given the nature of the problem, I am inclined to think that one solution could be to deal with it as 'criminal association' and (provided we catch them) to try those involved under this heading and implicate the accomplices.[28]

This is the first reference we have to the mafia in any official document. Gualterio had political considerations uppermost in his mind, and he was clearly seeking to deal with what was essentially a political problem by criminalising it. This intention was made yet more apparent in another report to the Minister of the Interior on 25 April 1865. In it he explained that the 'so-called *maffia* or criminal association' had recently grown in brazenness. This was particularly worrying, he said, because every political movement – 'the liberals in 1848, the Bourbons at the Restoration, the Garibaldians in 1860' – had made use of it, and the danger now was of a Bourbon conspiracy. What was needed, therefore, was a thoroughgoing drive against crime, which would 'disarm' the Bourbon party 'without the complication for the time being of political trials which . . . are always extremely exbarrassing'. The whole operation, he concluded, must be conducted in such a way as to appear 'nothing other than a drastic campaign against unpunished criminals'.[29]

This fusion of politics with the idea of the mafia was to remain a key feature of the Sicilian problem for many decades to come. When discontent took the form of the socialist International in the 1870s, the government spoke of 'the mafia'; when the Sicilian parliamentary delegation passed almost *en bloc* to the opposition benches in 1874, the talk once again was of 'mafia'; attempts were made in the 1890s to stigmatise the socialist movement known as the *Fasci* as 'mafia'; the mafia was said to be instrumental in the great wave of land occupations after the First World War; and when the fascist government tried to strengthen its hold on the island after 1925, it did so in terms of a major operation against 'the mafia'.[30] As Gualterio saw, the concept of 'the mafia' was a powerful instrument for dealing with political unrest. Those with power in Sicily invariably had contacts with people who might be described as *mafiosi*; therefore, if 'mafioso' was taken to indicate membership of an organisation called 'the mafia', a wide range of 'accomplices' could conveniently be charged with criminal association.

The Palermo rising of 1866

In addition to simplifying the problem of political opposition, the idea of the mafia helped to direct attention away from the social and economic causes of unrest in Sicily. It also offered justification for repressive measures of the kind that had worried foreign (and also domestic) observers in the early 1860s. The Palermo revolt of 1866 provided a good example of this process. The episode was an enormous embarrassment to the new state, but by highlighting its criminal aspects and suggesting that the mafia was behind it, the authorities succeeded in reducing liberal disquiet to a minimum. If cut-throats and bandits were to blame, what other solution was there but repression? Once more habeas corpus was suspended, and the late 1860s continued with the now familiar pattern of large-scale military operations to restore order in the island.

Many factors lay behind the 1866 rising. Ths dissolution of the religious corporations had increased unemployment, while the so-called 'corso forzoso' (inconvertibility of banknotes) was adding to the general economic malaise. There was continued resistance to con-scription; taxes were higher than they had ever been under the Bour-bons; and Piedmontese insensitivity and general maladministration had offended local amour propre. There was also disappointment at the government's failure to tackle public works or land reform. When, in the summer of 1866, the Austro-Prussian war led to a withdrawal of troops from Palermo, the old habit of insurrection quickly resurfaced. The peasant revolutionaries of 1848 and 1860 led their squads down from the hills, and for a full week the city was in the grip of perhaps as many as 40,000 insurgents.

The rising lacked both co-ordination and a clear political prupose. The insurgents apparently hoped that middle-class elements would come forward as in previous revolutions and guide the movement.[31] This did not happen and members of the nobility had to be forced to append their names to the rebels' manifestos. However, frustration did not lead to widespread lawlessness.[32] A few houses were sacked, but almost invariably, as in the case of the Marquis di Rudinì, the mayor of Palermo, the target was selected for political reasons. Eye-witnesses were particulary struck by the seriousness, as well as humanity, of the rebels: the wounded and those taken prisoner were treated with due respect. Most commentators also admitted that the rising was a spontaneous expression of resentment. Any Bourbonist or Republican instigation was quickly lost beneath a gen-eral surge of popular anger.

General Raffaele Cadorna, who was sent to suppress the rising, was convinced of the need for exceptional measures. However, the government wavered.[33] Cadorna sought to justify his view by highlighting atrocities that had allegedly been committed by the insurgents. He spoke, in a report, of the military hospital being sacked, of the sick being thrown to the ground, and of mainland soldiers being singled out for execution. The Istituto Garibaldi, he said, had been looted and stripped to its nails. He claimed that a soldier had been crucified, a wounded policeman burnt alive, and the flesh of *carabinieri* sold openly in the streets. At Misilmeri, a policeman had been bitten to death and his body torn apart by women, according to Cadorna.[34] He also tried to show that the insurrection had been planned by monks. He had no hard evidence for this, though undoubtedly many clergy sympathised with the rebels, and some may even have assisted them. The absence of proof did not prevent Cadorna from arresting the Archbishop of Monreale (an elderly philosopher of international renown), nor from accusing the eighty-year-old Archbishop of Palermo of moral responsibility for the rising.

The Prime Minister was unwilling to authorise the establishment of military tribunals (there was again concern about foreign, as well as domestic, liberal opinion),[35] but he backed down when Cadorna threatened to resign. To salve his conscience, he allowed the general's account of atrocities to be published in the *Gazzetta Ufficiale*.[36] This gave official endorsement to a series of allegations which Cadorna himself later admitted to be no more than gossip.[37] A subsequent enquiry seems to have confirmed Cadorna's confession, but its findings were never published. When the issue was raised in a parliamentary debate in 1875, the relevant documentation was discovered to have vanished.[38] Sicily was now branded as a region of cannibalism. Episodes of violence had certainly occurred in the rising, but the lurid stories related by Cadorna were almost entirely fanciful.[39] The claim that human flesh was sold apparently resulted from taking a local expression for a bloodbath literally. 'Meat was being sold at five lire a kilo' meant there was a 'butcher's shop', that is, a scene of carnage.[40]

One aspect of the criminal slant given to the 1866 rising was the notion of 'the mafia'. In a statement to parliament in December, the Minister of the Interior said that the stern repressive measures in Sicily in recent years had been a consequence of the 'discovery of a disciplined association of criminals'. The Bourbonist conspirators, he added, had failed to find support among the common people and had fallen back on

agreements with the *maffia*, that rival of the Neapolitan *camorra*, which, however, it far exceeds in ferociousness, and which sometimes, for the heinousness of its crimes, and the fear that it inspires in the population, brings to mind the secret societies that in the Middle Ages spread their mysterious and terrible statutes over many parts of Europe. Those affiliated to the *maffia* . . . constitute a shapeless mass of turbulent elements who are ready to hurl themselves wherever any fearless hand may push them.

This is what happened, he concluded, in the Palermo rising, 'with those horrendous and bloody depredations that we have no wish to recall'.[41]

The fashion for conspiracy and secret societies in the age of romantic nationalism had lent an aura of respectablility to conspiratorial theories of causation. For example, in England *The Times* reported the presence of bourgeois elements among the rebels, and added: 'Indeed, the Maffia, a secret society, is said to include among its members many persons of an elevated class.'[42] An article in a Florentine newspaper, the *Opinione*, suggested the rising was part of a European legitimist conspiracy, and that Palermo had been chosen because of the susceptibility of its population. The plotters, it said, came from all sections of the lower classes (the bourgeoisie was untouched); and next time the reactionaries would select another major city, somewhere else in Europe.[43]

The Palermo rising was, in part, the result of a popular social movement. Its most prominent figures were peasant leaders such as Salvatore Miceli and Giuseppe Scordato, men who had already distinguished themselves in earlier revolutions. Their exploits were celebrated in ballads that were strongly anti-governmental; so anti-governmental, indeed, that at least one Sicilian ethnographer found them too embarrassing to print.[44] The social dimension to the rebellion gave added piquancy to the term 'mafia'. The Sicilian élite had been threatened for nearly a century by the progress of democracy; and now they had liberalism to contend with too. Without the repressive machinery of the state they might not have survived. They accordingly needed to depict the unrest as, above all, an issue for the police. The concept of the mafia was useful in this regard.

The Marquis di Rudinì, the young mayor of Palermo, was a rich landowner. During the rising, his house had been sacked and his Piedmontese wife forced to escape across the roof. In a statement to the Pisanelli commission investigating the events of September, he highlighted the problem of law and order. 'The *Mafia*,' he said, 'is powerful, perhaps more so than we think; and in a great many cases it is impossible to expose and punish it, since there is no evidence with which to conduct prosecutions.' To fully appreciate its force, he continued, its structure ('*ordinamento*') would need to be known. Only those who were protected by it could move freely about the countryside. He admitted to having used 'some arbitrariness' in making arrests, but, given the situation he faced, he felt this was justified. He was not sure where 'the mysterious organisation' had its headquarters ('*sede prinicpale*'). Nor did he know how many chiefs ('*capi*') or members of the mafia ('*affigliati alla Mafia*') there were.[45]

A number of other people (mostly landowners or government officials)[46] who were interviewed by the Pisanelli commission claimed that the mafia had been instrumental in the Palermo rising. Sometimes they had the peasant squads in mind, and they spoke of the need to defend the upper and middle classes.[47] More often the word was used as a general synonym for criminals. Magistrates, policemen, and soldiers tended to link the term to the absence of civic morality. Only when 'the nightmare of the Mafia' ceased, said a former head of the National Guard, would people talk to the authorities.[48] 'Fear of the Mafia', according to the Military Commander of Palermo, dominated every class, and public morale would only improve when the mafia was destroyed.[49]

The idea of a criminal conspiracy was emerging as an explanation for many confusing aspects of the Sicilian problem. Political unrest, social tension, crime, and *omertà* could all be imputed to the mysterious workings of the mafia. At this stage no attempt was made to analyse the precise content of the term. After all, governments in the 1860s were preoccupied with political matters. Their main aim was to consolidate national unity, and an essential precondition for this was domestic order. If the unrest in Italy's most troublesome region was criminal, the obvious solution lay with the police and army. This suited the authoritarian cast of northern officialdom and dispensed with any need to consider the social question.

The mafia as 'manutengolismo': the parliamentary crisis of 1874–76

The notion of the mafia continued to gain ground in political circles in the years after 1866.[50] General Cadorna's repression of the Palermo rising had done little to generate stability. A period of economic buoyancy alleviated the worst symptoms of lawlessness, but political opposition became more persistent and organised. Red flags and insurrectionary manifestos gave the authorities sleepless nights, and in 1870 Giuseppe Mazzini, the great champion of Italian nationalism, turned up in Sicily to promote a republican revolution. As in the early 1860s, police, soldiers, and magistrates were assassinated, often in mysterious circumstances.[51] With the onset of the agricultural depression after 1872, the chaos in the island grew more intense. The socialist International spread, and far from being driven into the arms of the government, the Sicilian parliamentary delegation became dogged in its opposition. In the autumn of 1874, the Prime Minister, Marco Minghetti, announced the need for exceptional measures to deal with the mafia.

An increase in serious crime, particularly kidnapping, had been one factor behind Minghetti's decision. Political considerations were also involved. The Paris Commune of 1871 had been popularly ascribed to the International, and its bloodiness led many, including professional criminologists such as Cesare Lombroso, to equate socialism with lawlessness.[52] The Palermo rising had also been attributed to criminals. Accordingly, the growth in Sicily of both crime and the International greatly alarmed the authorities. Fears of a socialist insurrection increased during 1873, and in August of the following year, a number of presumed Internationalist conspirators were arrested and charged with criminal association.[53]

Police reports in 1874 often failed to distinguish between '*mafiosi*' and '*internazionalisti*'. Indeed the terms were used more or less indiscriminately. Prefect Rasponi of Palermo was among those who decried this confusion. He told the government in July 1874 that a number of recent kidnappings in Sicily had almost certainly not been intended (as some had supposed) to swell the coffers of the International. The mystery that surrounded such crimes, he claimed, together with their audacity, and the apparent involvement of so many local people made it easy to imagine that they were part of the 'subversive plan of a real association'. For example, a number of fires near Cefalù, he said, had been ascribed to the International, but they later turned out to be merely acts of local vendetta.[54]

The government's fears were not easily allayed. A report to the Justice Ministry on the condition of public order in Sicily in 1874 spoke of the political danger from bandits. 'The brigand Pasquale', the author said, 'has proclaimed himself a second Spartacus. . . . And I have heard of a small town in the Carini area where a lodge has been organised in which all the local brigands have enrolled. They are already announcing the approach of a general insurrection for the division of private property and all the fun and games of the *Commune!*' The government, the report went on, should beware, as workers organisations were merely fronts for criminals: 'These sinister associations have their leaders and principal bases in the cities, where the *maffia* also has its directors and "yellow-gloved" [i.e. affluent] protectors.'[55]

Another cause for governmental concern in 1874 was the growth of parliamentary opposition in Sicily. The exact character of this movement is hard to gauge. Indeed, one recent Sicilian historian has described it as *mafiosa* and reactionary, another as the work of a progressive élite.[56] Some of the confusion derives from the awkward overlap of principle and self-interest. The landowners denounced governmental illiberalism, in part because years of repression had (as the Sicilian deputy, Francesco Crispi, pointed out) helped engender in the island the very unrest that the state sought to control. There was also, though, a question of injured pride. By subjecting Sicily to exceptional laws, the government bruised the local élite's deep-seated patriotism; this was exacerbated by their repeated exclusion from government. Finally, there was a specific question of taxation.

The government's proposed fiscal reforms in 1874 threatened many *latifondisti* (owners of great estates) and helped precipitate their defection to the Left.[57]

In the late summer of 1874, with elections pending, the government declared itself in favour of exceptional measures for Sicily. The Secretary General at the Ministry of the Interior, Luigi Gerra, was sent to the island, ostensibly to deal with banditry, but some observers suspected that his real mission was to influence the course of voting. The fact that local landowners began to be arrested for *manutengolismo* (protecting criminals) lent substance to these fears.[58] In October, shortly before polling, the Prime Minister delivered a major speech in which he proclaimed the need to tackle the mafia. If he had hoped that this would win him support in Sicily, he was soon to be disabused. Moreover, an implied comparison with Ireland dealt yet another blow to the island's battered self-esteem.

In the November elections, only three of the forty-eight deputies returned in Sicily were firmly pro-government. Of the remainder, forty were in outright opposition, and these included all the Palermo delegation. The government sought to explain the rout by reference to the mafia, bandits, *manutengolismo*, the International, and the Bourbons.[59] Once again there was talk of exceptional measures and a bill was brought forward, article two of which stated that anyone suspected of being a 'protector or accessory' (*manutengolo o favoreggiatore*) to crime would be liable to summary arrest. *Manutengolismo* was now claimed to be an essential aspect of the mafia. Since those traditionally associated with this charge included landowners and middle class electors, there was a strong feeling that the idea of the mafia was being twisted to fit the government's immediate political need to discredit and intimidate its opponents.

In order, it seems, to bolster the case for exceptional measures, the government had asked the Sicilian prefects in the spring of 1874 to furnish information about the mafia. These reports were published in May 1875. They put the question of the mafia firmly on the map, and, though bewildering to read and inconclusive, they appeared to lend substance to an idea that had been in the air for some time. *The Times* referred to them in June 1875, and said that everyone 'acquainted with the subject [is] agreed in attributing the actual condition of Sicily to the *Mafia*'. Nobody, however, was able to give an exact explanation of what it was, but

> its mysterious influence is felt in all except the most private affairs of daily life....Whenever anything unusual occurs... anything, in fact, which is a departure from the common course of things, it is declared by the public voice to be the work of the *Mafia*. It pervades all ranks of society....No man knows but

that his dearest friend may be a *Mafioso*, or that the family into which his daughter is about to marry is not deeply tainted with *Mafia*. Such, in a few words, is this mysterious association . . . .[60]

The prefects themselves had not found it easy to answer the Minister of the Interior's questions about the mafia. Prefect Berti of Girgenti said he had heard the word bandied about on many occasions; but when he asked people what they meant by it, they always failed to come up with any precise definition. However, the mafia was clearly not an organisation, he said; rather, it was 'an overbearing and practical explication of what is called the right of the strongest'. A man gained the reputation of being *'maffioso'* through appearing courageous, carrying weapons illicitly, duelling, and taking revenge for any insult he had received. Indeed, 'the personal exercise. . .of vendetta is the first law of the *maffia*'. *'Maffia'*, Berti concluded, was to be found in all social classes, and the links between its exponents were hard to establish.[61]

Perfect Fortuzzi was more accommodating to the government line; so much so that when his report was published he was publicly assaulted in Caltanissetta.[62] The only way, he said, to get rid of the mafia was with exceptional measures; liberalism was a waste of time in Sicily. *'Maffia'* was an instinctive and general evil deriving from a horror of work, and was expressed in acts of intimidation. There were 'lower' and 'upper' levels, he said, and the 'upper' used criminals to carry out vendettas. Since *'Maffia'* was instinctive, it had no rules nor any need for bonds 'between those who form part of it', except in the generic instance of the upper mafia's dealings with the lower. Unfortunately, he said, it was hard to identify the main offenders, for the problem was so diffuse that anyone, peasant or duke, could be *'un gran maffioso'*.[63]

The other prefects felt equally uncomfortable with a term that seemed to imply some precise and concrete substance. After all, as Prefect Gualterio had noted in 1865, the word itself suggested an association. Prefect Cotta Ramusino of Trapani tackled the dilemma by claiming that the mafia had formerly been an organisation, and like the *camorra* it had once had a strict hierarchy and even special clothes ('a large cap with a tassel of silk, pulled down obliquely over one eye'). But today, he said, mafia and *camorra* were no longer to be confused. *'Maffiosi*. . .have no conventions or laws'; they indulge in acts of daring and arrogance; and though there might be a 'kind of sympathetic force of attraction' between them, it was wrong to suppose that there was any 'affiliation'.[64]

Despite the vagueness of these reports, the government was determined to press ahead with exceptional measures, and the protests from Sicily were to a large extent written off as the desperate cries of the mafia.[65] This interpretation of Sicilian opposition was to enjoy a long history. In the 1920s, Cesare Mori explained the campaign against his work by saying it was the result of the mafia trying to save its skin. More recently, resistance to the granting of special powers to General Dalla Chiesa in 1982 was dismissed by many non-Sicilians as criminally inspired. Attitudes of this kind coarsened the debate on the mafia, and polarised positions irreparably. Sicilians retreated into *sicilianismo*, that intense local patriotism that saw in every misfortune the operation of northern prejudice. Mainlanders grew ever more convinced that Sicily was beyond redemption, and 'mafia' not only became an easy, if disfiguring, synonym for the Sicilian problem, but also an expression of northern contempt for a region that had failed to endorse 'the values of the state'.

The bill for exceptional measures was debated at length in June 1875. The Prime Minister had considered dispensing with parliamentary approval altogether, but this, he felt, would have played into the hands of the 'supporters of the *Maffia*'.[66] The discussion in the Chamber of Deputies was remarkable for the quality of its speeches, as well as for the damning revelations that were made about fifteen years of inept administration in Sicily by the Right. Passions ran high, and on occasions the debate degenerated into bombast. At one point, for example, the deputy Tamajo leapt to his feet, seething with indignation. 'Gentlemen, it is true. Sicily *is maffiosa*', but 'this noble and beautiful *maffiosa*', he said, had been subjected to 'ceaseless persecution'.[67]

The problem of what 'mafia' meant cropped up a number of times in the course of the debate. Paolo Paternostro said that the word was fashionable, but it had been so abused that it was now applied to almost any offence. Yet the government wanted special measures to deal with 'suspected *maffiosi*'. Given the looseness of the term, this was surely dangerous, he pointed out, particularly as many Sicilians already had very little faith in the authorities. The island's prefects had been asked to define '*maffioso*'. The word figured in the newspapers as well as the bill, so it was reasonable to assume that it corresponded to something definite. But, he said, the prefects had found themselves hopelessly confused, and one had said one thing, another something else. The government complained that it did not enjoy the support of the local population, but what had it done to deserve it? Police and magistrates had repeatedly abused their powers, and now, to cap it all, the government wanted to introduce exceptional measures yet again.[68]

The deputy, and president of the Court of Appeal in Catania, Camillo Longo, said that 'mafia' meant 'everything and nothing', 'as with all terms that embody no definite idea'. He had recently asked people in Catania for their views on the subject, but no one had been able to help him. He was therefore pleased to have learnt the meaning of the word from the parliamentary commission reporting on the bill for exceptional measures. 'The mafia', the commission had said, 'is the solidarity in crime and defence against the law. Solidarity that is nevertheless not solemnised by any formal pact; solidarity that is based on an identity of interests in committing certain crimes and escaping punishment; solidarity that is frequently practised without the display of any marked actions.' Could anything be vaguer than this, asked Longo? Yet the government, he said, was demanding special measures to destroy something that was essentially impalpable.[69]

The question of *manutengolismo* was one that worried many deputies. If the government was intending to clamp down on this newly discovered dimension of the mafia, how would willing and unwilling protectors be distinguished? The Minister of the Interior, Cantelli, did his best to reassure the Chamber. The opposition, he said, was worried about innocent people falling victim to private feuds or misunderstandings. There were certainly dangers involved, which is why suspects would be referred either to the judicial authorities or to a junta composed of a number of local officials including the prefect. Would such a committee send someone to *domicilio coatto* (forced residence) on the basis of mere suspicion? 'Yes' came the cry from the opposition benches. Surely mistakes were not all that frequent, Cantelli insisted? 'Yes, yes' came the refrain once more, and one deputy singled out a recent episode in Sciacca. 'I do not deny that some errors could have occurred', Cantelli replied, 'but the errors have been corrected.'[70]

However justified the government's claim that without exceptional measures the authorities would have been powerless in Sicily, the fears of the opposition were also well grounded. The vagueness of the terms 'mafia' and '*manutengolo*' could, and often did, lead to political victimisation, and this was particularly damaging in Sicily, where a widespread feeling already existed that justice was partial. Furthermore, the unpredictability of the law fostered the practice of clientelism: for who could feel safe without protectors? It also lent substance to a well established belief that prosecution in Sicily often stemmed from political vendetta[71]. This meant that even the guilty could pose plausibly as hapless victims. The problem has continued to this day: when the former mayor of Palermo, Vito Ciancimino, was arrested in November 1984, he attributed his misfortune to political infighting. So too did the financiers, Nino and Ignazio Salvo. A number of people may have believed them, at least in private.

Though the Sicilian ruling class denied the existence of the mafia in 1875, they were certainly sensitive to the issue of crime. When the target was as ill-defined as the mafia it was hard to know which way the axe would fall; on the other hand, a campaign against bandits and petty criminals was circumscribed and less threatening to the land-owners. In both cases, however, it was important to see who would be conducting police operations. A government prefect in 1875 would hardly have listened to the promptings of opposition repre-sentatives, and the effects of this would have been felt at every level. The careers of both a rural policeman and a *pretore* (local magistrate) depended on keeping the authorities happy in the provincial capital, and that often meant bowing to the wishes of the local pro-gov-ernment faction, which was always eager to worst its enemies.

In 1874–5 the landowners were worried about social unrest. The economy had begun to decline, and banditry and kidnapping were once more on the increase. What they needed was a police operation to buttress their position; when the Left came to power in 1876, this is largely what they got. The Sicilian élite had always been am-bivalent towards the government that ruled them. Abandoned to their own devices on the fringes of successive empires, they had grown accustomed over centuries to a measure of autonomy. How-ever, they had always lacked adequate resources to fend for them-selves. They needed the repressive machinery of the state to put down *jacqueries* or urban risings. This was one reason why oppo-sition in Sicily was ultimately half-hearted. The landowners disliked government interference, but they expected to be helped when the going was rough.

The absence of firm political initiative at the top was one reason why social and economic unrest in Sicily was rarely channelled effectively. Popular frustration usually expressed itself in dull and fragmented anti-statism, interspersed with moments of violence. When the discontent threatened the landowners – as in 1866, or during the socialist *Fasci* of the 1890s, or immediately after the First World War – the notion of the mafia helped the Sicilian élite, as well as the government, to legitimise repression. Cesare Mori, a long-standing ally of the landowners, spoke of the turmoil and land oc-cupations of 1919–22 in terms of delinquency and mafia.[72] His appointment as prefect of Palermo in 1925 came as a great relief to the aristocracy. Prior to that the local fascists had been active against the mafia, and in their eyes the mafia was largely synonymous with the old élite. Mori focussed most of his campaign on the peasantry.

The problem of where the axe should fall with the mafia has persisted to this day. Discussion about 'upper' and 'lower' mafias, the involvement of the parliamentary parties, and, recently, the role of the so-called 'third level' bears witness to the interconnection of mafia and politics: not so much in the sense dear to the left (that is, that the mafia is essentially an instrument in the hands of the ruling classes) but rather that perceptions of the mafia, without any clear-cut entity to which to refer, invariably become coloured by political considerations. To the heirs of the nineteenth-century democrats, for example, the mafia is almost an extension of the state. For some Marxists, the question is one of capitalism run riot. Certain Sicilian patriots will still deny the existence of the problem, while the descendants of General Govone, General Medici, and Prefect Mori look on the mafia as a criminal aberration born of the state's weakness; in their view, the best remedy is force.

Despite the protests of Sicilian deputies in 1875 and the vagueness of the prefectural reports, the mafia was by then widely regarded as the main cause of the island's problems. The repressive measures of the preceding fifteen years seemed vindicated. Foreign observers no longer felt outraged, as they had in the early 1860s, at the illiberal treatment meted out to Sicily.[73] If the mafia was a deadly organisation that preyed on the weak and innocent, surely any means were justified in dealing with it? Sicilian crime now became a source of endless fascination to outsiders. When, for example, in 1878, three members of a brigand band escaped the clutches of the police, *The Times* attributed it to 'masterly' arrangements made by the mafia. 'It is well known', the paper added, 'that in Sicily the Mafia is every-where'.[74] Travellers to the island invariably sought information about the society; they almost always wrote of it in terms of a secret organisation that operated 'with knife, with gun, with dagger, with halter, with fire and with poison'.[75]

While repression established itself as the stock response to unrest in Sicily, so images of the mafia became appropriately horrifying. To the Procurator Royal, Gerolamo Floreno, writing in 1874, it was a 'Dantean she-wolf that [held] the petrified souls of those who might dare speak out against it in an iron grip'.[76] Many writers compared the mafia to a giant octopus (*piovra*) whose tentacles reached into every corner of Sicilian life.[77] This proved to be the most enduring image, and it helped reinforce the idea of a widespread organisation with a single co-ordinating body. Metaphors of disease were also abundant. Sicily was described as being infected with a cancerous growth that was destroying the body politic.[78] The only effective antidote to both monsters and tumours was violent intervention, a point which fascist writers were particularly keen to underline in the 1920s.

The mafia and racial degeneracy: the school of positivist criminology

The case for strong police action in Sicily was reinforced, and not altogether unwittingly, by the work of a large and influential group of positivist criminologists. Their ideas became fashionable in the late 1870s and 1880s, and coincided with the disillusionment felt by many intellectuals at Italy's failure to live up to the expectations of the Risorgimento. The desire to account for national weakness was one reason for a growing obsession with crime. Italy, it was discovered, enjoyed a 'sad primacy' in this field: the South, with its high incidence of violence, was particularly to blame. Moreover, the lawlessness of Italy's southern regions was only partly due to social and economic backwardness. The real root of the problem, it was said, was racial. Southerners were alleged to be descended from a 'Mediterranean race' that had originated in Africa. This accounted for their 'atavistic behaviour', and 'atavism' was seen by the new school of criminology as the main threat to Italy.[79]

Men such as Cesare Lombroso, Enrico Ferri, and Giuseppe Sergi were convinced that they had turned the study of crime into science. They packed their writings with statistics, graphs, detailed measurements, and photographs. Their work, however, is an object lesson in unconscious distortion. As with other systematisers of the late nineteenth century, a fervent secular faith inspired their perceptions. Signs of atavism were regularly 'detected' in men they defined as 'born delinquents'. These people had scant facial hair, narrow foreheads, large jaws and canine teeth, prominent chins, and handle-shaped ears. They gesticulated frequently, and their brains resembled those of madmen and savages. The most violent offenders had dark hair.[80] The main concentration of 'born delinquents' was in the southern regions, where the higher incidence of murder was taken as a firm indication of atavism. This led one criminologist to write a book about the South under the title *Contemporary Barbarian Italy*.[81]

Criminal associations were another sure sign of atavism. The barbarous races often produced secret societies, according to Cesare Lombroso. These might sometimes begin as defence movements against oppressors, as with the *camorra*; they could also be instruments for maintaining a moral code, as with the Mumbo Djembo tribe of Senegal. However, any appearance of nobility or altruism was deceptive, said Lombroso. All these associations were fundamentally criminal, and they indulged in violence whenever they could.[82] This was certainly true, he said, of the mafia, whose pretensions to generosity were simply a smokescreen. *Mafiosi* posed as revolutionaries in 1820, 'and worse still in our own times' (that is, 1866), but their aim was simply to 'conceal a criminal escapade beneath a political banner'. Members of the mafia were no more than common criminals, and this, Lombroso claimed, was evident from their dress, their jargon, and their preference for expensive rings.[83]

For someone concerned with scientific enquiry, Lombroso was remarkably naïve in his description of the mafia. His account of Sicilian crime was made up of half-truths and gossip; given the success of his work, both in Italy and abroad, this was unfortunate. He claimed the mafia was a variation of the *camorra*, and the differences were 'due, perhaps to the greater secrecy of the semitic race'.[84] However, the Sicilian organisation retained many features of its Neapolitan counterpart. In the prisons it had the same practices and hierarchical names; there was a livery (*'livrea'*) consisting of rings, a tie, a cap, and tassel; and the language of *mafiosi*, like that of the *camorristi*, was crisp and concise. 'To some extent they may have lost their strict organisation; but in certain circumstances they not only resume it, but resume it with a vengeance: for example in the Palermo revolution, or the Monte di Pietà theft.'[85]

Though Lombroso recorded in his bibliographies such serious works on Sicily as those by Leopoldo Franchetti and Giuseppe Pitré, he could not resist the temptation to sensationalise the mafia. This was largely because he viewed Sicily as a primitive culture, and the grotesque and the exotic were accordingly emphasised. *Mafiosi*, he said, followed the rules of *'omertà'*, a code that was 'fearsomely obeyed', and whose workings were 'revealed to us by Pitré and Vincenzo Maggiorani'. (Why Maggiorani should be mentioned in this context is far from clear: his writings on Sicily were limited to an account of the 1866 rising.) Anyone who broke the rules of *omertà* was killed, even in prison, where, in the absence of weapons, the victim was drowned in a basin of excrement. Sometimes, according to Lombroso, *mafiosi* would be told to commit suicide. This message would be conveyed by a cross on the door, or a shot fired at the house.[86]

Lombroso's sources for this pastiche are not certain. Like many writers on the mafia, he started from the premise of a criminal organisation and sucked into his account almost any aspect of Sicilian life that came to hand. He might have heard of a prisoner being drowned in excrement; this became a feature of the mafia. *Omertà*, which, as many observers pointed out, was a general feature of western Sicily, emerged as a sinister criminal code. The suicide idea is less easy to fathom, though crosses were sometimes chalked on doors as an act of intimidation or warning.[87] Occasionally Lombroso seems merely to have misinterpreted a metaphor, as when he says that the leading *mafiosi* of Messina used to wear yellow gloves.[88] The term 'yellow-gloved' was often employed in Sicily as a synonym for social superiority.

The followers of the positivist school had little specific interest in Sicily: their main concern was with a general classification of criminal types. Through the laborious accumulation of data they hoped to arrive at mechanistic explanations for crime that would dispense with notions of moral responsibility. However, they were by no means impartial. Their desire for a new secular culture was rooted in profound anti-clericalism (evident, for example, in Lombroso's claim that the strength of the Palermo mafia was directly related to the number of convents in the area).[89] Their studies of degeneracy were also tinged with fears about Italy's status as a great power. According to Alfredo Niceforo, the barbarian South would have to be civilised forcibly if the nation wished to become strong. Liberalism, however, was of no use here: primitive societies, he said, 'need the strong and sometimes despotic action of whoever would snatch them from the darkness'. Only if this were admitted would the state's 'wretched bankruptcy' be ended, and 'the new Italy', that 'pure dream of our poets and martyrs', finally be achieved.[90]

The precise influence of these positivist criminologists is hard to gauge. They failed to have an impact on the new penal code of 1889, chiefly, it seems, because their recommendations were impractical.[91] Their most important legacy was in the realm of attitudes. Northern views of the South as a degenerate region were reinforced; the language of atavism and race gave further justification to repressive action. It is perhaps not surprising that a leading exponent of the positivist school, Enrico Ferri, endorsed Cesare Mori's campaign against the mafia in the 1920s.[92] Mori himself was a nationalist, and shared many of Lombroso's and Niceforo's concerns about Italy's decline. Like them, he believed in the civilising value of strong police action. He paid lip-service to economic and social reforms, but Mori shared Niceforo's view that primitive people understood best the language of force, and this led him to regard repression not only as preventive, but also as something that necessarily induced morality.

Socialism and reaction: the mafia in the 1890s

The generation of the 1890s was influenced not by racial ideas, but by Marxism, and the most powerful minds thought in terms of materialism and the social question. Poverty, land reforms, education, and the class struggle became the focus of attention, and crime, far from being a cause of Italy's malaise, was now considered merely a symptom. When the mafia was discussed, it was to criticise Sicily's grinding poverty, the *latifondi* (great estates) and, above all, the government. For example, Napoleone Colajanni, the Radical deputy, said the mafia was the product of decades of bad administration and neglect. How, he asked, were Sicilians supposed to behave when they had been ruled for so long with partiality and arbitrariness? Crime and violence, he said, were natural responses to brutal circumstances, and the mafia could only be defeated by the provision of justice in the widest sense. That meant that the Italian government should take far more responsibility for Sicily than it had done in the past.[93]

The socialist deputy, Giuseppe De Felice Giuffrida, was more concrete in his anti-governmentalism. Addressing parliament in November 1899, he said that the mafia was composed of three levels: that of the people, that of the police, and that of the 'overbearing bourgeoisie'. Of this trio, the least important was the first. The poeple had always been 'victims rather than accomplices' of the mafia. It was the police and the propertied classes who were most to blame. As under the Bourbons, the public security forces constituted an 'official mafia' and they were not only directly involved in all major robberies, he said, but even headed criminal associations. The bourgeoisie, on the other hand, used the mafia in elections, and prisoners were even released from gaol on the eve of polling, to intimidate voters. 'The [electoral] practice of every government has been the explanation, indeed the cause and origin of the growth of this cancer that afflicts the wretched island of Sicily.'[94]

De Felice's view of the mafia dovetailed with the growing mood of anti-parliamentarism among intellectuals of the left. However, the attempt to stress Sicily's social rather than criminal problems was undermined by popular and official hysteria. This was evident in the reaction to the socialist movement known as the *Fasci* of 1892–4.★ The landowners and government were terrified by this expression of peasant militancy, and, as in 1866, they tried to criminalise it. The outbreak of social unrest in Sicily in 1892 was greeted with demands for the suppression of brigandage, even though there seems to have been only one bandit gand to speak of at the time.[95] The authorities produced reports on the *Fasci* that tried to link them with the mafia. For example, in September 1893, the Palermo Chief of Police said that local crime had assumed 'alarming proportions': 'I firmly believe that this situation stems directly from the evil influence of the *Fasci*. The mafia and the entire criminal class have enrolled in them, and can thereby impose themselves more easily on others'.[96]

The *Fasci* were, to begin with, too well organised and strong for repression to be readily countenanced. Furthermore, they had received a great deal of publicity. When Cesare Mori conducted his police operations in the 1920s, he was helped by strict press censorship. He also had the advantage of a political climate that made strong action acceptable: in the 1890s, authoritarianism was a much more contentious issue. Only with the growth of disorder at the end of 1893 could the Prime Minister, Francesco Crispi, justify interven-

---

★ Fasci (literally 'bundles') was the name given to the local organisations, usually socialist-led, that spread across much of western Sicily in 1892–4. Their goals were varied, and often not clearly defined, but in general they aimed at collective action to improve the pay and conditions of the peasantry.

tion. He claimed to have proof that the socialists were planning a revolution in Sicily, and that it was being backed by France and Russia. In a manner now familiar, 40,000 troops were dispatched to the island, and the *Fasci*, arguably the most disciplined expression ever of popular discontent in Sicily, were rapidly suppressed.

As in 1866, the government looked warily over its shoulder at reaction both at home and abroad. Foreign scepticism was certainly in evidence, though this time it seems to have been more muted. The reporter for *The Times* said that the *Fasci* had been the product of bitter discontent and desperate social problems. He was informed, however, 'on the highest authority, that the proofs of concerted revolutionary plans in the hands of the Government are abundant and decisive'. The great mass of Sicilians, he said, was being led, it seems, 'wittingly or not, into a scheme which the leaders of it intended to develop into a general insurrection, having as its object a social revolution in which Sicily was to lead and the Peninsula to follow'. All this, however, struck him as convenient for the government: 'This certainly makes the solution of the difficulty much easier than if there had been nothing beyond the distress from want to deal with'.[97]

The *Fasci* restored Sicily to the centre of the Italian political stage after more than a decade of neglect. However, two episodes – at home and further afield – ensured that crime continued to be regarded as the essence of the island's problems. One was the brutal murder in 1892 of Emanuele Notarbartolo, a highly respected Palermo dignitary, whose endeavours to expose corruption in the Bank of Sicily had earned him dangerous political enemies. The other was the assassination in October 1890 of a policeman, David Hennessy, in New Orleans. His murder resulted in an extraordinary outburst of hysteria and xenophobia that was to have tragic consequences, and for the first time the idea of the mafia penetrated the public imagination in the United States. Both crimes were shrouded in mystery. This allowed for the operation of fantasy as well as political manipulation.

Immigration formed the background to the Hennessy murder. By 1890 there were over 25,000 Italians in New Orleans. Many of them were prosperous merchants. The Sicilians formed the largest single community and they dominated the fruit trade.[98] In 1888, with business flourishing, the main importers formed a ring. This led to increased rivalry for jobs. Two factions in particular, the Matrangas and Provenzanos, vied with one another, and in May 1890 a number of Matrangas were shot at as they returned from work. Members of the Provenzano group were arrested and later prosecuted, largely on the basis of Matranga evidence.[99] However, a retrial was ordered. David Hennessy, the local Chief of Police, was thought to be better disposed towards the Provenzanos than the Matrangas, and there was a strong chance that his evidence would result in the acquittal of the Provenzanos. Two days before the retrial was due to begin, he was murdered.[100]

Though everything suggested a connection with the Provenzano – Matranga case, there was almost no evidence to go on. A wave of panic spread through the city. Some people thought Hennessy had muttered the word 'dagos' before he died; others that he had whispered, 'The Sicilians have done for me'.[101] A 'Committee of Fifty' was set up to take charge of matters. The mayor, a rabid, pro-papal Irish Catholic, raided the Italian quarter, and arrested several hundred of its inhabitants.[102] Of these, twelve were eventually sent to trial. Proceedings against nine of them began on 28 February 1891. Great care was taken with the selection of the jury, and 1,300 people had to be examined on oath before a quorum could be reached. The hearing lasted twelve days and, at the end of it, six of the accused were found not guilty. For the remaining three, a 'mistrial' was declared.[103]

Immediately after the verdict, the 'Committee of Fifty' met; the following morning a notice appeared in the local papers inviting 'all good citizens' to 'a mass meeting...to remedy the failure of justice in the Hennessy case'. They were told to come 'prepared for action'. The crowd gathered, and two main grievances were voiced: firstly, that Hennessy had been murdered by 'an organised band of assassins known as the Mafia Society', and secondly, that the accused had been acquitted by an 'infamous jury' of 'perjurers and scoundrels' who had been bribed.[104] The crowd then marched to the parish prison, in orderly fashion. A select group that included, it seems, a number of prominent local politicians, entered, and lynched nine of the Sicilian defendants, two of whom had not yet stood trial. Giacomo Caruso was shot forty-two times. Two of the remaining prisoners were then dragged outside and strung up. The crowd cheered, and the ladies, according to one report, waved their handkerchiefs from the balconies.[105]

The sources of such venom are hard to fathom. The Italian community in New Orleans had clearly retained a strong corporate identity. 'The lower orders', according to the British consul, greeted the verdict in the Hennessy trial with shouts and jeers. They ran up Italian flags, 'and some went so far as to hoist one on a signal-mast...with the American ensign – Union down – below it'.[106] The chauvinism may have stemmed from economic rivalry. The wealth of the Italians in New Orleans was prodigious. They ran 3,000 shops and a large number of successful firms. Poverty, petty crime, and vendetta appear to have been limited to Decatur Street, and it was largely in this marginal section of the community that Hennessy had conducted his enquiries. The great majority of immigrants, so the

Italian consul informed the Prime Minister, di Rudini, were respectable and prosperous. Might this not account, he suggested, for some of the hostility towards them? Could it not be that certain people had a vested interest in finding the Italians guilty?[107]

Hennessy's murder unleashed a wave of hysteria about the mafia. The idea of a large and deadly secret society gripped the American imagination. It was now accredited retrospectively with every killing in New Orleans since 1855 that had involved an Italian.[108] Its clandestine character, according to one newspaper, was shown by the persistent failure of the authorities to identify the guilty parties. The *New Orleans Times Democrat* reported in May 1891 that it was convinced of the existence of 'the secret organization styled "Mafia"'.

> The evidence comes from several sources, fully competent in themselves to attest its truth, while the fact is supported by the long record of blood-curdling crimes, it being almost impossible to discover the perpetrators or secure witnesses. As if to guard against exposure, the dagger or stiletto is selected as the deadly weapon to plunge into the breast or back of the victim and silently to do its fearful work.

The article went on to say that the society was composed largely of Italians and Sicilians who had crossed the Atlantic to avoid prosecution at home: 'These men knew the swift retribution of the law in Italy, for hundreds have been shot down at sight by the military in the mountains of Sicily without a second thought.'[109]

Several dozen American newspapers and journals carried similar articles. W.J. Stillman, the correspondent of *The Times* in Italy, produced a lurid piece for *The Nation*, one of America's most prestigious periodicals. 'The Mafia', he said, was a secret society that went back, in one form or another, to the Middle Ages. Anyone who injured an associate was killed and his hands cut off; if he had heard forbidden secrets, his ears were severed; if he had seen too much, the skin of his forehead was flayed and turned down over his eyes. In its simplest form, he said, the mafia engaged in brigandage and kidnapping. It boasted a large network of spies and informers. However, the Italian government was gradually paralysing the society through steady pressure; and it was probable, he concluded, that the organisation was now stronger in Louisiana than in Sicily.[110]

Stillman appears to have had no qualms about fuelling xenophobia. 'The flagrantly criminal character of a large portion of the Italian emigration to the Southern States', he said, 'is too well known here to permit their countrymen at home to doubt that the authorities at New Orleans have a knotty problem to deal with in the Mafia, and it is admitted that the extermination of the organization is necessary to order.' Drastic measures were needed, as 'every emigrant from Sicily is suspicious'. There were certainly honest Sicilians, 'but the proportion of such in the mass of emigration is very small'. The people of New Orleans, he concluded, would have to ensure that membership of the mafia was a criminal offence. Otherwise, the problem could only be solved by expelling all Italians from the state.[111]

Stillman may well have regretted this article. A fortnight later he wrote a far more circumspect piece on the mafia, also for *The Nation*. He had now consulted the best Italian authorities, he said, and found that the mafia was not a single, formal organisation, 'but a state of society, existing in every part of Sicily, which is in revolt against the law'. Only occasionally did *mafiosi* form bands, with oaths, statutes, and initiation rites, he said. The general tone of this article was sober. Nevertheless, Stillman could not resist ending with a sensationalist quotation from the sociologist, Giuseppe Alongi: 'Once the first nucleus of the brotherhood is constituted, it spreads rapidly, recruiting adherents among the criminals and evil-livers of every kind. This force of expansion, given the anthropological and historical circumstances of Sicily, is frightful.'[112]

In the charged atmosphere that surrounded the lynchings, there was little opportunity for objective analysis. This worried the British consul in New Orleans. Before Hennessy's death, he reported, the mafia had scarcely been mentioned. 'Since then any crime committed upon the body of an Italian has been attributed to its action.' Previous murders had been ascribed not to an organisation, but to 'personal, family, and business quarrels, and to retaliation by the friends of the victim'. He concluded:

> Mafia is a good word with which to conjure up prejudice and hide unpleasant truths. It has been, and is, so used by the press all over this country; but I think, if ever the real facts come out (and they may), it will be seen that the late Chief of Police was murdered at the instigation of individuals, out of fear that he would be instrumental in letting their enemies loose upon them, and not by any organized Society.[113]

Sicily's reputation was too low for international opinion to register much outrage at the lynchings in New Orleans. After all, as *The Times* reported in February 1891, the islanders were often 'deceitful, reticent, malicious and vindictive'; they would combine to hide each other's misdeeds, 'owing to the spirit of "mafia" and "*omertà*" which pervades all Sicily'. They also displayed 'excessive cruelty' to animals.[114] Such negative evaluations made it easier to accept the received view of the Hennessy murder. Heckethorn, in his 1897 encyclopaedia of secret societies, ascribed the murder unquestioningly to the mafia. The killers, he said, used 'muskets, sawn off behind the trigger, and with the butts hinged on, so that the guns could fold into the pocket'. These, he explained, were used 'only by Italian and Sicilian desperadoes'. The trial, he informed his readers, was a disaster: despite 'overwhelming evidence' against the accused, the jury was intimidated, and the culprits acquitted.[115]

The idea that the Sicilian problem was essentially one of crime was now as entrenched abroad as in Italy. The murder of Emanuele Notarbartolo, and the ensuing trial of the deputy Raffaele Palizzolo, added further grist to the mill. Commenting on the affair in December 1899, the British ambassador in Rome told the Foreign Secretary that the assassination had been the work of the mafia. This organisation, he said, began a long time back as a union of peasants protecting themselves against the oppressive weight of feudalism. Under the Bourbons it acquired 'a political complexion'; but since 1860, it had 'degenerated into an association of malefactors who seek to enrich themselves at the expense of the general community. . . .It is to be hoped', he concluded, 'that the energy shown by the Government in seizing one of the acknowledged heads of this association will lead to the complete suppression of the society'.[116]

The claim that the mafia had degenerated into a criminal organisation was to be repeated on numerous occasions down to the present day. Many police operations were prefaced by such an assertion. Cesare Mori, for example, justified his action in the 1920s by referring to the mafia's descent in recent years into pure criminality. After the Second World War, the mafia was said to have degenerated into gangsterism, and much of the blame was put on the Americans. More recently, the supergrass, Tommaso Buscetta, spoke of the mafia's decline from a noble organisation that protected the weak back in the 1950s, to an association of ruthless common criminals in the 1980s. The theme of 'degeneration' helped square some of the discordancy generated by the idea of the mafia. To placate Sicilian patriotism, it was necessary to pay lip-service to the mafia's nobility; to justify repression (or, in the case of Buscetta, collaboration) it was vital to say that this nobility was now a thing of the past.

The idea of degeneration grew stronger after the 1890s as anti-Sicilian feeling intensified. The Notarbartolo affair polarised national opinion, much as the Dreyfus case did in France; and though the evidence against the accused was circumstantial, in the charged atmosphere of the time, allegations stuck. As with the great trials of the 1920s and the 1980s,[117] the result was a verdict that breathed partiality, and prejudice of one kind or another had no doubt been at work. Palizzolo, according to *The Times*, defended himself 'in declamatory style with verbose eloquence and abundance of gesture', and 'seemed to lack that element of simple straightforwardness which carries conviction'. By contrast, Lieutenant Notarbartolo, the main prosecution witness, spoke with 'sobriety, scrupulous attention to fact, and careful separation of deduction from premise'. This difference of style, the paper felt, must have had an effect. 'The constant by-play with eyes and hands afforded daily demonstration of the impalpable methods of the mafia, and unquestionably helped to persuade the jury of the credibility of the evidence for the prosecution.'[119]

Palizzolo's conviction was hailed as a major victory for the state. 'The verdict deals a tremendous blow at the Mafia, both high and low', *The Times* recorded, 'and will enormously increase the prestige of Italian justice in the eyes of the people'.[120] The second half of this comment, in particular, was questionable. There was already a strong and growing feeling in Sicily that Palizzolo's conviction was another example of anti-Sicilian prejudice. When, in 1904, his sentence was overturned on appeal (it was now admitted that the prosecution evidence did not hold water), there was an outburst of exuberant celebration in the island. A boat was chartered to bring Palizzolo home in triumph. The streets of Palermo were decorated with banners, shops were closed, and a day of festivities was proclaimed.[121]

The noontide of 'sicilianismo': the age of Giolitti

The patriotism (*sicilianismo*) that swept Sicily in the early years of the century had a number of sources. Men such as Giuseppe Pitré and Salvatore Salomone-Marino had fostered pride as well as interest in local culture through their ethnographic studies. They were helped by the writers Giovanni Verga, Luigi Capuana and Federico De Roberto who, from the 1880s, turned to Sicilian themes and discovered in village life a tragic intensity to fit their interest in realism. Economic self-consciousness was also an agent of patriotism. The entrepreneur, Ignazio Florio, established a pressure group in 1900 to seek recognition for the island's particular agricultural and industrial requirements. The depression of the 1880s and 1890s had been a major cause of the *Fasci*, and many members of the Sicilian ruling class had become aware of the case for conservative reform. Simple repression was no longer regarded as the answer, and the government needed to be persuaded of this.[122]

Though *sicilianismo* was partly the product of wounded *amour propre*, it had the great merit of inducing a more sympathetic approach to the island's problems. Any radical reappraisal of the Sicilian question, however, would have meant the destruction of clichés; and, as Luigi Capuana suggested, old prejudices died hard. He said that his own and Verga's efforts to depict the sad reality of Sicilian peasant life counted for little: most mainlanders simply remembered the famous cry at the end of Mascagni's opera, *Cavalleria Rusticana* (based on a short story by Verga), '*hanno ammazzato compare Turiddu*' ('they have murdered *compare* Turiddu'). As for foreigners, they expected the island to be 'strange, fantastic, and deformed'. Consequently, what was commonplace elsewhere, he claimed, was regarded as 'lurid' when it occurred in Sicily.[123]

Capuana's essay, 'La Sicilia e il brigantaggio', was published in 1892. It was an early attempt to correct some of the more extravagant claims made for the island. Crime, he said, despite what was usually alleged, was not a distinctive feature of Sicily. Statistics showed, for example, that the increase in offences from 1863 to 1871 was less in Sicily than elsewhere in Italy, and relative to its population, the island stood seventh in the national league table of crime in 1871. In the years 1887–9, Livorno had the greatest number of offences reported to the *pretori*; Girgenti came 16th; Siracusa, 18th; and Palermo, 34th. Even on the question of acquittals for lack of proof, Sicily, in Caputana's view, was no worse than many other regions. In 1869 –70, more than 80% of trials in Milan had to be abandoned through the absence of evidence; in Turin the figure was over 70%; in Palermo it was around 65%.[124]

Sicily's evil reputation owed much, according to Capuana, to the recent distortion in the meaning of the word 'mafia'. Until not long ago, he said, the term had enjoyed a limited currency in western Sicily. It was an abstraction from '*mafioso*'; and referred to

> men, particularly young men, of overbearing character, who could be violent when the situation demanded, and who sported singular notions of chivalry. They were incapable of betraying their enemies, and would certainly never rob from an opponent they had wounded or killed. Circumstances might make them adept thieves, or savage brigands, but usually their carefree idleness and thirst for domination died out along with their youthful temerity.[125]

The popular idea that the mafia was a criminal organisation, he said, was quite simply nonsense. *Mafiosi* might have their own jargon but, as every Sicilian knew, anybody could become *mafioso* from one day to the next, provided he had the requisite effrontery. There was no admission ceremony, and what organisation there was, he claimed, stemmed from the simple fact that rogues the world over recognised one another instinctively.[126]

Capuana's arguments in defence of Sicily echoed some of those advanced by Francesco Crispi and his colleagues in the parliamentary debate of 1875. However, the sustained passion of his essay, and the fact that he was a writer rather than a professional politician, indicated how much deeper the current of *sicilianismo* was now flowing. It was ironic that this local chauvinism should have flourished in the period before the First World War. The twentieth century began with fresh departures in both liberalism and nationalism; these, it might have been hoped, would assist national integration. However, the social and economic concessions of the Prime Minister, Giovanni Giolitti (who dominated Italian political life between 1901 and 1914), were directed mainly at northern workers, while the Nationalists hankered after a strong state – and this, in crude terms, meant industrialisation. On both counts most Sicilians could feel that they had been cheated.

The failure of Giolitti's governments to see the problem of Sicily in social and economic terms ensured that the traditional criminal image remained. Two distinguished lawyers, one from Palermo, the other from Messina, took strong exception to this. Their book, *Mafia*, published in Rome in 1911, was a powerful *cri de coeur* and a classic expression of *sicilianismo*.[127] It set out to show that general notions of the mafia were entirely false and that Sicily had in the preceding half-century been grossly misrepresented. The mafia was not, they said, nor ever had been a criminal organisation. It was simply 'a way of feeling' that was inspired by generosity and nobility of spirit, and never by baseness: 'The Mafia...far from being a murky shadow, is, for the Sicilian, a virtue: it is his glory'.[128]

Much of the book was written by Salvatore Morasca. He regretted that the term 'mafia' had become so 'encrusted with layers of filth' as to be unrecognisable.[129] The word, he said, was now used for many different types of crime and social problem:

> But what link could there be between the criminality of the sulphur workers...and that of the men dwelling among the orchards of the Conca d'oro,...between the cattle-rustlers...in the terrifying and abysmal solitude of the *latifondi*, and the *souteneurs* of the Palermo brothels? Everything has been lumped together into a single word: Mafia. At the very most a distinction is made between the mafia of the city and that of the countryside.

Nobody on the mainland, said Morasca, seemed to be aware that in Sicily the word 'is almost always used in the laudatory sense so well illustrated by Pitré'.[130]

Morasca pointed out the peculiar tenaciousness of the idea of a criminal association. Writers such as Franchetti and Alongi, he said, conceded that there was no formal structure and yet wrote of the mafia as if it were a concrete entity. It was certainly true that *mafiosi* had friends and clients: men of authority were invariably asked to settle disputes or arbitrate. But did these social ties, he asked, amount to a criminal association?

It is indeed a peculiar *societas scelerum* that is composed of people who...have met once in their lives when one of them needed the support of the other...And is there any man of influence in Sicily who has not been induced, willingly, or unwillingly, to lend his good offices? Could it be that all these gentlemen are mafia chiefs, or simply *mafiosi*, in the bad sense of the word?[131]

The book by Avellone and Morasca was published at a time when the desire for autonomous rule in Sicily was strong. This mood of disaffection had been encouraged by several factors. The growth of a left-wing co-operative movement, as well as the influx of remittances from emigrants, was causing changes in the countryside that troubled the more conservative members of the island's élite. Also important was the persistent feeling that the government still had little interest in Sicily outside the sphere of law and order. The great strides in the national economy since 1900 had been visible largely in the North; the South was still characterised by archaic farming and huge disparities in wealth. Emigration was the only hope for many. In 1901, 36,718 Sicilians left the island; by 1906 the annual figure had risen to 127,603.[132]

An additional cause for grievance was the case of Nunzio Nasi, a talented and ambitious deputy from Trapani, who in 1903 was accused of misappropriating funds while Minister of Education. The judicial proceedings attracted great publicity and, as in the case of Raffaele Palizzolo, there was a suspicion that Nasi had been a victim of both political vendetta and anti-Sicilian sentiment. His arrest in 1907 was greeted with violent demonstrations throughout the island; when, the following year, he was sentenced to a term in prison, discontent became increasingly organised. A *Partito Siciliano* was set up, headed by a veteran Garibaldian who declared that autonomy 'would be the only way to repair 48 years of neglect by the government and scorn by the North'. There were demands that Nasi be amnestied; and article two of the party's statute proclaimed the need to 'champion the rights and interests, both general and particular, of Sicily, considered as an administrative unit within the organism of the State'.[133]

The *Partito Siciliano* enjoyed only a brief existence, but autonomist sentiment continued to flourish. Nasi himself went on being elected to parliament despite being ineligible, and in 1913 he brought out a radical manifesto in which he proposed to rectify fifty years of 'exploitation' by giving Sicily greater administrative control of its resources. He stressed, however, that he had no intention of endangering national unity:

What really, and continually, compromises the political, and above all, moral, unity of a state is that very situation of violence which has been created through disregarding the conditions and special needs of the people. Regional inequality and injustice are the perennial sources of discontent. The true separatists are those who seek to perpetuate these ills by raising the spectre of non-existent dangers.[134]

On the eve of the Great War, Sicily still posed a political problem for the Italian state. The island's western provinces in particular continued to be turbulent and uncooperative, just as they had been in the 1860s. The gap between the people and the authorities seemed to be as wide as ever. The philosopher Giovanni Gentile claimed in 1917 that Sicily no longer boasted its own culture;[135] but coming from an Hegelian, this sounded like wishful thinking. The island had yet to absorb 'the values of the state', or deal with the complex social and economic issues that beset it. The First World War, despite all hopes to the contrary, only accentuated the problems and once again the cry of 'mafia' went up. The fascist government, like its predecessors, responded with force; the justification once again was that there was a great criminal conspiracy at work.

3 THE STATE AND SICILIAN SOCIETY

Monopolising violence: the problem of omertà

The northern officials who arrived in Sicily after 1860 encountered a region whose culture and economy were markedly different from those to which they were accustomed. It also contradicted their expectations. Instead of the bucolic opulence suggested by Greek myths, they found a land of destitution. Politics were factional, and personalities often seemed to count for far more than ideas. Above all, this was a world of private violence where disregard for public authority and an exaggerated sense of personal honour drove men to take the law into their own hands. The new state found this frustrating. Unlike its Bourbon predecessor, it believed in the paramount importance of administrative efficiency, and yet, as Leopoldo Franchetti observed in 1876, the authorities were forced to operate in Sicily 'like an army in enemy territory'.[1]

The state's moral isolation was hard to understand. Was the new regime not manifestly superior to that of the corrupt, despotic Bourbons? Sicily's resistance to change after 1860 seemed to challenge the view of many northerners that liberalism was inherently natural. Given the opportunity, would anybody reject freedom if it were offered? The behaviour of the islanders was not only unsettling; it was also embarassing. If the legitimacy of the new order derived from the will of the people, how was the non-cooperation of Sicilians to be explained? Diomede Pantaleoni suggested in October 1861 that unfamiliarity with liberalism was only partly to blame. After all, he said, some mainland provinces were just as uncivilised as Sicily, yet they had not made such a mess of the newly introduced institutions. More important, in his view, was the moderate party's failure to win over the masses. The Garibaldians, as a result, dominated public opinion: 'This', he concluded, '. . .is the true reason for the Government's lack of support in the region.'[2]

Other observers felt that more sinister factors were involved, particularly as violence seemed to increase in the wake of unification.

Murders took place regularly in broad daylight, and yet (and this was particularly puzzling to northerners) no one would testify. According to the Palermo newspaper, *Il Precursore*, in September 1861, 'a diabolical organisation' was at work, with a 'hierarchy' and 'leaders', and this explained why people refused to talk to the authorities. Since 'every murder and robbery' emanated from its ranks, anyone who knew of its secrets was obliged to remain silent, 'for fear of being stabbed by the associates'. Admittedly, it said, reticence had been a feature of Sicilian society prior to the revolution: 'However, before 4 April 1860, crimes were punished, and it was possible to find witnesses who would talk'.[3]

It is unlikely that the situation had been much better under the Bourbons. In 1838, Pietro Ulloa, the Procurator General at Trapani, wrote a vehement report on the problems of administering justice in the island. 'There is no employee in Sicily', he said, 'who has not succumbed to the will of some overweening character (*prepotente*), and who has not considered using his post for feathering his own nest.' He claimed that the absence of sound administration had resulted in a widespread recourse to extra-legal measures. In many towns, people entrusted themselves to 'so-called parties'. These were informal groupings, dependent on a local notable such as a landowner or a priest, which acted to protect supporters from prosecution, or to persecute enemies. It was impossible, Ulloa said, to find witnesses even for crimes committed in public; and when thefts occurred, it was left to 'mediators' rather than the police to recover stolen goods.[4]

What changed in Sicily after 1860 was not so much the objective conditions of the island, as the set of assumptions about the practice of government. The Bourbons were far more tolerant of corruption and illiberalism in local administration than many northern officials after 1860. (Indeed, the Lieutenant of Sicily, Carlo Filangieri, claimed in 1852 that fear was an important ingredient of effective rule).[5] This led them to disregard many of the abuses that so troubled their Piedmontese successors. Pietro Ulloa was largely exceptional in his concern for efficient, centralised government. He noticed problems that many of his contemporaries either disregarded or failed to see. His outlook resembled that of northerners. It is interesting that his description of the island in 1838 has often been taken as evidence for the existence of the mafia *avant la lettre*.

In theory, the Piedmontese were averse to arbitrariness in government. However, intolerance, bewilderment, and, above all, fear that Sicily might be the springboard for a legitimist *revanche* drove them to adopt measures that were highly illiberal. Francesco Crispi claimed in 1875 that the new regime's methods of policing in Sicily were more savage than those of the notorious Bourbon official, Salvatore

Maniscalco. Was it therefore surprising, he asked, if people failed to co-operate with the authorities?[6] The persistence of old patterns of law enforcement certainly provided little incentive to drop the traditional view that crime and justice were personal matters, and no business of the state's. Consequently, as Franchetti observed, 'the majority of people accept and justify the use of forces and methods that elsewhere would be considered illegal'.[7] The reluctance of Sicilians to deal with the police was only partly due to fear of the injured party seeking revenge. Equally, if not more, important was a deep-seated moral imperative against it.

This attitude was generally known as '*omertà*', a concept soon to be linked closely to that of the mafia. The term apparently derived from the dialect word '*omu*' (man), and had connotations of strength and virility. It denoted not simply a disinclination to betray someone to the authorities, but equally the courage needed to exact justice oneself.[8] The deep-rootedness of *omertà* was shown by the number of proverbs and stories that commended it: 'Good is he who sees and is silent'; 'He is truly a man who reveals nothing, even under the blows of a dagger'. *Omertà* was additionally sanctioned by prudence: 'He who is deaf, blind, and silent will live in peace for a hundred years'. One popular story told of how Speaking and Eating once requested King Solomon to decide which of them should control the mouth. Solomon gave his judgement in favour of Eating, lest Speaking be the ruin of man.[9]

Most serious observers recognised that *omertà* was a general feature of Sicilian society.[10] It was more pronounced in the western half of the island than in the east, though quite why was never certain. One factor might have been the prevalence of vendetta in this area. Another, perhaps, was the strength of anti-statism in and around Palermo, which in turn may have been related to the presence in the capital of the aristocracy and their retainers. Giovanni Lorenzoni, in his major study of Sicilian society in 1910, said that most islanders agreed that matters of honour were private concerns. *Omertà*, he claimed, was 'a necessary consequence of the principle of personal vendetta'; and this owed its origin to 'the scant faith that public justice has managed to engender in previous centuries...and which has not increased much under the present national government'.[11]

Omertà posed an enormous problem for the authorities. Police and magistrates alleged time and again after 1860 that their work was being hamstrung by the absence of witnesses, or by false testimony. In the Damiani enquiry of 1884, 141 Sicilian *pretori* (local magistrates) described the conditions of justice in their towns. Ninety-four of them said that the depositions they received were in effect useless given the widespread habit of mendacity.[12] Ten years earlier, the Bonfadini report had produced similar findings. The problem of reticent witnesses, it said, was 'indeed peculiar to Sicily', and summed up all that was distinctive about criminality in the island.[13] Behind this non-cooperation could be detected not only fear of reprisal, but also 'that vague feeling of hostility towards the governmental system', and the 'false pride that forbids collusion with the judiciary and the law against one's fellow citizens'.[14]

Magistrates were among the first to talk of 'the mafia'. This may have been due to their frustration at the impalpability of the Sicilian problem, and many of them soon joined the police in calling for exceptional measures for the island. Several prominent lawyers used the term in their statements to the Pisanelli commission in 1867,[15] and by the end of the decade the idea of 'the mafia' was apparently common in Sicilian judicial circles. Vincenzo Calenda, Procurator General at Palermo, claimed in his inaugural address for 1872 that every criminal in his jurisdiction was 'a member of the mafia [*associato alla mafia*] or else had, in some way, secured its support'. This, he said, guaranteed that witnesses would have 'no eyes to see, nor ears to hear, nor tongue to speak', and that even the relatives of victims would deny knowledge of the culprit's identity: 'and when in the midst of so much darkness, a ray of light appears, and a criminal is dragged before a jury to answer for himself, he can be certain that the most important witnesses will retract, and that the victims will maintain a pitiful silence'.[16]

The frustration of the judiciary was evident in the reports elicited by the government while considering the introduction of exceptional measures in 1874. Many magistrates wanted a more rigorous application of *domicilio coatto* (forced residence, usually on a penal island). 'The facts', wrote one, 'demonstrate that the present laws are inadequate. It has not been possible for a government based on liberal guarantees...to destroy such a criminal association.... The many-headed hydra can only be slain with fire and sword!'[17] Similar sentiments were expressed by supporters of the Right in the parliamentary debate of June 1875. 'I intend to speak of the mafia', said Stefano Castagnola:

> You say to me, what is the mafia? Maybe it is indefinable, yet every single document that we have collected amply demonstrates that it is a huge and powerful organisation, an evil solidarity, an association of the guilty who seek both to profit from crime and ensure that the law never catches up with them.

He then quoted a former Procurator General who had said that the mafia existed everywhere in Palermo, and that it intimidated witnesses and accused alike.[18]

The problem of testimony continued to haunt the judiciary unabated after the 1870s, and the idea that the mafia was to blame became the received wisdom. Apart from simplifying a difficult issue, this had the added attraction of making the question easier to handle. If *omertà* was admitted to be a general condition of Sicilian society, stemming from ingrained mistrust, how was the state to respond? Furthermore, if popular diffidence had been reinforced, as Crispi and others alleged, by the government's illiberal behaviour, then a detailed analysis of the problem might entail an embarrassing admission of guilt. It was much simpler to impute the gap between people and authorities to a criminal organisation. Fear was accordingly billed as the essence of *omertà*: people were not co-operating with the state, it was said, because of intimidation.

The corollary to this view was that strong government action was indispensable. The mafia succeeded, so the argument ran, because the state was weak; the authorities must master the situation. Leopoldo Franchetti, who later became a leading imperialist, concluded his highly perceptive study of Sicily in 1876 with the uninspiring assertion that the government's isolation hitherto had been the result of its laxity: 'When the government has managed to impress on people its force, it will inherit the sympathy that is currently reserved for the overbearing [*prepotenti*].'[19] The state was undoubtedly ineffective in Sicily, but what was noticeable in Franchetti and other writers was their willingness to equate this with the absence of coercion. As a result, the moral dimension was frequently overlooked. Cesare Mori in the 1920s believed that the mafia could only be tackled with a massive display of strength; he was not, it seems, too concerned about judicial mistakes.

The idea that the Sicilian problem was the result of official weakness not only underpinned the use of exceptional measures, but also vindicated the frequent recourse to *ammonizione, domicilio coatto,* and its equivalent in the fascist period, *confino.* Given the difficulties faced by the police and the judiciary, it was always tempting for them to circumvent legal channels. If a man were suspected of some misdemeanour, he could be denounced to a local *pretore* by the police; and if the *pretore* felt there was any basis to the charge, he might impose *ammonizione.* This was a form of curfew, and its consequences were often disastrous. An *ammonito* was kept under surveillance, and had to remain indoors before sunrise and after dusk. This restricted his working hours, and as a result he frequently became unemployable. If he continued to arouse suspicions, he might be charged with 'contravening' *ammonizione.* This would make him liable to at least two years on a penal settlement.

As many observers pointed out, these measures (which, with slight modifications, remained in force throughout the liberal and fascist periods) were to a large degree counter-productive.[20] The 1865 law on public security prescribed *ammonizione* for 'idlers' (*oziosi*), 'vagabonds', '*camorristi*', '*manutengoli*', and '*mafiosi*'. These categories were very imprecise, and the scope for arbitrariness was accordingly considerable. What is more, the *pretori* were usually ill-educated and underpaid, and they were often beholden to the dominant local faction, which could exploit *ammonizione* as a weapon against its opponents.[21] The police, too, were susceptible, for they were rarely well-informed about the community they operated in. Moreover, like the *pretori*, they were frequently creatures of the municipal council, and failure to give satisfaction to those who ran the town hall often resulted in their being transferred.[22]

The risk of arbitrariness helped to discredit the law in the eyes of the local population. For one thing, it confirmed the traditional belief that justice was both personal and relative. A man with influence could be sure of impunity; the weak, on the other hand, were vulnerable. 'The law is for the fool,' ran one proverb, 'the gallows for the poor.'[23] Arbitrary measures also had the disastrous effect, as Franchetti observed, of 'infecting the doctor with the very disease he [sought] to cure'.[24] This was clearly visible, he said, in the 'sad experience' of the years 1860 to 1874, and above all during General Medici's term as prefect of Palermo when the authorities adopted a blatant policy of setting a thief to catch a thief.[25] 'At every stage in Sicily,' he noted, 'there is a dilemma between the ineffectiveness of legality and the dangers and moral damage of arbitrariness'.[26]

The issue of arbitrariness was to arise again and again in Sicilian history. Franchetti had discerned the crux of the matter, and though he hoped that strong, impartial administration might rectify the situation, he knew the auspices were not good. Good intentions were all too often vitiated in Sicily. Since the law was mistrusted, for example, the guilty could easily pose as victims of persecution. A barrage of protests followed almost any arrest. Police, prefects, politicians, and ministers would be harried with letters and deputations, protesting at the outrageous act of injustice. This was particularly so if the accused was a man of influence. The official who had brought the charges would find himself on the defensive. If he wished to avoid isolation, he would have to succumb to the blandishments of the arrested man's opponents. Concessions to the new allies would inevitably follow; one favour became two; two became three; and three, a whole succession.[27]

The difficulties involved in the pursuit of justice were well illustrated by Cesare Mori's operation against the mafia in the 1920s. In order to mitigate the problem of witnesses, the police were given a key role in the prosecution. This put them under considerable pressure, for to achieve results they often had to choose wholesale between one local political group and another. Sometimes the police would support one faction, the *carabinieri* (their military counterparts) another. At the higher level, Mori found that as soon as he attacked the fascists in Palermo for alleged affiliation to the mafia, he was then committed to their ex-liberal opponents. If he prosecuted any of his new allies, he ran the risk of total isolation. Indeed, his destruction of an erstwhile supporter, the influential former Minister of War, Antonino Di Giorgio, was almost certainly one reason for his removal from Palermo.[28]

Mori aimed, perhaps consciously, to out-mafia the mafia. He believed that a ruthless police operation could elevate the status of the law to the point where *omertà* was broken and crime destroyed. The logic of this policy, however, was by no means self-evident. Though he claimed in a moment of modesty that he was simply a state official, Mori's whole campaign was presented as essentially a personal operation. He took care to foster his image as a man of formidable strength. He could justify this, perhaps, by saying that Sicilians respected individual qualities more than dull, bureaucratic efficiency. The result, however, was that the fight against the mafia became Mori's, rather than the state's. A similar difficulty faced Medici in the 1860s, Malusardi in the 1870s, and more recently, Carlo Alberto Dalla Chiesa.[29]

The shortcomings of the Italian police in Sicily further widened the gap between the people and the authorities. In the first place there were administrative problems to contend with. After 1860, the island was divided into seven zones, and this made co-ordination more difficult than under the Bourbons.[30] In addition, the police were split into four categories: those under the control of the prefects and *questori*; the *carabinieri*, who answered to the Minister of War; those deployed by the judiciary; and those in the 'military zones'. The line of demarcation between these bodies was not always clear, and the result, frequently, was rivalry and confusion.[31] There were also communally controlled police, the rural guards, who were responsible to the mayor rather than the prefect, the Procurator General, or the local commander of the *carabinieri*. Despite this multiplicity, however, the public security forces were usually undermanned in Sicily. The government, it was sometimes said, preferred periodic military campaigns to consistent policing.[32]

It was the quality of the police in Sicily that evoked most criticism. In general, the Italian public security forces were not noted for excellence, partly because low pay tended to preclude those with talent or ambition. Moreover, a posting to Sicily was often regarded as a punishment, and this resulted in an unusually high proportion of incompetent personnel.[33] Brutality, arbitrariness, and collusion with known criminals became hallmarks of the island's police in the 1860s; once a pattern had been established, it was hard to break. In 1875, Diego Tajani, a former Procurator General of Palermo, revealed to an incredulous Chamber of Deputies how he had been forced to indict the local Chief of Police, Giuseppe Albanese, for protecting criminals and being party to murder. The whole affair had been hushed up. Albanese had been mysteriously cleared of the charges and promoted, while Tajani had resigned in disgust.[34]

Such revelations showed the extent to which Bourbon maladministration had persisted into the new regime. Prior to 1860, it had been common practice for known criminals to be enrolled in the police. The hope was that by giving them a share in the status quo, a repetition of the events of 1848 (when they had taken to the barricades) could be avoided. It was also supposed, and rightly, that such men were in the best position to know who the local lawbreakers were. This system, however, was dangerous, as it fostered the semblance of order at the expense of public morality. The police formed pacts with criminals, and thereby subjected them to a degree of control; but the resulting collusion, as well as the direct involvement of many policemen themselves in crime, did nothing to enhance the status of the law. Anyone with property was well advised to treat personally with bandits and thieves, or, better still, employ them.[35]

The new regime inherited a society with little confidence in the police. Unfamiliarity with Sicily and ignorance of the local dialect made the situation worse. The *carabinieri* were especially disadvantaged, as most of them came from the mainland. 'They live isolated amidst the population', wrote Franchetti, 'as if in a desert. They see and hear, but do not understand.'[36] The army was also very much out of its depth; and though the regular police had the benefit of a higher proportion of Sicilians in its ranks – about a third in 1875[37] – this branch of the public security forces was notoriously deficient in quality and numbers. Particular criticism was levelled, certainly in the early years of unification, at the Palermo *questori*. Their ineptitude resulted in gross, or even criminal, negligence (as with Felice Pinna, who ignored all warnings in the late summer of 1866 of an impending uprising), or in simple corruption. Given the problem of evidence, it was always tempting for them to resort to the policy of 'setting a thief to catch a thief'.[38]

The most controversial members of the police force were the *militi a cavallo* (mounted militiamen). This body was composed entirely of local Sicilian elements, and replaced the infamous *compagnie d'armi* (companies at arms) of the Bourbons. It was set up in 1863 and included in its ranks a high proportion of ex-convicts. Its shortcomings were proverbial and despite an attempt at reorganisation it eventually had to be suppressed in 1877. During the parliamentary debate of 1875, the deputy Vincenzo Cordova claimed that the *militi a cavallo* were the principal source of crime in Sicily:

Gentlemen of the government, the centre of the *maffia* lies in the ranks of your police force...And this should be no surprise, since our honourable colleague, di Rudinì, told you so in his report of 11 October 1866, when he defined the *militi a cavallo* as 'criminals who are paid to abstain from robbery and control other villains...'. Ramusino informed you of this when he said: 'The *militi* it must be confessed, are the first to give a bad example of *maffia*.'[39]

The dilemma for the government was that despite their failings, the *militi a cavallo* at least knew the environment. Local friendships often involved them in factional struggles, and that led to partial justice, but they could certainly not be accused of groping in the dark every time a crime was committed, unlike the *carabinieri*. For this reason, some people rued their suppression, and with the rising law-lessness of the 1890s calls were heard for their reconstitution. The *latifondisti* were among their stronger supporters, since a local force could reasonably be expected to do the bidding of the rich, at least on major issues. In 1892, with brigandage and social unrest on the increase, Francesco Agnetta proposed the revival both of the *militi* and the field guards. They should be commanded, he said, by honest and intelligent men 'selected from the land-owning class in each district'.[40]

Omertà and the resulting impotence of the police has remained a problem to this day. On occasions – as after the Great War, and in the early 1980s – it seemed as if the state had lost its grip entirely on the west of the island. This was one reason for the police operations of Cesare Mori in the 1920s, and Carlo Alberto Dalla Chiesa in 1982. Both men saw it as their duty to try to bridge the gap between 'civil' and 'political' society, and they both announced that *omertà* was col-lapsing.[41] Each was appointed by a government eager to instil into the island what Minister of the Interior Rognoni called 'the values of the state'. That Dalla Chiesa should be assassinated in terrorist style was a tragic reminder that, at root, the problem of the mafia was political.

Complicity and the problem of crime in Sicily

The isolation of the police was most noticeable when it came to serious crimes. The murder rate in the island, particularly in the west, was generally higher than elsewhere in Italy. In 1873 there were fourteen times as many killings in Sicily per head of population as in Lombardy.[42] The absence of evidence for such crimes was not only frustrating for the authorities, but also damaging, as every unsolved murder or major robbery underlined the fact of their weakness. This is why it was so tempting to dispense with hard evidence, and resort instead to *ammonizione* and *domicilio coatto*, which required no judicial proceedings. It also helps explain why the charge of criminal association★ (*associazione a delinquere*) was so appealing. If a murder was committed by 'the mafia' rather than individuals, the police had simply to define the collective body responsible. Mass arrests stood a good chance of hitting some malefactors, and they were a clear expression of the state's power.

When Prefect Gualterio first alluded to the mafia in April 1865, he was about to launch a major operation to establish order in western Sicily. He told the Minister of the Interior that a good way of dealing with the turmoil was to treat it with the charge of criminal association, and indict those arrested accordingly. One particular advantage of criminal association was that it constituted a 'flagrant' (that is, ongoing) crime, and so allowed for summary imprisonment. As Procurator General Interdonato told Gualterio: 'Since every criminal association is a continuous offence, arrest is always legitimate, provided only that one has evidence for the association, and indications of who its members are.' There was no need, he said, to worry about any specific transgression. The malefactors could be 'surprised and captured legally as soon as there is evidence that they have united and organised for the purpose of breaking the law, even though they have not been caught in the act of committing a crime.'[43]

This was the information that Gualterio had been angling for. Two days after receiving Interdonato's report, he sent an account to the Minister of the Interior of 'the so-called *maffia* or criminal association'. History, he said, showed that this society (which was particularly strong in the Palermo hinterland) had long displayed 'an uncommon tendency to commit crimes' and had an organisation 'that is perhaps the model for the associations of this kind known as "*camorras*" which were transplanted to the mainland'. As proof that the mafia was a true criminal body he said that it even had 'statutes'.[44] In the months that followed this report, an enormous number of arrests were made (the authorities had to contend with severely overcrowded prisons),[45] and the standard charge was criminal association. The scale of the operations pleased Gualterio, for, as he told the Minister of the Interior in July 1865, it was 'essential that force should gain the upper hand, and the government use every means to clean up the region'. He suggested that a few executions were needed, particularly in the small towns.[46]

★ According to the 1889 penal code, the crime of *associazione a/per delinquere* consisted of 'five or more people associating with one another for the purpose of breaking the law'. This was changed in the 1926 penal code to 'three or more people'. The maximum sentence for the act of association alone was also increased from five to seven years.

Criminal association became the most characteristic indictment in operations against the mafia, but it was a dangerously open-ended charge. That groups of criminals came together to commit particular offences was never in doubt: Sicily, in this respect, was no different from any other part of Italy. The peculiarity of the island (and particularly its western parts) lay in the reluctance of the population to consign offenders to the authorities.[47] This raised the awkward problem of complicity. If a murder were committed in a crowded piazza in broad daylight, and the assassin were seen and recognised, would the refusal to testify make a witness party to the crime? The police, in their frustration, were sometimes inclined to think so. In February 1883, Luigi Schillaci was shot at a christening reception in Favara. The bystanders were interrogated, but they all denied knowing the identity of the two killers. The police thereupon arrested them, on the grounds that their 'mysterious and unconvincing silence appeared to suggest complicity in the crime'.[48]

Complicity gave rise to important questions concerning the intrinsic character of Sicilian crime in general. The first aspect of the problem was normative. Did the values embodied in the new legal code after 1860 reflect those of the majority of the island's population? 'I am firmly convinced', wrote Giovanni Lorenzoni in 1910, 'that Sicilian morality is in no way inferior to that of other Italians or to Europeans in general. It is simply different.'[49] Sicily, he said, had suffered the misfortune of being suddenly thrust into a modern bourgeois world, and the process of assimilation was slow. As many other writers pointed out, the disparity was both material and cultural. Conditions of land-tenure and the structure of social relations still belonged in many ways to a world of feudalism. The obsession with honour, the cult of physical force, the belief in hierarchy, the importance of friendship – these were all facets of the Sicilian character that observers singled out as distinctive.

The attachment to honour and violence caused most difficulty with Italian law. Since status in this society depended heavily on personal authority, much energy was devoted to self-assertion against one's fellows. Honour pertained not only to the individual and his family, but also to his chattels. Theft was therefore frequently regarded as a slight, and could result in severe reprisals. Indeed, attacks on property often featured as stages in a feud. When a large landowner had cattle stolen, the motive was as likely to be vendetta as economic gain.[50] Fruit trees and vines could also be cut down in a dispute, or hayricks or woodland burned. In each case the principle at stake would be honour; and since the defence of reputation was an acknowledged right, these attacks on property – which in the eyes of the state were clearly crimes – might well be condoned by the community.

Theft for purely material gain was probably no more sanctioned in Sicily than in other rural economies. Indeed, the island often had the lowest incidence of petty robberies in southern Italy.[51] (*Omertà* might stop people divulging evidence to the police, but the fact of a crime was usually reported. Failure to do so could result in the victim's own prosecution.) The principal motive for this type of offence was poverty; as a result, according to some observers, it was regarded with a degree of sympathy.[52] Giovanni Lorenzoni said there was an element of communism in Sicilian peasant culture, and a belief in distributive justice; and this meant that thefts from the rich were not harshly condemned.[53] However, criminals who inflicted sufferings on their peers or inferiors might expect collective sanction. At Campobello in 1862, two particularly vexatious robbers were mobbed by the local population, their bodies riddled with bullets, carted away, and ignominiously dumped.[54]

The most serious crime connected with honour was murder. The failure to denounce assassins was a telling indication of the cultural gap between Sicilian society and the state. So too was the sheer incidence of killing. In 1873 there was one murder on the island for every 3,194 inhabitants: only Naples and Sardinia were at all comparable.[55] The west of Sicily had the worst record, and the statistics here were sometimes staggering, particularly at moments of upheaval. In the aftermath of the First World War, around 700 murders a year were committed in the province of Trapani; the small town of Marsala alone claimed over 200.[56] Such levels of violence naturally shocked northerners, and underlined their feeling that this was an alien culture. 'Sicily is more akin, perhaps, than any other part of Europe', wrote Bonfadini in the conclusion of his report, 'to the torrid sands of Nubia; in Sicily, the blood is hot, the will imperious, and the spirit prone to swift and violent paroxysms.'[57]

Part of the problem lay in the carrying of weapons. According to one writer in 1876, even priests and schoolchildren went about armed.[58] The motive was not simply self-defence: prestige and status may in fact have been more telling considerations. Humble people tended to sport knives, the wealthier guns. The bandit 'Nino' Leone was famous for his Winchester rifle, the first of its kind in Italy.[59] A more common firearm was the *lupara*, a short-barrelled hunting gun that was devastating at close range. Rich landowners would often supplement their weapons with a bodyguard, particularly when travelling in the countryside. There was certainly a risk of being kidnapped, particularly if there were bandits in the area; but most observers recognised that there was an element of sheer display in being escorted by a dozen or so armed and fierce-looking *campieri*.[60]

However, arms-bearing reflected, rather than created, the fact of violence. Without any tradition of impartial government, justice had become a matter of personal honour, and before 1860 no really concerted effort was made to alter this. Even the Church sanctioned the status quo with the practice of *componenda*: every year the Archbishop of Palermo published a *bolla di composizione* (bull of composition) which stipulated the financial penance for all offences, including murder. As horrified northerners said, this was tantamount to a tax on crime.[61] It was also, though, an admission of the Church's moral ineffectiveness. Secular practice in Sicily inhabited a sphere far removed from the tenets of both religion and state. When, in the 1960s, the social reformer Danilo Dolci asked the peasants of Partinico if it was wrong to commit murder, the response was far from unequivocal. The honour of one's womenfolk was declared to be a matter of life or death; vendetta too was inescapable ('"We're men and men we'll stay" – It's part of the old tradition in Sicily that has come down from the Middle Ages'). 'One may or may not want to kill,' said one man, 'but in some cases you have to.'[62]

The feeling that honour should, in the last resort, be defended with violence was an important factor in the reticence of witnesses. When a man was killed, the assumption was often that the murderer had a good motive for his action. Moreover, any retribution was felt to be the responsibility not of the state, but of the victim's family. As one proverb put it, 'Blood washes blood!'[63] The same attitude could apply to other violent crimes, such as kidnapping, rape, theft, extortion, and intimidation. Admittedly, few issues were clear-cut (no moral code is so rigid as to eliminate all shadow of doubt as to the correct response in a given situation); yet in general Sicilians felt that the individual victim, or his relatives, should decide on what steps to take. Justice was essentially a personal matter.[64]

The interpenetration of violence with honour did not arise from moral necessity alone. Many commentators remarked on the curious fascination with force *per se*.[65] Those with a reputation for brutality often won respect as well as sufferance, and they might, without cynicism, be known as 'men of honour'.[66] Franchetti was curious to note how Sicilians dwelt on the subject of bandits, and took them by and large for granted. One explanation may have been that ordinary people often regarded brigands as righters of social wrongs, who fleeced the rich and defended the poor;[67] but there was also what socialist writer Sebastiano Cammareri Scurti called 'the cult of brute force'.[68] Thus, as Franchetti found, incidents of violence were frequently reported without anger: even victims cold exude a measure of sympathy for those who had wronged them.[69]

Since violence was the ultimate sanction in many areas of Sicilian life, 'men of honour' were much in demand. A man with a reputation for strength, said Franchetti, became 'a social figure, and an instrument for every interest and pretension'.[70] Landowners, for example,

Vedi giudizio umano, come spesso erra !

Comm. CALOGERO VIZZINI

N. 24 - 7 - 1877   M. 11 - 7 - 1954

VILLALBA

POCO GENEROSI
SU LA SUA BARA NON ANCORA CHIUSA
INVANO TIRARONO GLI ULTIMI STRALI
L'ODIO E L'INVIDIA
IN QUELLA ESTREMA ORA DI PIANTO
FU PIÙ FORTE L'AMORE
E CON VOCE DI VASTA RISONANZA
DISSE
A TUTTI GLI ONESTI
LA GENTILEZZA SUA DEL TRATTO
LA NOBILTÀ DEL CUORE.

DI VEDUTE LARGHE
NEI COMMERCI NELL'INDUSTRIA
RAGGIUNSE ALTEZZE MAI TOCCATE
CON FELICE INTUITO
PRECORSE ED ATTUÒ LA RIFORMA AGRARIA
SOLLEVÒ LE SORTI
DEGLI OSCURI OPERAI DELLA MINIERA
E RACCOLSE SIMPATIE E PRESTIGIO
NEMICO DI TUTTE LE INGIUSTIZIE
UMILE CON GLI UMILI
GRANDE CON I PIÙ GRANDI
DIMOSTRÒ
CON LE PAROLE CON LE OPERE
CHE LA MAFIA SUA NON FU DELINQUENZA
MA RISPETTO ALLA LEGGE
DIFESA DI OGNI DIRITTO
GRANDEZZA DI ANIMO
FU AMORE

Pl. 3. A card commemorating Calogero Vizzini, distributed among friends and re-latives in America after his death in 1954. The last part of the eulogy on the right reads: 'He was humble with the humble, mighty with the mightiest, and showed with his words and deeds that his mafia was not delinquency but respect for the law, defence of every right, nobleness of spirit, love.'

needed resolute field guards to deter brigands and criminals; *gabelloti* used them to enforce their will, whether against proprietors or pea-sants. A strong individual could settle disputes, recover stolen goods, or even find jobs for the unemployed. As Don Calogero Vizzini said in the early 1950s, when explaining the function of a *mafioso*: 'Every society needs a category of men who can sort things out when they are difficult.'[71] Vizzini himself would hold court each morning in the small piazza of Villalba. People would approach him for favours, such as help with a bank loan or assistance with a court case – indeed anything in which 'authority' could be useful.[72]

The extent to which men of violence were part and parcel of Sicilian life perplexed the authorities. The dominant values in Sicily were clearly at odds with those of the new regime. The state's deter-mination to suppress crime was undermined by the Sicilian concept of honour and the belief that justice was something private. It was perhaps no coincidence that a common Italian word for criminal, *malandrino*, was often used in Sicily to indicate someone with verve and courage.[73] This disparity was bound to present difficulties. In August 1865, during his campaign against '*la Maffia*', Prefect Gualterio reported to the Minister of the Interior on the death of the brigand, Milanesi.

> At Altavilla, his home town, he was regarded as nothing less than a Garibaldi. Whether it was his many relations, inveterate complicity, perhaps, a degree of fear, or that by disturbing neighbouring villages he provided security for his own town, the fact is that the entire population can be said to have acted as his accomplice. I am not even sure I would exclude the mayor. At any rate, the Communal Secretary, believe it or not, had stood godfather to this bandit's son.[74]

How was the state to deal with a community of this kind? If Milanesi was guilty, who in Altavilla was not? Time and again when dealing with Sicily, the problem facing the authorities was who or what to blame. Should the landowners be condemned for employing violent *gabelloti* or *campieri*? Were they the accomplices or the victims of bandits, and should they be arrested for harbouring them? Did a field guard who witnessed a cattle theft without reporting it to the police become party to the act? Was a peasant who carried a black-mail letter for its author doing so out of fear or self-interest? (He might have been in trouble if he refused; but the advantages of complying could be great). To what extent was inept administration the source of Sicily's problems? Was *omertà* a result of bad policing or its cause? Were Sicilians mendacious by nature, or because the state offered them no guarantees? Such questions defied simple answers. As Franchetti said, those who studied Sicily were dogged by one perpetual nightmare: 'Who is to blame?'[75]

Arguably the most contentious aspect of this problem was the role of the Sicilian élite. *Manutengolismo*, the protection afforded by the powerful to criminals, lay at the heart of the parliamentary debate of 1875. It has remained a subject of controversy ever since. Given the absence of hard evidence, clear-cut answers have rarely been possible. In practice the apportionment of blame has often been politically conditioned: left-wing supporters of the peasantry, for example, condemned the landowners; their opponents blamed the criminal classes. Undoubtedly some property holders made money from kidnappings or from concealing stolen animals on their land, but others were receivers against their will.[76] Murders or major robberies could be 'commissioned' by aristocrats for reasons of vendetta; they might also, as Franchetti observed, be carried out by protégés acting in what they imagined was their patron's interest.[77] After all, the enemy of an influential man posed a threat to the notable's clientele, and many people accordingly had a vested interest in intimidating or even murdering the opponent. Once the crime had been committed, the underlings were well placed to profit from blackmail: if their patron denounced them to the police, they could accuse him of complicity or worse.

The problem of unsavoury allies confronted anyone in Sicily who entered the political arena. No man of influence could hope to be spared approaches from the ambitious and unscrupulous, and the overtures were not easily ignored. Franchetti wrote:

> Whoever enters the fray of national or local politics, will find it utterly impossible to avoid contacts with people who owe their authority to crime. A man might have the deepest horror of violence and bloodshed, and yet sooner or later he will be driven irresistibly to making use of the influence and ascendancy that comes from being known to be on good terms with people whose power derives from the fear they inspire.[78]

Treating with *mafiosi* was vital to political success, at least in western Sicily where such men were respected. To spurn their assistance meant either reprisal or failure.

In the last resort, as Franchetti admitted, the criteria for distinguishing legitimate (because imposed) from culpable *manutengolismo* were too crude to be adequate. 'When a drop of oil falls on a slab of marble', he wrote, 'it remains unaltered, and can easily be wiped off; but if it lands on a piece of paper, it begins to soak in. It spreads, and becomes as one with the surrounding material, and inseparable from it.'[79] What could the government do? The logic of Franchetti's analysis was pessimistic, particularly as he felt that no social group in Sicily was sufficiently detached and influential to spearhead the island's moral regeneration.[80] Men such as the Marquis di Rudinì who endorsed 'the values of the state' ended up as fish out of water, and left;[81] and if certain people did demand action against criminals, their aim was less likely to be the rule of law, than the furtherance of sectional interests. Sicily's only hope, Franchetti concluded, with a note of desperation, was for the state to secure moral ascendancy. How that was to be done, he did not say; but if all else failed, Italy, he announced, should abandon the island 'to its natural forces, and proclaim its independence'.[82]

The function of 'criminal association'

The harshness of Franchetti's logic was exceptional, since most Italian politicians in the 1870s and later regarded the fabric of the nation as indivisible. If mere exposure to liberalism did not integrate the island into the state, they felt it should be forced into line; there would be no truck with separatism. On what grounds, though, could coercion be justified? Sicilians might claim that they had been tricked out of autonomy in 1860, so the contractual argument (that they had approved annexation) was weak. If, however, non-cooperation with the state was due to a tyrannical organisation, the authorities could always say that they were liberating the islanders from the clutches of criminals. The idea of the mafia squared awkward circles (though the calculation, one must suppose, was for the most part unconscious). *Omertà* was now presented as the code of a criminal association: silence was said to be 'enforced' by the mafia, and people refused to testify because of 'intimidation'. If only the criminals could be destroyed, the argument ran, most Sicilians would turn spontaneously to the state.

Since men of violence were integral to Sicilian society, criminal networks could be easily inferred. In the first place, complicity was often easier to 'show' than it was to disprove. Secondly, once the idea had become established that the word '*mafioso*' implied membership of the mafia, social links between *mafiosi* could be used as evidence of criminal association. Correspondence, too, might serve this purpose: one of the most important mafia trials of the 1920s was based on a series of letters found in the study of an influential lawyer (see below pp. 234–6).[83] Sometimes, if zeal overcame discretion, the police ended up with imaginary criminal associations. Before he took up his appointment in Palermo as Procurator General, Diego Tajani read in the newspapers of how a vast criminal conspiracy had been unearthed in the Sicilian capital thanks to the vigilance of the *questore*. When he arrived, however, and made enquiries, he discovered that the whole thing 'was no more than a dream, or rather an ingenious invention by that official'.[84]

Every government report on Sicily found a simple definition of the mafia elusive, though they all agreed that it was not, in any strict sense, a criminal association. According to Romualdo Bonfadini in his official report of 1876, the term itself had been much abused. Its meaning, he said, was unclear, and it was almost easier to say what it was not, 'than to determine logically what it [was]'.

However, the Mafia is not an association with a fixed structure, or special organisms; it is not even a temporary union of criminals for a casual or specific purpose; it has no statutes, no sharing of profits, it holds no meetings, and has no recognised leaders, apart, perhaps, from those who are strongest and most intelligent. It is rather the development and perfecting of assertiveness for every evil intent; it is an instinctive, brutal, and self-interested solidarity that unites, at the expense of the state, the laws, and the regular institutions, all those individuals and social groups who like to derive their livelihood and comforts, not from work, but from violence, deceit and intimidation.[85]

Franchetti's observations, made independently of Bonfadini's and published a year later, suggested something even less concrete. Much of the first section of his report aimed specifically to scotch the view that the mafia was an organisation. The general belief on the mainland, he said, was that crime in Sicily emanated from a single source. This was wholly mistaken. The only way 'mafia' could be used at all collectively was as an abstract noun, to indicate a 'manner of being'. This, however, was vague and misleading; in order, he claimed, to have a clearer idea of what the concept meant it was best to look at the adjective. *Mafioso* was taken by Sicilians to indicate, not a professional criminal, but 'a man who is able to enforce his rights regardless of the means used'. Since people often gained respect in Sicily through force, *mafioso*, he said, might imply, but only incidentally, a propensity to violence.[86]

Franchetti did not write about the island with complete impartiality, but he was detached enough to accept that Sicilians used the terms 'mafia' and '*mafioso*' in different ways and often quite loosely. Violence, he suggested, was by no means the crucial component. A man who had the capacity to protect and promote his interests through patronage might also be considered *mafioso*. After describing the structure of clienteles in Sicily, Franchetti wrote:

> Thus are formed those vast unions of people of every rank, profession, and kind, who, without apparently any formal or continuous link, invariably unite to promote each other's interests, with no thought whatsoever for the law, for justice or public order. What I have just described is the MAFIA which an intelligent person who knows the island intimately, defined as follows: 'The Mafia is a medieval sentiment; a *mafioso* is someone who believes he can protect himself and his property through his own courage and personal influence without having recourse to the authorities and the law.'

Non-Sicilians, said Franchetti, equated the mafia with its violent and criminal aspects, but this was far from the truth.[87]

Opinions as to whether the mafia constituted a criminal association or not depended very much on the observer's viewpoint. If Sicily was considered from within, and on its own terms, clearly no large-scale organisation existed. Indeed, as Franchetti remarked, criminals in other countries were socially isolated – they needed an organisation for protection; but in Sicily, the ethic of private violence was widely accepted, and criminals could often dispense with formal safe-guards.[88] Many writers also pointed out that the concept '*mafioso*' implied an exaggerated sense of self-worth, and assistance, at least from one's peers, was to some extent despised. If, on the other hand, Sicily was looked at from a national standpoint, the mafia could easily appear both criminal and organised. This was the case, for example, with the positivist criminologists, whose northern perspective was reinforced by their concern for national integration. Cesare Lombroso observed:

> It might be objected that very often the mafia exists without any recognised hierarchy of real leaders; but this does not, at least for the anthropologists, invalidate the idea of an association...it shows merely its pervasiveness in every class, or, as the doctors would say, its endemic condition. They have no need of institutional pressure to keep their formation in being, and only resort to it in exceptional circumstances.[89]

Lombroso and his followers would not accept any subjectivism in crime. A lawbreaker was always, in their view, a criminal, and the impulse to recidivism a constant. The medieval heretic would, they argued, have been a terrorist or revolutionary in the nineteenth century; there was no place for cultural relativism. Accordingly, Sicily was seen not as different but as infected, and the bonds that composed its society were written off as intrinsically immoral: 'When [criminal associations] manage to exist', said Lombroso, 'even without leaders, it is a sign of the evil tendency and social sickness of the place that generates them.'[90] Such interpretations of the Sicilian problem were common from the 1880s; and as dissatisfaction mounted at Italy's failure to achieve strength and integration, and with nationalism, in one form or another, permeating the middle classes from the end of the century, so the idea spread that Sicily was a haven of criminality rather than a society with alternative values.

Concern for national cohesion was one reason why many writers on Sicily found it hard to accept that the mafia was not an organisation. This was particularly the case with magistrates and policemen, many of whom combined deep patriotism with a craving for effective action. The result was often a theoretical acceptance that the mafia did not exist, with an instinctual and simultaneous feeling that it did. A good example of this was Giuseppe Alongi, a Sicilian police officer, who published an important study of the mafia in 1887. Alongi was much influenced by positivist criminology: he concentrated on crime, used the word 'atavism' with some frequency, and did not balk at calling the islanders 'semi-barbarian'.[91] True, he conceded the importance of environmental factors, and avoided the extremes of genetic determinism; but for all his sobriety and intelligence, the impression left by his book was of the mafia as a large and insidious criminal conspiracy.

Alongi accepted, in his study of the mafia, that an adequate definition of the word was impossible, since it referred to 'a manner of being, feeling, and operating', and not to a criminal society; it was accordingly best considered, he said, in its 'manifestations'.[92] His book, however, was essentially a treatise on crime rather than a description of a particular form of behaviour. Despite his acknowledgement that no formal association existed, he nevertheless discussed mafia meetings, secret societies such as the *Fratellanza*, mafia jargon, and such specialities of the mafia as cattle-rustling.[93] The net result was to give the impression of an organisation that merely sported several different strings to its bow. As one critic said, Alongi aimed to destroy misconceptions, yet he inadvertently reinforced them by presenting diverse criminal phenomena as emanations of the mafia.[94]

Antonino Cutrera was a less intelligent observer than Alongi. He too was a policeman, and his study of the mafia was published in 1900.[95] He began by berating popular writers for their ignorance and irresponsibility. 'Unfortunately, we find Italian and foreign authors . . . describing the mafia as a huge, secret, criminal association, organised and regimented, with statutes, and perhaps even official places for public meetings!' Like Alongi, Cutrera dealt almost exclusively with crime, but his lesser intellectual reserves led him to succumb more swiftly to the spell worked by the concept of 'the mafia'. He claimed that the mafia had its 'main seat' in Palermo; its 'lowest grade' was the *ricottaro*, or *souteneur*, who protected a prostitute in exchange for her earnings; the mafia specialised in crimes of violence; it organised large-scale thefts; it ran elections; it found its members jobs on farms; it rigged auctions; and it had a jargon of its own. The inevitable impression from all this was of a single controlling entity.[96]

Cesare Mori was a near contemporary of Alongi and Cutrera. Many of his views on the mafia tallied with theirs. Like them, he was a policeman with nationalist leanings; but his concern for the observance of the law as the precondition of a strong state appears to have been more intensely felt. This may have been because his most conspicuous action in Sicily occurred during the fascist period when nationalist sentiment was at a premium. At any rate, in common with almost all other analysts of the island, he acknowledged that the mafia was not a criminal organisation; yet his operation in the 1920s suggested the contrary. Many thousands of people were arrested on the charge of criminal association; relatively few were accused of specific crimes. Underpinning his campaign was a belief that Sicily's problems derived from the weakness of the state, and like many of his predecessors, he regarded force as the best remedy. Criminal association was primarily an instrument for coercion; its legal appropriateness was probably of secondary importance.[97]

Mori, like Gualterio, realised the practical advantages of the charge of criminal association. It allowed him to make summary arrests and so avoid the need for prior investigations which had always been a headache for the authorities in Sicily. (Police enquiries were usually leaked, thus giving the parties concerned time to escape.)[98] Mori's main problem was to find evidence of criminal association. The penal code stated that a criminal association – which from 1926 was deemed to be made up of three people or more – had to exist for the specific purpose of breaking the law. Mori's round-ups embraced dozens of people at a time; but the relationship of the arrested with one another was often, it seems, merely familial or clientelistic. Even when a particular group did harbour known criminals, it was still difficult to maintain that the bond between its components was one of criminal intent.[99]

Some writers on Sicily argued that while the mafia itself did not exist, small nuclei of criminals, imbued with the spirit of mafia, did. The term applied to these groups was 'cosca', a dialect word whose literal meaning was a ring of artichoke leaves. This concept seems to have gained currency in the 1890s, and quickly entered the pantheon of mafia terminology. In 1900, Gaetano Mosca, the distinguished Sicilian political scientist, wrote an essay on the mafia in which he discussed cosche at some length. Sicilians, he said, used the term 'mafia' in two ways: either they wished to indicate a 'mode of feeling, which, like arrogance, pride or prepotence, necessitates a certain line of conduct in particular social situations'; alternatively they might be referring (and this, he said, was its only collective sense) to the totality of small, independent criminal associations that were common in Sicily, particularly in the countryside.[100]

These cosche, he claimed, resembled criminal groups that could be found anywhere in Italy. However, in Sicily they possessed peculiar vitality, as they fed on, and were in fact spawned by, the 'spirit of mafia'.[101] They were 'very simple organisms' and lacked any formal structure. They were usually run by three, four, or five people, whose age, intelligence, social position, or character gave them authority. These 'leaders', however, were rarely more than smallholders, tenant farmers, or stewards, and their followings consisted of a handful of youths, whose ambitions and boldness impelled them towards crime. Cosche had their own territory, and were usually self-contained. It was rare, according to Mosca, for a single unit to extend beyond one town or village.[102]

The goals of these cosche mafiose were not always the same, but as a rule, said Mosca, they sought 'the maximum prestige and illicit gain for the group or its most influential members'.[103] They preferred secret to overt crime, to avoid attracting the attention of the police. One of their most common offences was the imposition of protection money. This was usually demanded in terms of a 'gift' rather than an extortion, so making it possible to claim later that the victim had acted willingly. Another important *cosca* crime, according to Mosca, was *abigeato*, or rustling. This could entail co-operation between separate criminal groups, as the cattle often had to be transported some distance. A neighbouring cowherd might conceal the animals *en route* in his master's herd; friendly shepherds were a good source of information about police patrols; and 'understanding' butchers ended by slaughtering and selling the beasts.[104]

Mosca was writing chiefly about low-level criminality of a type that was familiar to many rural societies. *Abigeato* was often depicted as the mafia crime *par excellence*; certainly its incidence was uncommonly high on the island. This, however, was not necessarily the result of any organisational peculiarity – though *omertà* undoubtedly facilitated 'open' thefts. It was more that the pattern of animal grazing in Sicily allowed for this form of robbery: it was usual to allow herds to wander freely across the open *latifondi*.[105] Nor is it clear to what extent Mosca's *cosche* were self-consciously criminal. He admitted they varied in character and had different goals;[106] but he did not say how distinct they were from ordinary clienteles. In this society almost everyone was a patron or protégé; and many were both. Did a landowner who protected a clutch of bandits thereby become the head of a *cosca*?

This was a moot point, and one that caused a good deal of confusion. Mosca came from a middle-class family, and this may have been a factor conditioning his outlook. The leaders of the *cosche*, he said, enjoyed a 'social condition...somewhat higher than the poorest section of the Sicilian population'; but 'they rarely belong[ed] to the middle class'.[107] His own peer group, in other words, was beyond reproach. Cesare Mori, however, in the course of his campaign in the 1920s, raised the threshold considerably: the aristocracy, he said, was blameless, but the rural middle classes, in his view, and the *gabelloti* in particular, constituted the backbone of the mafia. The criminal associations that he arrested had, as their leaders, parvenu landowners, or the occasional member of the professional classes.[108]

The term '*cosca*' sounded intriguingly technical, but in practice there might be little to distinguish it from other social groupings. No man of influence was without his followers; and the network of dependents could be construed as criminal or not according, in part, to the disposition of the observer. Something illicit might usually be found nestling in every clientele. The question facing the authorities was whether to take action or not, and, if they did, how far to cast the net of complicity. Given the lack of firm evidence, the police often only had a hunch to go on. When a member of one political group was killed, suspicion tended to fall on the opposing faction. But at what level was the murder commissioned? Should it be assumed automatically that the leaders were responsible? What of ambitious underlings trying to bolster their own status through an act of violence? Furthermore, what constituted a 'commission'? If two men discussed an opponent within earshot of their boss, and murder was hinted at, did the patron's silence amount to a licence to kill? Such subtleties would inevitably elude the authorities.[109]

'Mafia' and political factionalism

In the 1920s, the police made up for their lack of evidence by assuming that the adjective 'mafioso' denoted involvement in a criminal organisation. 'Public opinion' (pubblica voce) became crucial to their enquiries. In the past, witnesses had been able to retract by claiming that their testimony was hearsay. The police now sealed off this escape route by declaring that anyone spoken of as mafioso must be a member of the mafia. This resulted in difficulties, as the term 'mafioso' was often loosely applied. It could refer to someone whose ambition had led him to commit crimes – and this might have been a common usage in the 1920s – but many people evidently still employed the word in a more general sense to indicate pride, assertiveness, self-confidence or even magnanimity.[110]

The main source of confusion, however, derived from the nature of local politics. Nearly all towns in Sicily were split between two parties. One of them controlled the local administration, while the other tried to win power by any means at its disposal. An important instrument in this struggle was the accusation of 'mafia'. Those out of power devoted much time to lobbying the authorities, either orally or in writing. They used the terms 'mafia' and 'mafioso' liberally about their enemies; the hope was that some mud would stick.[111] The need to do this was particularly pressing when a major anti-mafia drive was underway. Failure to convince the prefect or sub-prefect that it was the opposition that was responsible for local crime might, in these circumstances, prove disastrous.

The damage done by factionalism to local government was obvious, and it was frequently seen as a root cause of public immorality in Sicily. The maintenance of power was the supreme goal of the dominant party. The police were inveigled into harrying the opposition. Electoral registers would be doctored, voting cards issued selectively, and the ballot rigged. Communal funds were squandered to lengthen the public payroll, thereby increasing the clients of the town council. Power was there to be enjoyed, and the collectivity suffered accordingly. Taxes were imposed inequitably: the poor paid almost everything, the middle classes nothing, and dispensations were naturally given to supporters of the group in power. Jobs, too, were allocated along factional lines, and this was one important reason why control of local government was regarded as so vital.[112]

Many writers found this situation distressing. The lack of true political content in municipal affairs, and the widespread corruption, shocked northern officials who were educated to impartial administration and abstract notions of the common good. How, they asked, could people so unscrupulously push the interests of friends and relatives at the expense of justice? In 1894, Giuseppe Alongi wrote:

> Local factions have an entirely one-sided view of the law and legality...They attack their opponents and feather their own nests...Their friends receive arms permits, get acquitted of *ammonizione*, and break the law with impunity. Their enemies are...denounced for *ammonizione*, and even find themselves accused of crimes that have in fact been committed by the plaintiffs' supporters. Supposing the local policeman, or *pretore*, or sub-prefect fails to toe the line? In that case, specially tailored testimonials appear exonerating the guilty friend and condemning the innocent foe. There are floods of anonymous appeals depicting the official in the most false and lurid colours...And eventually the higher authorities, out of tiredness, credulity, or concern for the safety of the official, decide to transfer him.[113]

Given its emotivity and elusiveness, the charge of 'mafia' was a particularly powerful political weapon. Enemies were denounced as *mafiosi*, and any reciprocation of the charge was explained as a malicious slur by the opposition. The police then faced the problem of who to believe. In general they were best advised to support the ruling faction, particularly when the government was behind it, as any attempt to stamp out the abuses of the incumbent administration inevitably raised a dangerous storm. Complaints against an official (usually couched in terms of 'persecution') quickly reached Rome, and the policeman or magistrate in question would be forced to account for himself. If his case was watertight, he might live to fight another day; but in most instances he would end up transferred (to Sardinia if he had given particular offence) or even suspended.

The upward extension of the clientele system often made it hard for the police to manoeuvre. Each local administration supported a deputy, and in return for securing his election, the council would expect him to advance their interests. This might involve the allocation of a public works contract, a special subsidy, oiling bureaucratic wheels in Rome, intervening in a trial, or helping to remove a meddlesome official. Failure to gratify constituents could damage a politician, unless, perhaps, they had become too much of a liability. Dissatisfied clients might take their vote elsewhere; they could also, if particularly aggrieved, turn on their erstwhile protector and ruin his career. In the case of Piersanti Mattarella, a leading Christian Democrat politician who was murdered in 1980, the refusal to support some of his chief electors may well have cost him his life.[114]

Whether the contractual balance between local factions and deputies was significantly altered by the abolition of elections under fascism is by no means certain. From the 1880s a growing number of complaints were heard about electoral corruption. The government was using criminals unashamedly, it was said, to secure votes. Some writers even maintained that the mafia only survived because politicians in Rome offered protection in return for support at the polls.[115] This was naturally an argument that the fascists adopted: a number of prominent party figures stated that fascism could tackle the mafia for the simple reason that it no longer had electoral calculations to make.[116] However, fascism was not monolithic. It was split between different currents and factions that vied with one another, particularly in the early years, and the leading party figures often needed supporters lower down to buttress their positions. Apart from anything else, there was cachet to be gained from having a large clientele; and though the regime's authoritarianism implied control from above, the opportunities for blackmail and mud-slinging by disgruntled underlings was considerable. The bargaining power of clients under fascism may therefore have been less affected than is often supposed.

Because the chains of patronage ran from every small town, through the provincial capital to Rome, no decision about the mafia could escape being political. If a prefect decided to dissolve a local council on the grounds of public order, he needed great courage to do so without the highest approval. In 1923, Prefect Gasti and the leading Palermo fascist, Alfredo Cucco, together abolished many liberal and socialist administrations in the course of a drive against the mafia. This was evidently in keeping with government wishes. When Cesare Mori conducted his campaign against the mafia a few years later, he decided to turn the tables on Cucco. This was a dangerous move, and he sought reassurance. Mussolini backed him, largely because Cucco's current of fascism had become something of a liability to the regime. Mori, however, had dangerous enemies, and they did their utmost to have him removed. Letters of denunciation poured into the ministries. Mori took to counter-lobbying, and his spies plied him with information about developments, both in Palermo and Rome. In the short term he won; but he had engendered too much hatred to survive for long.[117]

The mafia as an emergent middle class

Since the boundaries of the mafia were unclear, decisions about whom to arrest were, in part, political. In the view of Cesare Mori, the great landowners had always been victims of the mafia, never its accomplices. He saw the rural middle class, and in particular the *gabelloti* and their dependents, as the chief culprits. This was a different choice from Franchetti, a Tuscan baron, whose conscience had forced him to upbraid his aristocratic peers in Sicily for their lack of civic awareness; the *gabelloti* hardly figured in his 1876 study.[118] When the Bonfadini and Damiani reports dealt with the mafia, they also had little to say about the middle classes. Giovanni Lorenzoni, in 1910, discussed the social and economic problems caused by the *gabelloti*, but did not suggest they were particularly criminal.[119] Mori's decision to strike at the *gabelloti* was to a certain extent politically motivated.

The Sicilian rural middle class was in some ways distinctive. To start with, it was numerically slight. For centuries the island had been divided between a mass of landless peasants and an élite of great landowners, or *latifondisti*. Before the abolition of feudalism in 1812, there was very little movement in the land market. The *latifondi* remained in entail, and this meant that despite multiple mortgages, the aristocracy were unable to sell their estates. In 1824, however, a law was brought in allowing creditors to take land in settlement of debts. A new class of parvenu proprietors began to emerge, many of whom bought titles and affected the lifestyle of lordlings. According to one estimate, there were 20,000 landowning families in 1860 as against only 2,000 fifty years earlier.[120] Nevertheless, this new bourgeoisie still represented only a minute fraction of the total population.

More important, perhaps, than its size was the character of the island's middle class. The medieval Sicilian towns had failed to challenge the dominance of the aristocracy (in part because foreign rulers found the local baronage indispensable), and this had deprived the island of a strong bourgeois ethic. The main culture remained that of a nobility obsessed with status, and accustomed from the fourteenth century to untrammelled personal rule. Attempts by the Bourbons to enforce centralised control were bitterly contested. Appeals were made to the island's liberties, and the Sicilian parliament on occasions emerged as a symbol of resistance. However, this spirit of independence was only half-hearted. The nobility never felt strong enough to stand alone against a rebellious peasant population. When social revolution threatened, as it did many times in the seventeenth, eighteenth, and nineteenth centuries, the aristocracy looked to the state to intervene and restore order.

The habit of personal rule and the belief that the government should cater to the interests of the strongest were passed on to the new bourgeoisie. The *gabelloti* were particularly liable to absorb these views. They filled a vacuum created by the nobility, whose need for cash and court patronage forced them to rent out their estates and move to Palermo or Naples. In their absence, the new men grew rich, and some of them rose to dominate their communities. They had no incentive to invest their wealth and become true capitalists:[121] the lease on a *latifondo* rarely exceeded six years, and the *gabelloti* profitted by subletting or squeezing the peasants mercilessly. In addition, markets, particularly in the west of the island, were often inaccessible, as a result of poor roads. (There was little reason to improve communications given Sicily's isolation from the main arteries of European commerce, which from the sixteenth century shifted northwards, away from the Mediterranean.)

The *gabelloti* were scarcely more than intermediaries with aristocratic pretensions. They accumulated capital through usury and speculation, and, like the barons, they resorted to private violence to impose their will. They employed armed *campieri* to help enforce contracts and control the peasantry, and in common with the great landowners, they used them also to bolster their status. Alongi wrote in 1887:

> I always remember seeing many of these lords of the mountain returning from their fiefs followed by half a dozen *campieri*, all on horseback, with boots, thick cloaks, and rifles on their knees. They would enter a town at full gallop...quite oblivious to whether someone might be trampled beneath the hooves of their mounts.[122]

Power in Sicily was personal, and it was there to be flaunted.

In the seventeenth and eighteenth centuries there was little opportunity for challenging the aristocratic ascendancy. During the Napoleonic Wars, however, the middle classes made a dramatic advance. Rapid inflation allowed the *gabelloti* to sell their goods at a premium, while the fixed cash rents paid to the landowners grew increasingly worthless. Many noble families found themselves bankrupt, and when the land market was unlocked after the abolition of feudalism, the parvenus took what they could.[123] A further source of enrichment came from the suppression of the peasants' feudal rights: the new men seized whatever acreage of the commons they could, and though the peasantry might legally claim at least one-fifth of any land where there had been a custom of ancestral usage, the king was persuaded in 1841 to make possession evidence of title. Villagers now had the arduous task of proving that the local despots had no right to what they had taken.

The revolution of 1860 that ended in Italy's unification provided fresh opportunities for middle-class advancement. The limited suffrage introduced by the new state meant that a few influential figures could dominate local government as never before. Taxes were easily adjusted to benefit the well off, and public funds were siphoned into private pockets.[124] The competition for land increased considerably after 1860. This was in part owing to a rise in rents, which made leasing highly remunerative. 'As a result,' wrote the Sicilian economist, Enrico Loncao, 'there was land speculation of every kind; and communal properties were ransacked.'[125] Commercial treaties and a strong demand for Sicilian wheat in Britain and France also added to the value of land. Sulphur too was a source of speculation in the early years of unity, with exports mounting rapidly. Given these various avenues to wealth, it is not unlikely, as one observer remarked in 1881, that most rich *borghesi* (small or medium landowners) in Sicily had been humble peasants fifty years before.[126]

The *gabelloti* enjoyed many economic advantages. For example, the absence of written contracts afforded great flexibility in dealings with the peasantry. An attempt was made, immediately after unification, to have agricultural agreements recorded, but in practice, business continued to be conducted by word of mouth.[127] This allowed the *gabelloti* to chop and change at will. One writer in 1873 mentioned a *gabelloto* of Villafrate who had sublet land in 1868 on the verbal understanding that the tenant should pay one *tumulo* of wheat (17 litres) for every *tumulo* of land (0.11 hectares). When it looked as if the harvest would be good, he changed his mind and opted for a proportion of the final yield. In June, however, the crop failed for lack of water, and the *gabelloto* reverted to his original arrangement. The peasants lost almost everything.[128]

Though some people disliked the *gabelloti*, their image was not uniformly bad in the first decades after 1860. In part this was due to a widely shared feeling that the creation of a strong middle class might help to solve Sicily's problems, and though the *gabelloti* were far from ideal, it was felt that they were at least better than effete aristocrats. Enrico Fincati spoke in 1881 of enterprising peasants who leased estates or mills from noblemen 'who would not, or could not, run them themselves'.

By living near to the breadline, and working daily like Trojans; by supervising employees personally, and exploiting to the utmost land taken *in gabella*...they succeeded in a decade or two in accumulating an independent fortune. Sometimes they themselves assumed ownership of the estate which the feudatory was too frightened to supervise at close quarters, or else was incapable of administering.[129]

This positive view of the *gabelloto* was partially shared by Sidney Sonnino in his famous study of Sicilian agriculture in 1876. He admitted that many *gabelloti* had little real interest in the land they farmed: some, indeed, took on an estate simply in order to re-let it to a '*sub-gabelloto*'. However, he felt that the best of them were a marked improvement on the aristocrats; and there was every reason to hope, he said, that the most dynamic and intelligent *gabelloti* ('whom I have been able to talk to in person, and whose many virile qualities I have seen') would gradually replace the current owners, 'without losing their enterprise, acumen, and energy'.[130] Like Franchetti, Sonnino reserved most of his vitriol for irresponsible *latifondisti*.

After the 1880s, the *gabelloti* suffered from an increasingly bad press. They came more and more to be seen as exploitative and as a source of social injustice, particularly when they were absentee speculators, like the landowners, and merely subcontracted. However, as Lorenzoni noticed in 1910, plenty of *gabelloti* took a direct interest in cultivation. They often resided on their estates, and were, he said, 'the true pioneer[s] of agricultural improvement and intensive farming on the *latifondi*'.[131] This dynamism may have been partly the result of peasant emigration: at the beginning of the century *gabelloti* were apparently finding it hard to attract tenants, and were now compelled to offer more remunerative terms. Better tools, irrigation, or even a farmhouse might be included in a new contract.[132]

The relationship between the rural middle class and the landowners was by no means simple. Marxist interpretations of the mafia (which were particularly popular after the Second World War) tended to reduce the problem to one of straightforward repression. The *gabelloti* and their dependents, the *campieri* and *guardiani*, were used by the *latifondisti*, so the syllogism ran, to keep order in the countryside. The rural middle class was the mafia *par excellence*, therefore the mafia had as its central function the preservation of the status quo. This line of thought underpinned the view that the mafia was controlled by big landowners and conservative politicians. It also meant that the fight against the mafia became a revolutionary struggle for the liberation of the peasantry. Not surprisingly, perhaps, many of the post-war writers who have endorsed the Marxist view of the mafia have themselves been active politicians of the left.

To regard the *gabelloti* as mere tools of the landed élite is to ignore the complexity of Sicilian class relations. *Gabelloti* and *latifondisti* were certainly united in wanting to keep the masses under control; but the *gabelloti* were, above all, ambitious peasants who disliked being subservient to anyone. Though they squeezed their tenants ruthlessly, they also pressurised absentee proprietors.[133] Indeed one of their chief sources of advancement lay in taking land, as well as money, from the aristocracy. On occasions this could lead them to exploit or even instigate peasant unrest, as, for example, in the 1890s, and more particularly after the First World War. Vito Cascio Ferro, later to be described as one of the wealthiest and most powerful mafia figures ever, had been a leading figure in the socialist *Fasci*.[134] Calogero Vizzini, another notorious *gabelloto*, was prominent in the Villalba co-operative movement in the early 1920s, and used it for his own advancement.[135]

The ability to spearhead local unrest presupposed a degree of moral authority over the peasants. However, the simplistic Marxist model that was usually applied to the mafia ruled this out: for if the *gabelloti* were exploiters, which they patently were, how could their victims feel other than oppressed? The *gabelloti* certainly aroused a good deal of grass-roots hatred, and this hatred was particularly strong among socialists, who saw the unscrupulous peasant *arrivistes* as class traitors. Nevertheless, the *gabelloti* embodied aspirations and values that were far from rare: only fools, it was often felt, wielded power in the interests of the collectivity, and only the weak had no capacity for violence. When men such as Calogero Vizzini, or more recently, Nino Salvo, died, the majority of the town turned out for the funeral.[136] Fear alone is unlikely to have been an adequate explanation for this.

Much of the power and also the wealth of a *gabelloto* derived from his local influence. Since few people dealt directly with officialdom, an authoritative *gabelloto* in a provincial town could often fill the role of policeman or magistrate. When a theft occurred in Villalba, Calogero Vizzini sometimes interceded for the victim: his reputation was such that some, if not all, the stolen goods would generally be returned to the injured party. A personal quarrel could be settled by appeal to a local *mafioso*; so, too, might a dispute with the tax collector, the *pretore*, or the *carabinieri*. A *mafioso* might negotiate or supply a loan, or perhaps arrange a job for a member of a needy family. For a man with authority, the scope for exercising power in this society was immense.[137]

Like the landowners, the *gabelloti* found it hard to escape contact with criminals. The *campieri* and *guardiani* they employed on their estates were almost invariably men of violence, and this raised the question of complicity, which, if hard to settle with the *latifondisti*, was almost equally so with the rural parvenus. Admittedly, *gabelloti* themselves often had to acquire a reputation for force in order to rise to, and maintain, their positions,[138] and this might involve them in crimes of 'honour'. Their power, however, depended chiefly on local government and avid speculation. They had little reason, once established, to deal in theft or overt extortion. Nevertheless, their extensive clienteles, and in particular their links with local bandits and petty criminals, made them vulnerable to the charge of criminal association. Mori exploited this situation mercilessly in the 1920s.

Prior to the final decade of the nineteenth century, the term 'mafia' rarely attached to the rural middle class. The historian Pasquale Villari claimed in an essay of 1875 that the *gabelloti, guardiani*, and grain merchants of the Conca d'oro were often the backbone of the mafia. He went on to say that they formed 'a kind of wall' between peasant and landowner, and '[kept] them constantly divided'.[139] However, this view was not explicitly shared by the major commentators on Sicily. Franchetti and Lorenzoni, for example, saw the *gabelloti* as facing similar problems to the landowners: they regarded them as men with property to protect, who had little choice, on the whole, but to treat with criminals. According to Bonfadini in his 1876 report, the *gabelloti* protected bandits, 'sometimes from calculation, often through fear'.[140] They also employed violent *campieri*; but, as was generally recognised, field guards were of little use if they had no capacity to intimidate.[141]

The advance of socialism in the last years of the nineteenth century brought greater awareness of Sicily's rural middle class. The exploitative behaviour of the *gabelloti*, and the harshness of the contracts they imposed on the peasants, became a source of grave concern. The aristocratic observers of Sicily in the 1870s had been worried about the landowners; the middle class writers who succeeded them gazed with horror at the island's nascent bourgeoisie. Socialists were particularly appalled: how could these ruthless entrepreneurs emerge from the peasantry? Sebastiano Cammareri Scurti, one of the most sensitive members of the Sicilian left, found this hard to square. In an article of 1899, he spoke of the 'necessity of the mafia' for success in life. He said that the peasants were so exploited that the only chance they had of gaining respect and wealth in this society was by violent self-assertion. However, he also defined the mafia as 'an instrument for the brutal control of the masses'. It was not clear, therefore, whether or not he wished to blame the rural parvenus.[142]

One solution to the moral dilemma was to condemn the landowners by saying that the mafia existed only because they willed it into being as an instrument in the class war. Alternatively (as with Napoleone Colajanni)[143] the government could be arraigned for cynical collusion. A simpler way out of the impasse, however, was to play down the connections between the new men and the masses. If the *gabelloti* were portrayed simply as brutal exploiters, it was possible to vilify them whole-heartedly. Furthermore, the awkward problem for socialists of how far the rural middle class embodied the values of the peasantry disappeared. If the mafia were a criminal organisation that terrorised others into submission, the behaviour of the *gabelloti* and *campieri* could be seen as alien to the true consciousness of most Sicilians.

The *locus classicus* for this idea of the mafia is Ruggero Grieco's statement to the Communist Party conference on southern agriculture, held at Bari in 1926.[144] The landowners, he said, leased their estates to *gabelloti*, or else administered them through stewards and *campieri*. These intermediaries 'exploit[ed] the Sicilian workers in the most ignominious manner'; taken together they constituted 'the managerial heart of the mafia'. The function of this mafia, he claimed, was to act as a 'solid defence for Sicilian rural feudalism', and to this end, it gathered into its hands all the necessary tools, including 'its own bodyguard, the communal administrations, the electoral circles, the deputies, and the banks'. It also employed a 'lower mafia' made up of peasants and impoverished middle-class elements, and it was on these that Grieco pinned his hopes for the future. 'In the dialectical process of the proletarian and peasant revolution in Sicily, we will see the displacement of the mass of lower *mafiosi* of peasant origin...towards the revolutionary proletariat.'

If the mafia were a defence force for the preservation of a feudal society, any attack on it would clearly have to be accompanied by economic reforms. The obvious premise for these was a division of the *latifondi*, and a number of left-wing writers in fact argued that the great estates were themselves the source of the island's social violence.[145] According to Napoleone Colajanni the brutality of the mafia stemmed directly from the iniquitous conditions of farming in the interior. Conservative critics retorted that lawlessness was just as much a problem in the Conca d'oro, an area of rich and intensive cultivation.[146] Many observers skirted the awkward question of the Palermo hinterland and its smallholdings and stated simply that the *gabelloti* and *campieri* were the backbone of the mafia, and that once the *latifondi* went, so too would organised crime. This view was particularly popular after 1945, when agricultural reform was the primary goal of the Sicilian left.

The fashion for Marxism in the 1890s was one reason for the growing identification of the mafia with the *gabelloti* and their field guards. Another was the shifting balance of power between the island's social classes and the threat this presented to the dominance of the big landowners. In the period leading up to the First World War, mass emigration strengthened the bargaining position of the peasantry. As a result, the fortunes of many *gabelloti* may well have been dented, for they relied on a surplus in the population to extract the most lucrative terms.[147] At the same time, the buoyancy of the fruit and sulphur trades, particularly in the first years of the century, guaranteed the *latifondisti* a healthy income.[148] The economic and social balance was inclined favourably towards the traditional order. The aristocracy had little to fear.

The First World War produced a drastic change. The closure of export markets entailed a serious loss of revenue for the landowners. More significant, perhaps, was the freeze on rents; for despite heavy inflation, the *latifondisti* were committed to leasing their estates at fixed sums. This gave the *gabelloti* a good opportunity for enrichment. They could demand payment from their tenants in kind, while giving the proprietor cash. Their profits after selling the surplus on the market were often huge. The gap between the established landowners and the rural bourgeoisie widened, and when, after the war, the economic crisis was supplemented by peasant unrest, many *latifondisti* felt they had little choice but to sell up. Those best placed to benefit were the affluent middle classes. They had access to both capital and credit, and could either acquire land themselves, or else act as speculator brokers.[149]

After the threat of the peasantry in 1919–22 came the challenge of fascism. The new movement made scant progress in Sicily before Mussolini came to power; but after October 1922, one local administration after another toppled to the new regime. Sicilian fascism was to a large extent radical, or intransigent, in character, particularly in the west of the island. Here the aristocratic order was still well entrenched, and young middle-class activists, many of them politicised by their war experiences, sought earnestly to sweep it away. They wanted new men to replace the old liberals and absentee landowners. They called for intransigence, and were angry when the government forced compromises on them during elections. They proclaimed a crusade against the mafia, and their target was the system of liberal clienteles.[150]

In the late summer of 1925, the leading Sicilian fascist, Alfredo Cucco, asked Mussolini to consolidate the victory of fascism in the island with an all-out campaign against the mafia. His motives were in part political: he wanted the final destruction of those groups that had profited most from the liberal system. The government had rather different ideas. Radical fascism was something of a liability by late 1925, and threatened to undermine the accommodation that Mussolini had secured with the conservative forces of big business, the Church, and landowners. Accordingly, the man appointed to conduct the operation against the mafia was a long-standing ally of the Sicilian élite. In common with many socialists, he regarded the rural middle class as culpable. Unlike them, however, his sympathies were with the old order. His campaign of 1925–9 had the effect of shoring up the beleaguered landowners at the expense of the rural parvenus and radical fascists. Once again the idea of the mafia was shaped to fit social and political ends.

The problem of secret societies

Though all serious observers agreed that the mafia was not a large-scale criminal society, evidence did emerge from time to time of local associations with formal hierarchies, initiation ceremonies, and rigid codes of conduct. This was particularly the case in the 1870s. However, the precise character of such organisations as the *Fratuzzi* of Bagheria, or the *Stoppaglieri* of Monreale is not easy to gauge. They appear to have been self-conscious groups; but whether they were glorified political factions, mutual aid societies, or true criminal bodies is unclear. As always, there is the problem of evidence. Unearthing dangerous conspiracies was a source of kudos for the police. 'Witnesses' could usually be found to provide lurid information, and sometimes it bordered on the absurd.

A good example of what sounds fantastical occurred in the summer of 1929.[151] Following the escape from the island of Lipari of the three leading anti-fascists, Emilio Lussu, Francesco Nitti, and Carlo Rosselli, the Messina police produced details of a 'supremely secret' society whose aim had been to occupy Nice and Savoy. The initiates, they said, took oaths on a human skull, wore rings in the shape of serpents, and covered themselves in black hoods during meetings. One of the alleged leaders of this society was Leonardo Bottari, an officer in the fascist Militia on Lipari, who had failed, according to the police, to stop the escaping anti-fascists after the alarm had been raised. Given the 'overwhelming evidence' against him, they said, he should not try to deny his guilt, because that would be 'clear proof that he belonged to an association that had secrecy as its cardinal rule'. Bottari duly confessed, and even supplied additional information about the society, including the fact that its propaganda was to be directed chiefly at fishermen, so that when the time came, they would have 'the means to prepare an expedition against France for the occupation of Nice and Savoy'. He also divulged the name of the society's leader, who on interrogation turned out to be an illiterate who had destroyed 'all the documents relating to the organisation'. This, said the police, indicated that he was 'in league with subversive elements', and confirmed their view that the Communist Party was infiltrating the Militia.

It seems that even the Ministry of the Interior found this hard to swallow.[152] Perhaps the Messina police had been embarrassed by the escape of Lussu, Nitti, and Rosselli, and sought to make amends for their incompetence by showing their efficiency in uncovering this secret society. However, the observer can only be guided in such cases by intuition and inference, and these cannot prove matters one way or the other. Probability dictates that true secret organisations have existed in Sicily. If nothing else, the mythology of the legendary eighteenth-century society, the *Beati Paoli*, is bound to have spawned self-conscious imitations at one time or another.[153] The difficulty is to know their frequency and extent. This is particularly true today after what Tommaso Buscetta has said about Cosa Nostra. If his account of initiation ceremonies and a rigid organisational structure is correct, there ought perhaps to be less scepticism about the societies of the 1870s.

Trials for criminal association have often been based on the evidence of police informers. This raises the question of motivation. If, as in the late 1870s or early 1980s, conspiracy theories are strongly in vogue, it is easy for interested parties to exploit them. Individuals can feed the police details about their opponents, and since almost the only leverage the authorities have in Sicily is through the charge of criminal association, the information is likely to be dressed in organisational terms. In 1926, Paolo Timpanaro informed the police that his enemies in Mistretta constituted the 'tribunal of the mafia'. He described their offices using such legal terms as '*presidente*' (president), '*procuratore del re*' (procurator royal), and '*giudice relatore*' (reporting judge).[154] Anonymous denunciations frequently used expressions such as '*una associazione segreta*' (a secret association), '*il presidente della detta società*' (the president of this society), and '*una setta di malfattori*' (a sect of criminals).[155] Such statements could be crucial in the construction of a police case.

Fashionable theories could easily determine the kind of evidence presented. At Bari in 1891 there was a much-publicised trial of 178 members of an association called the *Mala Vita*. This was said to be a structured organisation, whose members sported tattoos, and in particular, hearts transfixed with arrows.[156] Tattoos had been much discussed by Lombroso and his positivist school in the 1880s. They were seen as atavistic (through analogy with the body-painting of savages), and hence a good indication of criminal tendencies.[157] This might explain why they were so central to the *Mala Vita* trial. With little to go on, the police had to invest heavily in anything that seemed plausible. The police informers must have known this – a point underlined by the defence, which claimed that the evidence for the association had come from paid agents or from prisoners who had been offered an amnesty if they co-operated.[158] Though all but fourteen of the accused were found guilty in May 1891, the prosecution case collapsed a few months later on appeal, and only thirty-one of the sentences were upheld.[159]

Despite this sorry outcome, the idea of the *Mala Vita* had penetrated the popular imagination sufficiently for its existence to be accredited. Heckethorn, in his 1897 encyclopaedia of secret societies, described it as an offshoot of the *camorra*, whose initiates had to take an oath with one foot in an open grave, and the other attached to a chair. The name of the society, he said, allegedly derived from a popular novel by Degia Como (the influence of romantic fiction on organised crime is still uncharted country). Tattoos were a sign of membership, and any breaches of the regulations were punished by torture and death, after deliberations by the whole society.[160]

Belief in exotic conspiracies ran deep. This makes it hard to distinguish fact from fantasy, as those who wrote about secret societies usually did so in credulous good faith. They failed to discuss sources, but their thought often radiated sobriety and intelligence. This was the case, for instance, with Giuseppe Lestingi's article on the *Fratellanza* of Girgenti province, which was quickly taken as authoritative after it appeared in a learned journal in 1884.[161] A number of putative organisations such as the *Stoppaglieri* of Monreale or the *Fratuzzi* of Bagheria seem to have been extrapolations from trials.[162] Once they had been described in books, their status was assured. The evidence for the *Stoppaglieri*, however, derived from a single source, Salvatore d'Amico. He had been in prison for some years, and was the only witness at the 1878 trial who appeared to know about this 'sect' and its initiation ceremonies.[163] As with the *Mala Vita* trial, the prosecution case collapsed on appeal. Nevertheless, the *Stoppaglieri* continued to be spoken of by Alongi, Cutrera, and others, as a proven criminal association.[164]

The rituals and formulae ascribed to these organisations are often reminiscent of Freemasonry or the republican sects of the early nineteenth century. Among the functions of the *Fratellanza*, according to Lestingi, was the provision of jobs, help with funerals, and financial aid for families where the breadwinner was dead or in prison.[165] The province of Girgenti was an early stronghold of the International, and it could be that the organisation, in its initial form at least, was a rudimentary mutual aid society.[166] Its rituals, as revealed in a document unearthed by the police, were as bizarre as anything dreamt up by early nineteenth-century political conspirators. Associates recognised one another by holding an earlobe between index and middle finger, and saying: 'Greetings, *compare*, do you have a cigar stub, as my molar tooth is hurting me?' To which the answer was: 'I do.' When one member of the society was sent to contact another outside his own town, the following exchange took place: Q. Who is your God? A. Aremi [the name of a suit of cards] Q. What is your goal? A. Universal republic. Q. When they admitted you, who was there? A. Good people. Q. Who were they? A. [Names].[167]

The initiation ceremony that crops up most frequently in the context of the societies of the 1870s also suggests indebtedness to early nineteenth-century political or social organisations. It consisted of pricking a finger, smearing blood on the paper image of a saint, burning it, scattering the ashes, and then swearing an oath of absolute obedience and secrecy. Lestingi added that a thread was first tied round the finger to symbolise the 'indissoluble bond that linked the associate to his fellows'. The blood, he said, represented self-sacrifice, the picture of the saint, 'the divinity', and the ashes, the

irrevocability of one's commitments.[168] Whenever initiation ceremonies are referred to in Sicily, they usually conform to this model.
Tommaso Buscetta said in 1984 that members of Cosa Nostra were
admitted in the presence of at least three witnesses. They had to spill
blood on the image of a saint, burn it in their hands without com-
plaining, and swear to honour the principles of Cosa Nostra.[169]

A passage in Alongi's study of the mafia suggests that the societies
of the 1870s could well have had a political origin. He wrote in 1887:

> There has been much talk of initiation rites. People speak, in
> legendary terms, of some kind of missionaries, who after 1866
> travelled through various towns winning converts to a cause that
> was disguised as religious and political. In other words, they
> pretended to be seeking the triumph of religion and the destruction
> of a usurping and excommunicate government, but in reality their
> principal concern was crime. It was these people who introduced
> rituals that were part mystical, part sectarian.[170]

If there is any truth in this story, it could refer either to mendicant
clergy after the suppression of the religious houses, or to early
messianic socialists. Possibly, indeed, the two categories had been
conflated.

The societies of the 1870s (and they included, besides the
Stoppaglieri and the *Fratellanza*, the *Mano Fraterna* of Girgenti, the
Fratuzzi of Bagheria, the *Scaglione* of Castrogiovanni, the *Zubbio* of
Villabate, and the *Fontana Nuova* of Misilmeri) are ill-defined con-
stellations. Most of them are no more to us than names, and this may
well have been true also a century ago. Cutrera claimed in 1900 that
the *Fratuzzi* were divided into 'squads', each with a leader, called a
'*decimo primo*' (eleventh). However, when a recent scholar consulted
the relevant trial of 1887, he was 'baffled' at Cutrera's assertion. 'All
that is clear', he said, 'is that there were the usual two factions, one
headed by the mayor, Scordato, the other by Pietro Greco, and that
rivalry between them sometimes led to murder.'[171] Lestingi had
talked of the *Fratellanza* being composed of units of ten, each with a
chief;[172] Cutrera may simply have imagined this structure to be
generic, particularly as Alongi said that it was the *Fratellanza* that had
'spawned' all the other associations, including the *Fratuzzi*.[173]

The idea of an organisational structure similar to that of the
Fratellanza has from time to time been applied to the mafia. The
number ten has been particularly enduring. In 1937, when the fascist
police were conducting a major series of round-ups, Dr Melchiorre
Allegra made a confession in which he stated that the mafia was
divided into 'families', each headed by a chief, and that when a
family was too numerous, it was split into groups of ten. The leaders
of the mafia, he said, met in the Birreria Italia in Palermo.[174] In 1984,

Pl. 4. The 'bunker' court-room in Palermo, built for the equivalent of £15 million to house the so-called 'maxi trial' of Cosa Nostra. The trial, which began in February 1986, was based largely on the testimony of Tommaso Buscetta. Two thousand members of the security forces were deployed to guard the magistrates, the jury, the accused, and the witnesses.

Tommaso Buscetta revealed a much more elaborate structure for Cosa Nostra (the word 'mafia', he claimed, was a literary invention). It included not only families and chiefs, but also a 'commission' that co-ordinated the activities of the families in each province. However the unit ten is still present in the '*capo decina*', who operated below the '*capo*' (chief) '*sottocapo*' (sub-chief), and '*consiglieri*' (counsellors).[175]

How one interprets such elements of continuity is an open question. The idea of the mafia is a minefield of fact and fantasy, and the two are easily conflated. This is so for the authorities; it may also be true for the protagonists themselves. The testimony of Tommaso Buscetta has the hallmark of authenticity; but, as the recent trial of Enzo Tortora in Naples showed, false staments can be readily produced when magistrates are disposed to believe them.[176] Nor should it be assumed that such deceptions are always deliberate. Today's 'men of honour', like their forebears, are obsessed by power and self-importance, and in their minds, half-truths and illusions can easily acquire the status of certainty. This is no doubt particularly true when they are under pressure to provide evidence to the authorities that will condemn their opponents.

Myths have a power and momentum of their own, and can generate corresponding elements of reality. To many of those brought up in the slums of Palermo, the idea of a strong organisation that offers a path to riches and honour is appealing. This is particularly so as unemployment is high and resources are scarce. In the absence of legal channels to wealth, violence will retain much of its mystique, and those that practice it are likely to exploit existing myths. Initiation ceremonies, codes of honour, and hierarchies can provide a patina of respectability to men struggling for status. Accordingly, the idea of the mafia will at times overlap with the real world. The myth, however, is far stronger than any actuality, and distorts our understanding of the complex social, economic, and political life of Sicily. As long as this continues it will be impossible to achieve a correct balance between means and ends in the struggle to make Sicily an integral part of the Italian state.

PART II

4 SICILY, FASCISM, AND THE MAFIA, 1920–25

Fascism and the Southern Question

Mussolini told a deputation of southern fascists shortly after becoming prime minister: 'I have the power to solve...even the problem of Italy's *Mezzogiorno*. It is my most fervent aspiration to do so.'[1] This remark need not be taken too seriously: Mussolini had a gift for tailoring his words to his audience. Yet so much was made of the Southern Question (the social and economic backwardness of the South) in the first years of fascist rule, and so much said of the government's determination to resolve it, that it would require a great deal of cynicism to dismiss it all as mere rhetoric. Mussolini, as he himself admitted, was unfamiliar with the *Mezzogiorno*, and many of his statements on the problem of the South were simplistic.[2] However, his ignorance is no reason for supposing he was insincere. It might have been a case of naïvety fuelled by his excessive faith in the power of the will.

Mussolini had a strong political reason for wanting to solve the Southern Question. Fascism was a northern product, and it implantation into the South, and its growth there, proved difficult. Even as late as January 1925, Mussolini told his Minister of Public Works that the country was in danger of splitting in two, 'because in the *Mezzogiorno*, mistrust of the fascist regime can be considered total'. A massive programme of public works was vital, he said; and if the situation did not improve in six months, 'the regime will have trouble surviving'.[3] Three months later the same minister was again made to listen to Mussolini's extravagant claims: 'It is sad and extremely dangerous', he was informed privately, after the Duce had learnt of the trivial sums to be allocated to the South. 'The dignity of the fascist government is in mortal danger of being irreparably compromised....The question of public works in southern Italy is absolutely fundamental'.[4]

If in these early years Mussolini pledged himself to solving the Southern Question primarily to bolster his power, that does not mean that ideological considerations were altogether absent. Fascism claimed to represent national interests, and the themes of integration, unity, and centralisation were important weapons in the regime's armoury. In the long run, this led to a crude refutation of regional problems and an outright denial that a Southern Question existed;[5] but in the short term it produced a fairly concerted effort by the government to draw the South into the framework of the nation. The endeavour was buttressed by rhetoric: 'Banish every trace of regionalism', declared the prominent fascist and former socialist, Piero Bolzon, on the eve of the March on Rome, '. . . in a moment of supreme national synthesis, that must harbour the vision of a South framed proudly within the nation'.[6]

One reason why these good intentions ultimately came to nothing was that the Southern Question turned out to be a more complex issue than the government ever cared to admit. The resoluteness of fascism, so often paraded to point up the alleged weakness and moral lassitude of the liberal era, soon broke down in the face of political contradictions. The results were farcical and, ultimately, tragic. Having preached the need to find an answer to the Southern Question, the regime, ever image-conscious, dared not lose face: it simply declared the problem solved, and further discussion of the matter was forbidden. When in 1939 the party secretary, Achille Starace, learnt of the *Associazione per il Mezzogiorno*, he asked its president curtly why such an organisation still existed. 'The question of the South', he said, 'has been settled by the regime.'[7]

In the first half of the 1920s, however, a certain amount of constructive thought was applied to the *Mezzogiorno*. Mussolini even admitted in 1922, with uncharacteristic modesty, that the Southern Question was complex and that it was foolish to suppose that it could be solved overnight: 'Fascism', he said, 'is not a miracle-worker'.[8] Investment received particular attention, and in December 1922 the Sicilian, Gabriello Carnazza, introduced a major reform that provided for a separate ministerial department to deal with public works in the South. It was assigned over 2 billion lire for the period 1923–8, with an additional 307 million to be spent on railways in Sicily. However, any hopes of a southern renaissance were short-lived. Carnazza had to contend with mounting criticism from northerners who opposed his economic interventionism, and in August 1924 two decrees effectively put paid to his new measures.[9]

Since fascism was chiefly a product of the North, discussion of the Southern Question was always liable to be half-hearted. Furthermore, much of Mussolini's most influential support came from Italy's conservative élite, and this curtailed his freedom of man-oeuvre. He could not, for example, deal with the problem of land-hunger in the South by dividing up the great estates. One of the new government's first acts was to revoke the 1920 Visocchi decree, (which regulated property seized by peasants after the war) and make any land occupations that had already been recognised by the provincial authorities illegal. As one fascist intellectual explained, the *'feudi'* (fiefs) had their roots deep in history, and 'like all sad inheritances, we should accept them, even if it hurts to do so'.[10]

The division of the *latifondi* may have appeared impracticable, but fascism nevertheless had other ambitions for the South. In the absence of a strong socialist presence, corruption and clientelism became the dragons to be slain: 'Political life in the *Mezzogiorno*', exclaimed Piero Bolzon in a speech of 1922, 'is too much of a relativist quagmire...in which favouritism and compromise have time and again turned the temple into a brothel.'[11] Moral regeneration was to be achieved by dislodging the old political factions, and replacing them with men of purer faith. 'Fascism should concentrate the struggle on every local *camarilla*', said the party secretary, Roberto Farinacci, at Naples in March 1925: 'Our policies must be directed against every party, but favour the Italian people, especially the working classes.'[12] However, as this last remark suggested, radical fascism had no wish to confine itself to the sphere of ethics. It regarded moral renewal as the first step on the road to social and economic reform.

Among those who discussed what a fascist policy of reform might entail in the *Mezzogiorno* was Piero Bolzon. 'Some people claim', he said, 'that the question is technical, others that it is moral. To my mind, these two aspects of the problem cannot be separated.' Poverty in the South, he said, was not congenital, but stemmed from a 'poor distribution of wealth'. In order to advance towards a modern and rational system of agriculture, the present feckless owners would have to be replaced by a new class of farmers; and this would be achieved not by splitting the *latifondi* into small, uneconomic plots, but by 'evolution' towards 'a division into large holdings, based on modern and co-operativistic criteria of cultivation and exploitation'. Bolzon's programme was uncompromising. Its principal victims were to be the big landowners and the rural middle classes ('the former indifferent, the latter ignorant'), who between them, he claimed, had ruined southern agriculture.[13]

Although Bolzon's language was probably more extreme than his thought, his vision of the South under fascism was far from conservative. Admittedly he did not specify, at least for the short term, any major shift in ownership of property; but it is hard to see what place there could have been in his new order for the old élite. He wanted a capitalist middle class which would work the land 'for the benefit of the whole nation'.[14] The change would be gradual, no doubt to give time for moral as well as technical education; but change there would be nonetheless. For a movement that owed its success after 1920 to the more reactionary elements in Italian society, the views of men such as Bolzon were bound to cause problems. The period between 1922 and 1926 saw a long and often acrimonious struggle between the two tendencies, radical and conservative, for the soul of fascism; and it was the 'intransigents' (as the most hardline members of the party were known) who lost.

As the fortunes of radical fascism waned, the debate over the South lost not only intensity, but also intellectual credibility. More and more, the stress came to be laid on moral rather than strictly economic, social, or political matters: 'Why emigration? Why the backward condition of agriculture? Why the still inhuman agricultural contracts?' asked the fascist intellectual, Carlo Curcio, in August 1925. 'To answer all these questions we must confront...the moral issue which, at the end of the day, is the essence of the southern problem.' The solution, as he saw it, lay with education; but not with education of any formal or practical kind. 'It must be an education that...aims at the good of the individual for the good of the whole, in other words, the nation.' Social and economic change, in so far as it figured in the argument at all, took very much the back seat: 'The answer to the problem must be moved from the outside to the inside, from the environment so-called, to the individual'.[15]

Even more symptomatic of the growing conservatism of the debate on the Southern Question was a book published by Luigi De Secly in 1926, called *La conquista regia*. Like Curcio, De Secly stressed education rather than structural reform: 'The problem of the revival of the *Mezzogiorno*', he said, 'is above all moral and spiritual'. He believed that the minds of southerners needed to be 'moulded' to prepare them for national duties, and integrate them into the state. This would be achieved, he felt, largely through the 'psychological mediation' of the Crown. The aristocracy would also be important. It would be composed of 'men of thought, and the rich, nobles in the true sense of the word'; and its task would be to link the people to the monarchy. Thus constituted, the state would no longer require great social changes, but merely a 'spiritual transformation' to be worked through the new aristocracy 'We must...replace quantity with quality, the mass with individuality...In short, a return to the old European civilisation based entirely, as Guglielmo Ferrero suggested, on selection and ability'.[16]

Despite intimations of meritocracy, De Secly's vision was at root deeply conservative. It was a far cry, both in tone and substance, from Piero Bolzon's or Roberto Farinacci's heartfelt intransigence. In the years that followed 1926, discussion of the Southern Question became increasingly ill-focused until, in the 1930s, the literature on the subject was scarcely more than a collection of platitudes. It was now the received wisdom that the *Mezzogiorno's* problems would be solved through moral regeneration, and this, apparently, fascism had largely achieved: 'Today', Mussolini announced in 1934, 'the Southern Question is no longer the order of the day, because on the whole we have solved it, and we will solve it completely.'[17]

Fascism and Sicily

Part of the reason why intransigents such as Piero Bolzon believed in the moral education, or re-education, of the South, was that fascism had never been strong there. One way of drawing the *Mezzogiorno* into the fascist fold, they thought, was to teach people the new nationalistic values. However, there was a practical problem: could the movement make any headway in areas where politics lacked intellectual content, and where the burning issues were municipal and personal, without seriously compromising its ideals? And could it hope to succeed if it failed to come to terms with those often unscrupulous local notables whose cynicism was matched by their electoral indispensability? In Sicily, these questions, difficult enough in themselves, were further confused by the highly emotive issue of the mafia, which constituted a major theme in the island's politics throughout the 1920s.

It was often argued that since there had been no serious socialist presence in Sicily, fascism in the island lacked a *raison d'être*. There was clearly a good deal of truth in this. In December 1920, Alfredo Cucco, a leading Palermo fascist (who was also head of the local Nationalist group) reported to his superiors in Milan that the city was dominated by 'the most peaceful *quieto vivere*'.[18] A month later the situation was apparently no better, despite a great surge of support for the movement in the north of the country: 'I'm not sure whether fortunately or unfortunately, but at Palermo we still have no Bolshevism, and the little we have is insipid.'[19] As it turned out, there was to be no real improvement until after the March on Rome, when a combination of prefectural pressure and opportunism precipitated the island's conversion to fascism.

The absence of a 'red peril', however, was by no means universal in Sicily. Indeed in the east of the island, and particularly in the province of Siracusa, the working-class movement strongly resembled its counterpart in the Po Valley. Violent clashes occurred frequently. On 29 January 1921, a group of fascists destroyed the socialist circle at Vittoria, killing one man and injuring ten. Two months later, four people lost their lives and sixty were wounded in an episode at Ragusa; in July the following year, there were similar casualty figures at Lentini.[20] The towns in the south-eastern corner of the island were unusual by Sicilian standards in that they had a large number of day labourers, and the strength and militancy of the socialist movement produced, as in Puglia and northern Italy, a violent reaction from the local landowners.[21]

However, the presence of socialism was not the only reason why fascism had more success in the south-east of the island than elsewhere. Another important factor was the absence in the Ragusa area of any major politicians with established clienteles: in other parts of Sicily, the network of political patronage left the new movement with little space in which to operate. Equally significant, perhaps, was that the west of the island enjoyed a tradition of political violence that was frequently ascribed to the mafia. This helped dispel whatever fears of socialism there might have been among the middle classes (who were anyway numerically slight, compared to their strength in northern Italy). In March 1920, the peasant leader, Nicolò Alongi, was murdered at Prizzi; in October of the same year, Giovanni Orcel, the charismatic head of the metalworkers union and the man most responsible for the socialist action in the Palermo dockyards, suffered a similar fate.[22]

Some Sicilian writers maintained that the weakness of fascism in the island was due to the presence of the mafia: 'The failure of the movement to prosper in Sicily', said the author of an article in the autonomist paper, *La Regione*, in January 1922, 'proves my point: two identical institutions cannot coexist in the same place.' On the mainland, he said, socialism had been suppressed by fascism; in Sicily the mafia had fulfilled the same function.[23] This view was perhaps less polemical than it seemed, for the writer regarded the mafia as an organisation that supplied order and justice when the state failed. It was thus comparable, he felt, to northern *squadrismo*. Fascist orthodoxy, however, could not permit such niceties. A comparison between a movement of national regeneration and the mafia would not have been understood by many people, still less appreciated. It was much safer for the party simply to say that fascism had made little headway in Sicily because there had been no socialist threat there.

The weakness of early Sicilian fascism was a source of pride and, potentially at least, of political capital too, for advocates of separatism or autonomy. To northerners, however, the lack of enthusiasm for the new movement often appeared to be merely a symptom of Sicily's political and moral backwardness. In the long run, this view was to contribute to the island's increasing neglect by the government; but in the short-term, it helped focus attention on those aspects of Sicilian society – the mafia included – that stood in the way of the island's social and moral development. It also (as elsewhere in the South) provided the movement with its chief political objective: the destruction of the old liberal clienteles.

'We must fight tooth and nail', wrote a leading Palermo fascist shortly after the March on Rome, 'against all politicians, past and present, for they, and they alone, are responsible for our misfortunes. All they have ever cared about are their own interests and those of their corrupt followers.'[24] In the west of Sicily, the fight against the old clienteles was frequently presented as an attack on the mafia. After all, had Napoleone Colajanni and others not pilloried the liberal regime for its collusion with criminals and men of violence? And had the Prime Minister, Giovanni Giolitti, not been called the 'minister of the underworld'? And what was 'underworld' if not mafia? 'It is the mafia', wrote Alfredo Cucco in March 1923, in a savage article denouncing opportunist converts, 'that immense, and sinuous octo-pus...which, together with its accomplice and fellow traveller, the old deputy, is trying to worm its way into the fascist camp.'[25]

The mafia was a nebulous concept that carried with it a host of evil associations. This made it a useful weapon to hurl at opponents, but the vagueness of the term was also a source of confusion. At the beginning of 1923, Francesco Tiby was appointed as Palermo Chief of Police. 'I went,' he later recalled, 'with a specific mandate to fight the mafia'. However, he soon crossed swords with the local prefect, Giovanni Gasti, who, in close harness with the fascist *federale* (provincial party secretary), Alfredo Cucco, also claimed to be fighting the mafia. They clearly had different ideas about who to arrest, and Tiby was transferred to Bari in the autumn of the same year.[26] That these anti–mafia operations had a strong political charac-ter to them can be seen from the number of local administrations that were dissolved by the prefect for alleged immorality.

A good example of this process was provided by the town of Petralia Sottana. Here, shortly after the March on Rome, members of the municipal council started to hurl accusations at the local *fascio*. Prefect Gasti sent a police officer to investigate the charges. He also took the opportunity to conduct an inquiry into the administration itself. According to the ensuing report, the council (which had wanted to form a new fascist section in Petralia) consisted of men who ruined the town by running it 'for partisan ends...under the guise of socialism'. By contrast, it said, the members of the *fascio* represented all that was best in the region. On the basis of these findings, the prefect dissoved the Petralia administration and ap-pointed a special commissioner to oversee the work of reconstruc-tion. Elections were held at the end of 1923, and, predictably enough, the town's fascists came to power.[27] When Mussolini wrote to Gasti in May 1923, to express his pleasure at the 'enfeeblement of the mafia', much of his satisfaction no doubt stemmed from the political consequences of the prefect's work.[28]

The degree to which the opponents of fascism could be equated with the mafia was evident from a memorial written by Alfredo

Cucco after his fall from power in 1927. This was largely a catalogue of his former political achievements. At Bagheria ('one of the most dangerous centres of the mafia and delinquency, where *mafiosi* had misgoverned for many years...amidst every sort of malefaction'), Cucco said a group of 'honest men' appeared at the end of 1923 who made it their purpose to 'purify' the environment. With his support they managed to dislodge the old administration and set up a new fascist one. A similar process apparently occurred throughout Palermo province. 'Fascism's work of renewal...advanced step by step...driven onwards by one specific motive: outright aversion to the mafia.... In this way we systematically liberated almost every town'.[29]

There is no reason to be unduly cynical about Alfredo Cucco's opposition to the mafia. He was a young man of great political ambition, but he was also an idealist. He firmly believed that fascism could bring about the moral regeneration of Sicily, and to this end he was prepared to sacrifice expediency to principle.[30] This evidently caused some disquiet at Rome. In February 1924, not long before the national elections, a prominent under-secretary reported that Gasti and Cucco had between them created 'a situation that was far from simple or favourable' in the province of Palermo.[31] His concern probably stemmed from Cucco's moral inflexibility, and his spurning of such influential electoral figures as Francesco Cuccia, the notorious mayor of Piana dei Greci.

Cuccia, often referred to as a '*capomafia*', was a protégé of the moderate socialist deputy, Aurelio Drago. Time and again in 1923, he approached Cucco and sought admittance to the fascist party, but without success. On one occasion he gave the *federale* a list of names and suggested they be used to form a new section at Piana. Cucco was suspicious, and turned for advice to an acquaintance, Giovanni Silvestri: 'Silvestri assured me', he said, 'that they were all respectable; but when I asked him if they were effectively under Cuccia's thumb, he replied quite frankly that they were...So I dropped the idea of setting up a *fascio* at Piana dei Greci. It seemed a town that would remain impervious to fascism'.[32] Such high principles were not always politic. In the run-up to the elections, it looked as if Cuccia might oppose the government's National List, and the authorities grew alarmed: 'We should try somehow', said a report, 'to get [him] back, particularly as [he] has a brother in Trappeto, near Balestrate'. In the end Cuccia supported the government.[33]

However fervent Cucco may have been in his desire to keep immoral elements at bay, it was not always easy to do so, as Cuccia's doggedness suggested. Moreover, in an environment where accusations of criminality were a common political weapon, there were bound to be discrepancies: one man's ally and friend was often another's *mafioso*. One indignant fascist, for example, told Mussolini in 1923 that Cucco had become the 'marionette' of the big land-owners, and that in the Cefalù area he was enrolling in the party 'defeatists, sharks, protectors of criminals, *mafiosi*, and leading cattle-rustlers'.[34] This accusation was probably the result of political rivalry as much as of moral indignation. However, as the reference to the big landowners would suggest, Cucco was forced after 1922 to compromise some of his intransigence in the interest of votes. This was only to be expected: strategic, and sometimes unsavoury, alliances were almost inevitable given the weakness of Sicilian fascism prior to the March on Rome.

This state of affairs provided plenty of ammunition for the dis-contented. 'I have no desire', wrote the courageous Palermo fascist dissident, Maggiore Di Chiara, to Mussolini in July 1923, 'to play the anti-pope to that ridiculous pope of Castelbuono [i.e. Cucco] who pontificates...in a real *Babylonian captivity* at the beck and call of Scalea and Cirincione, servant of servants to all the Tartar dogs of the province'.[35] That Pietro Lanza di Scalea (a minister in Mussolini's government) and Giuseppe Cirincione (a deputy with his electoral base at Bagheria) had links with *mafiosi* was generally admitted. The problem, however, was whether to do anything about it. 'Among the components of Cirincione's party,' the Prefect of Palermo informed the Minister of the Interior in June 1923, 'there are, it is true, a number of individuals affiliated to the mafia. How-ever, they are not particularly dangerous, or at any rate could not provoke or instigate any demonstrations against His Excellency the Prime Minister'. In other words, for political reasons, they were best left in peace.[36]

The formation of alliances was often seen·as part of the necessary but unedifying spectacle of opportunistic conversions that followed Mussolini's accession to power. As a general rule the minority faction in each town would set up a party section, and then try, with the help of the prefect, to dislodge the incumbent administration. Sometimes, however, the process was more complicated, as the secretary of the Sciacca *fascio* revealed in a letter to the national party executive in November 1922: 'In an attempt to win power at the local level', he wrote, 'personal factions cobble together *fasci di combattimento.*' Whenever one party section had been set up, the opposition, he said, immediately followed suit. 'And wherever there is an old *fascio*, which is ideologically promising, it gets infiltrated by the agents of candidates who want to draw it into their own camp, or at least disrupt and confuse it.' The local *fasci* were thus, he claimed, 'irridescent': former democrats, social democrats, and reformist socialists jostled side by side with followers of Francesco Nitti and even Catholic *popolari*.[37]

This situation was obviously disheartening to those, whether intransigents or members of the Nationalist Party, who had hoped that fascism would regenerate Sicilian political life. The main problem was that idealism could not readily be reconciled with success. Achille Starace's reply to the secretary of the Sciacca *fascio* may have been laudable, but in the circumstances it was unrealistic: 'Fascism should march forward free of every and any link with past politicians, and old or new clienteles.'[38] This was easier said than done. By the following July, however, Starace was more cynical. The mafia now stood poised, he claimed, to go over to fascism, 'providing that it is left in peace'. He felt there was no point in confronting it 'because the results would be negative'. Instead he suggested removing all Sicilian magistrates, and replacing them with northerners.[39] Fortunately, this proposal came to nothing.

One reason why Sicilian fascism was forced to compromise with members of established clienteles was that it lacked 'personalities'. Many of the early *fasci* were founded by young men whose political pull was minimal. The section of Vita, for example, in the province of Trapani, owed its existence to a twenty-year-old demobilised soldier; that at Ragusa to a student in his mid teens.[40] Some of the first, and most ardent, Sicilian fascists had been inspired by activities in the north of the country. This may have left them with unrealistic expectations. Pippo Ragusa had been a *squadrista* in the Po Valley. In April 1921 he decided to return to Palermo, to further the cause of fascism in Sicily: 'I brought to my new *squadristi* brothers,' he later recalled, 'the Romagna perfume of the Lugo and Bologna *fasci*'.[41] His attempts, however, to reproduce the atmosphere of the North in Palermo, were markedly unsuccessful.

If the war and its aftermath helped to broaden the horizons of many young Sicilians, it must also have made provincial life seem unbearably dull and limiting. A number of the island's early fascists were clearly driven into politics (like many elsewhere in Italy) by a sense of frustration. The section at Polizzi Generosa, for example, was said in March 1923 to be composed 'almost entirely of young men who have as yet no social or economic position'. The executive consisted of five members, all aged between twenty-six and thirty-one. Two of them were 'unemployed accountants', another was 'a graduate without clients', the fourth and fifth were a small landowner and a cobbler respectively. The other members of the section were 'for the most part youngsters'. It was not surprising, as the report concluded, that the local population regarded the fascists as inexperienced, and ill-suited to running the town's affairs.[42]

To what extent early Sicilian fascism numbered criminals among its followers is hard to say. In 1927, when many of the island's *fasci* underwent radical purges, the claim was made that the movement had up until then been heavily polluted by the mafia. Surviving police reports for the early 1920s lend some credence to this; but, as in 1927, perception was inevitably clouded, and to some extent determined, by political considerations. The main complaint from party officials about the first fascist groups in Sicily was not about their criminality so much as their lack of influence. Trapani was particularly deficient in leaders,[43] but even in Palermo it was difficult to attract influential and respectable men, and only the fusion with the Nationalist Party in the spring of 1923 provided the provincial movement with a much needed social leavening.

In the mainland South, before the fusion, the Nationalists often constituted the local opposition to the fascists.[44] In Sicily, however, this was rare, except in Catania and to some extent Agrigento. One reason appears to have been that the Sicilian Nationalists were strongly élitist, and refused to became embroiled in what one of their spokesmen called 'the unhealthy and fetid bog of local squabbles'.[45] Another explanation could have been that in some places, notably Palermo, the fascist and Nationalist movements were run in harness, and this obviously precluded any competition for municipal spoils. In this situation it was often the Association for Servicemen (*Opera Nazionale per i Combattenti*) which formed the opposition group. The picture, however, was confused, for the Servicemen's movement in Sicily had, since 1919, been drawn into the orbit of electoral ambitions, and systematically dismembered. Thus in Gratteri and Castelbuono, the Servicemen backed Aurelio Drago and so opposed the fascists, while at Geraci Siculo and Bompietro they followed Francesco Musotto, and so supported them at least in theory; though by the time of the 1924 political elections, Musotto and the leading Palermo fascist, Alfredo Cucco, had fallen out, which complicated matters.[46]

Despite many good intentions, at the local as well as national levels, Sicilian fascism was far from robust, morally or physically, in the period down to 1924. The island's political regeneration was still not in sight. Opportunism had been the hallmark of the movement, and support was at best conditional, at worst expedient. The government secured 68% of the votes cast in Sicily in the 1924 elections, and had all its thirty-eight candidates returned; but, as Prefect Gasti said, most of the fascist poll came from 'the conservative forces of the big and small landowners'. In other words, old clienteles had merely shifted into the government camp. Gasti's explanation that the vote represented a reaction against left-wing demagoguery was more quaint than realistic. So, too, was his assertion that the opposition alone had made use of 'the mafia, family ties, friends, and personal contacts'.[47] In reality, fascism had plunged into the murky waters of Sicilian politics, and had failed to surface.

PROF. ALFREDO CUCCO
1° eletto nella Provincia di Palermo

Pl. 5. A postcard of Alfredo Cucco, issued after his success in the elections of April 1924.

The years from 1925 to 1929 saw the regime trying to salvage the situation, but its success was to be no more than partial.

Social and economic change: the 'new' mafia

In the decade and a half before the First World War, a combination of personal initiative and economic conjuncture resulted in a number of important changes in Sicilian agriculture. Emigration (particularly to the United States) creamed off the surplus population, and a new class of 'americani' appeared with higher expectations and money to spend. As wages rose, the more enlightened among the agrari (big landowners) resorted to intensifying production through investment in fruit and vines. There were also developments in the sphere of workers' organisations. The co-operative movement flourished, and such was the growth in industrial and agricultural leagues as well as Chambers of Labour that by 1914 Sicily could boast (at least on paper) the third highest level of unionisation in Italy.[48]

Though these changes were an apparent threat to the hegemony of the old ruling class, they were welcomed by a number of intelligent conservatives who saw in them a means of defusing the tension that had produced the socialist *Fasci* in the 1890s. As such they conformed to Tancredi's famous dictum in Tomasi di Lampedusa's novel, *The Leopard*, that things had to change if they were to remain the same. The early twentieth century was certainly a period of relative social harmony, with the doctrines of *interclassismo* and reform being accepted by most of the island's socialists.[49] This harmony, though superficial, was reinforced by the intense local patriotism, known as *sicilianismo*. It also found a potent symbol in the glittering social life of the *belle époque*. One Palermo aristocrat was to recall this era wistfully in a book entitled *The Happy Summer Days*.[50]

The onset of the First World War changed everything. The economic developments of the previous two decades came to an abrupt halt. Despite increased demand, there was a drastic fall in the output of sulphur, largely as a result of higher labour costs. The citrus trade suffered from the closure of European markets. Sicilian wine found itself above the regulated nine degrees of alcohol, and could not be consumed by the military; this ruled out a lucrative internal market, and during the war years production fell by 30% in the province of Palermo, and 46% in Siracusa.[51] Cereal growing was also affected, as price-fixing, commandeering, the abolition of the wheat tariff, and increased wages combined to reduce the area under cultivation: in 1917 it dropped by 21.7% in relation to the previous year.[52] Nor was livestock a beneficiary of the resulting spread of pasture, for though meat prices were high, local taxes and frequent requisitioning more or less decimated the island's animal resources.[53]

The social consequences of these developments were severe. The increase in the cost of living was not offset by the rise in wages. According to one set of figures, agricultural pay declined, in real terms, in the *Mezzogiorno* by around one-quarter between 1914 and 1918.[54] The simultaneous freeze on rents and increase in food prices might have afforded some compensation, but the peasantry were on the whole unable to benefit, it seems, as conscription often led to the collapse of their smallholdings, and a reversion of the land to pasture.[55] With the *agrari* themselves facing severe economic difficulties, the overall result was the breakdown of the relative harmony that had characterised the pre-war Giolittian era, and a reversion to the politics of confrontation, in which the question of the land was central. The stage was set for the crisis of what came to be known as the '*biennio rosso*' (red biennium).

The economic dislocation caused by the war in Sicily led to a great upsurge in crime and social unrest. Banditry and cattle-rustling reached epidemic proportions, and rumours began to spread that the island might be on the verge of revolution.[56] The problem of army deserters was particularly acute: there was talk of 40,000 of them, though this was almost certainly an exaggeration.[57] The government responded to the rising lawlessness by instituting a number of special *squadriglie* (squads) which were entrusted to an ambitious policeman called Cesare Mori. His successes against bandits and deserters (he may have made more than 13,000 arrests in less than a year[58]) earned him a substantial reputation and promotion to the ranks of *questore* (Chief of Police) and later, prefect. However, his severity was by no means unique: the man who succeeded him as head of the *squadriglie*, Augusto Battioni, used equally drastic methods.[59]

Demobilisation heightened Sicily's already intense social and economic problems. Well over 400,000 islanders had served in the army, and their psychological and material rehabilitation proved painful. Out of the turmoil there arose what was often referred to as a 'new mafia': 'The soldiers...returned home', wrote the judge, Giuseppe Loschiavo, 'unaccustomed to work and eager for quick enrichment. They joined up with outlaws...and formed...new mafias, which pitted themselves against the old. This young mafia shunned politicians and despised their protection, preferring to trust to the guarantees of their own shotguns.'[60] The violence that ensued probably exceeded anything that had gone before it in Sicily. According to Cesare Mori, it was like a 'hailstorm' that rained down on everyone and everything: 'There were no rules', he said, 'and no respect for anybody'.[61]

The difficulty, as always with the mafia, is to proceed from the general and schematic to the particular. Contemporary observers all too often took refuge in comfortable abstractions, and avoided what was perhaps the most crucial question and yet the one to which least attention was paid: who exactly were the *mafiosi*? The problem was not so much the lack of evidence, or the related question of mafia secrecy; it was more that *mafiosi* were defined by others, not by themselves. This meant that the phenomenon was hard to identify in any concrete sense. The very lack of objectivity, however, may have been the mafia's most telling feature, for its significance lay less in what it was, than in what it was thought to be, and why.

One commonly alleged reason for the rivalry between the old and new mafias was that the former had not only avoided military service, but had also taken advantage of the confusion of the war years to enrich itself by speculation and crime. There had certainly been no lack of opportunities for advancement. Don Calogero Vizzini of Villalba was said to have sold stolen animals to an army commission in Caltanissetta, and offered 'protection' to those who did not want their horses or mules requisitioned. He may also have been involved in cattle rustling: with meat prices high, this was a very lucrative business.[62] However, it is by no means clear that all those who profited during the war did so illicitly. With the freeze on rents, and high inflation, some people were in a position to make a fortune. The best-placed and most advantaged group was that of the *gabelloti*.

Many contemporaries pointed to the severe social changes produced by the war in Sicily.[63] Landowners struggled, as they had done a century before during the Napoleonic period, as rising prices destroyed the value of their cash rents. In addition, they had to contend with greatly increased taxation. According to one expert, levies on property at the communal and provincial level more than quadrupled in this period. For many *agrari* these were grim years, and the pill was made harder to swallow by seeing the *gabelloti* flourish. A man who sublet in kind, and then sold his surplus on the market at the new, inflated prices, might soon become rich. There were also many opportunities for usurious moneylending, as well as speculation on the transfer of land. As one senator reported from Sicily in the autumn of 1920, 'the *gabelloti* wax fat, the proprietors languish'.[64]

The unscrupulous, the astute, and the fortunate profited heavily in these years. According to the landowner and agricultural expert, Antonio Vacirca, writing early in 1921, a *gabelloto* in Terranova di Sicilia who rented a piece of land for 2,200 lire enjoyed, through direct farming or share-cropping, an average annual income of 25,000 lire; the owner, meanwhile, paid three times as much in tax on the 2,200 lire as he had done before the war. Another example given by Vacirca was that of a ten-hectare farm near Niscemi, which had been leased to a *gabelloto* in 1914 for nine years, at an annual rent of 2,500 lire. According to his own declaration, the *gabelloto* was making 40,000 lire a year from the holding, and he still paid the owner only 2,500 lire. In these circumstances, as Vacirca reported, many big landowners were being forced to sell land; and plenty of new men stood poised to buy them out.[65]

According to the economic historian, Emilio Sereni: '[In Sicily], even more than elsewhere, the aristocratic landowners always regarded the loss of their family estates as a blow to their prestige'.[66] In other words, land was not merely a source of income: it was also seen as an important indication of status. This might help to explain why many *agrari* were so bitter towards the new proprietors: 'Behold, there arose on the Sicilian *latifondi*', said the reactionary landowner, Simone Sirena, in 1927, referring to a period some ten years before,

a multitude of new men who knew how to *swell their coffers in various ways* and who became influential in politico-mafia intri-

gues. Meanwhile the traditional, broad-visioned Sicilian entrepreneur...who administered his farm directly, and provided
bread and work for those around him, disappeared...The mafia
harrassed him continually...The clique [*cricca*] took his lands or
forced him to leave them.[67]

Mori's campaign against the mafia led to the arrest of many *nouveaux
riches*, and the gratitude of such men as Sirena was great.

In the view of Cesare Mori, the unrest in Sicily after 1918 was
essentially criminal in character. The normal relationship, he said,
between mafia and *malvivenza* (criminality, usually of a petty kind)
was that of an army general to rank and file troops; but the First
World War had upset the hierarchy, and the result was chaos. Petty
criminals returned from the trenches with elevated ambitions, witnessed with indignation the prosperity of the old *mafiosi*, and
rebelled: 'Robberies, thefts, rustlings, murders, threats, and violence
of every kind rained down, as never before.' The mafia, he said, or
more precisely, the old mafia, was powerless: the *picciotti* (youngsters) no longer obeyed.[68]

This neat schema is often hard to match to reality, and the problem
was evidently shared by contemporaries, who had considerable
difficulty with their terminology. This emerged clearly from a series
of monographs on the mafia drawn up by the *carabinieri* early in
1924. One report said that while there was no old mafia in Collesano,
there was a new one, 'of criminal character'; however, its members
were few, were unassociated, and had 'neither leaders nor followers'.[69] In what sense, then, they constituted a mafia, was not clear. At
Campofiorito there was 'the so-called young mafia', composed of 'a
few rural thieves';[70] but at Bisacquino, the 'handful of criminals...
who rob and commit the occasional act of violence' were not to be
considered 'a mafia association' so much as a 'criminal' one.[71]

Confusion was often increased, if not caused, by political factors.
The 1924 report on Corleone rather curiously maintained that the old
mafia had been headed by the famous socialist leader, Bernardino
Verro:

> Seeing Verro's selfish opportunism...and also that their contri-
> butions [to the co-operative] were being squandered, the more
> intelligent went over to the landowner's party, which was opposed
> to Verro and his followers. There ensued, over the years, a
> succession of murders in both camps, along with related trials for
> criminal association, brought by Verro, who was mayor of
> Corleone, against his opponents. The conflict ended with Verro's
> murder, which was the work of his own disillusioned and cheated
> followers, rather than his enemies.

The report went on to claim that the old mafia was now headed by Verro's opponents.[72] Three years later, however, at the time of a major series of arrests in Corleone, the police said that the old mafia had 'for a long time' been led by Michelangelo Gennaro. Verro, it seemed, had been entirely extraneous to the mafia; he had fought it bravely, and 'paid for his boldness with his life'.[73]

Despite the self-confidence of his theorising on the mafia, even Cesare Mori could be opaque. In his memoirs, he said that the so-called 'siege of Gangi' in January 1926 was directed at 'the strongest and most impressive position taken and held by the mafia and *malvivenza*'.[74] However, in a report to the Minister of the Interior some months after the Gangi operation, Mori claimed that he had been attacking 'the armed bands' who had made the region of the Madonie mountains into 'the stronghold of Sicilian brigandage'.[75] These bands were led by the Andaloros, Ferrarellos, and Dinos, men whom Mori described unambiguously as 'bandits'. Nevertheless, he said in his memoirs that everything in the Madonie area was 'controlled by, and subject to, the mafia and *malvivenza*'. Indeed the mafia's power here was such that its superiority was recognised by 'all the island's criminals'.[76]

A year after the Gangi operation, Mori denounced the head of Palermo fascism, Alfredo Cucco, for his affiliation to the mafia. Cucco was from the Madonie, and through his ties with such leading Gangi fascists as barons Sgadari and Li Destri, he could possibly have been linked with local bandits. Was Mori saying in his memoirs that the mafia of the Madonie had one of its leaders in Cucco? He might have wished to imply this, but the case did not stand up to examination, for Cucco's allies, Sgadari and Li Destri, were described by Mori as victims of the mafia, through the imposition of tributes and protection money.[77] Once again, as with the 1924 set of *carabinieri* monographs, there seems to have been a confusion of terminology, with Mori defining Gaetano Ferrarello and his associates explicitly as bandits, and also, implicitly, as the local mafia.

Mori himself was not unaware of these semantic difficulties. He confessed in his memoirs that it was easier to describe the mafia than it was to define a *mafioso*.[78] As a result, he said, 'honest men were frequently called *mafiosi* in perfect good faith simply because they were exceedingly brave...and responded to criminal actions with ...extra-legal violence'.[79] The scope for judicial mistakes would seem to have been enormous. What is more, the confusion was not always the result of pardonable misunderstanding. 'The epithet '*mafioso*' was not only used with great prodigality, out of...ignorance or naïvety, but was often applied with utter maliciousness, in every walk of life, including politics, in order to carry out vendettas, vent grudges, destroy opponents, strike at rivals, or cripple initiatives.'[80]

Mori may have believed in his own impartiality, but were his choices really dispassionate? Was his claim, for example, that the big landowners had always been victims of the mafia not politically inspired? Was his use of the phrase '*malvivenza proletaria*' (proletarian crime) to describe the new mafia after the war not perilously close to the reactionary view of certain *agrari*, that what had been socialism on the mainland had, in Sicily, been '*delinquenza e malavita*' (delinquency and lawlessness)?[81] Was it just a coincidence that his elimination of the '*gabelloti mafiosi*' removed a section of society that threatened the dominance of the *latifondisti*? Finally, were the destruction of Alfredo Cucco, and the rebuilding of much of the island's fascism on a less radical, more conservative footing, not also political acts? Crime was certainly an aspect of the mafia; so too was a particular kind of behaviour. In the end, though, it was often political considerations that were crucial.

The Palermo local government elections

By the summer of 1924, hostility to fascism in Sicily was widespread. The killing in Rome of the socialist deputy, Giacomo Matteotti, in June of that year had a great effect on the island. The murder became a rallying cry for the opposition, partly because of its intrinsic brutality, but also, perhaps, because the ruling classes now grasped fully the extremism of the new movement and the dangers it posed to them. Their fears were compounded by a number of specific grievances. Business circles had for some time chafed at 'the shameful and ruinous excise tax', and when Mussolini failed to visit the Palermo Chamber of Commerce during his visit to the island in May 1924, their indignation turned to anger.[82] Many *agrari* were disappointed at the government's indifference to the problems of the citrus trade,[83] and the continuing high levels of rural crime, particularly in the island's western provinces, resulted in a succession of irate and anguished articles in the local press.[84]

The upshot of all this was a resurgence of *sicilianismo* and a feeling that what was rich and distinctive in Sicilian life was being wasted by yet another hostile government. By the time the crisis caused by the murder of Matteotti ended, early in 1925, the majority of the island's leading politicians had abandoned their support for fascism and gone over to the opposition. A form of cold war set in, and the Palermo newspapers pointedly refused any longer to comment on internal political affairs. However, as the French consul explained in February 1925, this was not altogether surprising:

Pls. 6 and 7. Mussolini's visit to Sicily in May 1924. *Top*: Mussolini and his entourage as guests of the mayor of Palermo. Third from the left, in a wing collar, is Antonino Di Giorgio. Next to him in the front row is Vittorio Emanuele Orlando. Prince Pietro Lanza di Scalea is on the far right. *Below*: Mussolini (in a bowler hat) visiting the Madonie mountains, accompanied by Alfredo Cucco.

This retreat by the local press is symptomatic of the state of mind of the majority of Sicilian people. Since the present government came to power, they have shown (after an initial wave of enthusiasm, which was quickly dissipated) a complete indifference to the fascist party...Many promises, in effect, had been made to them...and very few have been kept. They do not complain openly, but it is easy to discern their anger beneath their silence. They have been deceived.[85]

One result of the Matteotti crisis was a polarisation of political forces. Faced with a strong and inflexible opposition, many Sicilian fascists felt they had no choice but to become increasingly intransigent. 'Once again I remind you', said Alfredo Cucco in a circular to the provincial *fasci* in May 1925, '...that our ranks should never be polluted by unworthy elements, and that the policy of your *fascio* must be inspired always by absolute moral intransigence.' Though political expediency, he said, had once required 'contingent alliances', henceforward fascism was to have no truck with the 'detritus of the past' or 'present incrustations'.[86] Such inflexibility bordered on the impolitic, particularly as Cucco was at that time trying to persuade the Minister of the Interior, Luigi Federzoni, to agree to local government elections in Palermo.[87]

Federzoni consulted his colleagues on the issue, and, after a good deal of discussion, he consented. The trouble was that the opposition in Palermo included such personalities as the former Prime Minister, Vittorio Emanuele Orlando, and the social-democrat leader, Giovanni Colonna di Cesarò. Against them, the 'zeal' and 'spiritual values' of fascism's young supporters could be expected to carry little weight at the polls. Cucco must have known this, and he yielded (with great reluctance) to expediency, allowing the government to include on its slate influential 'fellow-travellers' (*fiancheggiatori*), as well as 'pure' fascists. It was important, after all, to confront voters with the inevitability of victory, and this the party could now do. In a society based on clienteles, personal prestige was at least as important as policy, for success in elections.

In addition to electoral considerations, there was another reason why Federzoni, and ultimately Mussolini too, was keen to bring in fellow-travellers. Farinacci's appointment as party secretary early in 1925 had reinforced the claims of the intransigents; but the more conservative party members (and they included the Duce himself) hoped that this state of affairs would be no more than temporary. Though intransigent fascists were useful in areas of strong opposition, such as Palermo, they were also a political liability in so far as their extremism and petty-bourgeois social base offended the sensibilities, as well as the interests, of big business, the Church, the *agrari*, and the Crown. The inclusion in the government list at

Palermo of such moderates as Empedocle Restivo, Count Tagliavia, and Giovanni Lo Monte, helped reassure the old order. Their fascist credentials were poor, but at least they had electoral pull. Together with the Sicilian prince, Pietro Lanza di Scalea, who had been Minister of the Colonies since the start of the Matteotti crisis, they constituted a formidable team.[88]

The government's campaign was run from two separate buildings. Cucco and his colleagues were based in the local party headquarters, while the less intransigent fascists operated from di Scalea's house, 'where the so-called fellow-travellers converged, mainly from the suburbs [borgate], to arrange the secret side of the elections'.[89] In Cucco's view, these 'so-called fellow-travellers' were probably mafiosi: Lo Monte in particular had a reputation for unsavoury ties.[90] Cucco kept his distance, literally as well as psychologically, and made it clear that he disapproved of what was happening. He stipulated that no member of the party executive should be included in the government list. To add insult to injury, the Palermo federazione (provincial executive) announced that it would go to the Fourth Fascist Congress unsullied by compromise: 'This is the grand idea that fascism of the Conca d'oro will bear to the Congress: moral intransigence, which brooks no monstrous ties, and repudiates every compromise dictated by contingent political needs.'[91]

Despite the alliances, the result of the elections was not wholly predictable. Cucco knew that violence would have been counter-productive, and he tried, on the whole successfully, to restrain his followers. However, other traditional tactics were not foresworn. The biggest worry was Palermo itself, where both of the major newspapers, and public opinion in general, were behind the opposition. In the borgate, the clienteles of Lo Monte and di Scalea made victory certain.[92] In a bid for votes, the government allocated 10 million lire for a local aqueduct; there was talk of 350 million lire being spent on the port of Palermo, and another 350 million on railways. More prosaically, the price of bread was lowered on the eve of polling, and the Pecoraino Mill made its customary distribution of pasta.[93] Employers allegedly threatened factory workers with the sack if they failed to support the government, and the police broke up opposition rallies, and found pretexts for making arrests – five lorry-loads in the case of one socialist rally in Piazza Calza.[94]

One important gain for fascism was Ignazio Florio, the most prestigious member of Sicily's leading industrial family. Cucco believed, or professed to believe, that this was the result of an elective affinity: 'I knew', he recalled in his autobiography, 'that some people had done their best to set Florio against me, as "that provincial boy who wants to dominate Palermo". But...no sooner had we exchanged ideas, than a bond of friendship was established.' Indeed, such was the attraction that Florio never missed a fascist rally: 'He was visibly in love with the battle.'[95] What Cucco failed to mention were the huge shipping subsidies that had been allocated to Florio earlier that summer.[96] His vote-winning presence at rallies may have been part of the deal; more likely, it was the spontaneous gesture of a grateful man.

While the government strove hard to win the elections by time-honoured means, the myth of a fascist revolution called for a less orthodox ideological debate. The polemic was intense and the battle lines clearly drawn. According to the former Nationalist, Francesco Ercole, fascism stood for 'faith in the Nation', and while it took as its premise the freedom of the individual, its goal was the greatness of Italy. It embodied, he said, the true spirit of Italian liberalism which could only flourish in the midst of peoples 'firmly governed and well-organised'.[97] Another candidate who dwelt on the theme of liberty was Pietro Lanza di Scalea. Before leading his audience to the church of San Domenico to pay homage at the tombs of General Cascino and Francesco Crispi, he announced that the freedom invoked by 'the false apostles of the Aventine' was a sham: in what sense could it exist, he claimed, 'when there was no freedom of work, industry and trade?'[98]

Although Ercole and di Scalea were trying to win over the establishment, many sections of the *agrari* and the Palermo bourgeoisie must have remained sceptical. Fascism could guarantee an end to social unrest and class warfare; but what of Sicily's interests *vis-à-vis* the North? If Ercole and di Scalea were not altogether reassuring, how much less so was Roberto Farinacci, who descended on Sicily in the middle of July, in company with the Minister of Communications, Costanzo Ciano? Farinacci's tactless speech at Messina (which angered Mussolini almost as much as it did the opposition),[99] spoke of 'absolute intransigence against the old parties, old politicians, and old clienteles'. Whoever thought, said the party secretary, that compromise with 'men of the past' was the only tactic in Sicily was wrong. Fascism would fight them all:

> I can...assure you that from this moment on, di Cesarò, Giuffrida, Guarino Amella, Pasqualino Vassallo, and others like them, will only be remembered by Sicilians when they wish to recall the blackest pages in Italy's political history. With the destruction of these men we will have dealt a mortal blow to all the mafias and counter-mafias that have strewn corruption and terror in various Sicilian provinces.[100]

The Sicilian opposition reacted to Farinacci's speech with volleys of patriotic indignation. According to one newspaper, the party secretary had given the impression that the island was 'a land of bandits and pillagers', and her leaders 'exponents of criminal factions'. Furthermore, it said, Sicily's social and economic problems had been discussed in crudely material terms: 'We are not a wretched people ...whom you can toss a crust of bread at...and then ignore. We have a great spiritual inheritance, and our difficulties are deep and noble.'[101] By far the most eloquent reply to Farinacci came in an election speech by the former Prime Minister, Vittorio Emanuele Orlando:

> People of Palermo, if by 'mafia' we mean an exaggerated sense of honour, a passionate refusal to succumb to the overbearing and arrogant, a nobility of spirit that stands up to the strong and indulges the weak, a loyalty to friends that is more steadfast and enduring even than death – if these characteristics, albeit with their excesses, are what we mean by 'mafia', we are dealing with ineradicable traits of the Sicilian character, and I declare myself to be *mafioso*, and I am happy to be such![102]

This speech had an enormous impact on the city. Alfredo Cucco tried to counter it by saying that Orlando was pulling the wool over people's eyes with his 'language of the *Beati Paoli*'.[103] However, a discussion on the nature of the mafia was not now in order; there were more urgent matters to be considered. According to almost every report, the government would win the elections but its majority might be small; and with international attention focused on Palermo, this would be embarrassing for the regime. Mussolini was aware of this, and voiced his concern to Cucco in a phone call, shortly before voting began. The elections, he exclaimed vehemently, needed to be won at all costs.[104]

On Sunday, 2 August 1925, the day of polling, the streets of Palermo were patrolled by truck-loads of fascists. 'The vehicle of victory', wrote Cucco in his autobiography, 'was the lorry...They had no specific purpose, but conveyed warmth, enthusiasm and patriotic songs.'[105] Their presence was no doubt far more menacing than this description implied. Cucco gave instructions that there should be no violence whatsoever, but although his own followers obeyed, about fifty Neapolitan fascists somehow reached Palermo and ran riot through the streets.[106] The ease with which order was restored was partly due to the fact that the police had received heavy reinforcements for polling day. They had also been issued, somewhat extravagantly, with special steel truncheons.[107]

Despite the power of the official electoral machine, the opposition managed to muster 16,616 votes. The fascist tally exceeded 26,000, more than the government or Cucco had expected, but hardly enough to justify Mussolini's description of the victory as 'clamorous'.[108] 'One should not conclude from this', wrote a senior French diplomat, 'that Sicily has became fascist', and his remark was justified.[109] In the first place, barely a third of the electorate had voted. Secondly, the government list had included the names of a good many non-fascists. Indeed, as one commentator said, victory had been achieved largely by putting Farinacci's intransigence 'in the attic' and making 'old fashioned' alliances. Some newspapers even maintained that the government had won despite the fascists.[110]

Fascism claimed to be a source of moral regeneration. The elections offered no proof of this. According to an anti-government pamphlet written shortly after voting, the real architect of victory had been the mafia. The alleged 85% turn-out in the *borgate*, where the vote was traditionally around 25%, was a clear indication, it said, that not all was above board. There were seven publicly recognised 'bosses' in the government list who a year or two earlier had been arrested by Prefect Gasti and charged with criminal association: 'And these seven, along with the noble Lo Monte, now glitter beside the austere and Pharisaic Prince di Scalea.'[111] Similar accusations could have been levelled at the opposition. The important point was that the government had won unconvincingly. Fascism, in both moral and quantitative terms, had still to make its presence felt in Palermo, and, indeed, in the island as a whole.

After the local government elections

The sober truth about the Palermo elections was played down by the regime. According to Mussolini, the victory demonstrated that the fascist government enjoyed 'the broad, solid consent of the Italian people';[112] and Farinacci spoke of a 'magnificent triumph over a past of ignominy'.[113] However, the celebrations were too strident to be convincing. Mussolini's position seemed strong in many respects in the late summer of 1925: he had been on a cordial visit to the king at San Rossore, and all four major pieces of legislation introduced that year had passed through the Chamber of Deputies without problems. However, the Senate was still proving resistant, and despite his apparent friendliness, even the king was known to harbour doubts about fascism.

The main problem lay with the party radicals, who continued to jeopardise the consolidation of the regime by demanding a thoroughgoing purge of the liberal state. The historian, Gioacchino Volpe, echoed Mussolini's own views when he wrote in an influential journal in August 1925 that Farinacci's attitudes were 'too simple, indeed simplistic'. Intransigence, he said, ought not to be dogmatic; nor should Italy be turned into a nation of automatons, 'all in perfect harmony with every party decision'. Fascism, he believed, was a movement with undefined boundaries, a spiritual force whose progress should be slow but sure, alluring rather than destructive.[114]

Towards the end of August 1925, Alfredo Cucco was granted an audience with Mussolini in Rome. It was three weeks since the local government elections, and the young *federale* was now eager to undertake a purge of Palermo fascism. He told the Duce that they should cap their success at the polls with 'the most rigorous intransigence'; he felt that there was no longer any need for compromise with the mafia. Mussolini was apparently surprised; he may also have been slightly alarmed. However, when Cucco alluded to a speech the Prime Minister had made at Agrigento the previous year, in which he had promised to restore law and order to the Sicilian people, Mussolini became more positive: 'What you are saying seems right'. He asked Cucco to return in five days time when the Minister of the Interior, Federzoni, would be back in Rome.[115]

In all likelihood, Mussolini and Federzoni discussed the matter carefully before Cucco returned. On the one hand, they must have felt the pursuit of intransigence in Sicily through a campaign against the mafia would please Farinacci. It would add prestige to the regime, and, if reports by Starace and others about the unpopularity of the mafia were true, it might help draw the masses into the state and overcome the apathy that had characterised the recent elections. On the other hand, there were serious political risks. Though Mussolini's understanding of the mafia was by no means profound,[116] he knew as a politician that the issue was one for discretion. A major doubt concerned the *agrari*, many of whom still had strong reservations about the government. Might a crack-down on crime not reinforce their hostility? The danger was real, for Cucco regarded the mafia as inseparable from the old political order, of which the great landowners had been leading exponents.

When Cucco returned to Palazzo Chigi, he was greeted warmly by Federzoni. The two politicians went for a meal at Ulpia's, and talked about Sicily and the proposed campaign against the mafia. The critical question was who should conduct it. Cucco thought they should appoint someone with a police background, and suggested the former prefect of Palermo, Giovanni Gasti, his ally from 1923. According to Federzoni, Gasti was unavailable. The name of Cesare Mori was mentioned. Federzoni apparently harboured doubts, and claimed that Mori was about to be pensioned off, 'because at Trapani he had caused a problem or two, politically'. 'I replied', said Cucco, 'that the situation in Palermo, from a political point of view, was completely stable'. Mori was accordingly agreed upon, though almost certainly Federzoni was less reluctant about the choice than Cucco suggested in his autobiography.[117] It is possible that the Palermo *federale* had been duped.

Pl. 8. Cesare Mori.

5   THE NEW PREFECT

Cesare Mori

Cesare Mori was born in 1872 at Pavia, in the north of Italy. He grew up in an orphanage, and was educated at the Turin Military Academy. His courage and taste for theatricality matured early: in 1895 he won a bronze medal for arresting an armed criminal, and the same year he threw in his commission for the love of a girl whose father refused to pay the statutory military dowry. After winning a national competition, he joined the police, and was posted to the Romagna. Following an incident here in 1904, when he frisked a leading Republican politician, he was transferred to Sicily, where he remained for much of the next thirteen years, gaining an enormous reputation in the western provinces for his courage against bandits. In 1917 he arrested the notorious Paolo Grisafi and his followers after a shoot-out lasting nine hours. Legends about his bravery were legion. He was called 'a man with hair on his heart', and was said to go about disguised as a monk when on the trail of criminals.[1]

The most important point about Mori's early years in Sicily was that he established close links with the *agrari*. The awe in which he was held by the peasantry made him an ideal instrument of social repression: 'Mori has shown exceptional qualities of tact, energy and prudence', ran a report in May 1914, recommending him for promotion, 'in situations of public disorder and disturbance...He has always managed...to restore calm, uphold the law, and keep the reputation of the police untarnished, without ever provoking anything untoward.' Particular mention was made of the demonstration by 1,500 agricultural workers at Trapani, in December 1913, when, almost single-handed it seems, Mori brought the rioters to bay, and arrested seventy of the ringleaders.[2] He adopted a similarly resolute approach to the land occupations in 1920. This raised his standing with the *agrari* still higher.[3]

Mori was authoritarian in character, and highly conservative. He had an intense moralistic streak and a rigid sense of duty. However, his severity could be offset by considerable charm. In so far as ambition and the fact that he was a public employee allowed him political sympathies, he was a Nationalist: he was devoted to the Crown and had friends at court.[4] His concern for individual strength left him little time or sympathy for the weak, though he was indulgent towards children and animals: in later life he became interested in the anti-vivisection cause.[5] He had a strong romantic side to him, albeit of a rather teutonic kind, and enjoyed the role the dutiful and adoring husband as well as that of the spartan adventurer. He liked poetry, and in gloomy moods would work out his depression by writing rambling, melancholy verse.[6] His speeches were full of rhetoric, and his favourite images were of sunsets, dawns, and morning stars. He called his first book on the mafia *Tra le zagare oltre la foschia* (Through the orange blossoms and beyond the mist). For his memoirs he toyed with such titles as 'Fascist reveille in the Conca d'oro' and 'Lictorial dawn over the flowering orange blossoms', but eventually settled for the more prosaic *Con la mafia ai ferri corti* (At close quarters with the mafia).[7]

Among the main components of Mori's character, it was his sense of duty, particularly towards the law, that caused him most trouble. After the Italian defeat at Caporetto in 1917, he was appointed *questore* of Turin. The stern measures he took to restore order in that city earned him the hatred of the socialists.[8] Later, in 1920, as *questore* of Rome, he faced not only unpopularity, but also political manoeuvring by the government after ordering his police to charge a gathering of Nationalist students who were celebrating the fifth anniversary of Italy's entry into the war. The confrontation left some dead and many injured.[9] Mori was sent for trial and was only saved from prosecution by a timely amnesty. Giolitti, who had always been well served by Mori, dispatched him to Sicily as head of a special anticrime squad. This was just a stopgap, however, and in February 1921 he returned to the mainland as prefect of Bologna.[10]

His attempt to uphold the law in Emilia landed him in trouble with the local fascists. He insisted that people be employed regardless of political affiliation, and to this end issued a decree prohibiting the free movement of workers. This thwarted attempts by landowners and fascists to impose what amounted to a monopoly on the labour market. Backed by Prime Minister Bonomi, Mori was able to stand his ground.[11] In November he was given 'extraordinary powers' over the whole of the lower Po Valley. This was the most disturbed area of Italy. However, the task of preserving peace proved too much even for Mori. In addition to the lawlessness of the fascists, he had to contend with the disobedience of his own police. After only a month he offered his resignation. Bonomi refused to accept it.[12]

Mori's relations with the local fascists grew steadily worse. In February 1922 they succeeded in pressurising the new Prime Minister, Facta, into withdrawing his exceptional powers. They were still not satisfied, however, and sought an outright end to what they called Mori's 'dictatorship' in Bologna. The crisis came to a head in the last week of May, when an order was given for a general mobilisation of the local fascist squads. Led by Aldo Oviglio and Leandro Arpinati, together with Dino Grandi from Modena and Italo Balbo from Ferrara, they occupied the centre of Bologna and besieged Mori.[13] According to one story, the prefect came out on to the balcony of Palazzo d'Accursio and said that he only received people in his office.[14] The government gave way, and on 23 June Mori was asked to choose another post. 'You do it', he replied, and he was sent to Bari.[15]

Mori's stay in Bologna had brought him into direct contact with some of the leading figures of the future regime. His inflexibility may have earned him their respect, but hardly their trust or affection. Henceforth a question mark hung more or less permanently over his name: he was a good policeman, but was he also a reliable fascist? The uncertainty persisted throughout the 1920s, above all among party intransigents, and a damning comment was almost *de rigueur* when they alluded to him.[16] Mussolini himself, talking to Yvon De Begnac in 1939 about the events of Bologna, displayed an evident respect, even admiration, for Mori. Nevertheless, he felt obliged to say that the prefect was not someone for whom he had any particular liking.[17]

Given Mori's notoriety within the fascist party, it was inevitable that he would be dismissed from service after the March on Rome. He left the prefecture of Bari in November 1922, ostensibly in disgrace, and moved to Florence. Here he spent the next eighteen months of his life in enforced retirement. To a man of Mori's energetic temperament, this must have been a period of deep frustration. He devoted part of his time to writing his first book on Sicily, *Tra le zagare oltre la foschia*. This was a detailed account of Sicilian crime, particularly in the post-war period, and it included a number of flattering references to the new government. It gained him some reputation as an analyst of the mafia (it was apparently admired by the famous criminologist, Enrico Ferri),[18] and may have been a factor in his eventual recall to service in 1924.[19]

Despite the humiliations of Bologna and Bari, Mori was eager to serve under the fascists. His chief asset was his devotion to law and order. Giovanni Furolo, a friend at court, told him in August 1922: 'You will surely find a way of refuting the myth that you hate fascists. Whoever applies the law impartially...restores the authority of the state. And the fascists, if they are in good faith, ought to be the first to acknowledge this.'[20] Throughout the winter and spring of

1923, Mori lived in hope of being rehabilitated. He pressed Furolo to intervene with the king's aide, Cittadini, but Furolo said Cittadini was 'as cold as the snow'.[21] He wrote to influential friends, and made plain his satisfaction with the new government: he even declared on one occasion that he had acted 'fascistically' throughout his career.[22] He had plenty of supporters who could lobby on his behalf, particularly in western Sicily; but the events of Bologna were as yet too recent. The government, wrote Furolo's wife in April 1923, was still afraid to employ him, 'for fear of raising a stink [putiferio] among the fascists'.[23]

Mori at Trapani

Mori was appointed prefect of Trapani on 2 June 1924, shortly before the outbreak of the Matteotti crisis. A few weeks earlier, Mussolini had visited the province and learnt, at first hand, of the confusion besetting local fascism, and of the crisis in the wine trade. He had also been told of the virulence of the mafia. A delegation of war veterans informed him that 216 murders had been committed in Marsala alone in the space of a year. They said that omertà was widespread, and that the presence of the mafia explained the 'implacable hatred' of Sicily's ruling class towards fascism. They begged Mussolini to take action to improve the situation.[24]

The prefect of Trapani at the time was Giovanni Merizzi. He had been the target of an unusual number of complaints and evidently did not impress the Prime Minister: no sooner had Mussolini left the province, than Merizzi's transfer was announced.[25] What damned him, apparently, was his close alliance with the recently disgraced provincial party secretary, Giuseppe Pellegrino, a man whom Achille Starace had advised the government in 1923 to 'liquidate with caution'.[26] Pellegrino had been accused of affiliation with the mafia. His failings, though, were evidently more political than moral: he lacked personal prestige, and his tenacious hold on Trapani fascism had resulted in the exclusion of many key figures in the province.[27] It was no coincidence that the person chosen to replace Merizzi as prefect of Trapani, Cesare Mori, was a long-standing ally of the local élite.

Mori, however, was sent to destroy the mafia, which was said to be particularly strong in Trapani in these years. What exactly did this mean? Perhaps the most striking feature of the province was its economic and social fluidity. 'In the last twenty years', wrote the agricultural expert, Giovanni Molè, in 1929, 'Trapani has succeeded more than any other Sicilian province in extricating itself from that suffocating shirt of Nessus, the latifondo.'[28] He suggested three reasons for this development. Firstly, the local landowners were businessmen, rather than aristocrats, which meant they were more interested in capital than in status. Secondly, the province had many well-funded co-operatives, with the resources to purchase and sustain new properties. Thirdly, a good number of the *latifondi* were small, and this made their transfer relatively easy.[29] Between 1907 and 1927, eighty-three *latifondi* were split up in Trapani, with a total area of 36,531 hectares. According to Molè, only the much larger province of Palermo could boast similar figures.

As elsewhere in Sicily, many of these developments in Trapani had come about as a result of the Great War. One striking feature of Trapani, however, was the prominent role played by brokers. According to the economist, Nunzio Prestianni, forty-fix of the fifty-seven estates that were divided up in the province after the war exchanged hands through 'intermediary speculators'. In Palermo, the figures were thirteen out of fifty-one. These brokers were often newly enriched *gabelloti*, who paid the hard-pressed landowners in cash, and then resold the property in small lots to peasants, or peasant co-operatives, at considerable profit. The process of sub-division was most in evidence at Marsala, Alcamo, Monte San Giuliano, Trapani, Calatafimi and Castelvetrano. These were all towns where the mafia was thought to be strong.[30]

The connection between social mobility, economic redistribution, and illicit behaviour was complex; there is no reason to suppose, as some contemporaries did, that the fortunes made in these years were invariably the result of crime. Robbery, intimidation, and murder were as much instruments of vendetta as of financial gain. Trapani province was certainly lawless in this period: according to one estimate there were 700 murders a year and thefts totalling 30,000 animals.[31] Undoubtedly a link existed in some instances between crime and social mobility. However, it was also the case that those who lost out in these years, and in particular the big landowners, had a vested interest in seeing their opponents as criminals.

Insinuations of criminality often went hand in hand with snobbery. A good example was an anonymous pamphlet, entitled 'The underworld in Sicily and the fascist response', which was serialised in a Trapani newspaper in 1923:

> They used to be called '*lu zu Vincenzo*' or '*lu zu Andrea*' but today they are pompously known as 'Don Vincenzo' or 'Don Andrea', wholesale merchants and knights of the Crown of Italy. Janissaries, friends and shoddy clients follow them around *en masse*. What services they render is not clear; but we do know that their so-called warehouses, and their great farms and farmhouses are frequented by foul brutes who in the country wear leggings, coarse

clothes, and caps like a cyclist's, pulled down at an angle over their foreheads. But in town they sport luxury clothes and often go around in carriages and even in cars.

The writer fervently admired Cesare Mori. In 1920, he said, when the island was racked with crime, 'Mori restored peace to the masses with his strategic arrests', and the peasants spoke of him in gratitude as their 'saviour'. The author had a strong propensity, it seems, for identifying his interests with those of the collectivity.[32]

Though the problems of post-war Sicily were largely social and economic in character, they were readily described in the language of law and order. The concept of the mafia was tailor-made for this purpose. It explained the unrest and simultaneously implied a response that was politically acceptable. As a result, social change tended to be dismissed as merely criminal. 'A new feature of the situation', Mori told Mussolini a few days after his arrival at Trapani,

is the attitude of the old mafia, many members of which (above all through unbridled exploitation of specific circumstances during the war) have now reached a comfortable economic position. Through self-interest they have grown conservative and law-abiding; they have withdrawn, or are tending to withdraw, from active life, and have assumed the curious garb of law and order fanatics. But others have remained at their stations and are fighting tooth and nail to preserve their power and prestige against the steady advance of the new mafia. This...sprang up in the immediate post-war period as a reaction to, and rebellion against, the inflexible and persistent domination of the old mafia. But it has the same characteristics...as the old mafia, except that its reflexes are quicker and its actions more aggressive.[33]

This sounded straightforward, but the application of the label 'mafia' at a grass-roots level was often complicated by local politics, which could filter and refract reality. In Alcamo the opposition group set up a fascist section immediately after the March on Rome. Its first secretary was Antonino Renda. He was described in a report as 'the implacable enemy' of the head of the municipal administration, a certain Lipari, and no one who was connected with Lipari was admitted to the *fascio*.[34] The new section announced that its aim was to stamp out crime, and Cesare Mori was asked if he would help by sending his 'notes' (what these were was not specified).[35] A few months later, Renda's successor as party secretary dispatched a long report to Mussolini on the mafia, saying it was high time the government did something about 'the old political caryatids' who 'protected *mafiosi* with every means'.[36] His sights were clearly trained on the local administration, and in the summer of 1923 it was dissolved.

Party politics and allegations of criminality were closely intertwined in Trapani. According to one newspaper, in September 1923 the province was on the verge of anarchy. There were spurious charges, it said, of 'state defamation'; the punishment of *ammonizione* was being widely abused for partisan ends; and the authorities were dissolving local administrations on 'pretexts of public order'.[37] The situation was not improved by the fact that the fascist provincial secretary was dismissed from his post for immoral conduct, after he had himself tried to purge the local party of the mafia: 'It is incomprehensible', he wrote in his defence 'that I, Pellegrino, should be accused of involvement with the mafia and criminals when I have fought [them] with such tenacious and fascist resolve to the point of becoming a target for persecution, threats, and gun-shots.'[38]

Trapani was in a chaotic state when Mori arrived in June 1924. The provincial party was riven with factionalism and lacked moral, as well as political, credibility. In the elections of April 1924, the fascist vote had been lower here than elsewhere in Sicily, and it was clear that the main liberal politician, Nunzio Nasi, was still well entrenched.[39] Mori's task was to fortify the government's standing in the province. His links with the big landowners were to some extent an asset, but their ties with Nasi and the liberal clienteles meant that he soon ran foul of parvenu fascists. 'Mori is misgoverning Trapani', wrote the brother of the Sicilian philosopher Giovanni Gentile, in July 1925, 'along with the demo-masonic clique... This is the Trapani of Nasi right to the core.'[40] A few months earlier, Giovanni Gentile had himself protested strongly to Federzoni. The government, he said, 'should never have given a position of responsibility to someone with Mori's past'. As a result, he claimed, the provincial *fasci* had been subjected to 'every kind of harassment'.[41]

In Mori's opinion, the provincial party was thoroughly infected. He referred in 1927 to 'the pseudo-fascist positions polluted...by the mafia' that he had been forced to destroy in Trapani.[42] His ruthlessness was to cause him considerable embarrassment in the longer term.[43] In the short run, it exposed him to charges of partiality: 'We need positive proof', declared an article in *Il Popolo* at the end of 1924, referring to Mori's operations in the province, 'that a real police force and true justice still exist in Italy. However, every day evidence emerges that...both are disappearing.' Arrests were being used, the paper claimed, 'to make hay of the opposition'; indeed some recent cases near Sciacca suggested that 'this and this alone was the ultimate goal of the proclaimed fight against crime'. It was sad, the article concluded, to see a man of Mori's calibre sink to the level of an ordinary policeman, 'slave of the local boss of any small town he finds himself in'.[44]

Mori's arrival at Palermo

Federzoni clearly had some justification for saying that Mori 'had caused a problem or two' at Trapani'.[45] Whether Mori was destined for retirement, as Cucco maintained, is less certain. The idea would probably have been mooted as Mori had antagonised influential party figures, and his credit, at least among intransigent fascists, was already minimal. However, the fact remains that Mori was promoted to Palermo, and Mussolini would surely not have authorised such a move if he had disliked what had occurred at Trapani. In telling Cucco of Mori's intended dismissal, Federzoni might have been fibbing to appease a party radical. Alternatively, he may simply have wanted to sound Cucco out.

Though Cucco was probably less pleased about the new appointment than he suggested in his autobiography, he was not downhearted. He had a strong belief that he was politically secure. He had won the August elections and been congratulated personally by the Duce. Farinacci, his spiritual ally, was still party secretary, and though all was not well between Mussolini and Farinacci, it was by no means evident in the late summer of 1925 that the days of intransigence were numbered. Additional security came from the fact that Mori had clearly been instructed at the time of his appointment to work closely with the party. After hearing of his promotion, he visited Cucco, embraced him, thanked him for his help and said that at Rome, 'the Duce, the Minister of the Interior, and the Minister di Scalea, had all told him that "he and Cucco would achieve great things at Palermo."'[46]

Mori was in a stronger position than the Palermo *federale* believed. Cucco had certainly contributed to the new appointment, but his voice had not been crucial: the former Minister of War, Antonino Di Giorgio, Federzoni, and perhaps di Scalea, were more influential sponsors.[47] Nevertheless, Mori was far from invulnerable: his chequered past had created a legacy of suspicion that the period at Trapani had done nothing to assuage: 'I remember very well', wrote Cucco in his autobiography, referring to the autumn of 1925, 'meeting Leandro Arpinati at Rome...He said to me in a tone of playful surprise and friendly rebuke: "So you have taken to being Mori's apologist?!"... He remembered what had happened at Bologna...and was always afraid that Mori might for some reason or other suddenly appear "averse" to the fascists.'[48] This was probably one reason why Cucco felt strong: a single mistake, he must have thought, and Mori would be out.

Mori entered the Palazzo dei Normanni as prefect of Palermo on the afternoon of 22 October. The local press had made much of his appointment. Cucco's newspaper *Sicilia Nuova* said that for the criminal world his coming resembled 'the unexpected arrival of a cat amidst a crowd of mice who are calmly munching away at a nice piece of cheese'.[49] *L'Ora* and *Il Giornale di Sicilia* were only marginally less colourful. Some newspapers exuded a near sadistic glee. The *Avvisatore*, an organ of the commercial classes, quoted approvingly from an article in *Il Giornale d'Italia* which recommended the wholesale deportation of criminals along with their families: 'This is what the English did with Canada. They thereby purged the nation, brought wealth to the colony, and enriched the deportees themselves with honest work.'[50] Such views were not uncommon in business circles, and there is no reason to suspect their sincerity.

One feature that was absent from the newspapers in October 1925 was a traditional concern for the reputation of Sicily. This may have been a consequence of tighter censorship. In April of the previous year, for example, the *Avvisatore* had denounced the removal of arms licences as a monstrous act, which gave the world the impression that Sicily was 'a haunt of brigands and robbers...a subject colony, governed by the mafia and the *camorra*'. What the island needed, according to the paper, was 'order, discipline and work', what it opposed were 'adventurers...and tin-pot dictators'.[51] Might not Mori's career, particularly his recent activity in Trapani, have put him in the category of adventurers? Or was this soubriquet reserved for fascists such as the *questore*, Francesco Tiby, or even Alfredo Cucco? Mori was a man of the old order; to readers of the *Avvisatore*, he may have been a source of reassurance rather than anxiety.

Mori set great store by the press. Like Mussolini, he tended to equate the absence of criticism with approval, or at least felt that the two were connected in some way. Shortly after his arrival at Palermo, he told the executive of the Union of Sicilian Journalists that his mission was to be regarded 'as a work of reintegration'; he wanted maximum collaboration between the population and 'local organisations', which in this case presumably meant the newspapers themselves.[52] In other words, the press was being asked to give its unqualified support. Mori later helped by providing annotated transcripts of his speeches, in which he described the applause as 'prolonged', 'delirious', or 'interminable'. According to Cucco, Mori's orations frequently met with dismay and silence.[53]

The Sicilian press cannot be taken as a reliable source for these years. In fact, its obsequious partiality was highlighted by Calogero Alajmo, the only fascist journalist to offer any serious criticism of Mori's campaign against the mafia. He claimed in an article in Farinacci's *Regime Fascista* early in 1930, that the local papers had 'failed to collaborate with Mori disinterestedly, and allowed the heroic island to be defamed...by giving pride of place to communiqués furnished by the police'.[54] Similar complaints could have been voiced about the mainland press: it either remained silent, or else toed the official line. The only newspaper that dared imply any hostility to Mori was *Il Tevere*, which was edited in Rome by the Sicilian, Telesio Interlandi.

In the weeks that followed his arrival in Palermo, Mori made it clear that he meant business. There was to be no equivocation or compromise; the hour of reckoning was at hand for the mafia. 'My main concern', he announced on the day of his installation, 'is to ...clear the ground inexorably of the nightmares, threats and dangers which...are paralysing, perverting and corrupting every kind of social activity.'[55] As if in augury, the end of October saw Palermo wracked by the worst storms in living memory: rivers overflowed, houses collapsed, and flood waters ran through the streets, to a depth, in places, of ten feet.[56] Whether heaven was angry with Sicily or the northern prefect might have been a point of discussion for the superstitious. Mori, however, was not supersititious, nor given to discussion: 'When you know you are right', he once wrote, 'you affirm and do not discuss.'[57]

In accordance with the wishes of the government, Mori and Cucco signalled from the beginning that it was their intention to work in harness. Whether theirs would be a partnership of equals, though, was far from certain. On 28 October, an estimated 50,000 fascists took part in celebrations to mark the third anniversary of the March on Rome. Portraits of Mussolini, the king, Farinacci and Cucco, were carried aloft on sticks, and some of the Palermo *federale*'s more zealous followers sported his photograph pinned to their shirts. The prefect received the salute of the party, but, as the local fascist newspaper, *Sicilia Nuova*, pointedly implied, this was a sign of respect, not devotion. Devotion, and by implication, loyalty, were reserved for Cucco. The political message was unambiguous: though *federale* and prefect would co-operate, the former had every intention of calling the tune.[58]

The same point was made again that evening at a banquet held in honour of Mori. The main theme of the speeches was the mafia. As usual, Cucco equated it with the old liberal clienteles. 'Fascism', he said, '...is today launching a full-scale attack on the system of political factions that were rooted in the mire...Mafia and counter-mafia will be routed, destroyed.' He stressed that Mori was the right man for the task: 'This distinguished representative of the government will restore peace, order, security and, above all, the law, which is stern, just, civil and fascist.' In his reply, Mori took refuge, as he was often to do, in verbiage and a paean of praise to Mussolini: the crucial question of the relationship between the mafia and fascism was left unanswered. With his pregnant reference to Farinacci's 'mafia and counter-mafia', Cucco had thrown down a gauntlet: Mori had declined to pick it up.[59]

A local clash between prefect and *federale*, dovetailing into the broader issue of state–party relations, was in the making, even at this early stage. For the moment, however, crime was the main focus of attention. 'It is clear beyond a shadow of doubt', wrote Mori to Federzoni early in November, 'that the time has come to pin the mafia to the wall.'[60] Miracles were not to be expected, he said, but a solution would certainly be easier than before. In the first place, he felt that the Great War had given many Sicilians a strong sense of the state, thereby making them less sympathetic to rival sources of authority.[61] Secondly, he believed that the mafia had degenerated to such an extent that it was now no more than a criminal organisation ('a kind of *camorra* pure and simple'). This meant it was isolated and could be crushed with confidence. He reassured Federzoni about the political consequences of repression: 'I am fully convinced that strong measures against the mafia can cause no serious political harm. Quite the contrary in fact.'[62]

Mori's campaign began in earnest at the end of November. On the 28th of that month, sixty-two wanted men were captured in the Madonie, a mountainous zone inland from Cefalù;[63] a fortnight later, the police arrested 142 people near Piazza Armerina.[64] Towards Christmas the so-called Palermo *viveurs* came into the firing line. These were elegantly dressed young men who frequented bars, and drove ostentatiously along the city's most fashionable streets. According to the authorities, their wealth could only have been ill-gotten. Certain night-spots were kept under surveillance, and on the evening of 21 December more than two dozen of these high-livers were taken into custody.[65] At the same time, an independent operation in the neighbourhood of Palermo led to the arrest of some 300 people with criminal records.[66]

On 9 December, Mori issued the first of his two ordinances.[67] It focused on various aspects of urban crime. *Zuinaggio* – the practice of picking up sick people and escorting them to rogue doctors, who fleeced them – was tackled by declaring a ban on suspects from hospitals and public places. All porters, janitors, and custodians now had to register with the police. So did garage owners and taxi-drivers, and personal identity cards, with photographs, were to be instituted from 1 January. *L'Ora* described these provisions as 'very practical', and reserved special praise for the attack on *zuinaggio*. *Sicilia Nuova* said the ordinance was 'an outstanding example of the new dynamism'.[68] Whether the measures were enforceable was something that was not discussed. *Zuinaggio* was still a serious problem two years later.[69]

6   THE SIEGE OF GANGI

The siege

Mori was determined to begin the campaign against the mafia decisively. He needed a dramatic victory to establish his authority and that of the government. He wanted to give heart to a population which, he believed, had for too long been ignored by the state. 'The alleged problem of crime is not of Sicily's doing,' he said. '. . . It has been nailed to it, like Christ on the cross.'[1] Only by making it clear that the era of neglect was over could *omertà* be breached, and the 'vicious circle' of impunity broken.[2] The mafia would then collapse, 'as the result of an inevitable reaction by all the healthy, pure, and strong forces which Sicily is particularly rich in.'[3] This was why the operation against the bandits of the Madonie, at the beginning of 1926, was so important for Mori: it was to be a watershed.

The choice of the Madonie was logical. For some years it had been the most crime-ridden area of Sicily, and a flagrant symbol of the impotence of the state. Some brigands had grown so powerful that they were known locally as 'the prefect', or 'the marshal'; 'an irony and an offence', said Mori, 'to the prestige of the authorities'.[4] Until 1919, the bandit Melchiorre Candino and his followers had been the dominant group in the Madonie. The payment of tribute money seems to have become institutionalised: through imposition, according to the police; willingly, in Candino's view. 'I did my best', he told the examining magistrate after his arrest in 1926, 'to see the landowners did not suffer at the hands of other *latitanti* [men on the run], and in return the owners gave me and my men what we needed to keep body and soul together.'[5]

Trouble had begun in 1919 with the emergence of rival groups headed by the Ferrarello and Andaloro families. Particularly prominent were Gaetano Ferrarello, a one-time follower of Candino, and Nicolò Andaloro, a young man of violent disposition who had escaped from prison in 1917 after being arrested for carrying a knife. Between 1919 and 1922, Candino's men were edged out of the picture as the new factions pressed to secure themselves jobs on the *latifondi* as *campieri, soprastanti,* and *guardiani.* Candino lost his mono-poly of protection money, and in 1922 he decided that the time had come for his retirement. His 'clients', he said, were disconsolate, and complained about being left at the mercy of *latitanti.*[6] He spent the next four years peacefully in his home town of San Mauro Castelverde. A police report of 1923 described him as spending his days 'between home and church'. In the spring of 1926, Mori had him arrested. He was nearly eighty, and sported, in keeping with his years, 'a flowing snow-white beard'. It was said that he was in tears as he was taken to the Ucciardone prison in Palermo.[7]

According to the police, the Andaloros and Ferrarellos 'domi-nated' the Madonie after 1922. To what extent groups of *latitanti* could control a mountainous region such as the Madonie is un-certain: the public security forces, like the press, were prone to hyperbole. Crime, however, was clearly widespread; and faced with *omertà* and protection, there seemed little the authorities could do. Mori was determined to break the deadlock. As prefect of Trapani, he had been authorised to set up a number of special police 'nuclei', which could operate across provincial borders.[8] In March 1925, he gave deputy-superintendent Francesco Spanò command of all the units operating in the area of the Madonie mountains.

Spanò was a conscientious official of Calabrian origin. He had been in Sicily since 1912, and knew the Madonie well. For some years he had conducted enquiries into the local bandits from a base at Polizzi, and in September 1925 he delivered a report to Mori, in which he claimed that local criminals enjoyed political support 'even at the governmental level'. He also said that the police were being hindered in every possible way.[9] Mori's indignation was apparently such that he promised to bring protectors and protected alike to book. This was easier said than done. The principal *manutengoli* in the Madonie – barons Sgadari, Li Destri, and Pottino di Capuano – were all prominent local fascists, and Mori, who was at times stubborn but never ingenuous, knew he could not arrest them. His transfer to Palermo was, after all, conditional on his collaboration with Cucco and the provincial party.

Spanò was in charge of the first *retata* (round up) in the Madonie which took place on the night of 28 November. Several 'interprov-incial nuclei' were involved, together with groups of *carabinieri.*[10] There were also about 100 members of the Militia, in keeping with a suggestion Mori had made to Mussolini while at Trapani. Fascists, he had said, ought to be involved directly in police operations; they should support the work of repression 'boldly, openly'; and what-ever hostility there might be to this at first would soon be offset by the gains, political and judicial: 'In view of the inevitable results, all this will amount to one of the most brilliant and best appreciated services rendered by Sicilian fascism.'[11] At Palermo, even more than at Trapani, Mori was obliged to rub shoulders with the party.

After the initial *retata*, Spanò somewhat foolishly took it upon himself to deliver the *coup de grâce* to the Madonie bandits. He approached Baron Sgadari, and through him arranged a meeting with Salvatore Ferrarello. The two men met on the night of 15 December. Spanò offered Ferrarello, in return for his and his companions' surrender, an end to inquiries, house searches, and sequestrations; there would also be an eventual amnesty. Ferrarello agreed to consult his men and report back. The offer was accepted, and Spanò conveyed the news to Mori, only to receive, instead of the anticipated encomium, a savage reprimand. 'The destruction of banditry', Mori is supposed to have said,

> 'must be made to appear the direct result of our own resolute action...You have acted too hastily, *cavaliere* Spanò. You should have told me beforehand what you had in mind. You might have damaged my reputation. You have almost presented me with a *fait accompli*. As if the last blow against criminality could have been struck without the personal intervention of the prefect, who is in Sicily for precisely that purpose, as you well know.[12]

The operation, known as the 'siege of Gangi', began on the night of 1 January, 1926. It was a slight misnomer, for other towns in the area were also involved. This was in accordance with Mori's tactic of working 'from a broad base and over a large area', to seal off all escape routes.[13] The main action, however, was at Gangi, and it was there that the operation's headquarters were set up. The peaks of hills were occupied by *carabinieri* and members of the Militia as look-out posts.[14] It was snowing heavily. The bandits had been driven by the cold to return to their families, and the police knew of their whereabouts. The only trouble was that Gangi was a bandit's paradise. The town was built into the side of a steep hill, and many of the houses had two entrances, one on the ground floor, and the other on the first, which facilitated escape. There were also hide-outs, skilfully constructed behind walls, under floors, or in attics, the work of a local artisan called 'Tofanella'.[15]

In these circumstances, the operation went more slowly than expected. The first bandit to give himself up was Gaetano Ferrarello, a tall, elderly man, with a long beard, much pride and some nobility of character. He had been a *latitante* for thirty years. He emerged from hiding on the morning of 2 January, walked to the house of Baron Li Destri adjoining the central piazza, and presented himself to *questore* Crimi, the man sent by Mori to head the operations. Mori had stayed behind in Palermo, in part, it seems, to monitor news-

Pl. 9. A panoramic view of Gangi in 1926. The photograph was taken a few months after the siege, at a celebration to mark the freeing of the Madonie from the mafia. On the left is a triumphal arch.

Pl. 10. The bandit Gaetano Ferrarello.

paper reports. Ferrarello, we are told, threw his stick on the table, and said slowly: 'My heart trembles. This is the first time I have found myself in the presence of the law. I am giving myself up to restore peace and tranquillity to these tormented people.' After shaking hands with the police and officials, as befitted a man who aimed at respectability, he was led away.[16]

Ferrarello was mistaken if he thought Mori would now desist. The object of the exercise was not simply the surrender of the bandits, but also their humiliation: 'I wanted to give the population tangible proof of the cowardice of criminals', he wrote in his memoirs.[17] The police were told to enter the houses of wanted men and sleep in their beds. The bandits' cattle were slaughtered, and the meat sold at cut-price to local buyers.[18] Orders were also given for hostages to be seized: as with later operations, the main targets seem to have been women and children.[19] Whether the women were maltreated, as critics of Mori later maintained, is not certain. It would undoubtedly have been in keeping with the spirit, if not the letter, of the exercise, for the purpose of taking hostages was to play on the man's sense of honour towards his wife and family: a little hardship would thus not come amiss.

Mori boasted subsequently that the bandits surrendered as the result of a telegram he sent to the mayor of Gangi at the start of the siege: 'I order the *latitanti* present in this territory to give up within twelve hours, after which time severe measures will be taken against their families, their possessions, and every kind of sympathiser.' The message was posted up around the town, and publicised by the local town crier. 'My simple telegraphic threat', he told Federzoni a few months later, 'caused the famous bandits to hand themselves over one and all.'[20] This was untrue for two reasons. Firstly, the arrests took place only gradually. Secondly, the ultimatum was intended as a *coup de theâtre*, and had little influence on the actual course of events. The real determining factors were the seizure of hostages and most crucially, the mediation of the Gangi *manutengoli*. Mori made almost no mention of either of these aspects of the siege in his reports to Rome.

The precise nature of the backstage negotiations is hard to ascertain. Almost certainly, however, Mori exploited the ambiguity of Baron Sgadari's position, and put pressure on him to surrender his protégés. Sgadari was the most influential of the Gangi *manutengoli*, and his collaboration with the authorities may well have been the price he had to pay for his own impunity. Spanò's enquiries in recent years had clearly made his life difficult for him. In December 1924, Salvatore Ferrarello had 'ordered' him to get rid of the troublesome policeman. Sgadari had agreed, and set off for Palermo – 'but naturally', it was later reported, 'his efforts...were directed instead to speeding up the operation that was so successful later'. He made a visit to Mori at Trapani, and also went to Rome. He was apparently engaged in an awkward double game. Despite this, however, Spanò could still say in September 1925 that everything was being done to hinder his work.[21]

During the siege of Gangi, Sgadari was instrumental in securing the arrest of several important bandits; but he was clearly forced to make promises that Mori subsequently felt no obligation to honour. This is apparent from a letter that Sgadari wrote to Mori in January 1927, the principal purpose of which was to testify against Alfredo Cucco, who had recently been disgraced:

> Further to our recent conversation, I can confirm that...I became the target of recriminations and even threats in Gangi, because the families of the *latitanti* I had forced to surrender thought I had deceived them. On the other hand those that turned to Hon. Cucco not only managed to get their relatives left in peace, but also secured the indemnity of their property. When I pointed this out to Hon. Cucco,...he almost reproached me for having put myself in such a vulnerable position by following the instructions of Prefect Mori whose actions were not meeting with popular approval, and...who would, he said, soon be dismissed.[22]

Luckily for Sgadari, Mori was to remain in Palermo long enough for the Gangi bandits to be safely convicted. Life, however, cannot have been easy for him, as there was strong resentment at his collaboration. During the trial in 1927, he was to be abused and threatened by several of the defendants. Salvatore Ferrarello felt particularly aggrieved, and when he later escaped from prison, Sgadari was apparently fortunate not to fall victim to vendetta: 'Have you ever heard of Ferrarello?' asked Calogero Vizzini, trying to explain to the journalist Indro Montanelli the true function of a *mafioso*. 'He began like Giuliano but finished like a saint. When he escaped from prison, he even refrained from killing Baron Sgadari, who had been responsible for sending him there. Somebody...arranged the matter.'[23]

Despite the embarrassingly slow results and the questionable methods being used at Gangi, ignorance and expediency combined to produce a more comfortable myth. On 6 January, Mussolini sent Mori a telegram (which appeared the following day on the front pages of the main Sicilian newspapers) congratulating the prefect on his 'magnificent' achievement, and urging him to 'carry on to the end without regard for anyone, however high or low'.[24] The local fascist press also did its best at this time to extol Mori and the Gangi operations: 'There is something legendary...in this action of the police,' wrote *Sicilia Nuova* on 4 January, 'and something mythological too. Hercules has succeeded in his twelfth labour. He has finally severed the last head, and cauterised every bleeding stump; and now serene and victorious, he passes amidst the cheering people who rapturously applaud the new conqueror.'[25]

In the course of the campaign against the mafia, Mori was often compared to mythical heroes. Perseus and Hercules were regarded as particularly apt. Mori did nothing to scotch this idolatry, partly, perhaps, because he believed the peasantry was deeply impressed by power; and it was the idea of a man of colossal strength, moral and physical, that he strove to project. His visit to Gangi on 10 January was in part an image-building exercise. To enter the town while so many bandits were still at large was in itself a demonstration of courage. Alfredo Cucco claimed that Mori's very appearance 'terrified' the Gangitani: he wore heavy military boots, a long thick scarf, and a 'magnificent' suit.[26] He also had the advantage of being tall and well built, and his deep and sonorous voice, with its unfamiliar Lombard cadences, no doubt added a note of awesomeness to the speech he delivered from a balcony on the second floor of the town hall, overlooking the main piazza: 'Rebel against tribute money, blackmail and imposition. . .Defend yourselves, counter-attack.'[27]

According to the account of the Gangi visit given in *Sicilia Nuova*, Mori was hailed as a hero. The whole population, the report said, turned out to fête him; he and Cucco were deluged with flowers; placards everywhere carried pro-fascist slogans, or reproduced the text of Mussolini's telegram; and when the prefect stepped forward to speak, the crowd bust into 'an interminable applause. . .a delirium that showed no sign of ending'. Mori's speech was apparently so much interrupted by clapping that the audience had to be told to keep quiet and let him finish.[28] A more sober version of the events was given by Cucco in his autobiography. His description offered no hint of a carnival atmosphere. The crowd, he said, consisted of 'a few people numb with cold'; Mori's speech struck the local inhabitants as unpleasantly terse and aggressive; and though there was applause, it lacked warmth and conviction.[29] This account was probably nearer the truth, though it should be remembered that Cucco had suffered at Mori's hand by the time of writing, and had an axe to grind.

Salvatore Ferrarello, the most dangerous of the bandits still at large, surrendered on 11 January. The previous day he had issued a threat to kill Mori and commit suicide. Baron Sgadari, who knew the bandit well, took him at his word, but in the event nothing happened, and after Mori's departure the police traced Ferrarello's hiding place to the house of the Communal Secretary of Gangi, a certain Paternò. An initial search revealed nothing. Paternò's family was arrested and the house surrounded. The bandit's sisters then came forward to announce that their brother would give himself up that evening, provided the hostages were released. This was agreed, and Ferrarello duly kept his word. He presented himself at the house of a local landowner, Francesco Mocciaro, dressed smartly for the occasion: he knew his photograph would be taken. As a final request, before being escorted off to prison, he asked if he could see the spacious house he was having built for him in the centre of the town.[30]

Mori's analysis of the mafia

During the next few days, the Gangi operation was brought to an end. In August 1926, Mori told Federzoni that 130 *latitanti* and over 300 'accomplices' had been arrested. He did not specify who these 'accomplices' were. For the most part, no doubt, they were relatives of wanted men.[31] 'As I had predicted,' Mori wrote, 'the success in the Madonie – which no one dared hope for – at one stroke...swung the situation in our favour. Nor could it have been otherwise, for the masses strongly favour any show of force, particularly in Sicily.'[32] This somewhat arrogant remark was matched in his report by others of more sinister drift. People, he said, had complained that innocent men were being arrested and women seized; that Sicily's reputation had been damaged, and the work-force reduced; and that in general the police were exceeding their powers. Such criticisms, however, came from 'the inevitable band of moaners' (*piagnoni*). His methods, he claimed, were not excessive: 'The pressure we exert is perfectly in keeping with the thrust of the enemy.'[33]

What was this 'thrust of the enemy' that justified the severe tactics Mori employed at Gangi and elsewhere? His interpretation of the mafia rested on two essential points. The first was his view of human nature: men, he believed, were fallen creatures, and needed to be kept on the straight and narrow with the threat of punishment. If the authorities were lax, 'that element of the vandal which is in every man' would well to the surface and produce chaos.[34] His second point was derived from the first: the mafia, he contended, was a moral degeneration that had been caused by the state's irresponsibility. Sicilians were by nature no less law-abiding than other people: it was simply that the Italian government had time and again washed its hands of the island and allowed anarchy to spread.[35]

Because of the state's indifference, what was noble in Sicily had been left to degenerate into baseness. This was the case with *omertà*. In its original form, said Mori, *omertà* implied self-confidence, no-bility, and a sense of personal worth, and it was expressed most characteristically in resistance to acts of injustice. In some measure it was a feature of all societies, but it was particularly strong among Sicilians, because they had a marked propensity for individualism. However, the virtue in *omertà* had gradually turned to a vice: if Sicilians once took justice into their own hands because they knew the authorities were corrupt, their non-co-operation now stemmed either from extreme pride or fear, or from the fact that among criminals, silence was known to be the best form of defence. The extent of this degeneration was apparent, Mori felt, in the tendency of *mafiosi* to justify their immorality by saying that men were evil by nature, and that nothing could be done about it.[36]

If the mafia were a degeneration of *omertà*, it would be logical to suppose that all Sicilians were to some degree *mafiosi*. Mori could not admit this, though at the gut level he may possibly have felt it. He had to be more concrete. The mafia, he said, mediated between criminals and the rest of the population, and thereby supplanted the state. It controlled *malvivenza* (criminality, usually of a petty kind) and simultaneously exploited it. Indeed, the two categories were spiritually united: 'Mafia and *malvivenza* form...part of a single faith: the mafia provides the priests, *malvivenza* the faithful.'[37] This structure was far from ubiquitous. The east of the island was almost entirely free of it, and in many places the mafia had been imported or imposed: 'There are few original centres of the mafia...They are invariably found where geography and traditional attitudes made it hard for the idea of the state, as well as the state's activity, to penetrate.'[38]

This was not altogether convincing. Mori had earlier claimed that the mafia derived from *omertà*; and *omertà*, he said, was originally a reaction to official injustice. This surely implied some awareness of the state, or at least of what those invested with power by the state could do. However, similar inconsistencies were commonplace in Mori's thought. He maintained, for example, that *mafiosi* could belong to any class, since all social groups had their moral degenerates; but he then claimed that the mafia had no base among the poor and weak, nor among the big landowners. The *latifondisti*, indeed, were invariably its victims, whatever people might think: 'Despite every legend to the contrary, it is a fact that the landowner, in one way or another, submits to the mafia.'[39] Necessity, and necessity alone, accounted for compromises: 'Obliged to see to its own protection, [the propertied class] was forced, under threat of ruin, to negotiate... with the mafia.'[40]

Who were the *mafiosi*? On the whole, according to Mori, they were not city dwellers. They belonged primarily to the rural middle class, and the *gabelloti* and their dependents – the *campieri*, *guardiani* and *soprastanti* – were the principal exponents.[41] They formed a parasitic group, which preyed on both the peasantry and the landowners. Their intermediary position and ruthlessness accounted, in Mori's view, for class warfare in Sicily: the rural masses regarded the mafia as the traditional enemy, but the landowners were also blamed for their collusion with it and were accordingly hated by the peasantry.[42] Social harmony would only be restored with the destruction of the mafia: 'The day the parasitic mafia is removed, the great proprietors and working masses will come face to face. The understanding will be such, that through the virtue, energy and spotless patriotism that both groups abound in, Sicily, at one stroke, will emerge at the forefront of national production and wealth.'[43]

Having identified the mafia as a parasitic middle class, Mori set out to demonstrate its collective criminality. His argument was somewhat confused. 'The mafia', he wrote, 'is not an association or secret society. It is a morbid form of behaviour peculiar to certain resolute individuals, that isolates them as in a kind of caste [casta].'[44] Nevertheless, the mafia was said to control malvivenza, and through 'catharsis' this resulted in 'coagulation', and 'connecting tissues woven of omertà'. 'Where there is mafia, there is association [aggregato]'.[45] Lurking in this fog of words was some notion of organisation; this was apparently confirmed when Mori spoke of the mafia as having 'local oligarchies' with 'areas of special influence and exclusive jurisdiction'. These oligarchies, furthermore, were linked, he said, 'as in a net made out of a single thread'.[46] Was the mafia an organisation then or not? Mori evidently had semantic problems. His difficulty stemmed from a limited conceptual framework, in which the idea of crime was equated whole-heartedly with a conspiracy against society and the state.

This is the reason why mafiosi were said to constitute 'a kind of caste': they had to be distinct from the rest of the population. However, there was an element self-deception here. If, as Mori stated, mafiosi were 'isolated' in the community, this presumably would have made the task of the police relatively easy; but in fact, he said, mafiosi were perceived only intuitively: 'The figure of the mafioso is recognised above all through intuition: he is divined, sensed.'[47] This was a rather alarming remark. More unsettling still, perhaps, was the admission that he himself had 'very frequently' mistaken honest men for mafiosi.[48] This may not have been surprising given the value he attached to intuition as a guide for assessing human character. What was particularly disturbing, though, was his apparent unawareness that one man's intuition could be another's prejudice. And was Mori entirely free of social and political bias?

The question of whether, or to what extent, the mafia was an organisation tended to be coloured by juridical demands. In his first book, written in 1923, Mori claimed that the mafia 'always falls just short of what is needed for it to be a criminal association in the eyes of the law'.[49] In his memoirs, published nine years later, he was apparently of a different persuasion: 'Whatever form it takes and however it acts, the mafia, by its very nature, constitutes...the typical kind [*la figura tipica*] of criminal association.'[50] This change of mind was probably due to the fact that in 1932 Mori was having to defend his *retate* against political opponents who had accused him of excess and arbitrariness. There was also, in the early 1930s, a legal debate about criminal association which seriously called into question the appropriateness of using this charge with the mafia.

Mori was above all a man of action. Unless he had a legal pretext for arresting and holding people against whom there were no specific indictments, but who were nevertheless regarded by the authorities as *mafiosi*, he knew that his campaign would founder. Criminal association had tactical advantages which he could not afford to overlook. As he explained to Federzoni in 1926, it allowed the police 'to move freely and act swiftly', and was particularly useful when it came to individual crimes that could no longer be considered 'ongoing' (*flagrante*). Criminal association constituted a form of permanent offence and the culprits could be arrested and held as if they had been caught in the act. Without it, Mori said, the police in Sicily would have been 'almost disarmed'.[51]

Mori was aware that his methods might lead to arbitrariness: 'Nobody is infallible', he told Federzoni.[52] Strict justice, however, was ultimately not his main concern. His primary objective was to demonstrate the power of the state. The mafia existed, he believed, because the authorities had been weak, and great *retate* would show forcibly how times had changed. In some ways this was a curious view. Could the problem really have been the state's weakness (in the sense of its incapacity to coerce), if Sicilian history had been punctuated by a succession of police and military operations of just the kind that Mori himself was undertaking? Might the real issue not have been, at least in part, the moral character of the state? For even after 1860, Sicilians had often viewed it as an alien force, which exacted and repressed, and gave nothing in return.

In fairness to Mori, police operations were only intended as one aspect of his campaign. He also set store by education and propaganda as means of influencing attitudes and behaviour, and he did his best to promote agriculture. Indeed, he sometimes claimed that the *retate* were just a way of creating the right psychological environment for moral growth,[53] but this was unduly optimistic. There was the same flaw in Mori's approach to the mafia as in fascism's response to the Southern Question. His operation had the effect of strengthening the *agrari*, and suppressing those elements (the intransigent fascists included) who threatened change. Was it realistic to suppose that the masses could be drawn into the state if the regime had nothing to offer them in economic and social terms? Was there not a case for saying, ironically, that Mori's campaign enhanced the need for the mafia? With such limited opportunities in Sicily, how else, as the socialist Sebastiano Cammareri Scurti said in 1899, could one hope to succeed in life?[54]

Fascism's attitude to Mori and the mafia

The siege of Gangi made Mori into a national hero. Mussolini's newspaper, *Il Popolo d'Italia*, described him as a man of 'strong and beautiful Italic cast'. 'Throughout his long apostolate', it said, 'he has maintained a position of intransigent inflexibility.'[55] The *Corriere della Sera* went further, and in a series of articles in February 1926 it mythologised not only Mori, but the entire Gangi operation. The meeting between Spanò and Ferrarello, the paper claimed, had never materialised: the bandit had lost his nerve and failed to turn up. The siege owed its success to Mori's ultimatum: his reputation was such that the brigands had dared not disobey. The local population loved Mori, and when he came to Gangi he was welcomed, 'almost like Garibaldi'. Some people, according to the *Corriere*, even referred to him as a 'saint', and when he was ill the women of Monreale lit candles in church and asked Our Lady to speed his recovery.[56]

Though such myths had an obvious propaganda value, they could not be carried too far. The campaign against the mafia had as one of its aims to draw Sicily into the state. If the national press made too much of the mafia, the ghost of *sicilianismo* might be raised. Telesio Interlandi, the Sicilian editor of *Il Tevere*, was in fact incensed by the articles in the *Corriere della Sera*. It was ridiculous, he said in a leading article, to inflate the police operations to heroic proportions and then add that it was only a matter of a few hundred common criminals; if that were the case, why titillate people with fantastic stories of whole provinces under the sway of a great criminal organisation?

> The mainland reader will be horrified; the Sicilian holds his tongue, proud but aggrieved, aware that he is paying the moral price for that touristic snobbery which permits people to switch with ease from a description of a famous lawn-tennis competition on the regal courts of Cannes to the examination of an ethnic problem whose roots lie very deep, and which has in some respects an unimagined nobility.[57]

Interlandi's anger was not just at journalistic insensitivity. He wanted to emphasise that the mafia was more than a problem of law and order: 'Instead of the mafia, we must talk of *latifondi*, malaria, lack of communications.' This, he said with a hint of admonishment, was already well understood. Mori had been entrusted with 'cauterisation', but a lasting solution lay with a programme of public works, 'which Mussolini's government has already studied and begun'. Interlandi was known to be close to the Duce – it is just conceivable that this article had received his blessing.[58] If there was an 'official' line on Mori, it probably lay somewhere between the sensationalism of the *Corriere della Sera* and Interlandi's indignant circumspection. Two articles on Sicily that appeared in *Il Popolo d'Italia* early in 1926 adopted this middle course.[59]

Between 1922 and 1925, the debate on the mafia was broadly divided between advocates of repression and those who believed in a socio-economic solution. Opinions were varied, but in general they conformed to political positions. Intellectuals of liberal formation, for example, emphasised environmental factors. According to Gaetano Navarra Crimi, crime in Sicily was a social phenomenon whose roots lay deep in the economic fabric of the island: the answer, he said, was to divide up the *latifondi* and improve communications.[60] A writer in *L'Ora*, at the end of 1924, agreed with Crimi in general terms, but attached greater importance to public works.[61] A less reductionistic approach was taken by the well-known agriculturalist, Giovanni Lorenzoni. It was impossible, he said, to deal with one Sicilian problem without tackling the others simultaneously. Mafia, *latifondo*, malaria, water, roads, and railways were all related: 'These factors, natural and social, are closely interdependent in the sense that they are at one and the same time both cause and effect.'[62]

Many people found the socio-economic view of the mafia unacceptable. The *agrari* disliked it; so too did many intransigent fascists, though for different reasons. The former admitted that lawlessness was the essence of the problem, but they would not accept that the explanation was social. Like Mori, they preferred to regard the mafia as a consequence of the state's weakness. However, after the March on Rome, the landowners were noticeably restrained in their demands for repressive action, despite the continuing high levels of crime in western Sicily. This was probably owing to the fact that radical fascists were now combining the issue of law and order with the idea of destroying liberal clienteles. Many landowners were accordingly wary, and, when threatened with anti-mafia action in the period from 1923 to 1925, they frequently adopted a defensive stance.

Some of the opposition's underlying concerns can be detected in an article published in the Palermo weekly, *Il Martello*, at the end of 1923. Fascism, it said, had no purpose in Sicily; accordingly, and for political reasons, it discovered the mafia: 'When Don Quixote

decided to attack the windmill he had to picture it as a noble knight.
. . . Sicilian fascism is being forced to do likewise. . . with that edifice
– if such it is – called the mafia.' Law and order, the article stressed,
was an issue for the policeman and not the politician. Moreover,
criminal activity was neither peculiar to Sicily nor its most pressing
problem: 'You should not erect, and certainly not just in Sicily, a
gaudy political scarecrow that will absorb the entire programme and
activities of a party, when questions of much greater importance
have for many years been awaiting a solution.'[63]

The drift here towards *sicilianismo* found its ultimate expression in
the idea that the mafia did not exist. Salvatore Cicala voiced this view
in a Catania newspaper shortly after the start of Mori's campaign.
Sicily, he said, like other regions, had its criminals and organised
crime; but the mafia was a figment of the popular and mainland
imagination. It was not only an error, but was also 'materially and
morally damaging' to the social prosperity of the island.[64] This
nominalist attitude has frequently been regarded as one of self-
defence on the part of the mafia. However, in this case the provenance
was almost certainly eastern-seaboard and commercial, a sphere not
noted for its criminal connections. The point Cicala wanted to make
was that by focusing on a largely illusory problem, the government
was avoiding the challenge of more complex social and economic
issues.

The debate on the mafia lost intensity after 1925, but fascism still
sought an official interpretation. The drift, as with the Southern
Question, was towards a moral and political perspective. The mafia
was now seen as a 'state within the state', with its own laws, tribunals, and taxes. It was thus an impediment to national integration,
and incompatible with fascism: 'Fascism and mafia', said Mori in
1928, 'are irredeemably antithetical. Fascism is the state in all its force
and prestige.'[65] On occasions, the depiction of the mafia as an autonomous political entity received elaborate treatment. The Procurator
General of the Court of Cassation said in January 1927 that the organisation had 'hierarchies, disciplinary powers, and a well-structured
tribute system of tithes, taxes, tolls and impositions'. It had extended
its sovereignty, he claimed, over the entire island, and it held the
state authorities in subjection.[66]

The corollary to this idea of a 'state within a state' was that Sicily's
absorption into the regime would only come about with the elimination of the mafia. This entailed making the island fascist. However,
the argument for greater civic and national awareness in Sicily and
the South also had a distinguished liberal tradition. It is therefore not
surprising that a writer in Piero Gobetti's *La Rivoluzione liberale*
could suggest in October 1925 that the answer to the mafia lay with
'an enlightened and clear-sighted process of political education'. It

was not a question, he said, of a particular mentality or a criminal association: the mafia was the 'spontaneous organisation' of that section of society 'which had failed to understand the basic reasons for the unity and centrality of the state'. The only way to get rid of *mafiosi* was to make the idea of Italy into 'a living experience'. Sicilians, he said, had to learn 'the necessity of the state'.[67]

The idea of Mori's campaign as an act of political and social education was particularly appealing to the criminologist and former left-wing firebrand, Enrico Ferri. In an article in 1928, he said that the decision to crush the mafia had been the result of Mussolini's 'lofty view of the fascist state and Italic civilisation'.[68] Ferri had been to Sicily and witnessed how, under Mori's guidance, a new climate was emerging in Sicily based on 'order, peace, hard work and belief in the state's authority'.[69] When he reported his impressions to Mussolini, Ferri was told: 'All is well: the wound has been cauterised: from now on we must see to the diathesis of the blood.' This remark, Ferri explained, was fully in keeping with positivist criminology which held that repressive measures had to be underpinned by social reforms.[70]

In practice, fascist political education had little time for social and economic change. Traditional views on the Southern Question were accordingly up-ended. Destroy the mafia, the argument now ran, teach Sicilians that they were first and foremost Italians, and the results would be the birth of political consciousness and a string of material benefits. This was naïve and also somewhat fraudulent, for the government knew well that an alliance with the *agrari* condemned Sicily to backwardness and reaction. Mussolini had to face up to this in later years. The *agrari*, he confessed to Yvon De Begnac in 1939, were not interested in collective social and economic needs; they had been much happier with the mafia than the rule of law: 'The day I set up a Piedmontese administration down there, I will be able to consider many problems solved. Mori will then belong to the prehistory of the island.'[71]

7 THE POLICE OPERATIONS

The arrests

Mori regarded the siege of Gangi as the most significant operation in the campaign against the mafia. That is why it received so much publicity. Though in reality the episode was unsavoury and in many ways ignominious, it was the myth that counted. The aim was to destroy any vestiges of romanticism surrounding men of violence, and make it seem that the state finally had the upper hand in Sicily. The illusion of success was important from a practical point of view, as it would give people the confidence, Mori believed, to renounce *omertà* and collaborate with the police. He felt that if the government were thought to be winning, the mafia would automatically lose face and hence power. This helps to explain his interest in the press: he saw it as an instrument for creating the climate of opinion most conducive to the state's victory.[1]

Mori had a firm belief in amateur psychology. He regarded most people as extremely manipulable, and this is one reason why he thought an understanding of human nature was important in the battle against the mafia: 'There is no need for books', he told a university conference in 1928, in explanation of how to solve Sicily's problems, '. . . nor dusty archives. On those cold and lifeless pages you would find the pale reflections of men who were all too often . . . spiritual eunuchs. What you need is a brief visit to the warm and vibrant regions of psychology, in other words, humanity.'[2] Mori's view of personal behaviour was somewhat mechanistic, and it bordered at times on the naïve. It led him to underestimate the intelligence and moral sensibility of others, particularly the Sicilian peasantry, and this dulled him to the complex relationship of means to ends.

In August 1926, Mori told the Minister of the Interior that the success at Gangi had stunned the criminal world into silence:

> In order to give the mafia and *malvivenza* no time to recover from the surprise, I went on immediately to attack every other position,

with tremendous energy, resolution, and speed. I proceeded from area to area, and criminal association to criminal association. The strongest, most terrifying members of the operational mafia [*mafia militante*] were my principal targets. Till then they had been considered untouchable.

He listed two dozen towns in the province of Palermo that had been subject to police action. They included Bisacquino ('notorious in the island's criminal history, and stronghold of a highly controversial deputy, Hon. Lo Monte') and Villabate ('a very dangerous centre, stronghold of Hon. Cirincione'). Major operations had also been conducted in the province of Messina, and in a number of towns in Catania, Caltanissetta, and Girgenti. Success had been so complete, he said, that public and judiciary alike could only look on in admiration.[3] How had all this been achieved?

The bulk of the police enquiries were carried out by the Interprovincial Service for Public Security. This was a mobile force which Mori had set up while prefect of Trapani. In structure, as well as personnel, it owed something to the *squadriglie* of the First World War. Each unit consisted of about two dozen men, and was assigned to a 'zone of action' of seven or eight towns.[4] The rank and file was made up of *carabinieri*, but the unit leaders were drawn for the most part from the police.[5] This was to cause a good deal of resentment. The *questore* of Palermo justified the imbalance by saying that the *carabinieri* had too many distracting duties to be entrusted with 'diligent' enquiries. Furthermore, he added, many of them were young and inexperienced, and 'unable to fathom with their intuition the more complicated forms of Sicilian crime'.[6] This may have been true, but it was conducive to neither harmony nor efficiency. As the campaign proceeded, and hostility to Mori increased, a number of *carabinieri* sought deliberately to undermine police enquiries, either from a sense of pique or for local political reasons.

Mori informed the Minister of the Interior in late-summer 1926 that 'those arrested for criminal association are always denounced for specific crimes as well'.[7] The last eight words were underlined in his report. This statement was in fact untrue. Nearly half of the accused at the Madonie trial, for example, were charged simply with criminal association, and this was by no means exceptional. At Corleone, only fifty-nine of the 128 defendants were indicted for anything other than criminal association, while at Roccella the proportion was even less: thirty out of 174.[8] Roccella may well have been more typical than either Corleone or the Madonie, which were both areas with notoriously high crime rates. However, specific charges did figure prominently in all the trials, and it was with these that the police usually began.

The first step was to reopen old dossiers. At Piana dei Colli more than a decade and a half of criminal activity was reinvestigated, and the enquiries took five months to conclude.[9] Many of the resuscitated cases related to the period immediately after the war, when crimes and acquittals for lack of evidence had been numerous. The sentence of the Corleone *istruttoria* (preliminary investigation), for example, contained many entries like that for Francesco Leone:

> The police have indicated him as affiliated to the mafia, and his criminal record shows that in 1919 he was sentenced by the *Corte d'Assise* of Palermo to three years and two months in prison, and a fine of 88,50 lire for private violence [*violenza privata*], inflicting gunshot wounds and carrying arms, while he was acquitted by the same court of two thefts.

Fresh evidence had apparently came to light in the course of investigations made in 1926, and on the basis of this Leone was re-arrested.[10]

Unlike Leone, the majority of the accused at Corleone had no criminal records and the evidence against them often seems to have been circumstantial. This may well have been the case, for instance, with Francesco Di Palermo:

> Son of the above accused, Calogero Di Palermo, he too has been denounced for complicity in the murder of Giovanni Gagliano (see attached document No. 9) – Although he has no criminal record, the police affirm in the report, on page 30 of the same document, that he has been of no small help to his father in his criminal activities. One gathers from the witness Andrea Rizzo on page 40 of the same document (No. 9) that Francesco Di Palermo has also been involved with his father in guarding the estates. He was 'extremely exacting and demanded his rights as a *campiere* in a *mafioso* way'.[11]

This statement formed part of the *istruttoria* of the Corleone trial. It was the product of more lengthy enquiries than the police would have made initially. It does however suggest the lines along which Mori's Interprovincial Service operated before the authorities proceeded to the issue of arrest warrants.

Precisely how denunciations were obtained remains a source of conjecture. At Villalba, the police were said to have employed a common criminal. They allegedly paid him for his services and he became a wealthy *campiere*.[12] Collusion of this kind was probably not uncommon. One of the more important sources of evidence at Corleone was an illiterate peasant called Gaetano Di Puma. He had been arrested by mistake, he said, 'because I got confused in giving my particulars, and instead of Di Puma, the *carabinieri* understood Pomilla'. However, he was sure that he would soon be released, 'because I have been an honest worker and have not committed any crime'. His denunciations were full and specific, and would certainly have caused him trouble with the local community. Reading between the lines, one can guess that collaboration with the authorities was the price he had to pay for impunity. [13]

Sometimes the prosecution case rested on different kinds of evidence. At Mistretta, for example, in the province of Messina, personal denunciations were supplemented by incriminating correspondence. Early in December 1925, the house of an influential local lawyer called Antonino Ortoleva was searched. The police already had their suspicions about him, and the following month he was taken into custody. After his arrest, another search was conducted, and this time ninety letters were discovered in his study. They apparently revealed the existence of a large criminal organisation of which the lawyer was the undisputed head. [14] It was chiefly on the basis of these letters that 161 people were later brought to trial for membership of what became known as the 'interprovincial mafia'.

Encouraged by Ortoleva's arrest, denunciations against him now began to emerge. As a rule in judicial proceedings, it was wisest to kick a man only when he was down. Early in February, an opponent of Ortoleva, Paolo Timpanaro, sent a letter to the sub-prefect of Mistretta. He confessed that he had once been involved with criminals, but after a spell of military service, he had returned to Mistretta and decided to get married, and go straight. However, his erstwhile associates had refused to leave him in peace. They had stolen his cattle, cut down his vines, burnt his hay-ricks, forced out his employees, and threatened his life. His enemies constituted the local mafia, and he claimed that its head was Antonino Ortoleva; indeed, he said, it was in the study of Ortoleva's house that the mafia assembled to deliberate and pass judgement. [15]

Though parts of Timpanaro's letter rang false (particularly in his description of Ortoleva's 'court'), the police used it to confirm their views about the local mafia and bring further charges. No doubt a chain reaction was set in motion, with arrests leading to more denunciations, and more denunciations leading to further arrests. This was clearly the case at Corleone where the initial *retata* in December 1926 was followed by additional police operations as fresh evidence came to light. [16] An important spur to collaboration with the authorities was the need to pre-empt opponents. Timpanaro had been closely involved with a number of Ortoleva's followers: he might have feared that they would denounce him first, convince the police of their own version of events, and secure immunity from prosecution.

Great insecurity must have prevailed in towns such as Corleone when police enquiries were underway. A circular sent by the Federation of the Palermo Servicemen to all its dependent sections at the end of January 1926 strongly suggests that fear was widespread. A number of 'criminals', it reported, had been spreading malicious gossip about Mori and his work. They had claimed that he was insulting Sicily and violating civil liberties. This, the circular said, was untrue. What is more, there was a rumour abroad that the police intended to arrest and deport anyone with a criminal record. Such allegations were as ruinous as they were unfounded: 'While many *latitanti* are giving themselves up, citizens, whom no one has accused, are abandoning their homes simply because of the rumours. They are thereby putting themselves in a position where they might commit crimes or else be accused by public opinion of misdemeanours which took place in their absence.' The local Servicemen's leaders were urged to persuade people of the truly 'patriotic' character of Mori's work, and make it clear that even those with criminal records were perfectly safe provided they did not commit fresh offences.[17]

Mori was naturally interested in the problem of *latitanti*; but he was more concerned to stop wanted men from escaping in the first place. The centrality of this issue determined the tactics of his *retate*. The police would conduct the initial enquiries secretly and then withdraw from the area for a time, to induce a false sense of security. After a while, they would descend, usually at night, and catch their victims unaware. To seal off the main escape routes, and minimise what Mori called 'waves of *latitanza*', the *retate* were spread over several neighbouring towns simultaneously.[18] All this made sense in theory; whether it worked in practice was another matter. At Corleone, the main body of arrests took place in the early hours of 20 December 1926. The police were searching for 159 men, but they found less than half of them; three weeks later there were still fifty-five people unaccounted for.[19]

Though Mori's *retate* were less successful than either his memoirs or his reports to the Ministry of the Interior implied, they were nonetheless effective. However, their success derived largely from the fact that hostages (usually relatives of the accused) were seized when a wanted man could not be found. Mori was reticent about this aspect of his campaign. In his memoirs there was merely a cryptic allusion to 'suspects' who were arrested along with those 'against whom there was evidence'.[20] He was only marginally less reserved with the Minister of the Interior. In August 1926, Federzoni was told that some women had 'inevitably' been taken into custody, 'for enquiries or to make a *latitante* or two [*qualche latitante*] surrender', but such instances were 'very few'.[21] In fact, Mori's *retate* included large numbers of hostages of both sexes.

A report sent by Vice-Prefect De Feo to Mori early in February 1927 gives some idea of what was happening. In order, De Feo said, to induce the *latitanti* of San Lorenzo ai Colli to surrender, their families had been taken in and detained at the Palagonia Hostel for the Poor in Palermo. The commissioner at the hostel had received the following instructions:

> For the time being, and until further orders, 69 women, 17 men, 65 boys and 62 girls are to be housed in this institute: in total 213 people, all from the area of S. Lorenzo. . . . Babies and children of both sexes under eight should stay with their respective mothers, who will be lodged in the female section in Via Malaspina. Boys over eight, and men, will be divided according to age, and housed in the male section in Via Malaspina. Girls of eight and over, and unmarried women, will go to Corso Calatafimi. . . . They will all be escorted by police who will furnish their particulars. These can be used to make the necessary distribution into categories.

Vice-Prefect De Feo concluded by saying that Mori's request that the hostages be treated as well as possible had been conveyed to the commissioner.[22]

Mori claimed that his tactics had an excellent effect on public opinion. After all, was the Sicilian peasant not strongly impressed by force? He told Federzoni that the *retate* were just what was needed in Sicily, for they generated 'the state of mind most conducive to success'.[23] Everywhere and in all classes, he said, there was 'enthusiasm' for his work. Not only was this destroying the mafia, but it was also making the island into a bastion of fascism: 'In the towns and the countryside, the majority of the population, from the aristocracy down to the peasants, now liberated and at peace, is turning with enthusiasm, in thought and spirit, to the national government and its leader.'[24]

Mori had obvious reasons for saying that his campaign was popular. It gave legitimacy to his work, and also helped to counter the accusations of his critics. Indeed, as complaints against him mounted, so too, it seemed, did the enthusiasm of the masses: 'The population,' he told the Ministry of the Interior in November 1927, when opposition to him was at fever pitch, '. . . is unanimously and enthusiastically with us, with the national government, in other words – and above all – with its head. The request is only that we go right to the end.'[25] Public opinion is naturally hard to gauge. Big occasions undoubtedly produced large crowds, and the crowds cheered. Quite what that meant, though, is not certain.

A sober picture of popular feeling towards Mori's work was given by the American sociologist, Charlotte Gower Chapman. In her study of Milocca (the small community in the province of Caltanissetta where she lived in 1928 and 1929), uncertainty, fear, and a degree of indifference seem to have been the main collective emotions. On her arrival in the town, bearing a letter of introduction

Pl. 11. The main street of Milocca in 1928.

from Mori, the rumour quickly spread that she was conducting criminal enquiries. The inhabitants went out of their way to please her, and every arrested man was described as 'entirely innocent and a true saint'. Nevertheless, she said that the government's work against crime in Sicily 'was always praised', and a few people 'went so far as to suggest that the cleansing had not been so thorough as it might have been'.[26] In an insecure world, it was clearly wise to humour one's neighbours.

The arrests were not greeted in Milocca with any evident sense of relief or enthusiasm:

The police descended in force, by night, and proceeded to make their arrests. Some of their victims escaped, in spite of the suddenness of the attack, but the members of their families were taken and held in their stead. If this did not produce the desired persons, all their livestock was confiscated.... No one felt safe. A bride who set out to make her nuptial calls was ordered back to her home, for this was no time to be abroad. Pity was mixed with fear, pity for the unhappy animals, the bereft families, the arrested men, and even for the police, who had come without adequate provisions and had to beg bread from the terrified townspeople. Finally the police and their captives set off to Mussomeli, a dis-

153

tance of more than ten miles over difficult country, taking with them the families and flocks belonging to the men who had not as yet given themselves up.[27]

Between thirty and fifty men were arrested in Milocca on this occasion: 'A few had been taken earlier, and arrests continued from time to time for more than a year, as bits of information implicated more persons'. By the autumn of 1928, about a hundred Milocchese were in prison awaiting trial. For a town with a population of around two and a half thousand, this was a substantial figure.[28] As a result of the arrests, the prevailing atmosphere, as described by Chapman, was mournful:

> Religious occasions were not celebrated with the usual splendor, for most of the men who had been active in such affairs were behind the bars. Prison-widows were numerous, and some were in serious financial difficulties so that for a time relief was administered to them in the form of free meals and condensed milk and flour for nursing mothers. The funds for this relief were soon exhausted. One woman had deviated from the path of virtue in the absence of her husband, and was condemned as much for her levity in a time of bereavement as for her unchastity.[29]

The arrest of the Milocca mafia was regarded not so much as a liberation, it would seem, but as a collective loss. It was as if a natural disaster had struck.

The arrested

Charlotte Chapman gave no indication that local attitudes towards the state were altering as a result of Mori's work. The *carabiniere* was still considered 'a stranger to the community', and villagers displayed their traditional mistrust of the police by being 'correct but uncooperative'.[30] She detected greater sympathy and understanding for the offender than the authorities: criminals were often regarded, she said, as the victims of injustice, as the law was held to be inefficient and venal.[31] Many crimes went undetected, while in general, the rich fared far better in their encounters with officialdom than the poor and weak. The law, in short, was not necessarily equated with justice in Milocca.[32]

The great majority of those arrested by Mori were of humble status, but the heads of the criminal associations were usually parvenus. Their wealth was said to have been ill-gotten: 'By birth, the leaders were poor,' said a newspaper account of the Palazzo Adriano mafia, 'but today they are all landowners. In order to gua-

rantee their positions, they imposed agricultural and livestock societies on honest proprietors, in an attempt to convince people that their
wealth had come from legitimate sources.'[33] An article in *L'Ora* in
February 1926 spoke in more detailed terms about the principal
mafiosi of Misilmeri:

> Giuseppe Di Palermo...was a humble cobbler in 1919; today he is
> worth more than half a million. Serafino Di Peri has assets of over
> 200,000 lire, but until 1919 he had barely five hectares of unre-
> munerative land. Giuseppe Di Silvestri had three or four thousand
> lire in 1920, but now has an estate worth about 100,000 lire.[34]

Such men were held to have prospered at the expense of the landowners. 'The activity of the mafia', said the Corleone *istruttoria*, 'was
most apparent in the concession of leases on estates, which were extracted from the owners at ridiculously low prices. No one could re-
fuse them for fear of reprisals...The *gabelloti* then sublet the land
to the peasants at an enormous profit.'[35] Additional sources of gain,
both at Corleone and elsewhere, were brokerage and speculation. It
was probably no coincidence that the towns that witnessed the greatest redistribution of land after the First World War were also those in
which mafia activity was considered to be most vigorous. The formation of small property in this period was much more intense in the
west of the island than in the east. Among the centres most affected
were Corleone, Mussomeli, Collesano, Caltavuturo, Piazza Armerina, Mistretta, and Palazzo Adriano.[36]

The dynamics of the redistribution process can be seen from the
case of the Belici *feudo* at Villalba. In September 1920, peasants
organised by the Servicemen, *popolari* (left-wing Catholic party), and
socialists occupied this and other estates in the area. The big
landowners were natually concerned. They approached Don Calogero Vizzini, and asked him to intervene on their behalf, and save
them from having to make too many concessions. Vizzini had no
wish simply to be exploited: he saw a way of turning the situation to
his own advantage by mediating between the two groups. Negotiations began, and in March 1921, Matteo Guccione, the proprietor
of the Belici *feudo*, sold the estate for 2,750,000 lire to the *popolari*
represented by Calogero Vizzini, his brother Don Salvatore (who
acted as president of the Agricultural Co-operative for Ex-Servicemen
of Villalba) and the archpriest, Angelo Scarlata, head of a local bank,
the Cassa Rurale S. Giuseppe.[37]

For Guccione, this sale was highly advantageous, at least financial-
ly. Earlier, he had been forced to surrender about 350 hectares to the
Servicemen for a peppercorn rent of one *terragio*, and the *popolari*
would probably have demanded similar terms. By selling the estate,
he had spared himself further dealings with the peasantry. He had

also secured an excellent price for it (2,300 lire per hectare), with payment to be made in cash by the following September. The savings of the Cassa Rurale – 400,000 lire – were given to him as a deposit, with the understanding that if the remaining 2,350,000 lire was not handed over by the following September, then the contract would be void; in that case Guccione would keep the deposit, 'as compensation'. This was a hazardous venture, as it was almost inconceivable that the Cassa Rurale could acquire over 2 million lire in just four months.

Fortunately for the peasants, Guccione did not press his case. Only in June 1922, with the money still unforthcoming, did he try to reclaim the land. However, at this point a loan was secured from the Bank of Sicily, and the sale went through. The Belici estate should now have been split up among the peasants; but for another four years the co-operative held on to the *feudo* as the self-styled 'provisional owner', and continued to receive rent for it. When anyone asked why the property was not being allocated to the members of the co-operative, he was told that it was because some of the land was held, through a prefectural decree, by the Servicemen. If the questioner persisted, and sought to know why their share – four-fifths of the whole – had not been distributed, he was probably asked to keep quiet. In 1926 the *feudo* finally began to be divided up, and only then did the peasants start to repay the loan.

It is not known what happened to the 6,000 or so quintals of grain which the co-operative received as rent between 1921 and 1926. Calogero Vizzini was alleged to have been a major beneficiary. He certainly did well out of the final distribution of the Belici estate. The only condition of sale was a down payment of 60% of the purchase price: this excluded all but the wealthiest buyers. As a result, 28% of the *feudo* ended up in the hands of twelve people. Vizzini himself bought thirty-eight hectares of the finest land for 70,000 lire. He also acquired a number of lots in his sister's name. However, his good fortune was short-lived, as in 1928 he went on trial for criminal association.[38] He was eventually acquitted, but he nonetheless spent five years in prison and lost, by his own admission, half his possessions.[39]

One feature of the Belici affair was the owner's apparent willingness to sell; yet throughout Mori's campaign it was continually stated that the *agrari* had been forced to part with their property. Perhaps the most frequent charge against *mafiosi* (apart from criminal association) was private violence (*violenza privata*), and this usually related to intimidation over land sales or to the imposition of personnel on the *latifondi*. However, the idea that the *agrari* were the hapless victims of men of violence was probably only partially true. Coercion was undoubtedly involved in some property deals, but it is also the case that owners could welcome the opportunity to acquire extra capital.[40] In retrospect, the sale price might seem paltry, as inflation was high after the war, and cash transactions soon lost their value. This made it tempting for the *agrari* to lay the blame for their financial plight at the feet of the *nouveaux riches*.

The imposition of personnel on farms was also not as clear-cut as the police made out. Demobilisation led to a great deal of confusion after the war. Competition for jobs was intense; and those who became *campieri* or *guardiani* may well have been unusually assertive. Furthermore, many landowners must have been under strong pressure to find additional posts for the friends and relatives of employees, but this was only to be expected. The important question was how far the *agrari* acted against their will. Estates, after all, needed protection, and violent field guards were a distinct asset when the peasantry was unruly and the crime rate high. Whether these field guards were criminals, or party to criminal activity, was by and large irrelevant. Indeed, the issue tended only to arise with a crack-down on the mafia when the police had to confront the awkward problem of complicity. In such circumstances, the *agrari* had an obvious interest in claiming that they had been the victims of private violence, and had been 'forced' to protect *mafiosi* or bandits.

Though the most influential and affluent of the people arrested by Mori were *gabelloti* and medium landowners, they constituted a small percentage of those implicated in the criminal associations. Of the 129 defendants in the Corleone trial for whom status or profession were given,[41] only twenty-two called themselves 'landowners' (*possidente, proprietario*). The remainder included sixty-three 'peasants' (*contadini*), five shoemakers, four shepherds, four carters, four farmers (*agricoltori*), two who held small areas of land *in gabella*, two 'wealthy peasants' (*borgesi*), two traders (*trafficanti*), and two bricklayers. The others had a variety of jobs ranging from shopkeepers to barbers. Only one man was described as a day labourer (*bracciante*).[42] The term 'peasant' (*contadino*) was no doubt broad, and this makes the precise status of half of the accused at Corleone difficult to establish. However, they presumably saw themselves as being distinct from proprietors and day labourers. It is important to note that the landowners (*possidenti* and *proprietari*) arrested at Corleone did not belong to the class of *agrari*. They were men of peasant origin, and were in some cases described as illiterate.

The social mix of the criminal association of Corleone was probably not unrepresentative of the rural mafia that formed the principal target of Mori's campaign. Of the thirty-five people wanted by the police at Contessa Entellina in May 1926, eleven belonged to a prosperous family of *gabelloti*, ten were peasant smallholders, and four were shepherds. The remainder consisted of two *campieri*, two artisans, one carter, two day labourers, one butcher, and two women.[43] The ten smallholders would probably have been classified at Corleone as 'contadini'. The family of gabelloti were parvenus who had begun to acquire property of their own and speculate on its transfer.[44] The local agrari had clearly suffered at their hands and apparently provided the police with evidence against them.[45]

Most of those arrested in the campaign of 1925–9 belonged to the intermediate levels of rural society. There were very few day labourers or proletarians (viddani). This tallied with Mori's succinct dismissal of any connection between mafia and poverty: 'Poverty', he wrote, 'can cause petty crime: produce mafia, no'.[46] This claim, however, was perhaps no more than partially valid. It was certainly true that those who remained poor were unlikely to be designated mafiosi: the word usually had connotations of power and authority. Nevertheless, the term could also imply a degree of ambition, and in western Sicily, where status was keenly felt and resources were limited, violence often appeared the only avenue to wealth. Fear of poverty arguably lay at the root of much mafia behaviour. This, however, was not something that Mori wished to highlight or perhaps even consider.

The police arrested 'mafiosi'; yet as Mori admitted a 'mafioso' was not easily defined. The issue was particularly complicated given the fact that mafioso was an epithet that people attached to others; rarely would a man apply it to himself.[47] How, then, was this epithet used, and what did it mean? Was it always synonymous with criminal activity? Giuseppe Pitré had maintained that 'mafia' and 'mafioso' only began to acquire evil connotations after 1860, prior to which the words signified beauty, grace, and perfection.[48] Gaetano Mosca claimed in 1900 that Sicilians still used the terms to describe positive attributes; and in 1925, Orlando was warmly applauded at an election rally for listing the virtues of 'mafia' and declaring himself happy to be called 'mafioso'.[49] With such different meanings of the word 'mafia' there was clearly room for confusion. Some of the semantic difficulties emerge from the transcripts of the hearings for the Corleone criminal association.

The Corleone 'criminal association'

Following the arrests in Corleone at the end of 1926, the police produced a long report on the town's mafia. It had been organised, they said, 'a long time back', and its undisputed head, until his death in July 1924, was Michelangelo Gennaro.[50] 'All this emerged from our first enquiries, and we realised how much power criminals had wielded here when we began to interrogate the victims. We noticed that even today, four years into the New Era, those that had suffered trembled (*tremevano*) at the slightest mention of the members of the vast association.' The leaders of the Corleone mafia met, according to the police, in the Agricultural Circle, 'otherwise known as the *Casino* [club] of the Mafia'. It was there that they organised 'the most atrocious crimes, and entrusted their execution to one of the others, commonly called *picciotti*.'[51]

The police were concerned to demonstrate that the Corleone mafia was an organisation with a strict hierarchy and a headquarters. The reason for this was clear: the majority of those arrested were charged simply with criminal association. The police based their arguments (and presumably many of their inquiries too) on the contention that the Agricultural Circle had for some time been known locally as the '*casino* of the Mafia'. The centrality of this point emerges from the *istruttoria*, where the accused were all questioned about their links with the Circle. Those that admitted membership were at pains to deny that anything illegal had ever taken place there. Witnesses, too, had to make statements about the Circle: 'The names I gave in my declaration', said Salvatore Labruzzi at the trial, 'belonged to people who frequented the Circle, and not to mafia people.'[52] However, the evidence that the Circle was indeed known as the '*casino* of the Mafia' was sparse and contradictory. Moreover, nothing was adduced to support the claim that it was here that the town's criminal activities were masterminded.

One problem, as the police themselves admitted, was that few witnesses could be found to testify before the arrests were made. Those that did come forward made full and dogmatic statements that at times seem forced. Leoluca Marsala was a member of the fascist Militia. As such, he said, he felt duty-bound to follow the orders of the Duce, 'who to the good fortune of Italy, rules the destinies of the country. Here, to the shame of Corleone, the mafia and crime have held sway'. He spoke of the Agricultural Circle, confirmed that it was known as the '*casino* of the Mafia', and denounced its members.[53] Another witness (whose patriotic declarations suggest that he too was a fascist) talked of the 'so-called group of the mafia', whose associates 'had a circle in the Piazza in front of the urinals'. Their building, he said, was 'commonly' known as the '*casino* of the mafia'.[54]

Assuming that the soubriquet '*casino* of the mafia' had been current before December 1926, what did it mean? The evidence is hard to interpret, but it looks as if 'mafia' and '*mafioso*' were highly emotive words that were often used vituperatively in Corleone. However, this was not always the case, it would seem: 'Most people did not regard him as *mafioso* if by that you mean a criminal', said a priest at the trial, 'because in Corleone the word also gets applied to someone who simply adopts a brazen manner [*un atteggiamento spavaldo*].'[55]

Pietro Cipolla, the local bandmaster, said that his pupil, Giovanni Ricciardi, could not have been a *mafioso*: 'I used to . . . clip him round the ear when he made a mistake in some piece of music and he never tried to hit me back. If he had been a *mafioso* he would have reacted differently.'[56] Even if such statements were only partial truths, it is nevertheless clear that scope existed for genuine confusion.

The police, however, were in no position to equivocate: they needed cut and dried statements. 'All the names that figure in my declarations', said a witness, Giovanni Palazzo, rather pathetically, 'were not given by me, but by the *carabinieri* and the judge. When they asked me if they were *mafiosi*, I said they were, not because I knew them personally but because that is what I had heard.'[57] The police were often inclined to present hearsay as fact, and many witnesses at the trial felt constrained to clarify exactly what it was they had said in the *istruttoria*. 'I reported what I felt to be the general view,' said Vincenzo Randisi. 'For my own part, I have no grounds for specific complaints against the people I named.'[58]

Some witnesses introduced a political note into their statements. 'When I named those men to the police', said Vincenzo Schillaci, 'I referred only to public opinion, according to which the opponents of the socialists were *mafiosi*.'[59] In Liborio Anzalone's view, Giuseppe Di Carlo was *mafioso*, because he had been active 'in the party opposed to that of the socialists'. In Corleone, he explained, there were two parties, 'that of the socialists and that of the mafia'.[60] However, another witness firmly denied that any such 'party of the mafia' existed. 'I cannot admit', he said, 'that I belonged to the party of the honest and that my opponents were dishonest. That is not true. The opposition list, like ours, was made up of respectable people. In every party, there are honest and dishonest. Giving the label "mafia" to the opposition is as outrageous as my being called a "social communist".'[61]

It is difficult to know what part fear played in these statements. Some witnesses may well have changed their evidence as a result of intimidation. However, that is no guarantee that they were now lying. Their panic might have been triggered by a feeling that their original deposition had been calumnious, and would therefore have provoked a just reprisal by the injured party, his family, or his friends. As it was, the majority of witnesses stuck by their statements in court. This too might have been out of fear, for the price of retraction was high. When Liborio Jannazzo refused to confirm what he was supposed to have said to the examining magistrate because his statement had never been read back to him, he was immediately charged with perjury.[62] Many of the witnesses must have felt caught between the hammer of the law and the anvil of the defendants and their supporters.

Very few people in Corleone testified against the accused. Of the four hundred or so separate statements made to the examining magistrate (almost all by different witnesses), only twenty-five denounced anyone as *mafioso*. The great majority simply declared that the defendant was hard-working, honest, and incapable of being a member of a criminal association. Most of these favourable depositions were given by peasants (*contadini*), many of them illiterate; a handful came from professionals and even local aristocrats. By contrast, almost all the denunciations were made by members of the upper classes and state employees. Among them were five landowners, two doctors, a teacher, the vice-prefect of Palermo, a lawyer, the communal secretary, the commanders of the local rural guards and municipal squads, a tax-collector, a broker, a shopkeeper, and employees of the local council and the Bank of Sicily.[63] In addition, there were thirty-four depositions from landowners, mostly dating from February 1927, which referred to individual cases of intimidation, threats, and the payment of tribute money.[64]

Although more than 90% of the accused who appeared before the examining magistrate at Corleone had no previous convictions, the police probably regarded many of those they arrested as seasoned criminals. The failure of earlier prosecutions could easily (and perhaps with justification) be attributed to *omertà* and protection.[65] Nevertheless, the police must have realised that there was a political side to their work. It was not just that they furthered the interests of the *agrari*; they also, through their arrests, became involved in local factional struggles. This was an important general aspect of Mori's campaign. As several witnesses at Corleone pointed out, the terms 'mafia' and '*mafioso*' were often employed as political weapons: they could be used not just against individuals, but also against administrations and other collective bodies. In these cases, the dividing line between moral and political concerns was hard to detect.

Corleone was in the electoral sphere of Giovanni Lo Monte, a somewhat notorious politician whom Mori once described as 'highly controversial'.[66] The fascist government had been eager to court him, not least because he enjoyed strong links with the industrial and commercial world. Shortly before the 1924 elections, Pietro Lanza di Scalea wrote to Gabriello Carnazza saying that Lo Monte should, if possible, be won over to the government side as he had some 12,000 votes in the Corleone area – 'where we have no candidates of our own'. He added that Lo Monte was 'a true gentleman' despite his reputation as 'an exponent of the mafia'.[67] Perhaps significantly, at this time the police also claimed that the real mafia in Corleone had been composed of the socialists, while the ruling faction (made up of Lo Monte's supporters) was 'obsequious to the authorities', and, by implication, beyond reproach.[68]

The two leading figures in the Corleone administration were Giuseppe Battaglia and the president of the Agricultural Circle, Marcello Bimenti. They had managed, with Lo Monte's support, to keep the local fascists at bay. According to the sub-prefect, writing in August 1926, the *fascio* in Corleone had never been very efficient, despite its membership of over 250.[69] One major problem was the executive: those who composed it, he said, were honest men, but they lacked influence. Furthermore, they were at the beck and call of the communal administration, which meant that any initiative by the party was immediately scotched. As a result, the *fascio* had been subject to dissension, apathy, and indiscipline. He thought that a special official should be appointed to rebuild it from scratch.

The sub-prefect knew that this was not the answer. Early in December 1926, he sent another report to Mori, which described the political situation in starker terms:

> Although the Corleone section is run by men of respect and influence,...they are clearly controlled through kinship, dependence, or some other bond, by the most terrible local *mafiosi*. In fact quite a few of them...have been enrolled in the section itself. This has created a bad impression, and many respectable citizens... who would have been an asset to the party have as a result refrained from applying for membership so as not to get involved in dubious company... The fascist section has for these reasons become run-down.[70]

'The party of the mafia', as Bernardino Verro liked to call it,[71] had clearly lost the goodwill of the authorities.

On 15 December, five days after this report was written, the protector of the Corleone administration, Giovanni Lo Monte, was indicted for involvement in a case of fraud. The charge related to the disappearance of a million lire from a co-operative in Sommatino, in the province of Caltanissetta. Though Lo Monte was eventually acquitted, his political influence in the mean time was neglible.[72] A major obstacle to the destruction of Corleone's dominant faction had been removed. Whether this was through design or chance, however, is impossible to say. On 17 December, Mori prepared the ground for the impending *retata* by ordering the closure of the Agricultural Circle, and the sequestration of its goods.[73]

The tight bond between the Circle and Lo Monte's faction was referred to by a number of witnesses. According to Bernardo Oddo, the 'party of order' received regular support from the Agricultural Circle during election campaigns. Furthermore, it seems that the links between the two groups had been sanctioned, if not encouraged, by the authorities. This made the closure appear strange to some people. One witness said:

The Agricultural Circle was made up of the middle class: notably teachers, farmers, and wealthy landowners. When it was shut, I was surprised because they called it a circle for *mafiosi*, whereas in fact its membership had always been respectable. . .It had never had a reputation as a mafia circle before its closure, but was actually well regarded by the authorities.[75]

Whether there was a tactical reason for closing the Circle only two days before the police moved in to make their *retata* is not clear. The idea might have been to lull Lo Monte's men into a false sense of security by making them feel that this was the storm itself, and not just its prelude. If that was the case, it was not successful, for only seventy-five of the 159 people for whom arrest warrants had been issued could be found in the early hours of 20 December. A few more were traced at the end of the month and early in January. However, many of the wanted men had evidently made a clean escape.[76]

It is not certain what, if any, political result was expected from the destruction of Corleone's 'party of the mafia'. Waiting in the wings was a certain Colonel Vinci. In the 1925 local elections he had presented an opposition list of candidates, but had withdrawn it at the last moment under pressure from the authorities.[77] He was *persona non grata* both to Lo Monte and to Alfredo Cucco, who mistrusted his left-wing background. 'For years,' Cucco wrote later, 'Vinci was a *popolare*, an anti-fascist, and head of the subversives. He was even cautioned by the military and political authorities.'[78] Despite this, he was asked in 1927 to head the rebuilt fascist section. That this could happen suggests that something drastic had occurred, and not just in Corleone.

8   THE FALL OF ALFREDO CUCCO

Alfredo Cucco was born in 1893 into a respectable middle-class family from Castelbuono. Like his father, he was an oculist by profession. His provincial origins help to account for the disdain in which he held much of the Palermo aristocracy. In 1924, he had spurned offers from the local nobility (who had hoped to appease this radical young man through a matrimonial alliance) and married a girl from Trieste. Cucco was small in stature and of pugnacious temperament. Among his leisure pursuits was wrestling. He was endowed with great courage and intelligence, and it was these qualities that had brought him to the leadership of the Palermo Nationalist Party, and then, in 1923, to the position of *federale*.

Cucco was unlucky in the timing of Mori's appointment to Palermo. At the end of August when he visited Mussolini in Rome, the intransigent wing of the party seemed relatively secure. Two months later, the situation was different. A wave of violence in Florence early in October led to Roberto Farinacci being sharply rebuked in the Grand Council for failing to restrain his followers. He was told to disband all squads and purge the *fasci* of undesirable elements: two leading party radicals were dismissed from their posts. 'It is high time', announced Mussolini, 'to make the necessary separation: the fascists with the fascists, the criminals with the criminals, the profiteers with the profiteers; and above all we must exercise moral, I repeat moral, intransigence.'[1]

With Farinacci's star waning, the balance of power between the party and the state began to tilt sharply in favour of the latter. On 27 November, a month after Mori's arrival in Palermo, a bill was submitted to parliament to increase the authority of the prefects. Just as Mussolini enjoyed supremacy over the executive in Rome, so, at the provincial level, each prefect would now have the right to issue orders to all other ministerial representatives. During the debate, Empedocle Restivo, head of the Palermo Chamber of Commerce, declared that 'the excesses of the democratic regime' had made people in Sicily mistrustful of the authorities. For this reason, he said, an extension of the prefect's power would be welcomed unanimously in the island: what was needed was strong government action, 'imbued with severity and justice'.[2]

In the middle of March 1926, three weeks before the bill became law, Mori had his powers in Sicily extended by decree. His control over the Interprovincial Service was broadened, and he now had effective charge of all the island's police. He was given the right to issue ordinances 'that can be enforced without additional authorisation in every province of Sicily', and the power to deploy policemen anywhere in the region after consultation with the prefect concerned.[3] Two days later, as if to explain this measure, Federzoni told the Senate that the drive against crime in Sicily would brook no compromise: 'We will ignore all considerations of expediency, and aim solely at the supreme goal, which is to restore fully faith, peace and security to the honest, who constitute, we can safely say, almost the entire population even in those areas that have been most ravaged by crime.'[4]

The government, and above all the Minister of the Interior, had unstinted confidence in Mori. In mid-April, Federzoni wrote to Mussolini and suggested that were it not for the campaign against the mafia, the prefect of Palermo would make an excellent choice for the position of Head of the Police: 'Unfortunately, however, Mori cannot relinquish his great work...in Sicily without irreparable damage.'[5] Two weeks later, Federzoni again took up the cudgels for Mori, this time in the Chamber of Deputies. He said that what fascism had 'dared' to do against the mafia 'represents something absolutely new in the history of united Italy'. Omertà no longer existed, he claimed, for citizens had rediscovered their faith in the authorities; there was now an unprecedented atmosphere, 'of confidence and of obedience to the law and the powers of the State'.[6]

This support for Mori and his work must have been worrying to Cucco. It put paid to any hopes he might have entertained of controlling the new prefect in the way that he had controlled Giovanni Gasti in 1923. The best he could do in the circumstances was to stick close to Mori and seek to exert some influence over him. However, the prospects for co-operation were not good, as neither of the two men was tractable; nor did they believe in compromise. Cucco insisted on calling Mori 'signor Prefetto', when everyone else used the more dignified 'Your Excellency'. This irritated Mori intensely, but Cucco's pride was unshakeable: 'I could not bear to appear too obsequious', he said.[7] The conflict of wills led not to mutual respect, but to a private power struggle, the intensity of which was increased by the fact that it dovetailed into the larger battle that was being fought at the same time between the party and the state.

Had the mafia been a circumscribed entity, there would have been little room for any serious divergence of opinion between the two men. After all, Cucco, like Mori, enjoyed a consistent record of opposition to the mafia and had attacked it regularly in his weekly newspaper *La Fiamma*, particularly in 1923 and 1924.[8] The *federale* certainly had an idealistic streak in him: when he talked of moral regeneration in Sicily, he clearly envisaged an end to opportunism and corruption. However, Cucco was first and foremost a politician. His aim was to destroy the old élite, and it is perhaps not surprising that he usually equated the mafia with the clienteles of the local liberal politicians. In his eyes the only possibility of any renaissance in the island lay with the political triumph of fascism.

During Mori's first months in Palermo, the *federale's* support was generous and seemingly unreserved. *Sicilia Nuova* (Cucco's second newspaper, which he had set up early in 1925 to counter the liberal dailies, *L'Ora* and *Il Giornale di Sicilia*) carried detailed reports of the police operations. It also showered a good deal of praise on Mori, albeit in a somewhat loaded form: 'There is something fascist...in the conduct of this extraordinary warrior,' said an article on 7 January 1926. 'His style is clear, precise, strong and intransigent.'[9] That final word was replete with significance. It was as if Cucco wished to warn Mori of his political responsibilities, and in case Mori had any doubt about what these were, *La Fiamma* spelled them out on 31 January: 'The men who have been, and the men who will be, arrested by Mori constitute the sum of the electoral clienteles of those that have been the eternal enemies of fascism, even if we have sometimes (or always) encountered them in the guise of devoted friends ready to offer any service, solicited or unsolicited.'[10] As five months earlier, Cucco's goal was still to purge Palermo fascism of opportunist infiltrators.

The connection between moral and political reform was highlighted by the party secretary of Cinisi, Dr Roberto Impastato. In a small book, published by Cucco's printing press, ATES, early in 1926, he declared that fascism should act 'intransigently and with intolerance' to clean out the town halls, and 'moralise their polluted environments'. To achieve this, fascism would first have to be purged of 'men without faith and character', who, out of opportunism, favoured 'alliance and compromise'. Secondly, all officials, including judges, were to be changed, and replaced with 'those who are...uncorrupted, incorruptible, and incapable of returning to the old partisan, and clientelistic, bureaucratic systems'. Favouritism was to cease; the problem of public works had to be resolved; and in order to save money, deputies should be limited to a maximum of two per province. Finally, the battle against 'crime, or the new mafia' had to be waged, if necessary, with deportation and the firing squad. It was lucky, said Impastato, that Sicily had its 'austere prefect, noble and intelligent', who would now see that justice was done.[11]

Despite their optimism, the intransigent fascists faced a serious obstacle in Mori. Cucco knew it, and tried hard to keep the prefect on a tight rein. In the middle of January he went to Rome, no doubt to gain reassurance about the character and extent of the police operations. The round-ups in the Madonie had affected families whom Cucco knew. Relatives of wanted men had solicited his help, and in some cases he obliged by ensuring that they and their property remained unmolested by the police.[12] However, his position was invidious. Some of his friends thought he had already committed himself more than was wise to Mori's cause. 'People I loved', he later wrote, 'tried to restrain me...saying that I was putting myself too much at risk....For although it was a holy crusade, it still had its dangers and responsibilities.'[13] As the *retate* escalated, Cucco came under increasing pressure to have the prefect removed. Apart from anything else, he had to shoulder some of the blame for Mori's original appointment to Palermo.

We do not know if Cucco received any consolation from his visit to Federzoni in Rome. He was certainly told that Mori would remain prefect of Palermo, despite any rumours to the contrary; and according to Cucco, such rumours existed, though these might conceivably have been 'invented' by him as a way of informing the Minister of the Interior that Mori was beginning to overstep the mark. On 19 January, Federzoni sent Cucco a telegram, presumably at his request, confirming what had been said at their meeting: 'I can give you complete assurance that the government has no intention whatsoever of removing Prefect Mori from Palermo. He has begun an operation there which is both salutary and necessary.'[15] This communiqué might well have heartened Mori, but it also told him (and perhaps this was its real intention) that Cucco had been to Rome and voiced doubts (whether his, or other people's, was largely immaterial) about the way the campaign against the mafia was being conducted.

On 24 January an article appeared in *La Fiamma* specifying some of Cucco's misgivings:

> One thing worries us, namely that when the war is over, the guerrilla action could persist; that after the criminal armies have been destroyed, their general staffs might not be fully eliminated, and could continue, with their oblique and underhand manoeuvres, to infect the moral and material life of Sicily...And we hope that when Mori has finished the grand offensive that he is now conducting against the lower ranks of the mafia organisation, he will finally turn his attention to the generals who pull the strings.

These generals, who were presumably to be found in the old liberal clienteles, dominated every sphere of civilian life, according to the article: 'The general staff of the mafia has its branches in the heart of the main economic, industrial, administrative, and even state institutions, of our island.'[16]

Whatever his misgivings (which he was careful not to make too public), Cucco strove to keep his followers on the right side of the law. He took firm disciplinary measures, and instructed the local party yet again to exercise 'the most rigorous selection' with its membership.[17] He also encouraged active collaboration with the authorities, and, in many towns, armed fascists joined the police in their search for wanted men.[18] This was a tactic that had been employed when Gasti was prefect of Palermo. According to Cucco it had paid off: at Capaci, Marineo, Vicari, and elsewhere, he said, the party had succeeded in dislodging once and for all 'the *mafiosi* entrenched in power'.[19] Mori seconded this collaboration with the police. He obtained special permission from the Ministry of the Interior to deploy members of the Militia, and in Palermo, some 300 were engaged in what were described as 'patrol and guard duties'.[20]

It was important for Cucco to retain support in Rome, particularly with Farinacci's influence declining. To this end, he combined a high moral profile with respect for political expediency. When the under-secretary of the Interior, Michele Bianchi, came to Palermo in January 1926, Cucco expelled a '*mafioso*' dramatically from a banquet held in the minister's honour at Corleone. There was an uproar, but Bianchi remained impressed.[21] A similar incident occurred in March in the presence of the Minister of the Interior. During a parade of the provincial *fasci* in the centre of Palermo, Cucco noticed that the section from Villabate was being led by a *mafioso*. He told a member of the Palermo executive to shout out in front of Federzoni that the Villabate *fascio* should be dissolved because it was 'infiltrated by the mafia'.[22] That Cucco resorted to such tactics suggests that he was trying to bypass the more conventional channel of the prefect.

Relations between Mori and the Palermo *federale* appear to have deteriorated steadily in the course of 1926. The dismissal of Farinacci in the spring of that year, and the concession of greater powers to Mori, gave a keener edge to the conflict. The tide was beginning to flow strongly against the intransigents. Their first major casualty in western Sicily was the provincial secretary of Caltanissetta, Damiano Lipani. His support for Farinacci was as intense as his opposition to Mori. 'The question of crime or the mafia', he wrote in March 1926, 'has been exaggerated.' The real issue, he said, was the old *politicanti* (corrupt politicians). Once they had been destroyed, Sicily would cease to be troubled by lawlessness, and this, in effect, had already been achieved: 'It is clear that the younger generation has solved the problem by denying the men of the past any say in our affairs.' All that was now needed, he maintained, was a spiritual and economic renewal.[23]

Lipani's difficulties had begun in February with the appointment of Pintor Mameli as prefect of Caltanissetta. The outgoing prefect had lasted barely four months, perhaps because Mori had thought him inadequate. At all events, Pintor Mameli was careful not to put a foot wrong. He referred to Mori publicly as his 'revered master', and said his task in Caltanissetta was to guarantee tranquillity in the countryside.[24] Lipani tried to win the new prefect's soul by making him an honorary member of the fascist party as soon as he arrived in Caltanissetta. It was not enough, and by the middle of March, Lipani's enemies were on the offensive. They published a pamphlet, listing various counts against him; Lipani dismissed them as the fabrications of *mafiosi* and 'vulgar slanderers'. However, the campaign escalated, and at the beginning of July Lipani decided to resign from his positions in the party. He wanted to be free, he said, to prosecute his opponents.[25]

Proceedings against Lipani's accusers began on 7 July. The trial was short-lived: on 1 August, Lipani informed the president of the court that he wished to abandon his suit for political reasons. He said that the case should have focused on himself alone; instead the defence had implicated other members of the party 'with the aim of damaging the regime, directly or indirectly'.[26] This, Prefect Mameli told Federzoni, was nonsense: Lipani had given up, for the simple reason that he had been defeated.[27] Lipani's behaviour certainly did not appear particularly high-minded. A few days before withdrawing, he visited Mameli and complained of being abandoned by the government and the party. He announced that he wanted at all costs to find a way out. Could he not be sent to some other province? He was even prepared, he said, to relinquish political activity for a year or two, provided he could retain his position as a deputy.[28]

Lipani's defeat was followed by the dissolution of the Caltanissetta party executive, and a deputy, Gaetano Pirrone, was dispatched from Rome to supervise the reconstruction. However, Lipani did not surrender without a fight. Several of his supporters, including his brother and brother-in-law, tried hard to win over the 'commissioner extraordinary', and even intercepted Pirrone's train before it reached Caltanissetta in the hope of making him see their point of view first.[29] They had no success. In October, following a review of the trial, Lipani was declared 'definitively expelled' from the party.[30] His opponents had triumphed. Their victory was a clear sign of which way the political wind was blowing.

One of Lipani's enemies was Paolo Savoca. He had been political secretary of Castrogiovanni until Lipani dislodged him after an investigtion early in 1926. Following his dismissal he had tried to convince Farinacci that Lipani was in league with 'notorious *mafiosi*'. What, he had asked, lay behind the accusations that had been levelled against him? 'A question of mafia and not of party'. The issue related to his dismissal of a number of *gabelloti* in the territory of Mistretta. Savoca said:

> It was painful to note how...some members of the fascist party in the province of Messina had become instruments of *mafiosi* who were trying to keep the price of rents very low on a number of *latifondi* that had been leased under pressure about twelve years ago. The truth is that I had had the courage to 'free' the *latifondi* of my father-in-law from the old *gabelloti*, who were all notoriously *mafiosi*.

To prove his case he pointed out that two of these *gabelloti*, Marcello Milletarì and Natale Di Salvo, had recently been arrested by Mori.[31]

Farinacci had disregarded Savoca's appeal, and upheld Lipani. However, with the arrival of Pintor Mameli as prefect of Caltanissetta in February, and Farinacci's dismissal as general secretary of the party in March, Savoca's position suddenly improved. Lipani was now vulnerable to attack, at both the provincial and national levels, and Mori (who sided readily with established landowners against *gabelloti* and their representatives) no doubt supported Savoca in his attempt to dislodge the radical *federale*. The result was the downfall of Lipani, the dissolution of the old provincial party, and its reconstruction on a more conservative footing.

Lipani was an intransigent fascist, and a political ally of Alfredo Cucco. The Palermo *federale* must have felt discomfited by his defeat. How far did Mussolini and the new party secretary, Augusto Turati, intend to go in Sicily with their elimination of the old leaders? Were the days of radical fascism really over? To add to Cucco's insecurity was the increasingly unsavoury turn that the campaign against the mafia was taking. Already in January 1926, as Savoca's letter indicated, Mori was hitting at fascists who would have looked directly or indirectly to Cucco for help. Not surprisingly, though a little unwisely perhaps, Cucco began to criticise Mori to his face. He suggested he take a more moderate line, avoid the mass round-ups, and concentrate on new rather than old crimes.[32]

Mori did not take kindly to such criticism: 'When these disagreements arose', Cucco wrote some years later, 'the conversation became increasingly fraught; and however much Mori used "his brakes of prudence", I noticed...that he grew detached, and began to feel revulsion towards me.'[33] The dissemination of malicious gossip did not improve matters. For example, Mori's wife was told that Cucco's two-year-old son had been taught to reply to the question 'What is Mori?' with the words 'filthy cop' (*porcu birru*).[34] Mori was too proud to swallow such gibes: 'Some people will call me a "cop" [*sbirro*]', he declared in a speech at Castronuovo in Cucco's presence. 'My reply is this: if to fight daily in defence of life and property, if to live by sacrifice and honesty, if to attack criminals and destroy them – if all this means "cop", then, my friends, "cop" is a word of praise and a title to be proud of.'[35] Here was a northern version of Orlando's famous phrase, 'I declare myself to be *mafioso*, and I am happy to be such.' No doubt Cucco and his friends enjoyed themselves with it at Mori's expense, mimicking his stentorian voice, his military gestures, and his Lombard accent.[36]

In the course of 1926, both sides raked up mud and dispatched it to Rome in the form of anonymous letters. Mori was denounced for his savage methods and illusions of grandeur. Particular reference was made to his entry into Piana dei Greci on a white horse, and to a triumphal arch inscribed: '*Ave Caesar, Greci et Albanenses te salutant*'.[37] Cucco was accused of excessive ambition and criminal connections: 'What is the DUCINO as he likes to style himself?' asked one letter sent to Mussolini. 'He is an ignoble and amoral profiteer: he makes a show of fighting the mafia and criminals, but exploits them basely, obliging them to take out subscriptions to *Sicilia Nuova*.'[38] Until the late autumn of 1926, Mori chose to ignore these attacks on the Palermo *federale*. In August, for example, a prominent local fascist, Roberto Paternostro, wrote a memorial accusing Cucco of corruption. It was dismissed by Mori as a collection of 'vulgar slanders'.[39]

Mori's relations with Cucco were not improved by his antipathy to many rank-and-file fascists. What Cucco saw as ardour or zeal, Mori regarded as little short of hooliganism. On 1 November 1926, a protest demonstration was held in Palermo following an attempt on Mussolini's life at Bologna. Several thousand young fascists took part, many of them brandishing *manganelli* (wooden clubs). Cucco led them towards the prefecture, 'to make clear to the government', he said, 'the city's feelings of indignation and outrage at this further attack on the Duce and the Nation'. By this time, Mori and Cucco were at daggers drawn, privately if not publicly, and since Mori was a career prefect with a poor fascist record, the rally must have had its malicious side. The chant went up of 'Mo-ri, Mo-ri', a conscious evocation, no doubt, of the chant of the Bologna fascists in May 1922: 'Mo-ri, Mo-ri, *devi morire*' (Mori, Mori, you must die).

Mori found the whole episode intolerable. 'He came towards us,' Cucco recalled, 'red in the face like a lobster and, as if seized by a dionysian fury, he said: "...I am fed up with these fascists. They are driving me mad!"'[41] The remark was fully in character, and reflected Mori's deep-seated dislike for a group of men whom a year later he described to the Ministry of the Interior as a 'conventional crowd of young political trouble-makers...trying desperately to leap on to the new bandwagon'.[42] The prefect's feelings for the Palermo fascists on 1 November were not improved when they followed up their demonstration by sacking the bourgeois 'Clubino' ('a circle for layabouts', as Cucco called it), at the Quattro Canti, in the centre of the city.[43] Here was another example of fascist 'faith' and 'ardour', the spiritual significance of which escaped middle-aged conservatives like Mori.[44]

The events of 1 November certainly added a nail to Cucco's coffin, but they were not as significant as he later claimed. In portraying his downfall as the result of a personal clash between a young idealist and a vindictive policeman, Cucco omitted two important factors. The first was his own attempt to dislodge Mori, by defamation and backstage manoeuvring. The second (and much more significant) was the regime's drift towards conservatism in the course of 1926, with the expulsion, under Augusto Turati, of unruly radicals, and the absorption into the party of 'fellow-travellers'. This process of so-called 'normalisation' left Cucco in a vulnerable position, for as long as he and his followers were in power, many of the agrari could, or would, have little to do with the regime. For economic as well as political reasons, the government found this increasingly unacceptable. Accordingly, when Cucco was disgraced there was a good deal of quiet rejoicing in Rome.

Until the beginning of 1927, Mori and Cucco maintained a façade of cordiality. They toured provincial towns together, exchanged glowing letters, swapped signed photographs, and patted each other on the back in public speeches. 'I join you fraternally', said Mori to a meeting of 'Fascist Tradesmen' in June, 'in professing love, affection, and sympathy for my most dear friend Alfredo Cucco.'[45] The following autumn, Cucco asked Mori for his photograph to grace the party headquarters: 'Here it is,' wrote Mori. 'I have expressed in the dedication what I feel for every fascist in the province.'[46] Cucco thanked him, and said that the photograph had been received with enthusiasm by all members of the executive, 'who regard Prefect Mori as their dearly loved eldest brother. Allow me', he concluded, 'to embrace you with all my heart.'[47] On 1 January, Cucco and Mori exchanged New Year's greetings and drank vermouth together. Two days later a denunciation was made to the police accusing Cucco of 'military corruption'. After hurried enquiries, the Palermo fascio was dissolved, and the following month Cucco was expelled from the party.

What exactly had brought about the rupture? The historian Arrigo Petacco, in his book Il Prefetto di Ferro, quotes a police report of 5 November 1926, in which Cucco was shown to be sending defamatory newspaper articles to a friend in New York. These highlighted Mori's brutality, the savagery of his police, the deleterious

Pl. 12. Cucco addressing a crowd at Gangi in 1926. Behind him, on the same platform, is Mori.

effect of mass arrests on the Battle for Grain, and the hostility of Sicilian public opinion to the campaign. According to Petacco, it was this document that convinced Mori that Cucco was a serious threat.[48] Undoubtedly, the Palermo *federale* harboured the views ascribed to him in the report (he had, for example, told Baron Sgadari not to kowtow to Mori, since his work was 'not meeting with popular approval [and] damaged agriculture'),[49] but Petacco's document (which, unfortunately, is at present untraceable) was not in itself significant.

Its date, however, was important. On 5 November, Federzoni resigned from the Ministry of the Interior, while the Sicilian aristocrat, Pietro Lanza di Scalea, lost his position as Minister of the Colonies. What would Mori have made of these changes? Might it not have seemed to him that the party radicals were returning to favour, and that he was in danger of being ousted? The seeds of doubt had already been sown in September when Francesco Crispo Moncada was replaced as Head of the Police by a less conservative figure, Arturo Bocchini. Giovanni Furolo was quick to alert Mori to the danger. 'Read this, then burn it,' he wrote. 'Bocchini has been imposed by Turati. Federzoni...has made *bonne mine à mauvais jeu*; but it was obvious that [he] was acting *ab torto collo*.'[50] Whether Mori himself had hoped for the post is not certain. The important point, politically, was that the new Head of the Police enjoyed the sympathy of the party in general, and of Farinacci in particular.

Federzoni's resignation probably semed to Mori like another turn of the screw, particularly as it was followed not long afterwards by the appointment, amid much publicity, of a new group of fascist prefects.[51] Mori must have felt severely threatened. The Minister of the Interior had been a mainstay for career officials like Mori against attacks by intransigents, and di Scalea, with his aristocratic ties, had been something of an ally too. An additional source of disquiet was that Cucco claimed friendship with the new under-secretary of the Interior, Count Suardo.[52] Mori's decision to heed the accusations against Cucco was determined by his search for security. He had no intention of being upstaged again as at Bologna. Removing Cucco would rid him of a troublesome, and now dangerous, critic. It would also force the government to declare itself openly for Mori, and make his removal very difficult without a serious loss of face.

As it transpired, Mori timed his move well. Fear of a general *revanche* by the party intransigents was unfounded, as Mussolini's Circular to the Prefects, issued on 5 January 1927, amply demonstrated. The prefect, according to the Circular, was now to be the guardian of the 'moral order'. It was his responsibility to point out 'harmful individuals', and ensure that all 'sharks' and 'profiteers' were removed from the party. Particular mention was made of the South, where the prefect was required to inaugurate 'an era of absolute administrative morality, and shatter resolutely the camorristic remains of old regimes'.[53] This statement provided the ideal backdrop for Mori. How could the government fail to support him against a man facing a string of criminal charges, even though he was the leading Sicilian fascist? There was one problem, however. In destroying Cucco, Mori was selling his soul to those very 'camorristic remains' that the Circular had so roundly condemned.

Mori needed to keep his cards close to his chest. On 3 December he sent a telegram, headed 'secret – personal – very urgent', to the sub-prefects of Corleone and Cefalù, and the commanders of the local *carabinieri*:

> I would ask you to tell me without fail by the 12th of this month, which, if any, of the fascist sections and trade unions in your respective jurisdictions might leave something to be desired, whether because of infiltration by mafia and *malvivenza*, or because of their political line, their internal rivalries and squabbles, or the shortcomings of their leaders or for other reasons....This telegram is of an absolutely secret nature and nothing whatsoever should be done or said that could in any way give rise to comments, assumptions, or alarms. Furthermore, I am sure that everyday experience and observation will enable each of you to make his report immediately and above all without having to resort to interrogations, external confirmations, and such like.[54]

Some days later, Mori and Cucco were present together at Valledolmo for the inauguration of a war memorial. The prefect was giving nothing away. 'The meal,' Cucco later recalled, '...was astonishingly good-humoured, and even my relationship with Mori was affected by it. Before we got up from table, we exchanged salvos of bread, mandarin peel, and so on; and when we got back to Palermo we said goodbye to each other as in old times.'[55] However, not everything could be kept secret. Towards Christmas, Cucco was informed confidentially that a lieutenant in the *carabinieri* had begun to make enquiries about him in Villabate. 'I attached no importance to the fact,' he said; but the reports grew more insistent. 'They told me that the *carabiniere* lieutenant returned almost daily, and summoned a number of people to the barracks; and they left it with anguished faces and their eyes red from weeping.'[56]

On 3 January 1927, the lieutenant received a denunciation against Cucco from Carmelo Calderone, the former head of the town council of Marineo and one of the victims of the local fascist party's drive against the mafia.[57] The charge against Cucco was military corruption for having allegedly induced the symptoms of trachoma in a certain Gaetano Di Liberto as a way of saving him from conscription. This was a telling accusation: not only did the regime attach great importance to military service, but Cucco himself, back in March 1925, had delivered a speech to the Chamber of Deputies in which he deplored the fact that trachoma was deemed legitimate grounds for exemption from the army.[58] The hilarity caused by Calderone's charge can well be imagined, and though Cucco was acquitted in December 1927, with the judge concluding that he had been the victim of 'a conspiracy hatched...for reasons of vendetta',[59] the damage was already done. His political career was in ruins.

Alfredo Cucco's downfall was symptomatic of a national trend. Augusto Turati had been appointed party secretary early in 1926 with instructions to bring the movement to heel, and in the spring and autumn of that year he presided over the expulsion of 7,400 militant fascists. Among them were five deputies.[60] Early in October, with the approval of the new party statute, the process of 'purification' was further intensified. The main victims, as before, were ex-*squadristi* and intransigents. They were replaced in increasing numbers by conservative middle-class elements.[61] Sicily, however, proved more resistant to this development than many other areas of Italy. Part of the reason lay in the strength of local instransigent fascism; but it was also related to the fact that politics here, as elsewhere in the South, were dominated by personalities.

One general difficulty was that the government found it hard in the *Mezzogiorno* to impose decisions dictated by ideology or tactics. A leading southerner could not be removed for political unsuitability without raising a storm of protest from his followers. A more specific problem was the extreme polarisation of Sicilian politics. By 1926, too much bad blood existed between the radical fascists and the old political order for there to be any chance of compromise. In Caltanissetta, the fall of Damiano Lipani had alleviated tensions; and in Girgenti and Messina the situation was considered satisfactory by the end of 1926. Elsewhere in Sicily, however, the party gave cause for concern.[62] In December, Turati announced the setting up of an enquiry into the state of fascism in Palermo, Trapani, Catania and Siracusa. The man appointed to conduct it was a northerner of military background, Ernesto Galeazzi. He arrived in Sicily on 31 December, three days before Cucco's indictment for corruption.[63]

A special commission was established in Palermo to receive and investigate charges against the local party. (It might, as Cucco suggested, already have been operating secretly in December.)[64] In an attempt to muster support for his cause, Cucco set off for Rome. On his way, he heard that the provincial executive had been dissolved: it would have been better, he told Mussolini in a note, if he had been given the opportunity to defend himself first. In the capital every door was barred against him. Only Michele Bianchi showed any civility.[65] He returned to Palermo, where he found that his house was subject to close surveillance. He reported the fact to the Head of the Police in Rome, Arturo Bocchini. Bocchini asked Mori if it was true, and Mori said that he had stationed his men there to protect Cucco against 'possible hostile demonstrations'.[66]

The commission investigating the local party met in the prefecture. It consisted of Galeazzi, a police officer, two *carabinieri* and the vice-prefect. Cucco described its proceedings in an appeal to the Grand Council in April 1927. His account was obviously partial; but since many witnesses were referred to, the document cannot be lightly dismissed. The commission, he said, met for two months: 'As if gripped by a satanic fever, it continued to summon, investigate, interrogate and probe.' Witnesses were threatened with arrest to make them talk. When Lorenzo La Viola refused to testify, Mori slammed his fist on the table and shouted 'like a man possessed: REMEMBER THAT THAT MAN ABSOLUTELY MUST BE DESTROYED!!!'. Cucco alleged that the police were under strong pressure to denounce him, and more than a dozen of them were transferred for failing to comply. Ten fascists, who said in conversation that Mori 'had become intolerable', were 'charged with spreading alarmism'.[67] After reading Cucco's account, it is not surprising that a Palermo fascist wrote to Mussolini saying: 'This is exactly like the Spanish Inquisition.'[68]

Cucco was allowed the semblance of a trial, but its verdict was a foregone conclusion. On 20 February, Mori reported to Rome on the proceedings: 'For three whole days Galeazzi has questioned Cucco, face to face with his accusers, on the charges they have brought relating to his political and moral behaviour. Having also heard defence evidence, Galeazzi believes that there is now irrefutable proof of his persistent and not disinterested links with major mafia figures.'[69] Among the prosecution witnesses was Giovanni Lo Monte, the deputy and political opponent of Cucco who had recently been indicted for fraud. Galeazzi seems to have been out of his depth. Lo Monte tried to show that Cucco had been a follower of Nitti in 1919, and used as evidence a speech by 'Dr Cucco'. Galeazzi apparently swallowed the bait, even though the Dr Cucco in question was Alfredo's father.[70] Lo Monte himself was hardly a model of consistency: he had stood as a 'democratic' candidate in 1919, and for the Agrarian Party in 1921.

The evidence for the defence was clearly kept to a minimum. None of the province's eighty political secretaries was summoned, nor were any members of the Palermo party executive. Cucco was desperate: 'President!', he wrote to Mussolini, 'I am being lynched! I beg you to intervene: this is a scandalous persecution and only you can prevent it!'.[71] He sent Galeazzi proof of his fight against the mafia in previous years. Galeazzi turned a deaf ear.[72] On 22 February Cucco was expelled from the party; two days later, a fresh set of charges was lodged against himself and thirteen of his closest followers. They included 'private violence', 'accessory to embezzlement' and 'fraud committed as a member of a criminal association headed by the convicted *mafioso*, Santo Termini'.[73] Henceforward, Cucco was to be referred to as a member of the mafia.

The *federale's* many enemies were naturally delighted at his fall. The aristocracy was particularly pleased. It went out of its way to entertain Galeazzi, and Mori became the darling of the salons: 'He passes from one drawing room to another,' wrote Cucco in April, in his appeal to the Grand Council, 'from receptions to parties, and swims inebriated in a new world, which had formerly shown itself to be hostile to fascism, or at least indifferent to it.'[74] There was no disguising his contempt and bitterness. Tina Whitaker, a member of one of Palermo's most influential families, wrote in her diary towards the end of January that Mori was doing 'splendidly':

> As far as Cucco is concerned, it is difficult to say how much truth there may be in what is probably based more or less on circumstantial evidence. His enemies are legion, and of late his swollen head made him most unpopular. Great pressure will no doubt be put on our Dictator to save him, but it is hoped that Mussolini will uphold the prefect.[75]

Whether the general public felt strongly one way or the other about the events in January and February is hard to say. Mori claimed that he had the entire province behind him: 'The mass of the population', he told the Minister of the Interior, 'together with fascists, Servicemen, War Wounded, and unions await further developments with supreme tranquillity and complete faith.'[76] How he arrived at such a conclusion, we do not know. The local press could no longer voice dissent, though it is sometimes hard to believe that the editorials of this period were not occasionally tongue in cheek. The *Avvisatore*, for example, commented on Galeazzi's bland decree of 12 February suppressing *La Fiamma* and *Sicilia Nuova*, in the following disproportionate terms:

> The finest wordsmith in existence would not have known how to forge stronger or more lapidary expressions. Every word seems to be synchronised effortlessly with an authoritative, clear, and incisive gesture that admits of no doubt, compromise or insinuation ...The truly piercing scream of faith and enthusiasm remains closed within us, crushed by its own force! In just such a way the apostles and the crowds must have heard the Word of Christ. O magical power of truths sublime![77]

During the next five years Cucco and his followers were to be systematically acquitted of all the charges against them. Their task was not made easy. In March, a short letter appeared in several national newspapers pointing out that Cucco had not been in Palermo at the time of one of his alleged offences. Mori denounced the letter to the Ministry of the Interior as a 'brazen, foolish manoeuvre, designed to influence public opinion', and the government published an official repudiation.[78] The following month, Cucco asked his erstwhile friend, Francesco Giunta, to deliver a typed appeal to the

Grand Council. Giunta wrote back saying he was sorry, but he could not do so.[79] In desperation, Cucco now turned to Mussolini. He had evidence, he said, that his accusers had been paid to charge him with military corruption: 'Summon me, Prime Minister, I can prove it all with documents, and were I to fail, I would deserve to be banished in shame for ever'.[80] Mussolini did not reply.

'Vendetta', Mori once wrote in a curious endorsement of Sicilian values, 'is firstly a duty, and secondly, a pleasure and a right.'[81] His pursuit of Cucco was single-minded and relentless. For nearly two years between the autumn of 1927 and the summer of 1929 (when he left Palermo), he tracked Cucco's every move with spies. Each day, a police superintendent issued him with a secret report on what Cucco had said, where he had been, whom he had met, and the contents of his mail.[82] Cucco and his supporters retaliated with equal determination. They lobbied Rome continually with letters, signed and anonymous, denouncing Mori and the political situation in Palermo. Mori tried to reassure the Ministry of the Interior, in November 1927, that all this was just characteristic mafia activity:

It makes no difference if the campaign [against my work] appears directed at one point, for example, at control of the fascist movement, at another towards the monopoly of land leases and contracts....Irrespective of particulars, immediate objectives, and individuals, there is essentially only one campaign, with a single, well-defined goal: to save the men and the positions of the mafia.[83]

Though Mussolini had apparently been pleased with Cucco's downfall, Mori felt far from secure. His attack on Palermo fascism had been the result of a personal initiative, and he badly needed to convince Rome of his own propriety and good faith. On the same day as Cucco's expulsion from the party, he sent Mussolini a report on the current state of the campaign. 'We have victory in sight,' he concluded. 'But for that very reason we must...press on unremittingly and with inflexible resolve.'[84] In Rome, Mori's friends worked assiduously on his behalf. One of them, a member of the fascist Special Tribunal, wrote to him in May and reassured him about the strength of his position: 'I have made a great many official visits', he said, 'to the supreme political and military authorities, and my advocacy for the greatness of your work has everywhere been persuasive and fervent.' The Duce, he said, was firmly on his side; so too was General Badoglio (a contemporary of Mori from Military school); and even Antonino Di Giorgio (whose loyalty Mori had felt was suspect) was unstinting in his praise. The only cloud, apparently, in this otherwise cloudless sky, was Bocchini's studied indifference.[85]

Rebuilding Palermo fascism

In the spring and summer of 1927, under Galeazzi's guidance, Palermo fascism was rebuilt from scratch. It proved a difficult business. The main problem, so Mori told the Ministry of the Interior in October 1927, was Sicilian fascism's sordid origins. The party, he said, had begun by being exploited by the unscrupulous, 'as a weapon...in local contests and faction fights that were at root personal, clientelistic, and *mafioso*'. Consequently, the best people – the 'men of faith' – had kept their distance or else been excluded, and the same situation applied to the masses. What was now needed, Mori claimed, was good leadership: the province had to be extricated forcibly from the quagmire of its recent past.[86]

During the first three weeks of 1927, neither of Palermo's leading newspapers was published. When they reappeared, they were under new editorship and both carried leading articles on the recently issued Circular to the Prefects. *Il Giornale di Sicilia* reported that the text of the Circular had been posted up around Palermo – a wise move, it said, given the great significance of the document.[87] *L'Ora*, in a long article by its new editor, Nicola Pascazio (who had been sent from Rome specially), hammered out the theme of centralisation:

A strong regime like this cannot support two separate theories and practices, one at the centre, the other at the periphery...the Circular concludes the era of indecisiveness. Give unto Caesar [presumably no joke was intended here], in other words, the Prefect, what is Caesar's. Without hesitation, reserve, or euphemism. Today, in each province, the prefect is the Law incarnate.[88]

On 26 January, Galeazzi announced that a 'triumvirate' had been appointed to oversee the work of reconstructing the party. It consisted of the Duke of Belsito, the Marquis of Spedalotto, and Dr Sgarlata. All three had been prominent in the Servicemen's or War-Wounded associations, but their fascist credentials were not beyond reproach. Spedalotto had only joined the party in 1926,[89] and Sgarlata had adopted a notoriously ambiguous position during the Matteotti crisis. He had also belonged to a dissident Servicemen's organisation.[90] None of the triumvirs had much strength of character or intellectual depth, which suited Mori after his experience with Cucco. Belsito was spoken of as a morphine addict and Spedalotto as a sybarite. However, they were aristocrats, and in the circumstances it was this that made them politically important.

Galeazzi stipulated that respectablility, war service, and fascist faith were the criteria to be applied in selecting new party members.[91] Twelve commissions were set up to represent various professional categories, and these decided who to admit on the basis of reports from the political authorities and the police. A further commission, presided over by Belsito, reviewed their decisions. Some of Cucco's closest followers were naturally debarred from the party, but many, perhaps the majority, were readmitted. The important point was that they were now politically impotent.[92] As to the *federale*, the names of Guido Jung and Vincenzo Arcuri, both ex-Nationalists, were suggested; so was that of Rosario La Bella – a former follower of Orlando, a leading figure in the Palermo War Wounded association, and a close collaborator of Mori at Trapani. He seems to have been the prefect's choice, but his faith in fascism had probably wilted too much during the Matteotti crisis to make him a serious contender.[93]

The man eventually chosen was the Duke of Belsito whose personal shortcomings were perhaps outweighed by his respectability. He was an aristocrat, and had been decorated during the war, and though there was talk of his opposition to fascism in its early years, his membership of the party dated from the Matteotti crisis, which suggested conviction. However, his appointment caused many raised eyebrows in Rome, where he seems to have been regarded as a rather lightweight figure.[94] Galeazzi pushed his nomination hard, partly because he knew Belsito from military school,[95] but the ultimate decision lay with Turati and Mussolini, and the Duke of Belsito was evidently the kind of man they wanted. 'A sweetener for the aristocracy' was Cucco's view of Belsito's appointment.[96] He was probably close to the truth.

The process of reconstructing the party was facilitated by a good deal of moral backing from Rome. The vice-president of the Chamber of Deputies, Francesco Giunta, was sent to the island in April. He reported his findings to Mussolini, and Mussolini pronounced himself satisfied. Giunta conveyed the news to Mori: 'He has authorised me', he said in a telegram, 'to ask you and Galeazzi not to heed rumours and insinuations, but to continue serenely and firmly along the lines hitherto followed, which he approves and commends.'[97] That same month, during an audience, the Duce congratulated Mori on his work and said that crime was 'the fundamental, indeed only, reason' for Sicily's backwardness.[98] The two men met again in May, and once again Mori felt reassured: 'I found him', he declared later in a speech, 'proud, upright, strong and secure. And in his eye there gleamed that light of certainty and of infinite goodness, which together produce the spell which entrances all who approach or behold him.'[99]

The biggest fillip to Mori's work was Mussolini's Ascension Day speech, which was delivered to the Chamber of Deputies towards the end of May 1927. This colossal review of the domestic political scene included a long section on the campaign against the mafia and a personal tribute to Mori. It also dealt Cucco a political *coup de grâce*: 'From time to time', said Mussolini, 'I hear sceptics imply that we are going too far in Sicily, that a whole region is being humiliated... Such suggestions I reject with scorn.' He listed some of the 'criminal associations' that had been rounded up by the police, and then congratulated Mori and offered him his 'cordial greetings'. Several Palermo deputies leapt to their feet at this point and applauded.[100] He quoted figures (which Mori himself had supplied)[101] to show the diminution of crime in Sicily, and said that these were the best tribute that could be paid to the prefect. As a final flourish he announced that the fight against the mafia would only cease 'when all memory of it has been blotted from the minds of Sicilians'.[102]

With this backing from Mussolini, Mori and the new Palermo party executive undertook a major reconstruction of local fascism. One problem was that all documents relating to the provincial *fasci* for the period from 1921 to 1926 had been stolen before work could begin.[103] In April, however, the sections at Bagheria, Cefalù, Ficarazzi, Lercara, Marineo, Misilmeri, Piana dei Greci, San Mauro Castelverde, and Termini Imerese were all dissolved. After June the momentum increased, and by the end of the year sixty *fasci* (three-quarters of the provincial total) had been, or were in the process of being, reconstructed. By the beginning of 1929 the figure had risen to seventy-nine. In only a minority of cases (twenty-one according to Belsito, writing in October 1927) were the former political secretaries reinstated.[105]

In the course of reconstruction, accusations and counter-accusations flew. Cefalù (where the *fascio* was dissolved in April 1927) was an example of the kind of confusion that could be generated, at least if we are to believe what the commander of the 15th *Centuria* of the Militia told Mussolini at the end of May. After the *fascio*'s dissolution, he said, a certain Rotolo was given the task of rebuilding it, although he was not even a member of the party. The town's '*quartarellisti*' (so-called after the area near Rome where the body of Giacomo Matteotti was discovered), who in 1924 had contributed to a monument in Matteotti's memory, received positions of power, while the old fascists were 'banished'. In May, the *podestà*, Colonel Stroppa, set up a committee to curb high prices. It included Giuseppe Matassa, who had formerly been expelled from the party; Giacomo Catalfamo, one of the contributors to the memorial to Matteotti; and Filippo Agnello, a member of a dissident group of Servicemen known as the *assisiani*.[106] When Mori was asked to comment on the situation in Cefalù, he said, somewhat curtly, that there had never been any anti-fascism in the town, and that the new leaders had always wanted to join the party, but had not been allowed to do so. He glossed over the specific charges against them.[107] However, as Cucco and others pointed out, Catalfamo at least was notorious for his opposition to the government in 1924.[108]

Despite two years of police operations, the second half of 1927 saw a stream of accusations of mafia involvement. Many of the charges were against those newly invested with power. In August 1927, Mariano Fazio wrote to Mussolini to express his horror at the stiuation in the town of Ventimiglia Sicula. His letter was written in anger, but its general tone was less partisan and querulous than many of its kind. The previous November, he said, Mori had proposed the dissolution of the communal administration, headed by a certain Calì 'who acted as mayor, and friend to the local mafia, and who had formerly been expelled from the *fascio* as an *assisiano*'. In April, however, 'to everyone's amazement', Calì was named *podestà*. Furthermore, the Communal Secretary, Brancato, was released from prison and now 'controlled the political and administrative situation on behalf of criminals'. He had earlier been denounced as affiliated to the mafia, and his brother was wanted by the police.

The key to this sorry state of affairs, according to Fazio, lay with a certain Miceli, who was a veterinary surgeon and close friend of Mori. Miceli was related to Brancato, and had managed, said Fazio, to secure Brancato's release and Calì's nomination as *podestà*. He had also engineered the dissolution of the local *fascio*, and had entrusted its reconstruction to Calì and his friends, who were *assisiani*. Miceli (whose skills as a vet Fazio doubted: he had been turned down for the post as director of the Palermo slaughterhouse after failing to recognise a four-month pregnant goat) was friendly with such influential figures as Lo Monte, La Bella, and Sgarlata. Mori's respect for him was shown by a circular of 31 December 1926, to all local officials, telling them to take out subscriptions to *Sicilia Zootecnica*. This periodical, run by Miceli, had become the official organ of the Animal Branding and Registration Service.[109]

Bagheria was another place that was chaotic in 1927. This town had been a political stronghold of Giuseppe Cirincione, a famous oculist and a friend of Cucco. In 1923, he had dislodged the administration of the radical deputy, Giuseppe Scialabba, in the course of the local fascist party's drive against the mafia. However, when Cucco fell from power the tables were turned. 'A cyclone of slanders', he wrote to Antonino Di Giorgio on 5 January 1927, 'threatens to hurl into the mud forty blameless years of hard work.' He had been suspended from university teaching, he said, and the reason lay, so he had heard, 'in my links with...the mafia!' Mori was to make an enquiry into his 'forebears and family' ('on behalf of [Govanni] Gentile and the Minister [of Education, Pietro] Fedele, who both have grudges against me'), and the starting point was a memorandum (which was subsequently passed to the Duce), 'drawn up by a *pretore* whom I had removed from Bagheria last year because he was a protector of the mafia, as was shown by an inquiry that I instigated'.

Cirincione believed that personal vendetta was largely to blame for his misfortune. However, it was not the only factor. Mori, he said, was viewing his case unfavourably,

> because the police have came across replies that I had written to requests for favours, in the homes of some of those who have been arrested. These are electoral letters, and in Bagheria they are an unmitigated nuisance, as the deputy has traditionally been considered a person you solicit for anything. Like my predecessor. . .I answered everybody, regardless of rank or character, and in my own hand.

How could such correspondence be a crime, he asked? Moreover, had he not always himself been a staunch opponent of the mafia?

> Everything I have done shows my hostility towards that rabble .... In my local administration (Bagheria), I chose the councillors personally, and not a single *mafioso*, or relative of a *mafioso*, has got in.... In order to make life harder for *mafiosi*, I had the rural guards replaced by sworn policeman. But I had to struggle manfully to get my way, and the prefect of the time sent me his warmest congratulations, and I still have them. From then on the countryside here has been free from crime. It is only because *pretore* Gestivo and the *mafiosi* hate me, that I have had to suffer the humiliation of seeing them credited rather than me.[110]

After Cirincione's fall, a special delegate was appointed to Bagheria, and Onofrio Corselli assumed control of the local party. This caused a good deal of surprise. Corselli had been an opponent of Cirincione; but he was also a follower of Giuseppe Scialabba, many of whose supporters had been arrested the previous year as *mafiosi*. This put the police in an awkward position. The local superintendent tried to explain the situation in a report of May 1927. It was true, he said, that at the time of the 1924 elections Scialabba had formed a bloc in opposition to Cirincione, made up of the local mafia, the fascists, the Servicemen, the War-Wounded and the ex-mayor, Galioto, 'cousin of the notorious brigand Salvatore Galioto': 'This bloc was actively supported by all the militant mafia, and is at present involved in the criminal association that was unearthed here'. It seems that Corselli had not kept good company.

Despite this, the police superintendent of Bagheria (who was writing in reply to an anonymous letter that had been sent to the *questore* of Palermo) believed Corselli to be 'of good moral and political character', and said that 'no criticism could be made of his honesty and probity'. 'Clearly,' he added somewhat lamely, because of his origins, [Corselli] was unable subsequently to sever his political ties with members of the old Scialabban party, composed, as I said, of the real militant mafia. However, he is disliked by the followers of Cirincione, who for obvious reasons find it convenient to hurl abuse at him. He is also disliked by them because he enjoys the confidence of the *podestà*, Colonel Nunzio Punzo.[111]

The superintendent's faith in Corselli was not shared by everybody. In September 1927, Giuseppe Gotta reported on the widespread discontent that had been caused in Bagheria by Corselli's reinstatement:

Colonel Punzo, a true gentleman, and now *podestà* of Bagheria, seems to have fallen completely under the spell of the courteous Cav. Corselli, who is causing real disquiet among the local population, who know his political background (Scialabban). It is with much sadness that they witness the reinstatement of the 1923 bloc, and of people who are anything but fascist – in fact real opponents of fascism – and the resulting re-emergence of the politics of 1922, that left the commune with 1,200,000 lire of debts and the mafia in control.

According to Gotta, 'the true fascists' had been prevented from collaborating with the *podestà* and also from entering the newly reconstituted local party. Bagheria, he concluded, was once more in the hands of the 'old Scialabban mafia'.[112]

In 1928, Cucco summed up the political situation in the province of Palermo as: 'Mafia and *quartarellismo* in power'.[113] This charge was not always easy to refute. The problem, in very general terms, was that those who had formed the opposition factions between 1923 and 1927 were now in power; and these same factions had sometimes furnished the backbone of the *retate* in 1926. Mori must have found this embarrassing, but he could do little about it. 'It is true that he is the half-brother of the criminal, Salvatore Di Bella', he told the Minister of the Interior in June 1927, after anonymous letters had been received attacking the new political secretary of Montelepre, Dr Vito Gaglio, 'who on 2 August 1926 was charged, while in custody, with criminal association...He is also the nephew of Giovanni Gaglio, brother-in-law of the *mafioso*, Michele Catalano.'[114] Mori evidently had little regard for Dr Gaglio, but he passed no judgement on him; and the following year Gaglio was still political secretary of Montelepre. As at Bagheria, the trouble seems to have been that the opposition group was too compromised by its links with Cucco to furnish an acceptable alternative.

The situation in Trapani

The upheaval in Palermo sent shock waves beyond the provincial boundaries. Early in February 1927, the prefect of Trapani, Giuseppe Sallicano, informed the Ministry of the Interior that since his last report at Christmas, relations between the local party leaders had seriously declined. The deputies Maccotta and La Bella had fallen out with the provincial secretary, Giuseppe Fontana, and all three were at odds with Giuseppe Rubino. Moreover, factionalism was on the increase again, particularly in such 'turbulent towns' as Alcamo and Castelvetrano.[115] The following month, with the situation still in disarray, the deputy, Manfredo Chiostri, was sent from Rome as 'commissioner extraordinary' for Trapani. On 24 May, Prefect Sallicano reported that all the provincial *fasci* had been dissolved, and delegates appointed to reform them within twenty days. In addition, 204 party members, 'who were criminal or notoriously *mafiosi*', had been expelled.[116]

Chiostri was no admirer of Mori, and this, as Mori himself lamented to the Under-Secretary of the Interior, inevitably caused problems:

I was aware – and I have a great deal of evidence for it – that ever since he came to Sicily, charged by the party with the supervision of fascism in the province of Trapani, Chiostri took it on himself to conduct, among other things, a kind of systematic defamation of me...I would very much have liked – and had hoped to be asked – to clarify matters, so that finally I could confound both him and the various Rubinos, Cuccos, Ciarlantinis and their like, who have been permitted to heap up so many foul lies, slanders and insinuations against me. But I was not allowed to, and I continued to keep quiet, even when I was told that the prefect of Trapani, Comm. Sallicano – for reasons that are easy to imagine – was in league with Chiostri. Now, however, I can no longer hold my peace.[117]

Mori considered that his good work in the province was being undone. At Trapani, he wrote, in August 1927, referring to the period 1924–5, 'I found myself confronting, after only four or five months, the pseudo-fascist positions polluted or weakened by the mafia. Naturally, I had to destroy them. It was logical.'[118] He now felt that under the influence of Chiostri and Sallicano, the local mafia was being reinstated: 'I had left the province of Trapani in perfect calm', he told Mussolini, somewhat petulantly, 'and in such a condition that all that was needed was to continue along the lines I had laid down in order to achieve a definitive solution.'[119] He had even heard that the *questore* of Trapani had said 'that there was no need to proceed against the upper mafia as its components had a vested interest in collaborating with the police to maintain order in the island'.[120]

The new situation in Trapani caused considerable difficulties for Mori's friends in the province. One of these, Alfredo Armato, wrote to him in July about the 'diabolical work that is being conducted in the prefecture of Trapani against those fascists who made the grave mistake of collaborating with you in the sacred task of re-generating this province in the period when you were its perfect'. Sallicano, he said, had even gone so far as to declare that Mori was 'liquidated', and that he had on his conscience 13,000 arrests, which he would 'sooner or later have to account for'.[121] Another of Mori's friends, Rosario La Bella, was more or less drummed out of the province at the beginning of August, with orders from the party secretary, Turati, never to involve himself again in Trapani politics. He took refuge in Palermo, where he was guaranteed a more favourable reception.[122]

What was Mori to make of this? Could it be that his position was not quite as secure as he had imagined? In August, he was summoned to Rome by Mussolini to discuss the situation in Trapani.[123] The Duce evidently took his side, as Prefect Sallicano was withdrawn from service a few weeks later.[124] The party secretary, however, (whom he apparently met at the same time) was evidently less sympathetic. 'A while back in Rome,' Mori told Count Suardo in November, 'His Excellency Turati asked me a significant question: *what the devil is going on in Sicily*? Then, after referring to the wave of denunciations and complaints that were pouring into the party executive from Sicily, he added: *I no longer understand anything.*' Did Turati not realise, he said, that the campaign against him was the work of the mafia?[125]

9 THE EFFECT ON THE ECONOMY

The imagery of the campaign

The replacement of Cucco and his parvenu friends with members of the landed aristocracy was a political move. It was convenient that the operation could be couched in criminal terms. The charge of 'mafia' or '*mafioso*' invested power struggles with an aura of altruism and respectability. That experts such as Mori had no clear idea about the precise nature of the mafia made little practical difference. Since the 1860s the word had become encrusted with sinister connotations, and any underlying substance had not only been lost to view, but had also become of secondary importance. The most powerful aspect of the mafia lay in the moral indignation that the term aroused. This indignation was such that despite little or no evidence, the collective imagination had created a secret society, criminal and violent in character, with initiation ceremonies, courts of justice, its own language and system of recruitment, and strict codes of honour and conduct.

Although it was intangible, the mafia was often described in concrete terms as a beast of terrifying proportions. Cucco referred to it in one of his newspaper articles as 'a huge and manifold octopus with long and impalpable tentacles',[1] while the writer, Guglielmo Policastro, spoke of 'a repulsive and mastodontic sphinx'. Sometimes the imagery of the Divine Comedy was used: Simone Sirena called the mafia 'an insatiable she-wolf possessed of every lust'.[3] Monsters were best destroyed by heroes, and Mori was often compared to mythical figures: Perseus and Hercules were deemed particularly apt.[4] Among the many gifts he received while at Palermo were a bass relief of Perseus cutting off the head of the Medusa and a painting of a human giant with, on one side, a group of workers kissing the hem of his cloak, on the other, 'a *mafioso* crushed and humiliated'.[5]

While the heroic image suited Mori emotionally, it did not satisfy him intellectually. He preferred to see his campaign against the mafia as a combination of repression from above and popular assertion from below. He wanted Sicilians to take responsibility for their own problems, and not stand passively by as the police did all the work for them. He expressed this idea in the phrase 'elimination through environmental auto-expulsion'.[6] The image that he found most useful was of a tumour attacking a potentially healthy body, for which the best cure was a mixture of surgery and prophylactic therapy. Medical analogies were used by a number of observers at this time, including Mussolini.[7] The logic of such imagery was conservative. A cure implied a restoration to a former state of health; it offered little scope for any change in the underlying organic structure.

Mori regarded Sicilian society as thoroughly infected. Shortly after his arrival at Palermo he announced that he intended to free the island from the ills which 'paralyse, pervert and pollute every form of social activity'.[8] One area to which he paid great attention was the economy. His 'surgery' here consisted of removing *mafiosi* from the Palermo bureaucracy and arresting troublesome *gabelloti*. He sought to underpin these measures by reinforcing the values of hard work and respect for private property. The government also contributed its share by initiating a programme of 'integral land reclamation' (*bonifica integrale*). Whether these means were appropriate, however, to the declared end of regeneration is uncertain. When viewed in terms of illness and cure, a campaign against the mafia tended to eliminate those elements that threatened not only the moral, but also the social order. Renewal, in other words, was to be a by-product of retrenchment and reaction. Was it possible, however, to combine these two ideas? Had there ever been a time when the Sicilian body politic was healthy, and to which fascism could restore it by clearing away the detritus of the mafia?

The Palermo bureaucracy

The Palermo bureaucracy began to be purged in the spring of 1927, but maladministration had been a long-standing evil. A particular source of concern was the disarray in municipal finances. According to the *Giornale d'Italia* in November 1925, the city was 'weighed down with debts like a young libertine of a good family'. Such, in fact, was the deficit, the paper went on, that 'so-called experts could not agree on its size: a few billion here, a few billion there'.[9] In January 1926, the *Avvenire di Sicilia* painted a similarly alarming picture, and suggested that Mori's operation against the mafia should focus on the city as well as the countryside, a piece of advice that resulted in the confiscation of the paper for propagating 'tendentious information'.[10] However, Mori's hands were to a large extent tied at this stage of the campaign by political considerations: he could not purge the city bureaucracy without raising a storm of protest that might prove unmanageable.

Some of the obstacles in the path of municipal reform can be seen in a vitriolic report sent to Arnaldo Mussolini in February 1926. Mori, said its anonymous author, was the kind of man Sicily needed; but he was in a difficult position:

> He sees his way ever more blocked, not by the mafia in the strict sense of the word, but by the exponents of Sicilian fascism who, in order to reach the high positions which they now hold, formerly had to come to some form of agreement with the mafia, represented in the city by the higher dignitaries who today sing hymns to the Duce, just as yesterday they fought him with drawn swords, and tomorrow will fight him with every weapon at their disposal.

To illustrate his argument, the author of the report considered the recent attempt by the Palermo administration to lower the cost of fish. The local speculator-traders, he said, had usually charged so much that the city council was able to acquire the produce from the wholesalers and sell it directly to the population at 50% of the normal price, and still make a substantial profit:

> The people rejoiced, cried out, and sang Hosannas to their redeemer fascism...But immediately, the fishmongers very cunningly formed themselves into a fascist union and, after one day, the market returned to the control of the speculators, who naturally not only restored the old prices, but also increased them...just a shade...Now people are saying that robbery and speculation can be legalised with a party card: the 'card–carrying Mafia'.[11]

The report blamed Cucco ('the most *mafioso* among the *mafiosi*') for this parlous state of affairs. As so often, however, a complex issue was personalised, and turned into a question of mafia. Why Cucco should have been held responsible for the shortcomings of an administration that was certainly not his puppet, nor even very sympathetic to him, is far from clear. Furthermore, the city council could hardly hope for complete domination of the market. There were pressures from below to contend with, as well as manipulation from above. Even the consumers were something of an unknown quantity: 'While in Piazza Caracciolo,' said one newspaper report, 'there was cheap fish on sale,...in Piazza Nuova a crowd of gallant people...was hurrying to buy expensive fish from the loathsome rabble whom it is in everyone's interest to force to surrender'.[12]

In December 1926, an erstwhile supporter of Orlando, Professor Salvatore Di Marzo, became Palermo's new *podestà*. At the inauguration ceremony to mark his investiture, Mori presented him with a steel pen with which to sign his name: 'It is not of gold', he said, 'It is of a nobler metal: of that same metal out of which warrior Italy shaped the sword of Vittorio Veneto.'[13] Di Marzo, however, was not noted for his bellicose qualities. Mori described him as 'universally recognised as being above all suspicion', but he had one major defect, he said: he was weak and was 'thus easily dominated by the communal bureaucracy'.[14] In March 1927, following Cucco's expulsion from the party, Di Marzo was granted exceptional powers by the government, 'to carry out a radical reorganisation of the administration and a purge of public employees'.[15]

It was Di Marzo's 'weakness' that created difficulties, since his own probity was not always matched by that of his colleagues. Among the most predatory of the city councillors was the Communal Secretary, Rosciglione: 'Di Marzo seems unable', the Under-Secretary of the Interior told Mori in September 1927, 'to free himself from the will of the Communal Secretary, who is generally regarded as the true *podestà* of Palermo, despite the fact that he has always shown a total incomprehension of the spirit of fascism.' However, the Under-Secretary went on, Di Marzo would be hard to dislodge as certain people had a vested interest in his continuing in power: 'It has been pointed out that the deputy, Guido Jung, would be strongly opposed to his replacement. Jung is a major exporter of nuts, and the excise duties agreed some time ago between him and the *podestà* (who was then mayor) established the lowest rate for this commodity.'[16]

The purge of the bureaucracy was regarded by some people as unduly negative. More than five hundred individuals were dismissed from their posts in the space of a year, and they were not replaced. According to Mori, this was because the remaining personnel was sufficient for the city's needs.[17] However, it might also have been that suitable substitutes were unavailable. Critics pointed out that the dismissals, together with the lengthy enquiries into every employee's past, lowered the prestige of the administration without remedying its defects. The situation might have been improved, one observer felt, if the new leaders of Palermo fascism had endeavoured to raise morale; but they did not: 'They denigrate rather than assist,' he wrote,' and they lack the prestige to make good what they honestly believe to be defective.'[18]

Mori was enthusiastic about the purge. He told the Ministry of the Interior in July 1928 that his enquiries had revealed a truly corrupt system. At election time, the city council employed 'a mass' of political supporters to act as 'agents and vote gatherers'. This, he said, explained the frequency with which the administration had in the past 'shelved' criminal enquiries, and why there had been such a poor attendance record among local bureaucrats. Employees 'pressurised' councillors into finding jobs for their relatives; as a result, 'family clusters' (*grappoli familiari*) had appeared 'dominating departments, and providing mutual help for personal advantage'. He believed that the dismissal of the five hundred employees had created a good impression in the city; henceforth, administration would be guided by sounder, more disinterested, criteria. Whenever an official failed in his duties, he would now be punished: public interests would prevail over private.[19]

The purge of the Palermo administration was particularly pressing in view of the large sums being allocated for public works. In May 1926, a royal decree spoke of 'the urgent and overwhelming need' for reform if the city was to carry out a massive programme of public works in the decade down to 1936.[20] How far did Mori's campaign succeed in establishing the necessary spirit of disinterestedness in the bureaucracy? Were the 'family clusters', of which he so much disapproved, eliminated? Given the dearth of solid evidence, any accurate assessment of change is hard to make. However, a superficial glance at the 1930s does not suggest any radical amelioration. One problem was that after 1929 the government refused to admit to the existence of the mafia. In order to avoid being shown up, the regime now had to suppress evidence of crime and corruption in Sicily. This meant a lowering of the threshold of accountability.

The situation in 1934 may have been exceptional, but it was nonetheless revealing. In February, the British consul in Palermo, Major Dodds, wrote to the ambassador to say that 'rumours too persistent to be ignored' were circulating about malpractices in the city administration. The government had appointed a 'commissioner extraordinary' to replace the *podestà*; and his first act had been to suspend the Communal Secretary, Rosciglione, and his assistant, Cosentino. Rosciglione had apparently accumulated 'a small fortune which he could not possibly have saved out of his meagre salary'. What is more, said Dodds the loan of 30 million lire a year for public works, 'by no means represents the amount... that has passed through the hands of the municipality'. For example, large sums had been earmarked for road building, 'yet the condition of the roads is little better than six years ago'. One of his colleagues had even seen a workman 'squirting coloured liquid instead of the bitumen contracted for on to the road'. Before dispatching this report to Rome, Dodds learnt that Cosentino had been reinstalled, and Rosciglione transferred to another department of the administration: 'This is probably all that will be heard of the matter. At all costs a scandal must be avoided.'[21]

That, however, was not the end of the affair. In March more evidence came to light of financial malpractice. One official, who had recently been forced to resign, declared that the losses sustained by the city council had been much exaggerated. They were due, he said, 'rather to the dishonesty of the contractors than to the officials of the Municipality'. 'According to Major Dodds' informant', wrote the British Ambassador to the Foreign Secretary in London,

> the contractors have for many years made a ring and agreed among themselves as to the amount of the secret tenders to be sent in, which were always considerably in excess of the real value of the contracts. Major Dodds says that it is difficult to believe that the municipal authorities could have been so ignorant of the value of the contracts as to allow such proceedings; and if they were not ignorant it must have been worth their while to remain silent.[22]

In November the 'commissioner extraordinary' announced that the municipal budget had been balanced. However, even this did not bring an end to the scandal. In January the new *podestà* revealed, to everyone's amazement, that there was still a deficit of 40 million lire. He demonstrated that the so-called 'balancing' had been achieved by juggling with figures for the 1926 loan from the Credit Association for Public Works. 'As far as Sicily is concerned', said Dodds, '[fascism] has done nothing to purify the administration. The officials are badly paid and, I am told by old residents, graft is as prevalent as it was under all previous regimes....Even when dishonesty is brought home to a Government employee he is not punished in a manner to deter others from following his example.'[23]

The changes in agriculture

Though the advent of fascism destroyed any immediate hopes for the breakup of the *latifondi*, the debate on Sicilian agriculture continued. After 1922, a number of intransigent fascists continued to argue that the condition of the peasantry would have to be improved if the spectre of Bolshevism were to be permanently exorcised. That meant saving them from what a writer in Cucco's newspaper, *Sicilia Nuova*, called 'the seigneurial yoke'. Fascism, he explained, aimed at 'the elevation of the worker and the defence of capital'. It was therefore imperative to 'destroy baronial tyrannies and save the proletariat from the twin evils of feudalism and communism'. The solution, he said, to both aspects of the problem lay in the formation of small-holdings.[24]

Some of the best argued and most radical views came from Caltanissetta, the province with the greatest concentration of *latifondi*. Damiano Lipani's newspaper, *Sicilia Fascista*, focused its attack on absentee landowners and *gabelloti*. An article in November 1925 suggested that the only hope of change lay in extending the terms of

contracts 'to give greater freedom of action to the tenants who usually have more entrepreneurial spirit than the owners'. At present, the
author said, nobody had an interest in improvement: the proprietor
clung to his land possessively 'like a husband', while the tenant exploited it 'like a lover'.[25] Writing in the same newspaper in March
1925, Nunzio Prestianni criticised the irrational manner in which
smallholdings had been formed in recent years. There had been
insufficient planning, he said: plots were too small and were often
widely scattered, and apart from greater use of the beans–grain ro-
tation, 'methods of cultivation have remained unaltered'. He claimed
that the only way to achieve 'true and lasting progress' was to settle
the farmer permanently in the countryside.[26]

While the radical fascists were not too worried about the effects of
economic reform on the position of the great landowners, the *agrari*
themselves naturally were. More intensive methods of production
might have resulted in the peasantry growing wealthier and less resigned, and this was obviously not in the interests of the *latifondisti*.
As it was, the situation had been bad enough in the war years when,
as one observer said in Contessa Entellina, 'the rich fell, and the
scrofulous ascended'.[27] Fortunately for the *agrari*, however, almost
all commentators were united in their opposition to these 'scrofulous' parvenus, many of whom were *gabelloti*. The meeting-point between the demands of the reformers and the fears of the landowners
was their mutual dislike for Sicily's parasitic middle class.

'Through imposition, pressure, and every sort of crime', wrote
Mori in his memoirs, 'the mafia had succeeded in buying or leasing
at knock-down prices many of the best fields and *latifondi* in the
island. Landowners – particularly the great landowners – thus found
themselves with their backs to the wall.'[28] The peasantry had also
suffered, he claimed, as they had been exposed to harsh and in-
equitable contracts. This militated against class collaboration, 'which
is one of the tenets of the regime'.[29] However, in proceeding against
the *gabelloti*, Mori had to face up to the fact that most of the existing
leases were valid. He solved the difficulty by arguing that they had
been entered into under duress, and could therefore be rescinded.
This inevitably opened the gate to arbitrariness. 'I admit', said Mori,
'that I set no store by the civil code, but I did rely . . . a great deal on
the reaction of the landowners concerned, and above all on my personal initiative'.[30]

In his second ordinance as prefect of Palermo, dated 9 January
1926, Mori instituted stern measures against the rural mafia. All field
guards, whether *guardiani*, *curatoli*, *campieri*, or *soprastanti*, would
henceforward have to be cleared with the authorities before taking
up their posts. They were to be issued with identity cards; and their
collaboration with the police in the fight against crime would be

mandatory. The ordinance also contained clauses dealing with 'un-healthy' latifondi. Whenever, it said, the local police, *carabinieri*, and Itinerant Agricultural Education Service (*Cattedra ambulante di agri-coltura*) considered an estate to be party in some way to criminal activity, they would declare it 'an infected centre'. Its administrators would then be summoned, and if they failed to give a satisfactory account of themselves, the authorities would proceed with 'the ne-cessary enquiries and take all the administrative and penal measures demanded by the situation'.[31]

The grounds for declaring an estate 'infected' were very broad. It was sufficient that there was 'action damaging to the free exercise of agricultural activities in the area, and to law and order'. Despite this vagueness, the penalties sanctioned by the ordinance were severe. In addition to criminal charges, personnel could be dismissed, arms li-cences withdrawn, and goods and animals 'of suspected provenance' confiscated. The problem of contracts and leases was tackled in an equally forthright way. Once the authorities had established that the mafia was in control of an estate, Mori would issue an edict, revising or rescinding any existing agreements. As he explained in his me-moirs, this was necessary 'in order to wrench from the mafia the control of landed property and the running of farms'. The task of purging the countryside was carried out, under the aegis of Mori, by a special commision composed of police, agricultural experts, and representatives of fascist unions.[32]

The most striking result of the commission's activities was the enormous increase in land rents. Mori claimed that in the province of Palermo alone, 320 estates were 'freed from the mafia', and 28,000 hectares 'resumed their true value'.[33] The difference between the old and new rents came to over eighteen million lire. In many instances the rises were of the order of several hundred percent. At Pallavicino, for example, the Castelforte *latifondo*, which had previously been leased for 14,000 lire, was revalued at 45,000 lire. On the *ex-feudo* Pirello the respective figures were 18,000 and 90,000 lire; on the *feudo* Modici, 25,000 and 75,000 lire.[34] A particularly dramatic increase occurred with the *ex-feudo* Ciambra, owned by the poet–baron, Filippo Agnello. The rent on this estate rose from 4,000 to 60,000 lire, an increase of 1,500%.[35] No wonder he described Mori, in one of his poems, as 'the most marvellous gift the Duce has given me'. Nor is it surprising to find him telling the new *gabelloti* on his estate to paint the words '*Viva* Mori' on the east wall of the farmhouse.[36]

Though statistical evidence is lacking, it seems that a good many of the old contracts had become worthless as a result of post-war inflation. In other words, the low rents received by the landowners may have been due to factors other than *mafiosi* imposing in-equitable terms. Another feature of the post-war economy that might have irritated some *agrari* was the upward spiral in land prices: those with estates *in gabella* were perhaps deprived of the chance to speculate on sales. One way of ecaping from contractual obligations was to have lessees denounced as *mafiosi*. This is what Paolo Savoca apparently did to remove a number of his father-in-law's *gabelloti*: for twelve years, he claimed, they had been paying ridiculously low rents.[37] A report among Mori's papers on ninety-five 'estates and *feudi* declared as infected zones, because occupied by mafia tenants', includes entries such as: '*Ex Feudo* Sagana...leased for a paltry sum to four *mafiosi* of S. Giuseppe Iato in 1922 for 18 years, has been freed.'[38] Sadly, neither this report, nor another on 105 estates with '*gabelloti mafiosi*',[39] furnishes any uniform data about the contracts.

The reports are equally unrevealing about the fate of the *feudi* after the *gabelloti* had been removed. In two cases discussed in the second report, cultivation is said to have been conceded directly to the owner, while in fifteen instances the land was to be farmed 'in accordance with the latest norms in agricultural leases'. What happened on other estates in the province is also far from clear. In a speech, probably in 1928, Mori talked of many owners 'returning to exercise their property rights, resuming the noble georgic [*sic*] traditions of their familes'. On 206 estates, he said, 'the proprietors have in effect taken possession of their land again, assuming its administration, and disproving once more the legend of their absenteeism'.[40] Did this mean that the figure of the *gabelloto* had disappeared altogether?

This was certainly the general intention, for the *gabelloto* was blamed both for the backwardness of Sicilian agriculture and for class hostility. In February 1927, the secretary-general of the Federaion of Fascist Agricultural Unions told a meeting of rural workers that the main enemy of the peasantry was not the *latifondo*, but the *gabelloto*. Fascism, he said, must 'defuse old hatreds,...restore harmony in the work place, and break the yolk of the *gabelloti*, that symbol of injustice and backwardness'. Luigi Ciardi, one of Sicily's most prominent labour officials, spoke at the same meeting of the difficulties that had been encountered in 1925 and 1926 in trying to ensure that agricultural agreements were honoured. He attributed this primarily to 'the obstacles placed in our way by rural crime'.[41] The answer, he suggested, was to destroy the mafia and above all its principal exponent in the countryside, the *gabelloto*.

Four months later, another meeting was held, this time with representatives of the provincial trade unions. At issue was the problem of agricultural contracts. The debate, according to Mori, was 'full' and 'serene', and the upshot was a five-point deliberation which demonstrated, he said, the resolve of owners and workers alike to combat the mafia.[42] The most important feature of this agreement was a declaration that all *gabelloti* 'who did not farm directly' would

be eliminated, 'in a decisive repudiation of every form of intermediary...and every kind of exploitation, direct or indirect, of property and labour'. Commentators regarded this clause as sounding
the death-knell of the 'parasitic' *gabelloto*. However, it was clear that
the *gabelloto* as such would not disappear. This left awkward questions about the distinction between 'direct' and 'indirect', 'parasitic'
and 'non-parasitic', unresolved.[43]

In 1928 the theme of the *gabelloto* was still very much alive. 'We
are faced with a grave situation today', declared the secretary of the
Agricultural Section of Palermo in June. 'Most owners do not wish
to lease their land to workers, but insist on giving it to *gabelloti*...
with a consequent return to the mafia mentality of tyranny, arrogance, and exploitation.'[44] At a provincial congress the following
month, a proposal was made to set up a commission to investigate
the situation on the great estates, 'looking at the *gabelloti*, one by one,
with a view to eliminating them permanently'.[45] Clearly many of
the hopes of 1927 had still to be realised, and there was every indication that the *agrari* were far less willing to relinquish their traditional practices than Mori liked to believe.

The main reason why the *gabelloto* proved so enduring was that
nobody had a vested interest in his elimination, except, perhaps, the
peasants, and arguably, even their feelings were mixed. The *gabelloto*
was extremely useful to the *agrari*. He saved them the bother of
humdrum administration and contact with the masses, and he left
them free to reside in the cities, where patronage was concentrated
and where the social life was more stimulating than in the small towns
of the interior. He also helped to discipline and repress the rural
work-force. The proviso, of course, was that he did not grow ambitious at the landowners' expense. The post of *gabelloto* was also attractive to ambitious and assertive peasants: it offered an avenue to
wealth and power, and, in a society where status was keenly felt,
many people were prepared to condone violence if it meant an escape
from grinding poverty and social impotence.[46]

In an article published in 1929, the economist, Nunzio Prestianni,
admitted that the hopes for the elimination of the 'intermediary *gabelloto*' had not been realised. He claimed that many *gabelloti* had
forced their subtenants to become sharecroppers, and this had allowed
them to pose as 'direct' farmers and so retain control of their land.
Others had 'handed back' estates to the owners, and had become instead 'proforma administrators', 'continuing wholly or partially with
the ruinous old methods'. Such changes had done nothing to benefit
Sicilian agriculture:

The transformation from subtenancy to sharecropping obliges
the lessee to take an interest in the production process; but it also

facilitates the pursuit of his own advantage. On the other hand, becoming the landowner's proforma administrator allows him to continue as an intermediary and often too as a parasite. The owner should not permit this latter system, while fairer conditions of sharecropping, to the peasant's advantage, would prevent those specious, administrative conversions from subtenancy to *métayage*.[47]

The much vaunted return of the *agrari* to their estates must have been either short-lived or very partial. In truth, few Sicilian owners had a serious interest in agriculture, at least from a commercial point of view. 'They were,' wrote Giovanni Lorenzoni in 1940, 'and alas, to a large extent they still are, absentee.'[48] The 'typical country gentleman of Sicily', who could 'cultivate plants and letters with equal love', and who had been driven from his property by the '*mafioso* speculator', was largely a figment of Simone Sirena's imagination. His mental landscape was closer to the bucolic vision of ancient authors such as Theocritus, than to the real conditions of the late 1920s. Myths, however, had a political function, and Sirena knew it:

> When a strong and benevolent government is in power, that protects the work-force and provides justice, . . . there is no need for special laws to split up the *latifondo*. Society's leaders find their rightful place. . . . The hierarchy is re-established. In transforming the face of Sicily, one gesture from Mori has been worth more than a thousand votes of ineffective assemblies.[49]

Sirena was clearly happy with the government's campaign against the mafia, and with good reason. The elimination of the *gabelloto mafioso*, the ensuing rise in rents, and the entry of the landed aristocracy into Palermo fascism, added to the gains that the *agrari* had already made from the introduction of wheat tariffs. If the revaluation of the lira in 1926 had affected exports or production costs, there was now ample compensation. The gratitude of the Palermo landowners was lavishly expressed. Receptions and parties were held in Mori's honour, and Mori himself was eager to reciprocate. 'The gathering had an aristocratic and most distinguished air', said a report on one of the prefect's galas in 1928, 'with the presence of our finest élite.' A similar function, in the same year, was attended by 'the most select representatives' of the aristocracy, and included a jazz band for entertainment.[50]

The official line on Mori's work in Sicily stressed the gains for ordinary people as well as the landowners. The mafia, the argument ran, had oppressed the poor as well as the rich, and the elimination of rural crime now allowed the peasants to travel to and from work without fear of being robbed. Their gratitude was said to be unbounded. According to one writer, Mori was honoured with votive gifts and his portrait graced every rural dwelling.[51] Whether there was any truth in such claims is not certain. If there was any gratitude, it was evidently not the result of economic gains. Between 1928 and 1935 official indexes showed a national decline of 28% in agricultural wages, and mounting unemployment and casual labour added to the problem. In 1934 it was reported that rural labourers in Sicily could not find work for more than 160 days a year; it is unlikely that the situation was much better in the late 1920s. Furthermore, the post-war boom in smallholdings slowed dramatically after 1924, and the revaluation of the lira forced some, perhaps many, of the new owners to sell out.[52]

The government set great store by its collective agricultural contracts, but the optimism was misplaced. To begin with, national wage reductions after 1926 were not offset by a comparable fall in prices. The situation appears to have been particularly bad in Palermo, where wholesalers and retailers indulged in what one newspaper called 'the usual game of pass the buck' in an attempt to keep prices up.[53] Secondly, contracts were frequently broken. In 1929 the sulphur workers of Riesi and Sommatino were paid only 12.7 lire a day instead of the stipulated 14.6 lire.[54] Nor were such injustices easy to remedy, as an appeal ran the risk of antagonising the employer, with possibly ruinous results. There was also no guarantee that a court action would succeed, however blatant the infringement. In 1934, a Palermo businessman was prosecuted for violation of contract. The judge decided that he was guilty, but also ruled that his twenty-seven employees were 'accomplices' as they had 'consented' to work under the illegal conditions. They were fined, and those who could not afford to pay were sent to prison.[55]

With the *agrari* in control of Palermo fascism from early 1927, the peasants were more vulnerable than ever to reactionary pressures. Their main union representative, Luigi Ciardi, was a man of integrity, with over twenty years of experience in labour relations. However, he was a northerner, rather unfamiliar, perhaps, with Sicilian problems, and by temperament, modest.[56] Against him were pitted such men as Simone Sirena, whose commission of agricultural experts were nicknamed 'the Firebreathers' for their ruthlessness with the new land rents.[57] Mori claimed that these rents were almost always fixed 'to the advantage of the unions', but there was probably not much negotiation involved.[58] The prefect himself was proud of the rises as he saw them as an indication of how repressive the mafia had been. It was also unclear what degree of impartiality could be expected from Sirena, who described the Sicilian *latifondista* as 'a true *patronus* in the patriarchal, and almost biblical, sense off the word, loved faithfully by his dependents'.[59]

The defence of private property

In his memoirs, Mori wrote: 'The campaign was not to be a police operation in more or less grand style, but a revolution in consciousness, a spiritual revolt, an action of the people.'[60] Though most of his time at Palermo was taken up with repressive measures, he also focused on education. He felt that if the mafia was to be destroyed permanently, Sicilians needed to learn respect for private property and appreciate the true value of hard work. He thought it was the failure of the local population to react more vigorously against parasitism and lawlessness that had given criminals such free rein, and he attributed this inertia largely to the absence of the state. Mori set out to strengthen the island's moral fibre, and one of the ways of achieving this, he felt, was through propaganda.

Mori made respect for private property, and its protection, into fundamental civic duties: 'It is the sacred task of every citizen', he declared in a speech at Castronuovo, 'to defend individual property, because it is an essential element of the nation's wealth.'[61] This idea dovetailed comfortably into the fight against the mafia:

> To make an assault on the life and possessions of a citizen, and to undermine the profitability of his work, is not simply a crime against an individual and his property, but also a betrayal of one's country...Therefore, friends, from this day on, let me no longer hear, as I did recently, the words: *down with the mafia! down with crime!* That cry, my friends, is now outdated. It is a fine cry, but it is the cry of vigilance. Today, friends, as we attack the final trenches, while the action is in full flow, your cry must be another, a cry of battle: *up and at the mafia! up and at crime!*[62]

Mori repeated this call to arms in defence of private property in many speeches.[63] Nor was he thinking in metaphorical terms only. He offered prizes to anyone who was prepared to resist criminals with force. At Bisacquino, for example, a peasant who had killed one thief and seriously wounded another was rewarded with a silver medal.[64] At least seventeen such prizes, ten of them in cash, were distributed while Mori was in Palermo.[65] In some ways, this was a rather curious aspect of the campaign. The dividing line between self-defence and self-interst was often hard to detect: an act of vendetta might readily be presented as an example of vigilance. Moreover, was there not a case for saying that Sicilians were already too prone to private violence?

The most dramatic demonstration of Mori's desire to reinforce respect for private property was the oath sworn by the *campieri* in May 1926.[66] The whole occasion was solemnised by giving it a military and religious character. Invitations were sent out to every *campiere* in the province of Palermo. Over 1,200 turned up, and the two

Pl. 13. Mori presenting a medal to a *campiere*.

who could not attend sent medical certificates to prove they were sick. They assembled on a small hill overlooking the railway station at Roccapalumba, and were placed, as if in battle formation, with the mounted men in front in double file and those on foot on the flanks. After being greeted at the station by local party representatives and a crowd of peasants chanting '*alalà*', Mori walked up the hill to review the assembled *campieri*. 'We need to give these people a new soul', he said to one journalist, 'because the material is there and it is good.'[67]

In his speech at Roccapalumba, Mori declared that henceforward the *campieri* were to defend private property on behalf of the state, not the mafia. They would retain their traditional character, he said, but now, more than ever, they should be prepared to give their lives for the land in their custody. Above all, they should have no truck whatsoever with criminals.[68] After the speech, an army chaplain said mass on an improvised altar. Mori stood with his back to the *campieri*, so giving anyone who wanted to, he said, a chance to leave before they swore an oath of loyalty to the king and the state. During the sermon, the chaplain reminded his congregation of the solemnity of the undertaking they were about to make. Mori then turned once again to the *campieri*: none of them had left. He read out the formula of the oath: 'A single voice', said the report in *L'Ora*, 'resounded through the huge plain: I swear'.[69] The mass was finished, the music of military songs and *Giovinezza* played, and the oath signed.

Mori was delighted with the full turn-out on this occasion. It symbolised, as one journalist put it, 'the revolution in rural consciousness which, under the insignia of fascism, has soared from the most petty and listless obscurantism of yesterday, to historic and luminous heights'.[70] Whether any *campiere* would have dared be absent is a question that few people, it seems, were prepared to consider. Mori was certainly too wise to believe that attitudes could be changed overnight, but he did have an exaggerated faith in the power of propaganda. In March 1927 he sent Mussolini some photographs of *campieri*, and told him that he was paying particular attention to their education. 'Public order', he said, could 'very soon' be safely entrusted to them.[71] Part of their training consisted of horse races in the Favorita park in company with members of the aristocracy.[72]

In the spring of 1927, Mori repeated the Roccapalumba experiment with the *guardiani* of the Conca d'oro. Since they constituted, in his view, a more homogeneous body than the *campieri*, he invested them with a semi-military character, with leaders, regulations, and a badge: a sprig of orange blossom over two crossed rifles. The ceremony marking their initiation into the service of the state took place in Piazza Politeama in Palermo, on 21 April 1927. 'Private property', Mori told them in his speech, 'is something we all have a duty to defend for the salvation of the country.' Like the *campieri*, the *guardiani* were asked to swear an oath of loyalty. 'Another three hundred men', said Mori in his memoirs, 'strong and courageous, passed openly, voluntarily, into line, alongside us against crime. The mafia, the blood-thirsty mafia of the Conca d'oro, lost at a stroke its strongest weapon.'[73]

In addition to the defence of private property, Mori sought to strengthen the ethic of work in the countryside. This was an aspect of the national policy of 'ruralisation' that fitted in comfortably with the struggle against the mafia; for the mafia, according to Mori, was 'essentially parasitic and exploitative', and was never to be found among those who treated labour 'as a means of subsistence, . . . civic dignity and human solidarity'.[74] He believed that all classes had a moral responsibility to work: 'It is not true that toil is the wretched duty of the poor and leisure a right of the rich. Leisure is a desertion from the most elementary duties of civil coexistence, and work is the noble privilege of men worthy of that name.'[75] Mori was pleased to have added four hours to the working day in summer, by making it safe for peasants to travel before dawn and after dusk.[76] Whether the peasants themselves saw this as intrinsically desirable, we do not know.

Public works

The fall of Alfredo Cucco and the injection of the *agrari* into Palermo fascism coincided with the moral rehabilitation of the *latifondo*. In

May 1927, while Galeazzi was still in Sicily, Count Lucio Tasca published a vehement article in *Il Giornale di Sicilia*, in which he claimed that only California could compete with Sicily in agriculture. In 1925, he said, the island produced 14% of Italy's wheat, 46.5% of its barley, 52.27% of its broad beans, 19.74% of its chick-peas, and 50% of its lentils: 'These figures demonstrate that if there is one region in Italy where there is no major agricultural problem, it is Sicily.' The *latifondi* were not undercultivated, he said; if anything, the opposite was true. 'The photographs published by trade union newspapers showing the lack of cultivation on Sicilian land are a cheap fraud designed to mislead the politically and agriculturally naïve.'[77]

Tasca, however, was no die-hard reactionary. He strongly supported Mussolini's Battle for Grain (the campaign started in 1925 to promote wheat production): 'In 1927, at least 500 tractors will shatter the silence of the *latifondo* with their beneficent roar, and all kinds of agricultural machinery, national fertilisers, and the intense fever of work, show how Sicilian farmers are responding to the appeal of the Duce.' He believed that under the conscientious guidance of the *agrari* extensive production could become more intensive, and the island's economy be transformed.[78] Mori was similarly persuaded. He claimed that it was only the mafia that had hampered the development of Sicilian agriculture; now that it had been destroyed, the *agrari* could return to their 'noble georgic traditions', revitalise their estates and, with some help from the government, produce an agricultural renaissance in the island.[79]

His faith was not shared by everybody. For example, Arrigo Serpieri, the under-secretary at the Ministry of National Economy, was profoundly sceptical. He wanted to foster intensive cultivation, with stable farms in place of scattered strips and short tenancies; and he doubted the capacity of the southern landowners to achieve anything themselves.[80] In May 1924 he introduced a bill on 'integral land reclamation' (*bonifica integrale*) which authorised the setting up of state-backed consortia, and the expropriation of those owners who did not co-operate. The *agrari* felt threatened. At the end of 1924, they established a 'Committee to promote improvements in the South and islands', and the following autumn they secured the repeal of the expropriation clause. They were also promised that owners' consortia would have priority in the allocation of public works and funds. Against Serpieri they argued that 'land reclamation' was not connected with the *latifondi* and the nature of production, but with the building of roads and other facilities; and these, they felt, should be entrusted to southern owners rather than northern 'speculators'.[81]

In its determination to solve the Southern Question, the government set great store by public works. The overriding consideration was political. As the Under-Secretary of the Interior told Mori in September 1927, fascism could not hope to make an effective penetration of the Sicilian countryside, unless there was first 'a vast process of moral and social reform'. He said that the question of political support from the masses was closely bound up with the fight against the mafia, the execution of public works, the spread of education, 'and above all, the absolute necessity of putting an end immediately to the abject conditions in which many peasants still live'.[82]

Though the situation in the Sicilian countryside still looked bleak in 1927, it was not altogether for want of initiative from Rome. In July 1925, the government had set up the Superintendencies of Public Works for the South, and the headquarters of the Sicilian branch was in Palermo. Later that same month, an interest-free loan of 10 million lire had been made to the city; in November, the Victor Emanuel III Institute for Land Reclamation in Sicily was inaugurated to promote general economic improvements, particularly in farming. In May of the following year, Palermo received a grant of 300 million lire for 'exceptional public works', to be spent, in the course of the next decade, on roads, sewers, schools, houses, and other amenities.[83]

At a meeting held in February 1927 to discuss land reclamation in Sicily, the head of the Palermo Superintendency, Pio Colletti, announced that between August 1925 and December 1926, 197 projects, worth 32 million lire, had been completed, and 423, worth 565 million lire, were under way. Priority was being given to roads and water, but other problems, he said, should not to be overlooked, for the well-being of Sicily depended on 'a general effort, born of the enthusiastic energy of all those elements, moral and material, that are needed to achieve the end'.[84] A good deal of pious rhetoric was exchanged at the meeting, but apart from a decision to appoint Prince Borghese to head and co-ordinate the island's land reclamation committees, nothing of any concrete value was agreed on. Perhaps this was not surprising, for the *agrari* had little incentive, with their political position and incomes assured, to initiate change.

Public works, moreover, might have seemed unduly hazardous to some landowners, as they risked elevating the material and moral condition of the peasantry. This may have been one reason why, in the end, so much was said and so little done. It might also have accounted for a curious disequilibrium, for while in theory the Sicilian problem was acknowledged to be complex, in practice attention was focused almost exclusively on roads. In the wake of the 'Mussolini Law' on land reclamation in December 1928, the *agrari* held a meeting in Palermo to establish consortia: of the nine set up, all but one were pledged to road-building.[85] Two years later, the Duke of Belsito suggested to Serpieri that the law on integral land reclamation be changed in Sicily to deal solely with roads.[86] Serpieri was not to be persuaded: the basis of the island's land reclamation, he said, lay in 'the irrigation, transformation and colonisation of the *latifondo*'.[87]

Roads did not endanger the existing social order. Indeed, by lowering transport costs and making the countryside more accessible to the police, they benefited the big landowners almost exclusively. However, sectional interests were easily confused with general ones. Why was so much of Sicily uncultivated, asked Guglielmo Policastro in 1929? The answer, he said, lay in the absence of roads: 'We need roads, means of communication that will in a flash turn a desert into an oasis'.[88] This view was endorsed by writers in *Il Resto di Carlino* in January 1929, and *Il Messaggero* in February.[89] Nor, it was argued, would agriculture alone benefit from a better system of roads. Tourism would increase; so too would the population, as new sections of the countryside were opened up and made habitable. For, as one university professor explained, 'the road is an instrument of cohesion and social grouping, as well as of travel...The road is like the furrow stamped on us by God's gaze: therein we feel protection, security, joy and life.'[90]

Between August 1925 and March 1929, the Palermo Superintendency authorised over 100 million lire for road building in the province. By contrast, only 10.5 million lire was allocated to irrigation and the search for water. Hydraulic works received 7 million lire and building works 5.5 million lire, of which 300,000 lire was spent on enlarging the prison at Termini Imerese, and the rest on the construction or improvement of *carabinieri* barracks. 'Hygienic' works (including the provision of aqueducts for drinking water), were given 150 million lire, and maritime works 176 million lire, of which all but one million was to be spent on the port of Palermo – neither of these two categories, it might be said, was politically or socially sensitive for the *agrari*. Education, by contrast, was: only 7 million lire was set aside for the building of schools and it seems that none of this had been spent by March 1929.[91] In the ensuing years, the allocation of funds for public works became even more tellingly disproportionate. By 1936 the Palermo Superintendency had authorised, in all, nearly 380 million lire for roads, 50 million lire for hydraulic works, 177 million lire for maritime works, and a mere 8 million lire for irrigation, an apparent cut-back of 2 million lire on the period down to the spring of 1929.[92]

The 'Mussolini Law' of December 1928 earmarked 7 billion lire for land reclamation and improvement, to be spent throughout Italy over a period of fourteen years. It was claimed at the time that this would 'transform the face' of Sicily.[93] However, the results were disappointing. Inefficiency, misappropriation of funds, and above all, a lack of will on the part of the big landowners, who dominated the consortia, were chiefly to blame for this. By July 1936 work had been finished or almost finished on less than 5% of the 500,185 hectares in Sicily destined for land reclamation.[94] One problem was that members of the consortia tried to avoid their mandatory private contributions by subcontracting, or simply not paying their share. In 1938 there were nearly 40,000 hectares on which the public works had been finished, but those 'of private initiative' had yet to begin.[95]

Many opportunities also existed for speculation. The landowners had access to easy credit in order to help them pay their contributions to the reclamation schemes, and it was often the same landowners who dominated the banks. Simone Sirena and Ettore Pottino di Capuano, for example, were members of the administrative council of the Cassa Centrale di Risparmio, while the Prince of Spadafora was a director of the Bank of Sicily. Lucio Tasca was the Bank of Sicily's representative on the Central Commission for Agrarian Credit.[96] In the late 1920s, there was an enormous increase in the flow of credit in Palermo, and Mori took this as a sign of an economic renaissance. Whatever the original intention, however, it is clear that very little of this money was spent on land reclamation.

The rural mafia was not, as Mori professed to believe, the main reason for Sicily's agricultural backwardness. Violent crime might, it is true, have done something to hamper freedom of movement in the countryside. Mori certainly liked to think so. 'You only have to talk to the peasants and farmers', he told the Ministry of the Interior in October 1927, as evidence that the mafia was being destroyed, 'or look at the traffic in the countryside, or the increase in agricultural and livestock credit.'[97] However, the main reason for any rise in rural activity after 1925 was not so much the destruction of the mafia, as that land, previously uncultivated or left to pasture, had now been turned over to grain production. With prices artificially high, even areas of low yield became profitable. The amount of land under wheat in Sicily rose from 677,600 hectares in 1923–8, to 789,500 hectares in 1936–9.[98]

This extension of arable land, however, did nothing to benefit the island's economy. Monoculture was reinforced at the expense of diversity, and this led to a deterioration in the quality of the soil. There was also a serious decline in lemon, wine, olive, and nut production, and though this was due mainly to the international depression, the Battle for Grain was certainly a contributory factor. The elimination of fruit trees in turn added further to the process of soil erosion. As pasture was replaced by arable land, there was a dramatic fall in the number of farm animals: 'The decline in Sicily's livestock patrimony constitutes a very serious phenomenon', said one expert in 1934.[99] This decline meant a reduction in manure and traction power, not to mention protein in the diet.

The collapse of livestock must have been particularly galling to

Mori. He believed that cattle-rustling had seriously hindered the development of animal husbandry in the island; and since, officially, rustling declined sharply between 1925 and 1926, it might have seemed that livestock farming would now enjoy a revival.[100] There was an apparent rise in the number of cattle in the later 1920s – 12.28% in the province of Palermo, according to one set of statistics;[101] but this figure may simply have reflected the more rigorous system of registration that was being introduced in these years. Either way, the increase cannot be related directly to the campaign against the mafia. The same statistics indicated a greater rise in the east of the island than the west – 56.87% in Siracusa – and yet the impact of Mori was hardly felt here. Clearly factors other than crime determined the quantity of livestock in Sicily. One such was the grain tariff, which in 1928 rose to 11 gold lire, and the following year to 14. In these circumstances, few landowners could resist sacrificing cattle to wheat.

Though Mori's confidence in a resurgence in animal husbandry was misplaced, he devoted considerable energy to livestock shows. (The one held at Petralia Soprana in June 1928 saw the Mori Cup being awarded to Baron Sgadari of Gangi.)[102] Part of Mori's interest in this field derived from his analysis of the mafia. The landowners, he claimed, had been forced into renouncing their georgic traditions; therefore once the mafia was crushed, and cattle-rustling, its most characteristic crime, eliminated, the *agrari* were free to recover their interest in husbandry. There was also, however, an element of conscious self-deception in his concern for livestock. Herds grazing in safety became a symbol to him of his success: 'In a short time', he wrote in his memoirs, 'I had the pleasure of seeing again in the island's once deserted countryside, flocks and herds of every kind standing alone and tranquil in the calm and peace that had finally been won.'[103]

Bucolic fancies, it seems, had conditioned Mori's perception of reality; but he was not the only one to be thus affected. The destruction of the mafia, said the Procurator General of Palermo in 1927, had brought 'peace and security to the countryside, so that herds now freely graze this most fertile of lands'.[104] Simone Sirena – whose capacity for self-deception was considerable – said that Mori ('that new John the Baptist of the Sicilian people') had prepared the way 'for the re-emergence of those herds that from ancient times enjoyed such enormous fame, beginning with the Theocritan idyll'.[105] Where all these new herds were is not certain. We do know, however, that large loans were granted for the purchase of livestock. In 1924, the Bank of Sicily lent 7.5 million lire for this purpose. By 1928 the figure had risen to 22 million lire.[106] Could all this money have been spent as it should have been?

10   EDUCATING SICILIANS

Towards a new culture

Leopoldo Franchetti and Sidney Sonnino were two Tuscan noblemen. Their report on Sicily, published in 1877, remains the most astute ever written. In defiance of official wisdom, they revealed that unification had failed to improve the cultural and material conditions of the island. Their high moral vision of the state spurred their curiosity, and since they had been nurtured in an environment that found vendetta abhorrent and egoism repellent, they were naturally fascinated by Sicily. The contrast between the island's natural beauty and what they felt to be its underlying evil was a source of particular curiosity: 'After a number of such stories [of violence]', wrote Franchetti, 'all that scent of orange and lemon blossom begins to smell of corpses.'[1] The beautiful and the good were clearly not always at one.

Mori lacked the Tuscans' analytical gifts, but he shared many of their convictions. Like them, he believed in the sacrosanctity of the centralised state. He accordingly agreed with Franchetti in seeing governmental weakness as the prime cause of Sicily's problems. Islanders had to be taught that they were Italians with duties towards the nation. The law needed to be enforced, and the exercise of justice removed from the hands of the individual and lodged firmly with the police and magistrates. In short, civic values of the kind Tuscany and the North had long boasted would have to be exported south, and Sicily drawn into the framework of united Italy. The trouble with this approach was that it was potentially one-sided and somewhat arrogant. Were the values of Franchetti, Sonnino, and Mori as self-evidently superior as they liked to believe? It was all very well to talk of teaching Sicilians to be good citizens, but how were Sicilians expected to view the process of re-education, particularly when it took a repressive form, as in the 1860s, 1870s and 1920s?

Mori had little regard for the intelligence of the Sicilian peasants. In general, he thought them simple and superstitious. For example, he described how a young policeman made a suspect talk by taking a headlamp from a truck, shining it in his face, and saying: 'Beware, this is the eye of Mori, and it can read even your stomach'. 'Comic, incredible', Mori added; 'But the fact is that, whether through confusion or hypnosis, in front of that eye, the *latitante* broke down and confessed.'[2] Elsewhere in his memoirs, Mori gave a series of vignettes to show how Sicilians were good at heart, despite their moral and intellectual shortcomings. The tone, however, was predominantly patronising. On one occasion, he said, he met a shepherd boy, 'alone in the murky solitude of a *latifondo* of ill repute'. He dismounted and spoke to him: 'His father? Wanted, and in America. His mother, sick and alone in the village with two babies. The village? Far away. How far? He did not know; he never went there. God, prayer, school? Nothing. The King, Italy, the nation? Nothing. Rights, duties, the law, good and bad? Nothing.'[3] As Telesio Interlandi commented, the reader might have been forgiven for thinking, from such anecdotes, that he was 'in the heart of darkest Africa'.[4]

The story of the shepherd boy formed part of Mori's speech to the First Regional Congress of Fascist Teachers, in June 1926. Mori used this occasion to issue an appeal to the schools for their support. He told the teachers that if the mafia was to be destroyed for good a new mentality was needed in Sicily, and already, he said, there were signs of change:

> The great soul of Sicily, that once was lost in a moonless night, whose sole illumination was the sinister flash of revolts, and where the only guide was compromise, has found itself again, and now blazes forth in all its beauty, in all its purest energy. . . like once the Spartan virgins on the sand.

However, the durability of such progress depended on indoctrination. It was the duty of the island's educators, he said, to fashion a 'new soul composed of love and inspired by one faith: God, King, and Country'.[5] Mori was proud of this speech and sent a copy of it to the Minister of the Interior. He also had it circulated to every school in Sicily, as a kind of teacher's vade-mecum.[6]

In October 1926, Mori launched a competition for a school text book, 'with a view to realising concretely those criteria of collaboration. . .announced at the First Regional Congress'. All primary and secondary school teachers were eligible to compete. The book was to be between 150 and 200 pages, and had to be suitable for peasant and working-class children. Its subject matter, said Mori, should treat principally of 'the phenomena of the mafia and *omertà*'; the aim was to correct the 'spiritual and ethical errors that these produce'. In addition, it should 'instil in the masses, through the masculine and Roman idea of the citizen, the precise nature, and correct evaluation of the relationship, which. . .must exist between the individual and the social order, if the supreme goal of the nation's prosperity and greatness is to be achieved'.[7] Sadly for Mori, the competition 'did not have the outcome desired', and no prizes were awarded. This may have meant that nobody, or too few people, had entered.[8]

It is hard to say exactly how much support Mori received from the schools. Among his papers are a few letters from teachers expressing their enthusiasm for his campaign. A schoolmistress from Prizzi sent him various tributes written by pupils. 'Miss has told us', said one, 'that in Sicily there were lots of robbers, brigands and men who always stole and killed other men, and you have been right to put them in prison.' Some of the children mentioned a portrait of Mori in the classroom.[9] The situation at Prizzi was in all likelihood typical of many rural communities. The teachers belonged, on the whole, to the petty bourgeoisie who made up the backbone of the party, in the South as well as the North; this, as well as a practical concern for job security, is likely to have made them obedient to state directives. The Milocca schoolmaster (who was the brother of the *podestà*) dutifully taught his pupils that they were Italians, and that Italy was one of the greatest nations in the world, with a glorious past and a brilliant future. He also told them to say 'Etna' and not 'Mungibeddu', in keeping with fascist strictures on dialect.[10]

Mori set great store by education. He liked to think of the children imbibing what he called 'the word of liberation and redemption', going home, and preaching the gospel to receptive parents.[11] However, his hopes may well have been misplaced. Even the most zealous teachers had a necessarily limited influence on the young. In the first place, school attendance was poor. This was partly because most peasants saw little value in academic learning. During the autumn season, children were often kept at home to help with the grape and almond harvests. In winter, the bad weather took its toll, and in early summer there were further agricultural chores to be done. Less direct economic factors also contributed to absenteeism. For example, girls were apparently not allowed to attend the second year of school unless they had underwear: very few peasant women possessed, let alone wore, such garments, and they usually saw no good reason why their daughters should have them.[12]

Many schools lacked adequate facilities. At Milocca there were six small classrooms, each of which was located on the ground floor of the teacher's home, and had to be rented by the town council. In 1927 an effort was made to enforce attendance, and eighty-two girls turned up for the first grade alone. There was not enough space for them, and as a result vigilance had to be dropped. In 1928, the same class began with just fifty-one pupils and fell to thirty later in the year.[13] This sorry state of affairs was in part a reflection of the general political situation. The *agrari* and rural middle classes had no wish to encourage the education of the peasantry, and preferred to use communal funds for less creditable purposes. Consequently, little was done in the 1920s or 1930s to reduce absenteeism or improve school facilities. One expert reported in 1941 that truancy was still 'intense' in Sicily.[14]

Other circumstantial factors contributed to the Milocca school's scant influence in the community. For one thing the teachers had little corporate identity. They taught in separate buildings, and had no common room where they could meet. They also participated in the town's factional struggles, and this helped divide them from one another, as well as from many of the parents.[15] Legal restrictions also proved damaging. For example, the school's film projector could hardly be used, as the only available electricity was generated by the local mill, which had no licence to distribute outside its own walls. Furthermore, a law existed which said that films could only be shown in buildings with fixed seats, and Milocca had no such building. 'Under the present system', concluded Charlotte Chapman, 'the school results in no solidarity between teachers, among the students, or in the community at large. It is a thing apart, pertaining to the government'.[16]

Mori thought that Sicilian parents rather neglected their offspring. 'The islanders', he said, '. . . tended by tradition to be somewhat disinterested in children and adolescents, perhaps because of the high birthrate.'[17] He was particularly worried about street urchins, for he felt they were especially prone to crime, and he tried to set up a 'hostel' that would cater for them.[18] This, according to one writer, was an excellent idea, as it would afford 'an oasis, a sincere refuge of honesty, a kiss of righteousness', where the child could encounter the discipline and morality which his family, through irresponsibility, had failed to teach him. It would be a step, he believed, on the road to the elimination of juvenile delinquency.[19] The Procurator General of Palermo agreed, for in his view, juvenile delinquency stemmed from the 'lack of parental care and education for children.'[20] Mori launched a public appeal for the hostel, but it did not bring in enough money; and when he left Palermo his project had still to be realised.

Another idea, which met with greater success, was the distribution of subsidies to the wives and children of arrested men. Mori was particularly keen on these doles, and between 1927 and 1929, he gave out 72,000 lire to more than nine hundred families.[21] Admittedly, this was not much; but in fairness to Mori it should be said that he had to rely exclusively on donations, chiefly from landowners, as the government provided no more than verbal support for the scheme.[22] The ceremonies marking the distributions received much publicity. One was held on Christmas Day 1928, and was attended by many of the province's leading figures.[23] Other acts of largesse by Mori included the presentation of 1,000 food parcels to poor people on New Year's Day 1929.[24] Whether these gestures of goodwill did anything to alter the character of the state in the eyes of the masses, we do not know.

Mori always claimed that his campaign had popular backing. He was proud of being called the 'peasant prefect', and toured the province assiduously, rallying support. Many of the places he went to had never before been visited by a prefect (a fact he stressed),[25] and the receptions given him were lavish: 'Everywhere, in the streets and in houses, there were flowers and laurel wreathes', said an account of Mori's trip to Roccamena. 'Balconies were draped with carpets, hangings, embroideries and silk; at every street corner and in the piazza there were flags and arches decorated with greenery.' The band from Corleone provided music; the banner of the agricultural union was baptised, first with holy water, then with champagne; and Mori ('greeted as always by frenetic applause and cries of joy') smiled as he began his long speech, and 'almost chatted with the peasants'.[26]

Cultivating the peasantry was important for Mori personally, as it strengthened his political position. Whatever hostility there was to him in party circles in Rome, he could always claim that he enjoyed popular support in Sicily: 'It has got to be true – and it is', he told the Ministry of the Interior in October 1927, 'that fascism's penetration into the countryside is concrete, tangible and undeniable, and in a continual state of progress.'[27] It was probably no coincidence that Mori's tours of provincial towns became more frequent in 1928. By early spring of that year, he had to contend with the hostility not only of Cucco and his associates, but also of the former Minister of War, Antonino Di Giorgio, whom he had accused of involvement with the mafia. The cheers of the masses were a good antidote to the vitriol of his enemies.

There was also a more general political purpose to Mori's courtship of the peasantry. It was an aspect of the government policy of 'ruralisation', which became something of an obsession with the regime from the middle 1920s. In Mussolini's view, the strongest nations were those based on a population of smallholders: peasants were obedient and hard-working, while city-dwellers were refractory and comfort-loving, a disposition that he thought resulted in small families. Mori (who in one of his modest moments admitted that he was only 'an executor of the head of the government's orders')[28] sought to articulate the Duce's wishes, and in June 1927, at the installation of the new Palermo party executive, he proudly declared that fascism in Sicily would be 'substantially rural'.[29] To many people this stress on the countryside seemed logical: 'In no other region', said Luigi Chibbaro in 1928, 'does the need for ruralisation ...tie in so closely with the material condition of the land, the de-

Pls. 14 and 15. Mori's visits to provincial towns. *Top*: The people of Piana dei Greci greeting Mori with a fascist salute (some with their left hands). *Below*: Mori at Valledolmo.

mographic distribution, and the primitive farming methods of the people.'[30]

Mori reserved some of his most florid prose for the peasants. At Termini Imerese, for example, he waxed eloquent on his love and admiration for them, and on their importance to Italy:

> In the figure of the Sicilian peasant...silent, industrious, and riveted to his place of work on the sun-baked *latifondo*, I see not only the worker of today,...but also the bold pioneer who affirms the primacy of Italy beyond its shores. I also see the heroic infantryman through whose valour the warrior tradition of Italy was yesterday born again, and which will re-emerge tomorrow and shine forth for ever amid the flash and lightening of legends and epics.[31]

This was good fascism. Even the language was such as Mussolini himself would have used in talking of the peasantry. Mori was watching his step very carefully after 1927, for he could not afford to give any ammunition to his opponents: 'To start with all seemed well,' he said in some rough jottings on Antonino Di Giorgio, 'then bit by bit he tried to get the upper hand with the old methods of intrigue. I pulled the rug from under him by polarising everything on fascism and the Duce.'[32]

The policy of ruralisation stemmed not only from Mussolini's belief in the moral superiority of the peasants, but also from his concern for a higher birth-rate. He thought that the rural population was naturally fecund, and he looked to the South in particular to lead the way in the 'Battle for Births'. Mori did his best to pass on the regime's demographic message. In December 1928 he distributed 26,300 lire to 101 prolific Palermo families, and in his speech he said that strength lay in numbers, that children had always been and would continue to be Italy's greatest asset, and that everyone should persevere in the work of procreation, 'mindful of Christ's instructions...and the Duce's wishes'.[33] The fact that Mori himself had no children may have caused him some embarrassment; but he carried on doggedly with his propaganda nonetheless. Sometimes his logic was decidedly tortuous: in a speech in 1928 he argued that a clampdown on swearing would increase the population. Blasphemy, he said, undermined religion, and (as Korherr's book had shown, 'with that marvellous preface by Benito Mussolini'), 'the extinction of true religious sentiment is the cause of a declining birth-rate'.[34]

In an interview in 1922, Mori said that the he believed in 'the state above everything else'; he added that a good soldier invariably made a good citizen.[35] One notable feature of Mori's campaign was the way in which he linked the establishment of the state's authority in Sicily to the inculcation of military values. Here too, he was broadly in step with the regime. Nothing, he believed, could be gained without a fight, and there was no shortage of opponents to contend with: 'There is an enemy in the house...It is called "mafia"', he once said, 'To battle! We must march against it.'[36] Economic backwardness was another formidable opponent: 'Friends, even peace today means battle, battle for the economic salvation of our land; it is a battle that requires faith, courage, discipline and work.'[37] Other aspects of Sicilian life were also considered to be hostile: 'Today,' he told a university audience in 1928, 'the four amazons of the apocalypse – mafia, *malvivenza*, *omertà* and vendetta – arè silent, disarmed, and beaten, but not yet tamed.'[38]

Mori had been trained as a soldier. He regarded courage, discipline, sacrifice, assertiveness, and obedience, not only as qualities supreme in themselves, but also as the virtues that most befitted a citizen. Whether he intended a political, as well as moral, purpose to his martial rhetoric is unclear. He never explicitly mentioned, for example, a link between military values and national integration. However, he did make repeated reference to Sicily's experience of the Great War in the hope of inciting the kind of fervent nationalist spirit that he (and the regime) admired. 'The Italy of Vittorio Veneto', he said at Gangi, 'advances irresistibly towards that future greatness... which was the radiant vision of six hundred thousand men, nobly slain...and which we have the inescapable duty to convert into firm and acknowledged reality.'[39] Nearly half a million Sicilians had been called up between 1915 and 1918; it was reasonable to suppose that patriotic appeals would have been welcomed.

However, if the town of Milocca is any indication, military service would not appear to have been a source of pride in Sicily. 'The 1914 –18 War seems to have been unpopular in Milocca and the surrounding region', observed Charlotte Chapman:

> No criticism was heard of the two men who had permanently blinded themselves with the medicine they put in their eyes to make themselves unfit for military service. Another man told at length the devices he used, first to avoid being taken for the army, and later to keep from being put in active service....He would have resented being called a coward; that was not the question. His life was very useful to himself and he saw no reason why he should risk it. To resort to artifice to avoid military service was simply the exercise of proper Sicilian astuteness. No one was pointed out as a hero of the War. Disabled veterans were preferred for employment in minor positions connected with the local government, but their war records were never cited in their praise.[40]

There seems no reason to believe that Milocca was exceptional, at least among rural communities.

Whatever the reaction of his audiences, the theme of the Great War certainly inspired Mori to poetic heights: 'Here speak the noble spirits', he said in a speech at the war memorial in Balestrate,

> rising beyond all human sorrow, along the purest paths of feeling, in the blaze of unbounded faith, toward the sacred flame of the Ideal, which is called Italy. These dead can only be honoured by making ourselves worthy of them by our deeds. And because this is so, I rejoice today before this monument, wreathed in super-human light, which is the light of glory, truth, and the future. For, citizens, from this, as from the other monuments, leap such brilliant flames, that idiotic myths and foul slanders are reduced to nothing; such brilliant flames that from the murky shadows... Sicily has finally leapt forth, the true Sicily of the Vespers, warrior Sicily, monarchist and fascist.[41]

The Church and Mori's campaign

Though the regime's formal reconciliation with the Vatican did not occur until the beginning of 1929, Mori received a good deal of help from the Church throughout much of his campaign. This was not altogether surprising. His belief in authority, class-collaboration, and the family endeared him to the ecclesiastical establishment. Equally, Mori knew that any attempt to change the spiritual climate in Sicily would have been the poorer without the backing of the clergy. Co-operation was never made into an article of policy (he did not discuss the matter in his reports to the Ministry of the Interior), but it was practiced nonetheless. Many of Mori's visits to provincial towns took place on Sunday, and priests were often involved in the celebrations. On occasions he wove religious symbolism into his speeches. When he visited the mainly Greek orthodox town of Piana dei Greci on Easter Monday 1926, he dwelt on the theme of resurrection: 'Yesterday, Easter of resurrection. Today resurrection in progress... Yesterday, crosses raised in devotion to heaven. Today the fascist banners proudly unfurled in the wind.'[42]

It seems that the Church's support for Mori became marked only after Cucco's downfall. Throughout 1926, there was little sign of official approval. In February 1927, however, Archbishop Lualdi of Palermo wrote to Mori saying that he had nothing but 'the most heartfelt thanks' for his work.[43] Ernesto Filippo, Archbishop of Monreale, was similarly enthusiastic: 'The people of my archdiocese, together with their priests and all the clergy, bless the work of Your Excellency which has allowed them to enjoy the inestimable benefits of peace and tranquillity, which in the past they never knew.'[44] A few months later, on the feast of the Assumption, the bishop of Cefalù joined Mori and the Duke of Belsito on a visit to Gangi and Petralia Soprana. In a speech, the bishop declared that everyone should be grateful for the island's liberation from criminals; and he went on, somewhat curiously, to consider the achievements of Imperial Rome, and the parallels that could be drawn between the heroes of the ancient world and 'the great figures of today'.[45]

Perhaps the highest accolade paid by the Church to Mori was an article in the authoritative journal, La Civiltà cattolica, in the summer of 1927. Its anonymous author applauded Mori's analysis of the mafia, and in particular his view that Sicilian crime had stemmed from governmental weakness and complicity. History, he said, proved this thesis, for the mafia had flourished under the 'corrupt leadership...of the old Masonic liberalism'; and now, 'a new, legitimate, but more resolute exercise of authority' was destroying it. However, force was not the full answer, as Mori had realised: education needed to be carried out 'by schoolteachers, all honest citizens, and especially by priests'. As to the latter, the author said that Mori's judgement was again sound; for in contrast to the 'agnosticism' of the liberal era, he had called on the clergy to aid him in his fight against crime. Who could forget the ceremony at Roccapalumba, and the part played in it by 'a passionate army chaplain'?[46]

There is little to suggest that Mori was inherently religious. Though his speeches contained many references to God, their general tone was pagan. His main concern was for social order and discipline, and, like Mussolini, he tended simply to indulge the Church's susceptibility to form. He lent his weight, for example, to the campaign against swearing, and personally authorised the appointment of 'inspectors' to watch out for offenders.[47] In 1928 he became president of the Palermo branch of the National Anti-Blasphemy League. In his acceptance speech, he claimed that blasphemy 'sabotaged' morals and that its suppression would lead to 'the elevation of religious sentiment and the formation of a religious consciousness'. He also found room for a diatribe against female fashions, which were inclined, he felt, to overstep the boundaries of elegance, and enter the domain of 'exhibitionism'.[48]

Though Mori's work against the mafia received the blessing of the Church hierarchy (at least from 1927), the attitude of the parish clergy is harder to evaluate. Giulio Virga, a priest, was probably exceptional in his enthusiasm. On the occasion of the oath of the Conca d'oro guardiani, in April 1927, he marched at the head of one of the local contingents; when Mori visited San Giuseppe Iato and San Cipirello in 1928, Don Virga figured prominently in the reception committee, and presented Mori with a 'symbolic' bunch of grapes. Most priests, however, were less conspicuous. Local ties must often have made it hard for them to support Mori's campaign actively, particularly if they were linked to a vulnerable faction. This was clearly the case with Don Benedetto Biffarella of Castelluzzo. He was suspended *a divinis* in 1924 but continued to minister to the people, 'among whom', said Mori, 'he carried out acts of incitement against the ecclesiastical authorities with the support of the local mafia'. The priest sent to replace him was continually harassed. In the end Biffarella had to be almost forcibly removed, though this immediately prompted a petition from over a hundred townspeople protesting at the maltreatment of a 'model priest'.[49]

Biffarella's ties with his community were undoubtedly political as well as spiritual. Such factional involvement could, and did, lead to clerics being caught up in criminal proceedings. Cirino Latteri was charged by a certain Don Versacci with membership of the Mistretta mafia. 'I am innocent,' said Latteri. 'The priest Versacci had links with the mafia . . . and is accusing me because I made him dissolve the town council: he was mayor, and since he did not run things properly, I attacked him and won.'[50] Some priests (though not enough, it seems, to worry the ecclesiastical authorities) appeared as defendants. There were two in the Madonie trial, and one in that of the Mistretta association. They may have been treated with special leniency, as only one of the three was found guilty.[51] There was little sense, after all, in risking a breach with the Church.

Palermo fascism after Cucco's fall

In October 1927 Mori sent a long report to the Minister of the Interior on the political situation in Sicily. Circumstances, he said, were still far from perfect, especially from an organisational point of view; but it would be wrong to conclude that the island was not fascist. There was an 'imposing phalanx of men of thought, faith and responsibility', and though the rural masses were 'perhaps unconscious' in their loyalty to the regime, they were 'undoubtedly' reliable. Centuries of bad rule, he explained, had affected the islanders profoundly; the result had been the 'emergence – albeit unawares – of a spirituality and outlook that are at root clearly fascist'.[52] All this sounded a little strained. The truth was that despite Mori's propaganda, and the purge and reconstruction of the provincial *fasci*, the countryside was still largely impervious to the new order.

Some aspects of party organisation were more deficient than others. Mori admitted (in the same report) that fascist trade unions hardly existed in the province of Palermo. 'There is still', he said, 'some misunderstanding and scepticism on this score. Therefore, as I have

repeatedly told the leaders, we must conduct a detailed and intensive campaign of popularisation.' However, the youth organisations,
the *Balilla* and *Avanguardisti*, were more successful: 'Everyone. . .
agrees on the need to mould the character of young people.' As for
party membership, reliable statistics were hard to come by in 1927,
as many *fasci* were being reconstructed. However, official figures in
July suggested a total for the province of around 6,000.[53] The island
as a whole, according to an estimate in November, had the ninth
highest party membership in the country, ahead of such regions as
Puglie and Liguria.[54]

Although some progress occurred with the provincial party organisation in 1928, it was not remarkable. The number of unionised
rural labourers increased by 3,000 to 12,800. However, in the same
year there were 15,000 industrial workers in trades unions, and yet
the province was overwhelmingly agricultural. As for *Dopolavoro*,
membership was officially put at 8,000 by 1928,[55] though this was
probably a gross exaggeration as such figures often existed merely
on paper,[56] and even if true, an average of about 100 enrolments per
commune was not very impressive. The overall party membership
had risen to nearly 12,000 by the spring of 1929, but the Palermo
fascio alone accounted for well over a third of this total, which meant
that the average membership in each provincial town was less than
100.[57]

We have little hard evidence for the social composition of the provincial party after 1927. However, there seems no reason to suppose
that it was any less middle class than it had been earlier. Among
Gangi's hundred and seventy fascists in February 1926 were twenty
landowners, thirteen members of the professional classes, twenty-
three state employees, fourteen *campieri*, eighteen traders, forty-six
skilled labourers and artisans, three students, seventeen 'countrymen' (*villici*), two shepherds, and two unskilled workers.[58] At Isnello
in 1925, the middle classes were even more preponderant. Of the
seventy-seven party members, only one was described as a 'day labourer', and two as 'peasants'. The rest were landowners, professional men, artisans, and traders.[59]

However, membership of the party by no means implied active
involvement. Lethargy and indifference could easily prevail, particularly in remote rural centres where there was likely to be a shortage
of adequate leaders and where nobody was at hand to give proper
guidance. Big towns, too, could succumb to inertia. In 1932, it was
reported that the Palermo *fascio* was undertaking no new activities,
and 'existed solely to recruit members'.[60] One important source of
confusion and degeneration was factionalism. At Milocca, in 1928
and 1929, all the leading women in the town were members of the

fascio femminile; 'but', said Charlotte Chapman, 'only those from the faction in power took part in political processions or in the other activities of the group'.[61]

The situation in Milocca would suggest that fascism had merely brushed the surface of the Sicilian countryside by the late 1920s. Most of the townspeople, according to Chapman, knew the fascist salute and stood to attention when *Giovinezza* was played. The youth organisations, however, like the *fascio femminile*, functioned 'rarely', and embraced only a small part of the population. Furthermore, there was little evidence that affairs outside the community aroused much interest. News of border incidents on the Riviera, for example, merely confirmed 'the legendary hatred between the Sicilians and the French', and the story was considered less interesting than that of the patriotic rising of the Sicilian Vespers in 1282. The theme of Italian glory excited a number of the younger fascists, but the local school's attempts to instil patriotic sentiments met with little success. The various quarters of the town received new names such as Roma, Piave, Balilla, and Crispi, and the streets were similarly rechristened; but 'these high sounding names were used by no one, and known or understood by only a few'.[62]

One declared aim of Sicilian fascism was to elevate principles above personalities. This seems to have been most acutely felt after the fall of Cucco. The Duke of Belsito said, in September 1927, that the time had come to 'depersonalise the party';[63] he repeated this view the following month in the presence of Michele Bianchi.[64] However, the tendency to submerge policies beneath individuals was deeply rooted in Sicily. Thus, while fascism seems to have meant little as a concept, the cult of the Duce was strong. Mussolini was the subject of many popular ballads, and he was often depicted as a man of superhuman strength, with the capacity to destroy or regenerate at will.[65] It could even be, as one writer claimed in the early 1930s, that the Duce was more romanticised in Sicily than anywhere else in Italy.[66] The process of idolisation certainly began early: the episode on the slopes of Mount Etna in 1923, when the lava apparently stopped flowing on Mussolini's arrival, was soon part of local folklore.[67]

Mussolini was often seen as occupying an exalted position, above his party. No doubt many Sicilians agreed with the father of writer Leonardo Sciascia, who trusted in the Duce but had no faith in fascism itself.[68] This attitude might have had a number of political advantages, but it also tended to encourage resignation to inefficiency and corruption. If only the Duce knew the true state of affairs, the feeling ran, he would put matters right; since he did not, there was little to be done. At Milocca, where the local party barely functioned, Mussolini was referred to as 'a saint out of paradise'.[69] He was also the object of invocations: 'Duce, give aid to the poor unfortunates, to the little old people who suffer hunger.'[70] Sometimes the divorce in the popular imagination between the regime and its leader reached pathetic proportions. One writer told of a Sicilian woman who went to Mussolini to ask for the release of her son who had been sentenced to thirty years in prison: 'He is master', she said calmly, 'He can do what he likes. He can even free my son.'[71]

Mori, like Mussolini, was the victim of a personality cult. However much he regarded himself as the embodiment of the state ('*Lo stato sono io*', (I am the state), he once declared, a little infelicitously),[72] it was unlikely that others would see him merely as a government official. His task was certainly difficult: how much of an impression could he hope to make in Sicily as a faceless bureaucrat? However, there is little to indicate that his self-obsession was purely tactical. He relished the thought that peasants murmured 'It is him!' (*Iddu è*), as he passed. 'How many times', he commented, 'did I hear that exclamation, and how many times must it have been uttered even in my absence!'[73] Sometimes his egotism could reach extraordinary heights: 'There remains the man,' he said in his farewell speech to the Palermo party executive, in the summer of 1929,

> There remains, as I said, Mori, citizen Mori, fascist Mori, Mori the soldier, Mori the man, alive and vigorous, who today sets out on his journey towards the horizon. . .I have my star and I watch it with faith, because it shines and will continue to shine along the path of work and the path of duty. I will walk along that path which is the light of the fatherland, and there, my friends, we will meet again.[74]

Mori's obsession with his image makes it particularly hard to evaluate the popularity of his work. Almost certainly it was less than he and the press maintained. However, there was a tactical reason for reports of ecstatic crowds and prolonged applause. If newspapers claimed (as they did) that Sicilians had unlimited faith in Mori, and were disregarding *omertà* to denounce all manner of crimes, might this not become self-fulfilling?[75] Such a calculation, though, required a fairly low estimation of human intelligence; and intelligence, or at least a variant of it, was highly prized in Sicily. 'Every Sicilian', said Charlotte Chapman, 'likes to think of himself as *scaltru* (shrewd or clever). This is the term of praise which is most frequently heard. *Scaltrizza* involves quick-wittedness, intuition, the ability to deceive others and not to be taken in by them.'[76] Who, then, would have been so foolish as not to proclaim himself an ardent supporter of Mori and of Mori's work?

11 THE TRIALS

The character of the judicial proceedings

Already, in the second half of 1926, Mori's mind was turning to the problem of the trials. He was determined to make them succeed. He was firmly against their being held outside Sicily, as this, he felt, would be both insulting to the islanders and psychologically damaging.[1] The important thing was to show that a mafia trial could be successfully conducted with a local jury. This would give Sicilians self-confidence and also greater faith in the legal process. As Mori wrote in 1923, campaigns against the mafia should be seen as going not 'against', but 'towards Sicily'. Trust was all important: 'Sicily has the feeling that it has too often been treated indiscriminately. Therefore: look, see, understand and distinguish. Identify the criminals clearly, isolate them with precision, and destroy them with the most resolute energy.'[2]

Mori thought that three main obstacles hindered the operation of justice: the restriction on police action, the tendency to grant 'provisional freedom', and the hastiness of the preliminary investigation (*istruttoria*).[3] The problem of police action was largely resolved, in Mori's view, by the charge of criminal association, for this allowed an arrest to be made even when there was no positive evidence for a specific crime having been committed.[4] The problem of provisional freedom (which had enabled the accused to intimidate witnesses) was settled more peremptorily: it was abolished and replaced by 'preventive custody'. That this could lead to instances of gross injustice, Mori was well aware; but, as he told the Minister of the Interior in August 1926, the fight against the mafia had to be conducted with weapons as powerful as those of the enemy.[5]

The problem of the preliminary investigation could not be dealt with so easily. In the first place, there were simply too many defendants. Mori told the Ministry of the Interior that on average, fifty people were arrested in each town.[6] However, this was probably a conservative estimate, as the total figure for Palermo province alone was unlikely to have been much under 5,000 in 1926.[7] The result was endless interrogations and paperwork. Secondly, the magistrates, in Mori's opinion, were deficient, not only numerically, but also morally. As he told Federzoni:

> There are still too many magistrates who, for physical reasons, their connections, or their mentality are either unsuitable, or else do not feel the necessity for the present campaign. There are still too many who indulge in juridical abstractions, too many who are unable, or do not want, to live in the real world, too many who – loyalty apart – cannot feel the dynamism, the spirituality, the will, the rhythm, of the regime.[8]

In other words, they appeared to be more concerned with purely legal problems, than with winning the fight against the mafia.

Mori was aware that the trials would inevitably produce some acquittals (it was only 'natural and logical', he said), but they had to be kept to a minimum.[9] The Procurator General of Palermo, Luigi Giampietro, agreed with Mori. He declared that the mafia should be destroyed, 'with methods strong and potent, like the surgeon who, with steel and fire, penetrates the patient's flesh in order to cauterise the infection from which the malignant bubo springs'.[10] Victory, he felt, would be hard to come by, and he therefore wanted particular weight to be given to police testimony: 'It seems exorbitant', he said in a speech in 1926, '...to discount statements made by the police which refer to facts they may not have witnessed themselves, and for which no sources are given'. Mori heavily underlined this remark in his copy of Giampietro's address.[11] He also underlined his general comments: 'Study the evidence calmly, but also with diligence and firmness; no inopportune release of prisoners, no granting of parole, no light sentences.'[12]

Luigi Giampietro had been sent to Palermo in 1924 to replace the more liberal minded Marsico as Procurator General. His severity was almost proverbial. 'Kindness', he used to say, 'is regarded as weakness, and makes criminals cocky [ringalluzzisce].'[13] Small in stature, thin, with cold eyes and a prominent Roman nose, he shared with Mori a moralistic temperament. He was troubled, for example, by the degeneration of female attire, as he felt it threatened woman's natural position as the 'tutelary angel of the family'.[14] Like Mori, he was highly ambitious, and on one occasion he described the judicial liquidation of the mafia as constituting his 'Roman aspirations'.[15] However, his firmness and zeal made him a difficult colleague. Mori referred in August 1926 to 'a certain ill humour' against him,[16] and in January 1927, after a tactless speech in which the Procurator General criticised some of his fellow magistrates, almost the entire

Pl. 16. Mori with Procurator
General Luigi Giampietro.

Palermo bench banded together and sent a telegram to the Minister
of Justice, protesting at Giampietro's lack of respect.[17]

His forthrightness was apparently not conducive to harmony and
efficiency. Nor, it seems, was his unapproachability: 'Sometimes',
said Giuseppe Loschiavo, who worked with Giampietro in the 1920s,
'those who should have briefed him on the completed preliminary
investigations...kept quiet about, or distorted, their contents. As a
result, people who had been held in prison for many years were later
cleared sensationally.'[18] However, the real problem with the judicial
proceedings was not so much Giampietro's character as that of the
campaign itself. After thousands of arrests amid so much publicity,
Mori dared not risk the humiliation of mass acquittals. Yet the
evidence against many of the accused was flimsy, and the chances of
making a mistake were high. Cucco mentioned the case of a group of
travelling salesmen who were caught up in the Corleone *retata*
entirely by accident. He also referred to a member of the criminal
association of Piana dei Colli who was discovered to be three at the
time of his alleged offence.[19]

Given the atmosphere that prevailed during the campaign, the
police must sometimes have felt they had *carte blanche*. At the time of
the Corleone *retata*, Leoluca Cortimiglia claimed that he and Giuseppe
Fedele were in Vincenzo Di Carlo's butcher's shop. He said that the
police entered and arrested Fedele: 'But Di Carlo begged the brigad-

ier to release Fedele, pointing out that he was his employee. And because Di Carlo insisted, the brigadier told him to come along to the barracks too.'[20] The dangers of interceding for someone were also evident from the statement of a local marshal in the *carabinieri*, Annibale Palumbo. Giuseppe Di Carlo, he said, was the *carabinieri's* butcher; he knew him well, and had no grounds whatsoever for suspecting him: 'So much so that in the list of *mafiosi* I drew up at the request of the senior authorities, I did not include this Di Carlo. But he later figured in the list made by the police after the superintendent had ordered me to detain [Di Carlo] for having come to the barracks to plead on behalf of a lad of his who had been arrested earlier.'[21] Giuseppe and Vincenzo Di Carlo were both sent to trial. The evidence against them was supplied by Liborio Anzalone, the most effusive of the prosecution witnesses. Vincenzo was judged to be *mafioso* because 'it was in his butcher's shop that the worst *mafiosi* met and chatted';[22] and Giuseppe because he had been actively involved 'in the party opposed to that of the socialists, which in Corleone was said to be made up of *mafiosi*'.[23]

It was not only opponents of Mori and his work who talked of injustices. Giuseppe Loschiavo (who was in a good position to know) admitted in later life that the campaign had been plagued by arbitrariness: 'As a result, many innocent people suffered, at least during the pre-trial period, and they never forgot or forgave.'[24] Giovanni Guarino Amella, a former liberal deputy from Agrigento, wrote to Mori in July 1929, to offer his condolences on hearing of the prefect's retirement. He hoped that the good effects of the campaign would not be undone; but he also hoped there would be an end to what he called

> the nights of St Bartholomew, when in order to arrest fifty criminals, a similar number of innocent people were dragged into the abyss, whose only fault, in the worst hypothesis, was that they had not been heroes in darker times; but often they were not guilty even of this. I know that when you learned of such errors, you intervened to put things right. But it was not easy to reach you, and much harder still to give you definite proof of the mistake.[25]

During the campaign, there was almost no public criticism of Mori's work, either at home or abroad. For example, in England, *The Times* merely repeated the views contained in the Italian press.[26] In private, however, there seems to have been a good deal of disquiet, even at the highest levels. In a report to Austen Chamberlain in August 1928, the British ambassador in Rome said:

> To put it briefly, it would appear that Signor Mori has defeated the Mafia by making terms with the big guns of the organisation and

persecuting, along with the lesser villains, a large number of people whose only connection with the Mafia was that they had been forced to obey the orders of its leaders when these were all powerful...Signor Mori has certainly restored order. He has eliminated numerous Mafiosi and Rasses and also a number of innocent people by very doubtful means, including fabricated police evidence and trials *en masse*. But many of the 'capintesta' are flaunting in his train, among them Barone Sgadari, the new Podestà of Gangi.[27]

Eighteen months later, the ambassador forwarded a memorandum from Mr McClure, who had been speaking to Antonino Di Giorgio and Count Platamone, *podestà* of Trapani. Both men, he said, were uneasy 'regarding the ultimate effect of wholesale arrests which have involved hundreds of practically innocent people'.[28]

Another well-informed British observer, Tina Whitaker, confided similar thoughts to her diary in November 1930:

Grave injustices have been inevitable in the wholesale imprison-ments that have taken place under this repression, and the trials have been totally inadequate. The innocent have been left lying one or even two years in lurid prisons, owing to the insufficient number of judges. Although legislation in Sicily has not been divorced from that in the rest of Italy, the methods employed – alas! – have been drastic and merciless. The sparing of the upper classes has led to grave discontent, and important *Mafiosi* have been left at large, some actually in power – while underlings and their dependents, far less to blame, receive heavy penalties and long years of imprisonment. So the Mafia is not yet destroyed. Under the ashes there burns and smoulders the fire of resentment ...At Enna for instance 100 people were arrested and thrown into prison, and then only 14 finally convicted. The innocent men returned home to find themselves ruined, and faced with starva-tion.... Mussolini's work in Sicily is but begun and he has not been so well served at the outset in the carrying out of this vast undertaking as he himself thinks.[29]

The Madonie trial

The arrest of the Madonie bandits had been regarded by Mori as a watershed; the trial, in his view, was equally important. It received enormous publicity, both at home and abroad, and the verdict, according to many people, sounded the death-knell of the mafia. Preparations went on throughout 1926 and into 1927, and it was not until the autumn of that year that the work of the examining

Pl. 17 The interior of the court-room at Termini Imerese during the trial of the Madonie bandits. Many of the accused have placed their caps on top of the cage.

magistrate was finally complete, and the stage set for the trial to begin. Of the original accused, about seventy had been released. Four had died in custody, including two of the most famous bandits, Melchiorre Candino and Gaetano Ferrarello.[30] The latter almost certainly committed suicide, though at the time it was made out that he had met his death ignominiously while trying to escape from prison.[31] Among the 154 defendants were two priests and seven women. One of these was the mother of the Andaloro brothers, Francesca Salvo. The press related endless lurid stories about her violence and masculinity.[32]

The Madonie trial began on 4 October 1927 at Termini Imerese. The prisoners were transported under heavy armed guard from the newly built gaol to the church, which had been converted to act as a court-room. The operation took two hours.[33] Down one side of the nave a cage had been built, fifty metres long, to house the bandits. It was divided into four sections. Maps were available to show the judges and jury the whereabouts of the accused. Unfortunately, the first day's proceedings were marred by the absence of many potential jurymen. This was rather embarrassing. The non-attenders received heavy fines, and the selection of the jury was deferred. It was not until 8 October that the interrogation of the defendants could begin.[34]

The trial was given an enormous build-up. The two major Sicilian newspapers ran extensive feature articles on the accused and their crimes. According to *Il Giornale di Sicilia*, the ignominious past now finally stood revealed: 'For many years...our countryside was subjected to the shameful slavery of those villains who at last have been identified and brought to justice through the wise and firm action of the National Government.'[35] The examining magistrate, the director of the gaol, the commander of the prison guards, and many other protagonists in the trial received glowing write-ups. The fourteen jurymen (there were four *supplenti* (stand-ins), twice the usual number, as the trial was going to be long) had their photographs published; in what was clearly a repudiation of *omertà*, their names and particulars were also given. Seven of them were state employees, one was a landowner and two were professional men. The others included a photographer, a bank official, and a businessman.[36]

The trial got off to a lively start, with many of the accused vigorously denying the charge of criminal association. 'I have never associated with anyone', said Santo Ferrarello proudly.[37] Salvatore Ferrarello explained the difficulties of being a *latitante*: 'You have to watch out for the police and enemies, and take care of yourself. There's no way...I could have considered a close accord with someone.'[38] When Nicolò Andaloro was asked of his relations with the Dino family, he replied vehemently: 'I don't even know them. While I was on the run, the Dinos were in prison here at Termini. They couldn't be associated with me.' He also denied being associated with the Ferrarellos. How could he be, as there were 'serious quarrels' between their two families?[39] Superintendent Spanò dealt swiftly with such objections. It was true that the bandits often fell out, he said; but their disputes were like family rows, and far from invalidating the idea of an association, they confirmed it.[40]

Some of the accused were clearly eager to defend a self-image as well as a reputation. Nicolò Andaloro (the most notorious of the bandits) insisted on speaking Italian, while his brother, Carmelo, used dialect. When asked of his relations with the Albanese family, Nicolò replied: 'The Albaneses, poor things, were my sharecroppers.' However, the Albaneses also had their pride. Antonio fastidiously spread a newspaper under him before sitting down in court, so that his clothes would not be dirtied.[41] Pietro was highly indignant at a photograph being passed round the jury as evidence of his violent character. It showed him with a proud demeanour, sitting on a fine horse, clutching a rifle. The photograph, Pietro said, had been taken at a party in the farmhouse where he worked; he had had to bor-

Pl. 18. A photograph of Pietro Albanese, used in evidence against him at the Madonie trial.

row the horse and rifle specially.[42] Mori later published this photograph in his memoirs, with the simple caption: 'The bandit Pietro Albanese'.

As far as specific crimes were concerned, most of the accused pleaded innocent. A few, however, confessed. Nicolò Andaloro admitted responsibility for the murder of Carmelo Battaglia, but claimed it had been justified: 'Battaglia was an uncontrollable bully', he said, 'and had assaulted me and members of my family'. 'Why these assaults?' someone asked. 'For political reasons. Battaglia supported a party opposed to mine.'[43] This crime, like many others in the trial, dated from the immediate post-war period. Some were older still. When asked about the robbery of a certain Gagliardo, Carmelo Andaloro said that it had occurred ten years before when he was only seventeen; at that age, he claimed, no one had the spirit to commit such an offence. He added that the accusation against him had been made by a woman who had killed one of her own children and subsequently been confined to a lunatic asylum. No refutation was made of this.[44]

At one point during his examination, Giuseppe Andaloro said: 'As you can see, President, the police used to attribute every crime in Gangi to the Andaloros.'[45] The ascription of crimes was certainly a problem for the police. After all, the local population had never helped with enquiries. Even the authorship of blackmail letters was far from certain: it was quite common for people to fake the signatures of notorious bandits in order to extort money.[46] Nicolò Andaloro may therefore not have been lying when he disowned two notes that had been attributed to him. He claimed they had been written by one of the prosecution witnesses, a certain Lo Dico: 'I even wrote to Lo Dico', he said, 'telling him not to use my name'. The prosecution admitted that this was true. Lo Dico was perhaps not the ideal witness: he had himself been suspected by the police of extortion, and had, on one occasion at least, been arrested and imprisoned.[47]

With 154 accused, there was little chance of thorough cross-examinations. The members of the jury must have been hard put at times simply to remember who was who. In the last few days of October, seventy-five defendants were questioned, while in the second half of November, 300 prosecution witnesses gave evidence. Two factors helped explain this haste. The first was the government's belief that fascist justice, in contrast to that of the liberal era, should be swift and decisive. This was an issue that particularly concerned Mussolini. At the end of November, he sent Mori a telegram saying: 'It is my conviction that we should impress a more rapid, in other words more fascist, rhythm on the Termini trial. Otherwise the judicial liquidation of the mafia...will not be completed before the year 2000. Make the necessary arrangements with the local judicial authorities.'[48] Six weeks later, when the sentences had been passed, he returned to the same theme. The proceedings, he said, had been 'interminable': 'We must study ways of ensuring that future trials are conducted with a rhythm more in keeping with the times, in other words, more fascist.'[49]

The second reason for haste was the trial's political character, which made the proceedings a formality, and the outcome essentially a foregone conclusion. The mafia, so the argument ran, had flourished through impunity: fascism would now demonstrate that the era of acquittals 'for lack of proof' was over. The press was unashamedly partial. No opportunity was missed to paint a dark picture of the defendants, and every more or less plausible attempt at exculpation was denounced. When, for example, Nicolò Andaloro accused Lo Dico of having written the blackmail letters with his name on them, *Il Giornale di Sicilia* pointed out that such 'calumny' was 'a typical mafia trick'.[50] Much coverage was given to the case for the prosecution, particularly to the statements of superintendents Spanò and Bonelli. The defence witnesses, who were admittedly few, were ignored by the press: their evidence, according to *Il Giornale di Sicilia*, was 'of very little interest'.[51]

The prosecution witnesses consisted mostly of peasants who had allegedly been terrorised into collusion with the mafia: 'Victims of criminal abuse, they were forced to save their lives and property by withholding information from the police, and meanwhile the truth was straining to escape from their honest souls.'[52] How the authorities distinguished between willing and unwilling accomplices, we do not know. In many cases it must have been difficult. What, for example, made Francesco Paolo Cerami a defendant rather than a witness for the prosecution? The charge against him was criminal association, for having received members of the Albanese and Andaloro families into his house, and for having collected 'tribute money' on their behalf. He was unlikely to have had much choice in the matter, as he was related to the Albaneses by marriage. That, however, may have been the decisive factor.[53]

Among the most important prosecution witnesses were the big landowners of the Madonie. Baron Sgadari's evidence was awaited with particular eagerness. He had been the victim, he told the court, 'of all the island's criminals'; he had suffered threats, violence, and extortion; he had been forced to pay Salvatore Ferrarello and his men 10,000 lire in tribute money; he had been 'ordered' to remove Spanò from Gangi; and he had been compelled to employ people against his will. His overall financial losses were prodigious: they amounted annually, he said, to not less than 100,000 lire.[54] Sgadari was barracked fiercely during the trial by a number of the defendants, and in particular, it seems, by Salvatore Ferrarello. However, as Il Giornale di Sicilia explained: 'Baron Sgadari has been among the most courageous of the landowners who have helped the police in the difficult task which has now been happily concluded; this is the reason why the criminals dislike him so much.'[55]

Towards the middle of December, two months after the trial had begun, the court heard the concluding speeches for both sides. Commenting on those for the defence, Il Giornale di Sicilia said:

> No honest citizen, even if he has been summoned by the law to the hard task of defending the guilty, will ever contemplate obstructing the glorious work of purification carried out by the National Government to free Sicily from crime. And this is certainly understood by the lawyers who are now defending the accused.[56]

A few advocates had the courage to mention the lack of firm evidence against their clients, but in general there was little point in risking a career when the verdict was a foregone conclusion. Lawyers who were too zealous in the defence of mafiosi risked being branded as such themselves.

On 10 January, after three days of voting by the jury, the sentences were delivered. Only sixty of the accused bothered to turn up in court. With one or two exceptions, all were convicted of criminal association. Nicolò Andaloro, Pietro Palazzolo, and Salvatore

Ferrarello were in addition found guilty of being the association's heads. Seven of the accused received life sentences; a further eight, thirty years. Forty-nine other were given ten years or more, and fifty-eight between five and ten years. Only eight were acquitted.[57] This was the outcome that Mori had wanted. 'The verdict of Termini', he said, 'is a virile affirmation of calm justice, of civic awareness, and Sicilian dignity. And it will serve as a warning and as an example.'[58] Had justice really been done? And was this the kind of 'warning' and 'example' that was going to restore confidence in the state, and break what Mori called the 'vicious circle' of non-co-operation with the authorities?

The major newspapers certianly thought so. *La Stampa* called the verdict 'one of the most important events in Italian life under the fascist regime'.[59] *La Tribuna* seconded this, and added that even though the trial had been held in Sicily, the jury had felt protected; it had thus been able, it said, to reach its decision 'with a free and clear conscience'.[60] The main national party newspaper, *Il Popolo d'Italia*, declared in a prominent front-page article that with the Termini trial, the mafia had received a mortal blow; soon, it claimed, 'the prophy-lactic work of justice' would be finished, and the mafia spoken of no more. The paper reminded its readers that Sicilians were a virtuous people who had long endured the mafia against their will: 'No writer's pen, no poet's song, could do justice to the hard work, the disinterestedness, the generosity, and the upright feeling for thrift and family life, as Sicilians understand and practice them. On this magnificent social foundation had been built a superstructure, a wretched compost heap of criminals.'[61]

The Madonie trial brought Mori's campaign to international at-tention. On 20 January 1928, *The Times* devoted a leading article to the subject. 'Mussolini', it said, 'has dared to threaten the monster in its native haunts, and has throttled it with success.' The mafia, it went on, began with the demise of feudalism, when retainers of the nobility were taken on by the Bourbon monarchy in an attempt to keep order.

> They found the employment lucrative, grew in numbers, and perfected their organisation. Nothing succeeds like success. Men of all classes, from the ancient nobility to the lowest ruffians of Palermo and the half-starved peasants, joined an association that gave protection to its members and to its tributaries, and inflicted summary and ruthless punishment upon its enemies.[62]

The same issue of *The Times* carried a brief report on the Madonie trial which stated that although the accused were dressed in various styles, they 'all wore caps, which the Mafia appear to prefer to hats'.[63]

Other newspapers had even more exotic comments to make on the mafia. The *Daily Herald* announced on 12 January the condemnation of 147 members of 'the notorious secret society', and added: 'The society observed all the rules and traditions of secret societies of romance. New members were qualified by trial of skill with the dagger and were all pledged to a code which was in defiance of the laws of the State.'[64] The *New York Times Magazine* carried an article early in March entitled: 'The Mafia dead, a new Sicily is born'. The mafia, it said, may have begun as a philosophical group among Greek settlers, with Pythagoras as one of its most influential early members; but from a patriotic movement of self-defence it degenerated into a 'criminal organisation', of which the landowners were the chief victims. Mori, it claimed, began by dismissing 'all police heads, judges and public prosecutors – and they were the large majority – who were suspected of having even indirect contacts with the mafia'; with new officials 'from Italy', he managed to restore confidence to the people, and to break 'the rule of secrecy' on which the mafia depended.[65]

The great majority of foreign newspapers depicted Mori's work as a brilliant police operation against a dangerous criminal organisation. Occasionally, however, there was a note of dissent. *The Observer*, while in general approving Mussolini's 'draconian measures', pointed out that the mafia was not an association which could be dispelled by the police: 'It is more an attitude of mind, a tenet of a perverted code of 'honour', a token of an independent spirit, which combine to drive Sicilians to carry out their own justice in primitive fashion, because of the contempt they have nurtured for the law through countless years.'[66] A less orthodox view still was expressed by *L'Interprete*, an Italo-American newspaper whose readers included immigrant Sicilians. 'The Mafia', it said in a leading article in March 1928, was an irresponsible fiction: 'The word 'Mafia' used in connection with the arrest and conviction of ruffians has only served to aliment and perpetuate a prejudice based on a lie.' The *mafioso*, however, undoubtedly existed; but far from being a criminal, he was a 'characteristic sensitive type, rebellious against any act of injustice and oppression'. One indication of this, the paper said, was that immigrant Sicilians translated the word 'with the equivalent "sport or sportman" which in their colloquial Italo-American slang they pronounce "spuortu".'[67]

The Mistretta trial

Only one other trial received as much coverage as that of the Madonie bandits. This was the criminal association of Mistretta, otherwise known as the 'interprovincial mafia'. It began in August 1928 and continued, with a number of interruptions, until the spring of the following year. There were 161 defendants, 250 injured parties, and 500 witnesses.[68] The principal defendant and alleged head of the association, Antonino Ortoleva, was dead by the time proceedings began, but this was not regarded as a drawback. The trial ended with the conviction of 148 of the accused. The terms of imprisonment were slightly less than for the Madonie trial, and ranged from twenty-three years to ten months. The average was between seven and eight years. There were thirteen acquittals.[69]

The Mistretta trial was based on a series of letters discovered in the study of Antonino Ortoleva. This correspondence, according to Superintendent Spanò (who, as at Gangi, headed the investigations), revealed the existence of a vast and centralised criminal organisation. Additional evidence came from a letter sent to the local sub-prefect shortly after Ortoleva had been arrested. It was from Paolo Timpanaro, a self-confessed *mafioso*, who, knowing he was a marked man, had decided to speak out before he died. 'He related', said Spanò, 'how the Mafia Tribunal met in the study of the lawyer, Ortoleva, and how its president was Ortoleva himself; its Procurator Royal, Di Salvo; its Reporting Judge, Antonio Tata; its Deputy Reporting Judge, Giuseppe Ortoleva; and its Counsellors, Giuseppe Mammana, Stefano Pittari, Marcello Milletarì, Felice Stimolo and his brothers, Mauro Biondo, and Giuseppe Calandra.' The letter also disclosed the names of some twenty *bravi* (henchmen).[70] The police used Timpanaro's confession and Ortoleva's correspondence to unearth the structure of the interprovincial mafia.

Although, said Mori, the letters found in Ortoleva's study were written 'in a kind of conventional language', they were nevertheless 'of moving transparency'.[71] In other words, they seemed commonplace, until it was realised that their subject matter dealt with the internal workings of a criminal organisation. For example, the key to Vincenzo Abbate's letters, according to the police, was cattle-rustling. In one of them, Abbate mentioned sheep being lost, and asked Ortoleva 'to lend his good offices'. In another, he referred to a certain 'Raimondi', who felt himself 'taken in' (*infrullato*). As Spanò explained, 'Abbate was head of the Castelbuono mafia, and Raimondi, his cousin, is Giuseppe Raimondi from Pollina, a dangerous *mafioso*.'[72] At times a curious interpretative logic seemed to be at work: the letters were construed as criminal *because* they were written by *mafiosi*. Spanò talked, for instance, of a note from Antonio Farinella: 'Although the witness was unable to offer an explanation, its contents undoubtedly relate to crimes...Farinella is a terrible villain with a long criminal record.'[73]

From the Ortoleva correspondence, it was possible to deduce, said Spanò, that the system of animal rustling was organized by eight men. The structure was vast and complicated, with 'bosses', (*mandanti*) 'henchmen' (*mandatari*), 'trusted *campieri*' (*campieri di fiducia*), and receivers ('who in the event of any unpleasant surprises could say the stolen animals were their own'). The association, he claimed, was headed by Ortoleva; its goals were 'the monopoly of the *latifondi*, large-scale animal thefts, the appointment of friends to positions on estates, unconditional help for those who fell foul of the law, and extortions'.[74] Spanò's exposition was vague, and the logic of his arguments (at least as it was reported) far from convincing. Was the organisation deduced from the correspondence, or was a preconceived model imposed upon it? The most quoted letter in the trial was one from Cataldo Piscitello, in which he asked Ortoleva to help a young Mistretta man who was 'at his studies' (a colloquial way of saying 'in prison'). Ortoleva was a lawyer, and it was perhaps not altogether surprising that he received such a request. However, since he and Piscitello were regarded as *mafiosi*, the correspondence acquired a sinister complexion.

The shortcomings of the prosecution case were highlighted by the deputy, Adolfo Berardelli.[75] Speaking in defence of his client, Antonio Farinella (one of the eight alleged leaders of the Mistretta mafia) he said that the police had failed to prove the existence of a criminal organisation:

From the written sections of this trial, in other words, the long police memorandum (almost all of which was compiled by Cav. Spanò), I learnt, as we already knew, that there is a mafia, and that there are leading *mafiosi*, and I saw a collection of rumours and allegations against Y and Z. But there was never any mention of a formal association to which these defendants might voluntarily have belonged. Where are its statutes? What rights and duties does each member have? Which actions were deemed to be private, and which collective? For all of this, there was no evidence. Nor did anything new emerge during the trial itself. Cast your minds back to what Cav. Spanò and his subordinates said in previous sessions: we had endless recollections, vague affirmations, and comments on letters found in the study of the lawyer Ortoleva; but was there any specific evidence against Y and Z? No. But what would one expect? How could citizens from different towns, miles apart, many of whom neither knew each other, nor even had dealings with each other – how could they have been united in an association, and acted in accord? The imagination can do anything: the dreams of Cav. Spanò. . . could create new myths, and even summon up in Sicily the horrors of the Middle Ages, with the Companies at Arms and Brotherhoods. But for God's sake, every exaggeration has a limit.

Berardelli (who incidentally published this speech in Rome, under the ambiguous title 'Against the mafia and for justice') went on to consider the evidence against his client, Antonio Farinella. It was not enough, he said, to call someone 'head of the mafia'. A more specific charge was needed, 'and this, in many cases, was lacking in the present trial'. A *mafioso* was not *ipso facto* a criminal: 'You can be *mafioso* for an act of daring, or exceptional arrogance, without ever having thought of an agreement with others to commit crimes.' This was so with Farinella, he claimed. Spanò had not found one item of hard evidence against him. He had been acquitted of previous charges, and charges were always brought against a man who rose in the world: 'If Antonio Farinella had continued to work his fields and run his small family farms, and had never become involved in politics and administration, not only would he have been spared former indictments, but he would not find himself here today before you answering to such slanderous charges.' Farinella's fortunes had improved noticeably during the war, and in 1920 he had become mayor of San Mauro Castelverde.

According to Berardelli, the only piece of evidence against his client was a letter signed 'Your most affectionate friend', which Farinella had written to Ortoleva, on 1 April 1923. In it Farinella had asked Ortoleva to tell one of his *campieri* to return a mare, 'without further ado'. This letter, said Berardelli, had been used to show that Farinella was a *mafioso*, and yet none of the witnesses or injured parties had made a single accusation against his client. 'The only person to suggest that the defendant is a *mafioso*, or rather that he got rich through the mafia, is Cav. Spanò, the *deus ex machina* of this trial.' The prosecution claimed that Farinella had become a millionaire through criminal activity; the truth, said Berardelli, was that Farinella had started poor and made his way up by hard work and luck. He had done well out of the war, and in 1921 he had bought a piece of land for a few hundred thousand lire. However, he was not, as Spanò liked to believe, a millionaire.

Berardelli ended his speech with a plea for justice. He praised Spanò's diligence, but added: 'One cannot swear by his word as if it were the Gospel'. Judicial mistakes, he claimed, would have dire consequences; for the mafia had begun as a response to injustice, and any new injustice would only reinforce already widespread feelings of resentment:

That [mafia] which was based on overweening arrogance could be contained and crushed; but that which might emerge from suffering, hatred, political injustice, and grievances would be beyond control. Then indeed sad times will lie in store for your island, which requires instead, if it is to be reborn and make constant progress, discipline, work and peace.

Farinella was not the only defendant whose rapid enrichment had been viewed with suspicion. According to the police, many of the accused had risen from poverty to millionaire status in the space of a few years; this they ascribed to mafia activity.[76] Crime, however, was far from being the only avenue to wealth in Mistretta at the time. Market forces had created a general situation of flux, as the economist, Giovanni Lorenzoni, pointed out: 'Almost half of the properties [in Mistretta]', he wrote, 'passed [in this period] from the old land-owners to peasants returning from America or the war.' The scope for speculation had been great: 'Olive groves, which had been worth 500 lire a hectare before 1915, were sold subsequently for 10,000 lire.'[77] Among those who had benefited, it seems, was Mauro Biondo, a former *gabelloto* of the landowner, Paolo Velardi, who now accused him of kidnapping and extortion. Biondo claimed that he had always been on good terms with Velardi, and that his wealth had resulted not from crime, but the war, 'which caused the value of goods to rise'.[78] Spanò evidently saw matters in a very different light. The Mistretta mafia, he said, was 'a vast association of criminals, cleverly directed by Antonino Ortoleva, whose aim was to force all the owners to give up their lands at derisory prices'.[79]

The economic climate in post-war Sicily was severe. In Mistretta, the battle to succeed, or merely to survive, was hard-fought, and the results were often confusing. Among the injured parties giving evidence at the Ortoleva trial was a landowner, Bettino Salomone, who claimed to have been the victim of 'private violence'. However, the defence pointed out that Salomone was himself indicted for criminal association, extortion, and private violence by the court of Messina. Salomone admitted this was true, but added that the charges against him were politically inspired: they came, he said, from Paolo Savoca, the former party secretary of Castrogiovanni, who had once tried to compel his uncle to surrender land to a co-operative in Mistretta, a move Salomone had strenuously resisted. Spanò endorsed this. Salomone, he said, was the victim of political vendetta, and was 'beyond suspicion'.[80] Evidently not everyone agreed, and Salomone's fortunes might easily have been different.

'Criminal association': critics and advocates

Between October 1927 and the summer of 1929, when Mori left Palermo, at least fifteen major mafia trials were staged. The six largest of these involved between them over 1,000 defendants.[81] However, this was not the complete picture. The legal work was arduous, and many of the accused did not appear in court until 1930 or later. One reason for the delay was the shortage of magistrates at every level: '*Preture*, such as that for Palermo, Castelvetrano, Castellammare del Golfo and Partanna, not to mention others, possess a wholly inadequate complement of magistrates and officials for the business they have to conduct', said Luigi Giampietro in 1930.[82] The consequence of this was that several years could elapse between the initial *retata* and the final verdict. At Corleone, the bulk of the arrests were made at the end of 1926. The preliminary investigation was not completed until July 1928, and the trial itself only took place in 1930.

Such delays caused a good deal of disquiet in legal circles; so much so that three articles appeared in the criminological journal, *La Scuola positiva*, which strongly criticised various aspects of Mori's campaign. This was remarkable considering the general mood of censorship, but *La Scuola positiva* probably counted as too technical a publication to warrant any official interference. Furthermore, it did not speak with one voice. In July 1928, it published an article by Enrico Ferri, praising Mori unreservedly. The old jurist had learnt on a recent visit to Sicily (where he had talked to Mori) of how the Madonie bandits had been forced to surrender through the simple expedient of a telegram; of how the peasants could now work longer hours than before; of how the land had reacquired its true value; and of how ordinary people were becoming aware of 'a judicial system that is impartial between rich and poor'. Ferri not only committed his findings to paper, but also conveyed them directly to Mussolini, with whom he had an audience on his return.[83]

Ferri's enthusiasm contrasted strongly with the sobriety of the other articles on Mori's campaign in *La Scuola positiva*. The first of these appeared in the later summer of 1928, and was by a Messina lawyer, Filippo Manci.[84] His argument (supported by an imposing array of statistics), was that repressive action alone could not settle the problem of Sicilian crime, and that the best chance of a permanent solution lay with economic improvement. Manci included in his article a striking assessment of Mori's work:

> The authorities have not yet succeeded in destroying the evil in its entirety. Instead they have crushed, or rather tried to crush, just one criminal faction – or rather some of those disparate warring groups into which the mafia is notoriously divided in Sicily... Hatreds and vendettas smoulder beneath the surface, and they grow stronger with restraint... The liberated masses who can be seen cheering at ceremonies are simply the victorious faction, disguised, but unrepentant, which has won a position of power

and privilege without disowning the past or assuming responsibility for it.[85]

The other two articles in *La Scuola positiva* focused on more specific, but equally fundamental, aspects of Mori's campaign. They were both by a Palermo lawyer, G. M. Puglia. The first, which appeared in March 1930, dealt with the problem of preventive arrest. This, said Puglia, was an issue that had attracted his attention through the case of Ernesto Rodriquez, an engineer from San Giuseppe Iato, who spent twenty-one months in prison before being declared innocent. Such episodes, Puglia claimed, were common, and the results could be disastrous.[86] He mentioned the example of a taxi-driver who was held in custody for several months before the examining magistrate realised that a serious mistake had occurred. In the mean time, the accused's family had been forced to sell his car, 'to pay for urgent domestic expenses and the service of lawyers'. As if that was not enough, thieves had broken into his house while the family was out and had stolen all they could, 'and this poor wretch, the most honest and harmless of workers, found himself, when he regained his freedom, plunged into poverty'. To cap it all, his fiancée had left him for another man.[87]

Puglia maintained that the moral, as well as economic, effects of imprisonment were severely damaging: 'Who will ever believe that [the taxi-driver] was innocent? Surely people will say that he took the authorities in, and that he was acquitted because he knew how to circumvent detailed police inquiries?' In other words, once a man had been charged, he was effectively tarred for life. 'The problem', Puglia went on,

> is one of human error; and if judges often make mistakes despite their moral probity and legal training, how can we give a policeman the right to send a citizen to prison (albeit in perfect good faith) by simply filling in a charge-sheet, without having some arrangement whereby his work can be subjected to direct scrutiny in order to ensure the legitimacy of the arrest? Nobody should be allowed to make an indictment, blindly, without thinking, and often on the basis of false information.

Puglia's article was cautious and restrained, and he may in fact have underestimated the problem of preventive arrest. At Corleone, 128 of the accused were sent for trial by the examining magistrate. Seventy-six others were acquitted and of these, sixty were released from prison.[89] Many of them had been detained for over eighteen months, and their conditions of confinement must have been unpleasant. Not only was there severe overcrowding, but the gaols were also, as Puglia pointed out, hotbeds of brutality and vice. One particular problem, it seems, was bribery: 'Given the wealth of some of the inmates', said Mori in August 1926, 'ever kind of corruption is possible. In fact we have had to dismiss the doctor and substitute many of the warders.'[90] A year later he complained that prison guards were being offered as much as 100,000 lire to help the Ferrarello and Andaloro bandits to escape.[91]

Puglia made no mention in his article of violence on the part of the police. However, there were endless complaints, allegations and rumours of this. One reliable witness said in the spring of 1928 that accusations of police brutality in Sicily reached 'to the antechamber of His Excellency Mussolini'.[92] Mori dismissed such claims: 'Violent methods', he informed the Ministry of the Interior, 'are not used in this province, nor are violent acts committed by the police.'[93] In order to support his case, he secured letters from several prominent local figures. 'I have received no complaints from anyone of mal-treatment being inflicted on those arrested during the present police operations', said Procurator Malaguti of Termini Imerese. 'For all its thoroughness', wrote the Archbishop of Monreale, 'Your Excel-lency's work has given rise to no kind of unseemly behaviour.'[94]

It is hard to arrive at a simple verdict on police violence. There were undoubtedly many episodes of brutality, but it is rarely clear how far the authorities were to blame. One Francesco Monteforte was said to have been so badly beaten by the police that he had to be escorted to hospital where he received treatment for 'severe injuries to his forehead and nose'. The official version of the incident read as follows:

> Monteforte, a dangerous criminal, was arrested in the act of breaking and entering. Whilst being escorted inside the gates of the local police station, he smashed, with a blow of his head, the glass in the door that separates the guardroom from the security cell, and was injured.[95]

Rumour had it that torture was used, and this may have been so. 'Methods of torture were allegedly devised that would have dis-graced the Inquisition', wrote Leonardo Sciascia in *Le parocchie di Regalpetra*.[96] In particular, Mori was credited with the reintroduction of the *cassetta*, a small wooden box to which the prisoner was bound, drenched in brine, and then whipped.[97] No hard evidence has emerged to substantiate such allegations, but none, perhaps, should be expected.

Two observations could be made about the behaviour of the police in this period. Firstly, the persistent rumours of torture were indi-cative of a climate of deep fear and mistrust: talk of Sicilian army recruits being castrated might have been comparable.[98] Secondly, the whole character of Mori's operation was conducive to police violence. His claim that the mafia derived from the state's weakness sanctioned a solution based on force, and since the police were vital to both the trials and the arrests, any excesses were likely to be condoned. In addition, the prefect's determination to destroy *omertà* may have encouraged the authorities to extract confessions by any means they could. Twice in 1926, Mori had to issue circulars urging the police to watch their behaviour, particularly with women.[99] In the circumstances, however, calls for restraint were unlikely to be heeded.

Puglia had raised an important point when he drew attention to the plight of the arrested man. In his second article for *La Scuola positiva*, which appeared in October 1930 under the title 'The "*mafioso*" does not belong to a criminal association', he focused on another significant issue. Quoting Pitré in support, he claimed that the term '*mafioso*' did not always imply criminality. In the past (and to a large extent this was still true, he said) a *mafioso* had been thought of as someone with exaggerated self-esteem, enormous pride and an assertive manner; he was by definition an individualist. This made the very idea of an association repellent to him:

> Should a *mafioso*, who has sunk to the level of a common criminal, decide to join with others to break the law, he would thereby destroy his reputation; and by forming a *pactum sceleris* with others, he would automatically cease to be '*mafioso*', as he would have clearly confessed his own personal inadequacy. '*Mafioso*' and 'member of a criminal association' are thus terms which cannot coexist in the same individual.

An organisation required a leader and a structure; but a *mafioso* was incapable of obeying orders, said Puglia, 'because he refuses instinctively to recognize anyone as superior to himself'.[100]

Though Puglia was to some degree, perhaps, playing the devil's advocate, he might have been closer to popular perceptions of the mafia than other less disinterested writers. When he described the nature of the bonds between *mafiosi* he was beguilingly straightforward. They were human beings, he said, and like everyone, they took pleasure in the company of like-minded people:

> And the various groups – politely termed '*petits comités*' – that you see at large receptions: what are they but the product of a reciprocal attraction between like-minded individuals? The lawyer will prefer to chat with the magistrate; the philosopher, in the absence of a colleague, will fall to talking to the man of letters; the playboy will take refuge in a group of attractive ladies; and the same thing applies to *mafiosi*.[101]

Among those who agreed with Puglia was the lawyer Vincenzo

De Bella. In 1933 he published a short treatise in Turin on criminal association. Citing Pitrè, Mosca, Franchetti, Bonfadini, and Alongi, he attempted to show that the mafia was not an organisation but a form of behaviour which placed personal gain above considerations of legality. He quoted Mori's observation that the mafia was essentially 'a morbid form of behaviour' which set certain individuals apart 'as in a kind of caste'. De Bella endorsed this line of argument: 'In my opinion the mafia is a sect which can generate criminal association without being such itself.'[102] A sect, he said, was based simply on a similarity of ideas; but an association required a specific, and formulated programme. 'To confuse the concept of mafia', he concluded, 'with that of criminal association could lead to very serious judicial errors, where people are sentenced, sometimes severely, for a crime with which they ought not to be charged at all.'[103]

Views of the kind put forward by De Bella did not pass unchallenged. F. U. Di Blasi, a magistrate whom Mori singled out for his achievements in Sicily, wrote a technical (indeed almost incomprehensible) article in *Giurisprudenza Italiana* in 1930 on the question of criminal association. In a footnote he referred to the mafia:

> The new conception of the ethical state...could not tolerate associations stemming from particular interests, nor the continuance of secret hierarchies, which, even if they did not have criminal aims, appeared incompatible with the sovereignty of the state...All discussion, therefore, of the sociological content of the phenomena of the mafia and the *camorra*, must be considered finished: their character is now to be seen as essentially that of a criminal problem.[104]

This was a surprising assertion. Di Blasi appeared to suggest that the mafia's crime was that it detracted from the sovereignty of the state. Indeed he went on to say, paraphrasing Luigi Giampietro, that it was not the mafia, but 'the society of *mafiosi*', that was criminal or rather a criminal organisation.[105] Did this ultimately mean anything except that particular people with specific attitudes, interacting socially, could be prosecuted, even though they had not broken the law?

One of Di Blasi's colleagues in Sicily was Giuseppe Loschiavo. He defended the idea of the mafia as a criminal association in a booklet published in 1933. This was a somewhat abstract work, and it may have been intended primarily to justify the judicial side of Mori's campaign *ex post facto*. Contrary to what Puglia had written, Loschiavo said that *mafiosi* did constitute an organised body: 'The "aggregation of *mafiosi*" [*aggregato dei mafiosi*] had as its main aim reciprocal help and mutual assistance among its associates.'[106] By the turn of the twentieth century, 'every town had its mafia, in other words its "aggregation of *mafiosi*", dependent on one or more chiefs [*capi*], who were in turn subordinate to a supreme chief', and each communal mafia was answerable to 'an intercommunal, provincial, or even interprovincial chief'. As evidence for this he cited the Mistretta, Borgetto, and Piana dei Colli trials which, he claimed, had shown the mafia to be so well organised as to have 'tribunals'.[107] To illustrate the authority of a 'chief', he referred to the case of Vittorio Calò: everybody on the Palermo-Monreale tram, he said, offered him their seat; not even the local archbishop commanded such respect.[108]

Loschiavo maintained that from a legal point of view it was unnecessary to prove that *mafiosi* came together specifically to commit crimes. All that was required was to show that *mafiosi* entertained 'a willingness to break the law'. This was easily done, since 'one cannot be *mafioso* without having a mind that is disposed to perpetrate every legal violation, from the least serious to the most grave; and one cannot be part of the "assembly of the mafia" [*consesso della mafia*] without being aware of, and agreeing to, the whole programme which the mafia habitually conducts against civil society.'[109] The trouble with this argument was that it depended upon two unproven assumptions. First, that an assembly of the mafia existed, of which *mafiosi* felt themselves to be part. Secondly, that there was a particular type – known as a *mafioso* – whose cast of thought was intrinsically criminal. Even if this latter point could be proved, it is not clear that there was any offence involved; and might it not be argued that everyone, in theory at least, has a mind 'disposed to perpetrate every legal violation'?

After its self-confident start, the weakness of Loschiavo's argument was soon apparent. Having described the mafia's structure, with its communal leaders, and tribunals, he then claimed that *mafiosi* were only recognisable through 'a series of often subtle indications that form one of the ethnic manifestations of the Sicilian. The *mafioso* is sensed [*si fiuta*]'.[110] Not surprisingly, this placed the magistrate in an invidious position: 'It cannot be denied that the task of the judiciary in making such an assessment is very difficult'.[111] However, the recent campaign had undoubtedly been successful, he said: 'Enquiries were able to show, once the cases had been stripped of inevitable inaccuracies and exaggerations, that in general the police operations had accurately picked out the most criminal members of the "mafia aggregates".'[112] Loschiavo's pronouncements in later years were more circumspect.

Pl. 19. Antonino Di Giorgio

12   THE FINAL YEAR

The clash with Di Giorgio

Antonino Di Giorgio was a brilliant soldier and a good politician. He fought at Adua, in Somalia, and in Libya, and he received five medals 'for military valour'. He was a hero of the Great War: he conducted the defence of the Isonzo and Piave at the head of the Special Army Corps, and he went on to distinguish himself further at Grappa and Montello. His political career began in 1913 when he was elected as a right-wing liberal for Mistretta. In 1919, he stood again, this time in the provincial college of Messina. He withdrew from parliament in 1921, but was returned as a government candidate in 1924, and became Minister of War. He held the post for a year until forced to resign over his army reform bill. In August 1926, after a spell at Florence, he went back to his native Sicily to command the island's military forces.[1]

His view of Mori was initially positive. When in January 1927 Mussolini had asked him what he thought of Cucco's disgrace, Di Georgio replied (without reservation, it seems) that Mori had acted with credit and should be supported.[2] However, in the course of 1927 his opinion changed. Relations between the two men grew frostier. Talk of their mutual hostility began to reach the government, and on 7 March 1928, while Di Giorgio was at Rome for the funeral of Marshal Diaz, Mussolini sent for him, and asked for an explanation. Di Giorgio said he had fallen out with Mori because the prefect had lost all sense of proportion. Mussolini apparently sympathised, saying he had been disturbed by the official figure of 11,000 arrests in Sicily. There was even talk, it seems, of Mori being dismissed, and Di Giorgio suggested he be replaced by a *carabiniere* general. Mussolini demurred, and the conversation ended inconclusively.[3] However, he told Di Giorgio to put his criticisms of the prefect in writing. Di Giorgio did so, in a long letter dated 19 March 1928.[4]

Di Giorgio's main complaints related to the character of Mori's arrests. 'The mafia', he said, 'had its leaders, its followers and its victims', but no distinction was made between them. 'The victims were rounded up with the criminals at the time of the so-called *retate*, for no other reason than that they had had contact with them.' This naturally made the task of the magistrates much more difficult. How could they deal adequately with so many accused? 'To observe all moral and practical guarantees prescribed by the law, when conducting criminal proceedings in which hundreds and hundreds of people are being examined simultaneously, is not humanly possible. As a result, there have been hair-raising stories of individuals who have been victims of wrongful arrest.' The moral consequences of such mistakes were far-reaching: 'As a result of the inevitably numerous judicial errors, the verdicts were deprived of any salutary effect.' Honest men were condemned, while the guilty could credibly protest their innocence: 'So all the sentences...are wrapped in the same cloud of suspicion and disrepute, and the judiciary, partly because of one or two shameful decisions by the political authorities, is openly accused of being under the thumb of the police.'

The arbitrariness of the arrests had not been the only reason for widespread disquiet, Di Giorgio explained. There was also the question of partiality: 'Ordinary people', he said, 'were offended in their sense of fairness and justice when the rich were spared (they, toò, are victims of the mafia; as is well known, they deal with it, and are forced to be its protectors) and yet poor illiterates were investigated, arrested and then sentenced, simply because, under threat of death, they had delivered a blackmail letter.' There might have been some point in saving the rich and powerful, 'if the aim was to make them into committed supporters through gratitude and fear; but in practice things were spoiled and, in terms of salutary governmental action, ruined, when these people, and these people alone, were let off, and the poor persecuted; yet the latter group, if any, should have been treated with indulgence.'

All this, according to Di Giorgio, was very damaging to the regime's reputation. The covert anti-fascists (who were numerous, he said) were profiting from the general resentment to stir up trouble:

They praise fascism to the skies, applaud the fight against the mafia, and make themselves hoarse cheering for Mori. But when they are alone with their friends and family they comment adversely on what is happening and whip up anger against the regime ....The long lines of handcuffed people you see on lorries, trains and stations, the disconsolate crowds of women and children who wait in the rain outside the prisons and courts, all lend themselves perfectly to damaging remarks and the propaganda of hatred.

In these circumstances, *sicilianismo* inevitably reared its head: 'Sicilians feel wounded, offended, and defamed by the continual parading of this problem of theirs in the Italian and foreign press.'

After Cucco's disgrace, Mori had been carried away, Di Giorgio said, by the false scent of victory: 'In order to fight the mafia, he sank to its level...and success went to his head.' The whole point of the campaign became obscured: 'The mafia and crime were no longer regarded as ills to be cured or tumours to be cut out, but as enemies to be beaten.' The waters grew muddied with revenge: 'Whoever had disputes to settle, vendettas to conduct, or positions to conquer, suddenly had a golden opportunity by providing the police with secret information, making denunciations, or giving false testimony.' Once again the moral consequences were disastrous: 'The mafia threatened to turn the Sicilian people into cowards; with these police methods we could make them all delators as well as cowards.'

Mussolini had asked Di Giorgio about public opinion: 'What, you enquired, is the response of the masses to all this?' The peasants were content with security in the countryside, he said, 'and they request no more'. 'Closed in the fierce egoism that is his hallmark the world over, the peasant shows a wary sympathy for the most wretched cases and for friends who have been the victims of judicial errors, and he is delighted when his enemies are wrongly arrested. Otherwise, he watches with indifference. It is something of no concern to him.' However, the more civilised and humane Sicilians were appalled by what was happening: 'They look on with horror, and distance themselves in spirit, if not bodily, from fascism. Yet it is precisely on these people that fascism should be counting if it really wants to penetrate the island and take hold there.'

Such dissatisfaction was undoubtedly widespread given the extent of Mori's *retate*. Mussolini himself had learnt of 11,000 arrests ('a figure that made me shudder', said Di Giorgio), and this, the general pointed out, did not include those sent to *confino*. Furthermore, the police operations had been concentrated in particular towns, which intensified the hardship: 'With lawyers' fees, prison living expenses, visits from relatives, usurious interest rates on money borrowed, and the damage done to business when no one is in charge, arrest means complete ruin, even for those who are acquitted.' Whatever benefits had come from Mori's work had been entirely vitiated by his excesses: 'If you then consider that for each of the eleven thousand arrested, and for every person in *confino*, there is a family, a network of relatives, and a circle of friends and associates, we can conclude ...that the operation against the mafia has not had, because of the way it was conducted, a beneficial effect on society.'

Criticisms, such as Di Giorgio's, gained added poignancy from Cucco's recent acquittal: 'Of course the total collapse of the accusations against Cucco and twenty-seven others on the score of dishonesty', wrote Tina Whitaker in mid-April, 'have made a great impression on many people, and no doubt on Mussolini himself.'[5] This was probably true. After receiving Di Giorgio's complaints against Mori, Mussolini summoned two *carabinieri* generals and several leading Sicilian fascists, including Francesco Ercole, Guido Jung, Salvatore Di Marzo, and the Duke of Belsito.[6] These four (and Belsito, in particular, as he had a long-standing quarrel with Di Giorgio)[7] in all likelihood gave the prefect their support. Nevertheless (and despite a meeting with Mori himself on 27 March), the Duce was not entirely won over: '*Signor Prefetto*', he wrote to Mori brusquely on 30 March,

> Further to our recent conversation, I hereby confirm the instructions I gave regarding your future work. That is: forget the business with Cucco and his followers, . . . see to the judicial liquidation of the mafia as quickly as possible, and restrict your retrospective enquiries. . . . The operation is well in hand and must be finished. Your Excellency will see to it.[8]

Though Di Giorgio had never before voiced his opposition so openly, Mori had been aware of it for some time. One symptom may have been the restiveness of the *carabinieri*, who seem on occasions to have been at odds with the prefect. 'I have become convinced', the *questore* of Palermo told Mori in September 1927,

> that the *carabinieri* are pursuing a programme that does not accord with Your Excellency's instructions. At Cefalù, Campofelice and elsewhere, they are supporting, and blatantly, Cucco's disbanded cohorts, and are in opposition to the local police. At Gangi they have been trying to ruin the trials, and a secret enquiry is underway against Spanò. At Palermo there is that livid-faced Emmanuele. . . and that is not all.

His advice to Mori was simple: 'You must eliminate every enemy, or else, we cannot proceed'.[9]

Mori did not need to be told this, but he had little desire to take on Di Giorgio so soon after his clash with Cucco. Apart from anything else, the general had influential connections with the Palermo aristocracy through his marriage to Norina Whitaker. However, Di Giorgio's criticisms had stung, and Mori felt compelled to retaliate: 'In life's battles,' he once wrote, 'non-vengeance is desertion'.[10] As he had with Cucco, he aimed to demonstrate that his opponent was in league with the mafia. This tactic had the advantage not only of liquidating the enemy, but also of invalidating his criticisms; for talk of excess and arbitrariness seemed comic on the lips of a *mafioso*, and could even be taken as proof of the campaign's efficiency. As Mori told Mussolini on 7 April, only those with 'something of a vested personal interest' resorted, like Di Giorgio, to intrigue and complaints.[11]

Mori decided to attack Di Giorgio by exposing his relations with the Mistretta mafia. When he returned to Palermo after the bruising encounter with Mussolini on 27 March, Mori asked Spanò to send him a report on the Ortoleva trial that would demonstrate Di Giorgio's guilt, if only by inference. This he hurriedly sent off to Rome on 7 April, along with several other documents of a more general nature. He also enclosed a set of statistics showing how much crime had diminished in Sicily since the start of the campaign. In an accompanying note, Mori said he would execute 'scrupulously' the orders contained in the Duce's letter of 30 March, but added that he would like to go over – 'simply for clarification' – what they had discussed at the last meeting. As for Di Giorgio, he said that the report by Spanò would reveal the man's true character as well as his motives for attacking him.[12]

Spanò referred in his report to the difficulties he had encountered while pursuing the Mistretta mafia, that 'huge, dense network that involved some highly influential people'.[13] The head of the association, Antonino Ortoleva, had formerly been (as Mori pointed out in a marginal note to his copy) 'His Excellency Di Giorgio's chief elector'.[14] In Spanò's view, everything had been done to hinder investigations, and there was a rumour that Di Giorgio might have been partly to blame, though he could not vouch for this. One thing he was sure was that the head of the Castel di Lucio mafia was Domenico Di Giorgio, Antonino's brother: 'He became part of the mafia after marrying a sister of one Stimolo, a priest and *mafioso*.' Domenico Di Giorgio's name had appeared on an inventory found in April 1926 in the house of Serafino Di Salvo, who was currently facing trial on a number of counts. 'All the most dangerous mafia chiefs in the island figured on this list', said Spanò, and he was certain that the general knew the document was in the hands of the police.

Spanò's report, together with a claim that Di Giorgio had made the War Office buy a new army hospital simply because his father-in-law disliked living next to the old one,[15] had the desired effect. Michele Bianchi's mistress, the Marchioness De Seta (who regarded herself as the arbiter of Palermo politics), apparently informed Mori that he was safe.[16] On the strength of this, he publicly cut Di Giorgio at a ceremony on the afternoon of 10 April. Di Giorgio telegraphed Mussolini that evening and requested another audience. An appointment was fixed for 19 April.[17] This time the Duce was terse: Di Giorgio had deceived him, he said. The general was furious. The accusations against his brother were pure speculation by the police: the inventory had been written by Di Salvo's wife, 'to remind her of who to notify about someone's death', and contained 'unimpeachable names'. As to the new hospital, it had only been built, he claimed, out of urgent necessity, as official enquiries had shown. His father-in-law (who anyway lived a mile from the old hospital) had had nothing to do with it.[18]

Mussolini appears to have been somewhat taken aback by the plausibility of Di Giorgio's explanations. However, he had decided to support Mori, and could not afford to change his mind again. Would the general accept a command somewhere outside Sicily? Di Giorgio, whose pride was as proverbial as his probity, said no, and tendered his resignation.[19] He returned to Palermo, where he had a violent altercation with the prefect. He may even have slapped him in the face – there was certainly talk to that effect.[20] Mori, however, was already the victor, and there was little that Di Giorgio could now do. He retired from public life and settled in his home town of San Fratello Acquedolci, where he died a few years later, in 1932.

Mori had clearly despised, and perhaps feared, Di Giorgio. He listed the counts against him in some rough jottings: 'Old clientelistic and masonic mentality – meddler – intriguer against the Militia – anti-fascist – told Restivo that I had threatened the jury at Termini – has always accused me of hegemonic aspirations.'[21] He was delighted at Di Giorgio's fall, and his elation was shared by a number of leading Palermo fascists, and in particular by the Duke of Belsito. Di Giorgio had for some time suspected the local party of intriguing against him.[22] Quite what the bone of contention was is not clear. As far as the Duke of Belsito was concerned, it seems that he blamed Di Giorgio for his undistinguished military career. The general certainly had no great respect for him.[23]

On 13 May, in the wake of his success against Di Giorgio, Mori visited Agrigento. After hearing the provincial *campieri* swear an oath of loyalty to the government, he proceeded to the Regina Margherita Theatre where he delivered a long speech, extolling Mussolini and denouncing his opponents. 'I join with you, fellow blackshirts . . . in a blaze of gratitude, faith, and love that rises to him, to Benito Mussolini, who willed, who promised and who kept his word.' He quoted sections of the Ascension Day speech, and then turned to the problem of his enemies. He declared that he had no time 'for men who endeavour, in the most subtle and oblique manner, and with every means . . . to sabotage and defeat'. Nor could he tolerate the false patriots who 'feign indignation when they speak of the insult to Sicily, or shed crocodile tears as they talk of repression . . . For these people felt no indignation when Sicily was really being defamed by bands of criminals.' Admittedly it was disturbing to see so many people going to prison; but what of all the families who had been 'forced to cross the ocean in search of security, peace and work'? Did Mori really regard the mafia as the cause of emigration?[24]

Some people might have wondered, listening to this speech, whether the prefect had not become slightly unbalanced. There was certainly a hint of megalomania in the way he condemned all those who had any doubts whatsoever about his campaign. In all likelihood though, he relished being surrounded by opponents. 'You cannot be truly strong in this world except when you are alone' was one of his aphorisms; 'the man of courage may achieve unanimity of dissent. Unanimity of consent is reserved for the complete and utter fool' was another.[25] His defeat of Di Giorgio no doubt gave him a sense of elation. It was a victory for political astuteness as well as muscle: 'To start will all seemed well, then bit by bit he tried to get the upper hand with the old methods of intrigue. I pulled the rug from under him by polarising everything on fascism and the Duce.'[26]

The last year

In the speech at Agrigento, Mori announced that his work of repression was coming to an end.[27] The writing had been on the wall for some time. In the autumn of 1927, he had complained to Rome about the lack of forces at his disposal: 'I will not speak of the grave difficulties that I have encountered, in particular from the gradual and almost wholesale reduction in the complement of policemen'. He said that of the original twenty-five officers in the Interprovincial Service only six remained; there was no longer a *carabiniere* general; and the number of horses had been cut by a fifth. All this made his task very difficult: 'The success achieved hitherto is recognised by all, and is tangible and extensive, but it must be followed up and affirmed.'[28] The government, it appears, thought otherwise. Two months after sending his report, Mori had still received no reply. Had Mussolini read it, he asked towards the end of January? Yes, came the terse answer from the Ministry of the Interior.[29]

In February 1928, Mussolini's brother, Arnaldo, wrote a leading article in *Il Popolo d'Italia* under the title 'Sicily'. Now that the mafia had been destroyed, he said, fascism should aim to improve the island's economy: 'Land reclamation must be the order of the day'. Roads, rational farming, drainage, the fight against malaria, and the promotion of tourism: these, he stressed, were the regime's new concerns in Sicily.[30] The article made it clear that the government saw the work of repression as over; Mussolini himself confirmed this to Mori in his letter of 30 March.[31] At the end of May, Michele Bianchi declared in the Senate that a million lire was being cut from the police budget for Sicily: 'It is not a great saving', he said, 'but it is highly significant: it shows that the fight against the mafia...has already produced results of a permanent character, and such as to influence the behaviour of the islanders, who, after so many years, have turned again, with faith and spontaneity, to the state.'[32]

Mori went out of his way during his last year in Palermo to court the masses. He probably had a political motive for doing this. His attack on Di Giorgio had in all likelihood alienated sections of the Palermo élite; his best course now was to foster his image as the 'peasant prefect'. Furthermore, Mussolini had specified in his letter of 30 March that Mori should 'help those families that are innocent, particularly the children'. It was partly in response to this, perhaps, that he used his *onomastico* (saint's day) on 2 May as an occasion for distributing food parcels to orphans. Among the provisions were 700 kg of meat, 3,275 kg of bread, and 1,025 kg of pasta.[33] Di Giorgio's relative, Tina Whitaker, was not impressed by this populism: 'Mori's Saint's day, and he is being treated like royalty by the shopkeepers of Palermo who have sent him presents of food, which he had distributed to the poor. . . . What a very dangerous man he is and how he knows how to curry favour with the illiterate masses of the province.'[34]

Mori devoted much of the early summer of 1928 to agriculture. On 3 May he visited the Sicilian Zootechnical Institute at Baida, together with his friend from the Madonie, Baron Pottino di Capuano. The institute had recently imported a number of Swiss bulls, and Mori was full of praise for the initiative.[35] He was no less effusive at a ceremony on 15 May, when he distributed prizes to the most successful wheat growers in the province. Among those honoured were Simone Sirena, Lucio Tasca, and Prince Spadafora. The prefect himself received a gold medal from the head of the Bank of Sicily and a bunch of roses and carnations from a 'representative' peasant. In his address he emphasised the virtues of the island's landowners and peasantry (the vast majority of whom, he said, were untainted by the mafia), and declared once again that his work of repression was coming to an end.[36]

In the autumn of 1928, Mori concentrated on propaganda in provincial towns. In October, he visited, among other places, San Mauro Castelverde, Cefalù, Roccamena, San Giuseppe Iato, San Cipirello and Bagheria. The following month he was in Ustica, Casteldaccia, and Santa Flavia. As always on these occasions, a carnival atmosphere prevailed. 'This morning our little town woke up all decked out for a celebration', said an account of events at Casteldaccia. 'The tricolour fluttered from every balcony along the main streets, and such a huge display of flags had only been seen ten years before. . . on the day of Victory.' Mori was greeted with 'rapturous applause, an incessant rain of flowers, and the singing of fascist hymns'. In his speech he claimed that it was the first time, so far as he knew, that a prefect had been to Casteldaccia; this showed, he said, the determination of fascism to have direct contact with the population.[37]

During these propaganda tours, Mori sometimes abandoned his car and made his entry into a town on horseback. This may have helped to foster his image as the 'peasant prefect'; it might also have reinforced the military character of his visits, which could be very marked: 'He immediately mounted a horse', said a report from San Mauro Castelverde, 'and at 11 was at the entrance to the town, where the Unions, the Associations, the Balillas, the *Piccole Italiane*, the *Avanguardisti* and the pupils from the primary schools were all assembled in fine array. . . . His Excellency wanted then and there to pass in rapid review the Associations, which were drawn up in military formation.'[38] There was often an attempt to increase the solemnity of proceedings by adding the sacred to the profane. At Roccamena, for example, the new banner of the agricultural union was baptised by a local priest, Padre Stagno, before being doused in champagne.[39]

Mori's growing international reputation may have contributed to a false sense of security, particularly as the local press dwelt lovingly on the tributes he received in foreign newspapers. Sir Percival Phillips' remarks in the *Daily Mail* were widely reported,[40] and *L'Avvento Fascista* referred in July 1928 to the 'serene and enlightened' articles in *The Times*, 'the British newsapaper with the largest circulation'.[41] 'In England', said the *Corriere Marittimo Siciliano*, with an unfortunate misprint, 'people still continue to speak of the mafia as a truly miraculous achievement of Mussolini's government.'[42] Feature articles on Mori appeared in countries as far apart as Norway and Argentina. Those by the former American ambassador to Italy, Richard Washburn Child, seem to have been widely circulated. This was hardly surprising given their sensationalist billing: 'First thrilling account, from the "Inside", of the uprooting and throttling of the world's deadliest secret society, which for centuries terrorised four million people with the "dark, the knife, silence!" – written on the ground in Sicily. . . after access to official files and the order's oaths, rituals and records of vengeance.'[43] These pieces in fact contained nothing very original, and much that was fictitious.

In Italy, the press was considerably more guarded. Several major tributes to Mori had appeared in 1926 and 1927 (for example, a large front-page feature in Mario Carli's *L'Impero* in May 1926),[44] but after 1927 the campaign received very little attention. The focus shifted increasingly from Mori and the fight against the mafia, to the economic and social problems of the island. Alfredo Armato's article in *Il Giornale d'Italia* in December 1928 was symptomatic of this change. The mafia had been subdued, he said, but not destroyed: 'To the surgeon's treatment we need to add the prophylaxis of the sociologist.' An extensive programme of 'social improvement' was required: 'We must plan for, and intensify, the completion of public works, which will all contribute to social reform: schools, roads, aqueducts, and easy agricultural credit facilities.'[45] Views similar to Armato's were expressed in *Il Resto di Carlino* in January 1929,[46] and *Il Messaggero* in February.[47]

While the press in Italy was quietly easing Mori (and the mafia) off stage, the government took care to ensure that neither he, nor the public, inferred that anything was wrong. After all, the campaign had officially been a complete success. In July 1928, Mori received a decoration from the King of Spain.[48] Later that same year he and Luigi Giampietro were both made members of the Italian Senate. Among the tributes on this occasion was one from Mussolini's biographer, Margherita Sarfatti, praising Mori as a 'fascist' and a 'courageous surgeon'.[49] The satirical paper *Piff Paff* (which had lost much of its sense of humour since 1925) took the opportunity to comment: 'How times have changed! Do you remember? In the past Palermo used to be nicknamed the "prefects' graveyard". Indeed, as soon as a prefect gave a hint of carrying out his duty, he was as good as transferred, that is if he wasn't dismissed.'[50]

In March 1929, the government held a national plebiscitary election, the principal aim of which was to show the outside world that fascism enjoyed widespread popular support. Mori was determined to do his best by the regime. His principal worry was abstentions: 'We will have the plebiscite that we want. Is that not so?' he declared, addressing a meeting of *podestà* and political secretaries at the end of February. 'We must ensure that people really do go to vote. Do you understand me?' He said that every scrutineer should possess 'sure faith' and 'a broad outlook', while attempts to sabotage the ballot boxes (did he seriously envisage this?) would be dealt with firmly by the police. However, the prime responsibility for vigilance, in his view, should rest with local fascists. They were to make sure that the 'wishes of Italy' were truly reflected, and should remember how they used to affirm their will, 'by appealing where necessary to that piece of wood that is called a *manganello*'.[51]

Mori was in an uncompromising frame of mind, as his speech to representatives of the Palermo suburbs (*borgate*) at the beginning of March made clear. A 'no' in the plebiscite, he declared, or an abstention, were to be considered 'acts of treachery'; those who did not support the regime would have to brave his wrath: 'Since a little spice is always needed, I will find time afterwards to look at the lists. Whoever has been lax will settle accounts with me.... This is a parade that is being conducted in the open. Either here with us, or over there against us.' Voting, he said, was to be carried out in a carnival atmosphere, and the Church (which was now formally reconciled to the regime) should be exploited: 'The priests will do what we have the right to demand of them'. In case there was still any doubt as to the character of the event, he admitted bluntly that it was not an election, but 'a display of consensus'. He concluded by saying that the plebiscite should be 'totalitarian', 'not only on paper but also in reality'.[52]

Mori could hardly have anticipated better results. The poll in the province of Palermo was 92%: 190,797 voted 'yes' and only 320 'no'. Two hundred and seventy-seven of the negative votes were cast in Palermo itself, and the remaining forty-three in only seven rural centres. This meant that in more than 90% of the towns not a single 'no' vote was recorded. Other Sicilian provinces claimed even more startling figures: Enna registered a 96% turn-out and not one vote against.[53] In the circumstances, however, such results were broadly predictable, and most people probably realised this: 'In the old days of local elections', said Charlotte Chapman, who observed the plebiscite in Milocca,

> election days were exciting occasions, but now that local affairs are administered by appointive officials, it requires effort to get the voters to the polls. When the list of Deputies was elected in 1929, speeches were made on the preceding evening, and Fascists paraded to stimulate general interest. On the election day, men were collected in groups and marched to the polling places escorted by the band. Voting was set forth as a patriotic duty for every Milocchese...The government list was unanimously approved.[54]

Before the plebiscite, Chapman heard someone saying: 'We will vote as they tell us, but God knows what is in our hearts.' She was unable to discover exactly what he meant.[55]

Throughout 1928 and 1929, Mori continued to chart the movement of Cucco and his followers. His spy network was highly efficient. He learned, for example, that the fall of Di Giorgio had left Cucco and his friends surprised, but not dismayed: 'They assume that His Excellency the prefect will have been much weakened by this victory', said Superintendent Nicolosi, the head of Mori's espionage unit, in May 1928: 'They are therefore interested to see what action Bianchi and Federzoni will take in the next Council of Ministers, and they point in particular to the discontent that has been caused in the army, and to the fact that Di Giorgio has the support of His Majesty.'[56] Federzoni, according to a report in April, was now convinced that Cucco had been the victim of a 'political frame-up'.[57] Michele Bianchi's hostility to Mori had been known about for some time.

Although it was thorough, Mori's spy network was not always discreet. 'Cucco is proposing to present to the local police', said Nicolosi in June, 'a denunciation for *zuinaggio* against Giovanni Marsala, who usually sits in front of a bicycle workshop opposite Cucco's house...Cucco has realised that Marsala is there to watch him and report to us.'[58] However, this was hardly a set-back as Mori had agents everywhere. They shadowed Cucco continually, intercepted his mail, and even succeeded in penetrating his home. Conversations with his wife were often reported; so too were dealings with his lawyer, Scimonelli: 'Paternò', said a communiqué in April 1928, '...made a statement to Scimonelli at Cucco's house about sums of money he had been offered to take part in the "plot" against Cucco.'[59]

In July, whilst in Rome, Cucco heard that Mori would not be withdrawn for some time. He now contemplated, it seems, the idea of a *rapprochement*,[60] but this was hardly possible, as the prefect was still in full cry. On 20 July, Mori had a certain Captain Franchina of the *Bersaglieri* transferred to Verona. Franchina came from Di Giorgio's home town, and had visited Cucco on a number of occasions in the preceding weeks.[61] A few months later, the chauffeur to the Palermo party executive was in trouble: he was godfather to Cucco's driver, and the two men had been caught talking together.[62] Cucco does not appear to have been deterred by Mori's relentlessness. He had an influential and loyal circle of friends in Palermo, who helped sustain him throughout this period. Many were political allies from early days; but some, such as the Marquis De Seta, had entered his sphere more recently. De Seta was the husband of Michele Bianchi's mistress. The fact that he was shuttling to and fro to Rome on Cucco's behalf worried Mori.

Cucco initially believed that Mori's appointment to the Senate at the end of 1928 signified that the government had faith in the prefect.[63] However, he soon changed his mind. In January, he was told by a prominent lawyer that he now enjoyed the support of the party;[64] shortly afterwards, he heard that the Grand Council was to review his case at the instigation of Rocco, Federzoni, Turati, Arpinati and Giunta.[65] In February, a member of the national party executive was sent to Palermo to conduct an enquiry: 'I can tell you', Cucco wrote to a friend, 'that after a thorough investigation he has realised the full and painful reality of the situation. It seems that he will sweep away the present order. As to my position, everyone has told him that the issue is one of political persecution and a judicial frameup.'[66] On 1 March, Cucco was reported as being 'extremely pleased':[67] a number of his friends had been placed on the list of candidates for the plebiscite elections, whilst Rosario La Bella, Mori's close ally, had been excluded, 'despite the pressure exerted on his behalf by His Excellency the Prefect'.[68]

After the plebiscite, the Duke of Belsito was replaced as Palermo *federale* by Robert Paternostro: 'He comes across to those who know him superficially,' said one newspaper, 'or have met him only rarely, as a likeable sceptic who disparages everything that has its *raison d'être* in the sphere of idealism.'[69] Such impressions, it seems, were wrong: Paternostro was an interventionist with a good war record, and had joined the party as early as February 1922. He was also a successful lawyer with a reputation for energy and intelligence. However, his subtlety of mind and strength of character were unlikely to have endeared him to Mori. Furthermore, despite a venomous attack on Cucco in 1926, he had never been one of the prefect's strongest supporters. In June 1922 he had voted through an 'order of the day' protesting at alleged proposals to send Mori to Palermo: it would have been, he said, 'a provocation and insult to the province of Palermo, which still remembers the criteria and methods which this official used when applying his ideas on the liberty of citizens.'[70]

Mori was known to be unhappy about Paternostro's appointment.[71] He might have felt that it boded ill for his own position, and if so, he was right. On 23 June a brief telegram arrived from Mussolini informing him that his career was finished: 'By royal decree Your Excellency retires for reasons of seniority as from 16 July. I thank you for your long and commendable services to the country.'[72] A recent law had stipulated retirement for prefects after 35 years of public employment. Mori, however, was only 57; he must have felt that an exception could have been made in his case, had the government wanted to. He looked for reassurance; the following day he received a second telegram from Mussolini:

> At this moment when Your Excellency is concluding the period of his official activity, I wish to express to you once again my sincere praise and most fervent congratulations for what you have achieved in Palermo and in Sicily in the last four years. These years will remain sculpted in the history of the moral, political and social regeneration of the noblest of islands.[73]

This telegram was released to the press.

Mori was still not happy, and asked for an audience with Mussolini. He was granted one on 8 July.[74] What passed between the two men is not known; in all probability very little. Guido Jung, a close ally of Mori, saw the Duce a week later.[75] 'Mori. . . can and must still be employed', Mussolini told him. 'I will make sure he is given a job in one of the para-state organisations.' As to the reasons for Mori's withdrawal from Palermo, however, 'not a word', said Jung, 'except that it was necessary to educate Sicilians to the idea that the state and the regime exist independently of the officials who momentarily represent them. . .I believe therefore,' he concluded in an attempt to reassure Mori, 'that you have no cause for concern.'[76]

EPILOGUE

Mori was bitterly disappointed at his retirement from Palermo. His friends tried hard to console him. Luigi Giampietro wrote to say that he should be grateful that his career had ended 'with the applause of the Duce and the respect of the great majority of honest men'. It was also good to remember, he said, that 'it was Roman not only to do, but also to suffer great things'.[1] A few months later, when Mori was still feeling badly let down, the Archbishop of Monreale told him that it was right not to trust too much to 'mortal contingencies': 'But to lose all faith in men and the highest ideals of life...No, Excellency, no!'[2] Mori evidently found it hard to adjust to normal conditions after the heady experiences of Palermo.

Among Mori's most ardent well-wishers on his departure were the landowners. No sooner was his retirement announced, than a number of *agrari* started a subscription fund to buy Mori a farm or a villa. According to one report, 400,000 lire was collected in a little over a week. This, however, was almost certainly an exaggeration.[3] When the government learnt of the scheme, it ordered the contributions to stop, and the money to be refunded: the state alone, it said, should be responsible for the welfare of its officials. Mori was slightly hurt. It had been merely an informal gesture, he told the Ministry of Interior, by a few landowners 'grateful for my work' and eager to show their 'true feelings'.[4]

After a brief spell at Bari, Mori moved to Rome. He tried hard to keep the issue of the mafia alive. In a forthright speech to the Senate in March 1930, he spoke of the urgent need for employment and land improvement schemes if the problem of crime in Sicily were to be settled definitively.[5] His remarks were not appreciated: as far as the government was concerned, the question of the mafia was solved. Mori must have realised that he stood to contribute little in the capital. He accepted a post in Istria, in the far north-eastern corner of the peninsula. Here he spent the remaining years of his life as president of a land reclamation consortium, superintending irrigation works, building roads and canals, and draining large tracts of marshy ground.

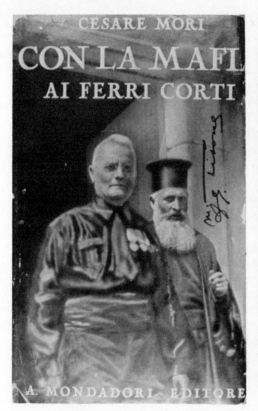

Pls. 20 and 21. *Left*: The dust-jacket of Mori's memoirs. In the original photograph (*right*), Alfredo Cucco appears behind Mori's right shoulder.

Mori had always nurtured literary ambitions. In the spring of 1932 he published a volume of memoirs, *Con la mafia ai ferri corti* (At close quarters with the mafia). They were written in an opaque style, which alone might have guaranteed them a poor reception. When combined with Mori's unpopularity in party circles, the result was disastrous. On 6 May, several deputies asked Mussolini if there should not be a ban on state officials recounting their experiences in 'unauthorised publications'.[6] The following day *Il Tevere* published a front-page review of Mori's book, dismissing it as 'ridiculous': 'There are no facts', it said, 'no ideas, and no argument. It is a collection of arrogant, cynical, and unbelievably stupid anecdotes'.[7] The dust-jacket was a particular irritant to radical fascists. It showed an armed bandit peering menacingly from beneath a heavy cloak. This was deemed to be morally offensive to Sicilians, and the book had to be withdrawn after publication. It was reissued with a new front cover featuring Mori in a black shirt, standing beside a Greek Orthodox priest at Piana dei Greci.[8]

Mori might have gained some consolation from the English edition of his book. It appeared in the spring of 1934 despite a half-hearted attempt by the party secretary, Starace, to have it stopped.[9] *The Last Struggle with the Mafia* differed from its Italian counterpart. The translator had been asked to turn Mori's rather ponderous text into 'a spirited story...with real popular appeal'.[10] He condensed and revised it, and the result was a more accessible book than the original. It was widely, and on the whole, favourably, reviewed, though some commentators guessed that Mori had not told the full story. 'Presumably,' said *Time and Tide*, 'the Prefect was possessed of emergency powers which enabled him to disregard strict legality'. However, desperate remedies were clearly in order: 'If the facts be as stated, the use of the strong hand would seem to have been inevitable; a widespread tyranny whose weapons are blackmail, theft and murder cannot be tackled in kid gloves.'[11]

Mori's career as a writer effectively came to an end with his memoirs. He decided not to go ahead with a French edition of the book: it would have been unwise, he told his publisher, Mondadori, in April 1933, even though 'everyone realises that my work is a hymn to Sicily, Fascism, the Regime, and the Duce'.[12] While in Istria he wrote short stories and poetry, and submitted work to the fashionable literary review, *Pan*, but without success. His subject matter was perhaps too odd a mixture of the brutal, the bizarre, and the heroic. One projected story involved a 'timid scholar' whose sister was raped by an 'exceptionally bold aviator'. Among his poems was an account of a witches' sabbath, in which the narrator discovered that the demons were 'ordinary women' and the opening to Hell, a sewer.[13]

Mori spent his last years peacefully with his wife, Angelina, to whom he was deeply devoted. His energies were given up to the land reclamation work in Istria. In October 1940, during a rare visit to Rome, he was overheard saying that in three or four years Italy would lose the war: 'The English newspapers are right'. He was denounced for defeatism.[14] This was the last documented episode of his career. He died in July 1942, a few months after his wife. News of his death went almost unreported, and what obituaries there were, were laconic. He had no children, and his few possessions (including a trunk full of private papers) passed to distant relatives.

In contrast to Mori, Alfredo Cucco enjoyed increasing success after the 1920s. In the summer of 1931 he was acquitted of the last remaining charges against him. Scenes of rejoicing greeted the verdict, together with cries of '*Viva la Giustizia*', '*Viva il fascismo*', and '*Viva il Duce*'.[15] According to one report, the degree of sympathy for the former *federale* could only be explained in terms of 'a retaliation against something that [was] hard to define'.[16] Throughout the 1930s, Cucco continued his career as an oculist. He also taught demography at Palermo University, and published several works on the dangers of birth control and racial degeneration. Whether these books improved his standing in the party is not known.

For all his professional interests, Cucco was at heart a political animal. A year after his acquittal, he wrote to Mussolini and asked for readmission to the party. Mussolini forwarded the request to Starace, but Starace turned it down.[17] Apart from anything else, it seems that the new prefect of Palermo was worried that Cucco's rehabilitation might cause 'turmoil and vendetta'.[18] In the years that followed, Cucco continued to press his suit, and among the leading fascists who supported him was Federzoni.[19] In 1936 his wish was finally granted, partly through the good offices of Farinacci.[20] However, an application for an audience with Mussolini was unsuccessful: Starace was 'absolutely opposed'.[21] Certain party figures in Palermo clearly had a vested interest in preventing Cucco's comeback.

In the late 1930s the regime began to revert to its radical origins. Cucco's brand of fascism came back into favour; and with the conquest of Abyssinia and the approach of war, Sicily's position in the Mediterranean gave it a political importance it had hitherto lacked. Cucco's name started to circulate again in the highest circles. In December 1942, the vice-president of the Chamber of Fasci and Corporations told the party vice-secretary that Palermo was 'short of strong men whom we can trust'. He had noticed, he said, on a recent visit to Sicily, that Cucco ('whom the notorious Mori persecuted relentlessly') was 'profoundly respected by the mass of Palermitans'. Might it not be sensible to appoint him to the Chamber?[22] In the spring of 1943, with the Allied invasion of Sicily pending, Cucco became a vice-secretary of the national party.

Cucco remained loyal to fascism throughout the war. He joined Mussolini's puppet government in Salò as Under-Secretary for Popular Culture: Farinacci's support again appears to have been instrumental.[23] He devoted much of 1944 and 1945 to helping Sicilian refugees in Rome, and the services he gave were long remembered. With the end of the war and the fall of Salò, he was condemned to death *in absentia*. He took refuge in the Vatican until his sentence was commuted to thirty years imprisonment. He was later pardoned. In 1946 he helped found the neo-fascist party, the MSI (Movimento Sociale Italiano); and from 1953 until his death in 1968, he was an MSI deputy in Rome. His career as an oculist flourished, and among his clients was Sophia Loren. It was partly because of his contribution to science that a large piazza was recently dedicated to him in Palermo.[24]

Sicily in the 1930s

Mori's successor as prefect of Palermo was Umberto Albini.[25] He was thirty-three years old, and was one of a new generation of state officials drawn from the party. He had little in common with his predecessor except that he was a northerner. Albini possessed ability (he was to enjoy a distinguished civil service and party career), but he cultivated a playboy image. He made a flamboyant entry into Palermo by seaplane, and there were soon reports that the prefecture had transferred to the beach of Mondello.[26] Anonymous letters to Rome spoke of his lack of dignity, his inexperience, and his refusal to live in accommodation befitting his office. A particular source of grievance was that he continued to flirt shamelessly with women although he was engaged to a member of the local Florio family.[27]

Albini declared on his arrival that he would continue the fight against crime with 'energy, resolution and courage'.[28] He received the same powers as Mori for co-ordinating police action throughout Sicily, but it was clear from the start that the government wished to be rid of the mafia. The press was instructed to play down reports of criminal activity, and particularly murders. This was frustrating to those who believed that the answer to Sicily's problems lay in exposing them to public gaze. 'The newspapers only print now what the prefect likes to hear', said one indignant Sicilian to Mussolini, 'namely that...we are living like Adam and Eve in perfect peace.' Just a few days before, he said, three people had been brutally murdered in a town near Palermo; yet Albini would not be informed, 'because everyone here is quite determined that he will never, never, never know anything'.[29] Whether this was from a desire to conciliate the prefect, or because local people were worried about a resumption of Mori's methods, is not certain.

Albini resorted more than his predecessor to the expedient of *confino*. This was a much simpler way of tackling the problem of crime than *retate* and show-piece trials. Two or three times a week, the prefect received lists of suspects, and with his authorisation they could be sent to penal islands for up to five years. One of the attractions of this procedure was that it saved resources. Albini lacked police, and his requests for reinforcements went unheeded. Many of the *carabinieri* were deployed in guarding those on trial. Furthermore, Albini could no longer use members of the Militia to supplement his depleted forces, as the government had cut his budget for this to almost zero. As a result, Palermo in particular was seriously underpoliced; and yet, he said, 'traditional forms of criminal activity' were at best dormant.[30]

The 1930s are devoid of adequate documentation for the true state of Sicilian society. Newspapers closed their eyes to all that was unpalatable; even government officials seemed reluctant to disabuse their seniors in Rome. Perhaps they were unaware of the truth themselves. In December 1934, Albini's successor, Prefect Marziali, spoke reassuringly of the 'continuous improvement' in public security, but he admitted that he had been forced to conduct an 'energetic purge of the many criminals...of every social category who were still roaming loose in all spheres'. He also alluded to the problem of *mafiosi* who had finished their sentences or earned remission. Many of them were public menaces, he said, and in the preceding year more than 400 had been sent to *confino*. Nevertheless, the general situation was good: he claimed that 'associated crime' had been definitively destroyed.[31]

The little evidence we have for the early 1930s suggests that crime was still a serious problem in Sicily. The dire economic situation had not improved matters; nor too had the censorship in the press. In June 1932, the poet-baron, Filippo Agnello, wrote to Mori from Cefalù about the difficulties the island was facing.

> I have been thinking...of the glorious days of the redemption, when the *gabelloti* began to pay, and wealth once again, after so long, entered our coffers. Now, my illustrious friend, albeit for other reasons, we have fallen once more on hard times....There is hunger, and you know what a bad influence that can be in some quarters. The roads are once again dangerous. There have been hold-ups, highway robberies and violent thefts; the only thing we seem to have been spared is cattle-rustling....God preserve us, for we are going through a wretched time; and what is particularly bad is that the newspapers have been ordered to keep quiet.[32]

Agnello was not alone in his despondency. The lawyer, Giuseppe Sciarrino, wrote to Mori in December 1931 about the growing chaos around Termini Imerese:

> As for public security, strong orders are issued but people go ahead regardless and murder and rob at will. Where is it all going to end? Even the *podestà* of Termini...has been held up and robbed. I realise that hunger, after two bad harvests, has not improved things; but it is above all the general lack of faith in the authorities that is to blame. In almost every town, the *capi-mafia* have had their sentences reduced and are back from *confino*, leaving the small fry behind. In Caccamo, a dangerous place, the Azzarello brothers, *capissimi-mafia* of Sicily ...were proposed by the local authorities for *confino*, but were then let off by the Palermo Commission. Scandals such as this make honest people sick, and do nothing but encourage the criminals.[33]

Despite Mori's drive against urban crime, Palermo continued to be a trouble-spot after his departure. Many of the city's problems in the 1930s stemmed from increasing decay and poverty. Peasants desperate for work moved in from the countryside and swelled the ranks of unemployed and marginal workers. Between 1931 and 1936 the population of the capital rose by nearly 40,000. Housing was in extremely short supply. A good deal of substandard accommodation was demolished, but it failed to be replaced quickly enough. In 1931, 54% of the city's inhabitants lived in only one or two-room dwellings, double the figure for ten years earlier.[34] A report of 1938 spoke of how 'huge working-class quarters' had been pulled down and the population resettled in 'hovels without sun or light'. In these cramped conditions, it said, tuberculosis was common and poverty 'absolute'.[35]

This was the squalid backdrop for the widespread corruption in Palermo during the 1930s. The city's administration was racked by deficit and embezzlement. Private building contractors exploited political ties and speculated on housing.[36] Lower down the scale, there were familiar complaints about fraud in the Palermo markets: Albini had to deal with 'an organisation of dishonest fish wholesalers' who took a cut of more than a fifth on their transactions.[37] The problem of *zuinaggio*, which Mori had been so determined to stamp out, flourished as the main state hospital ground almost to a halt. A report of 1939 said that the only activity which the nurses performed with relish was transferring patients to private doctors. Moreover, money was in such short supply that syringes had to be bought singly in cases of emergency.[38]

What was distinctive about Sicily in the 1930s was not that the mafia had been destroyed, but that the authorities could no longer use the word to describe the chaos. The annual reports of the Procurators General of Palermo referred to persistent high levels of crime, but they were forced to dispense with the traditional explanation. Rodolfo Loffredo, who succeeded Luigi Giampietro, claimed in 1932 that there was no longer 'any specific form of crime' in Sicily, as it had been destroyed for good. Nor, he said, was he being unduly optimistic, for 'that climate of lawlessness was above all the consequence of the political environment which fascism has destroyed'.[39] Two years later, Procurator General Bartolini expressed his concern at the 'vast scale' of Sicilian crime. He found it hard to account for, but suggested it was the result of the appalling economic and social conditions in the island.[40] Both magistrates studiously avoided using the term 'mafia'.

If lawlessness continued to flourish, so too did other features of Sicilian life that the government had hoped to suppress. One of these was clientelism, and in the worsened economic climate of the 1930s, the bitterness of factional struggles could well have been intensified by the competition for resources. No sooner had Mori left Palermo, than his opponents moved on to the offensive. 'The rabble and anti-fascism together', a Palermo judge told the former prefect in April 1930,

> are trying to destroy those who were closest to Cesare Mori, and not even I am spared, despite my position as a magistrate. An anonymous letter was sent to my Minister in which I was accused of protecting the mafia of Castellammare [del] Golfo for nine years!...If Your Excellency had been at Palermo, who would have dared to attack me in this way?[41]

The early 1930s were a familiar battleground of denunciations and counter-denunciations. Those who had lost out in the 1920s attempted to make a comeback, and because Albini knew little about Sicily (and was therefore, perhaps, susceptible to persuasion), they had reason for optimism. In March 1930, a magistrate wrote to Mori from Misilmeri about the turmoil that had occurred since the new prefect's arrival:

> People have become obsessed here and see *mafiosi* everywhere. There is not a *carabiniere* lieutenant who has not appointed himself a scourge of the mafia. Men of unblemished character, who in the past risked having their heads shot off for standing up to the mafia, are now in grave trouble with the *carabinieri* simply because some trouble-maker decided to have them branded as *mafiosi*...Much of the work that Your Excellency achieved in the province of Palermo has been undone through ignorance or ineptitude.[42]

The problem of factional rivalries and false denunciations became severe enough for the issue to be raised in parliament. In April 1932, the Sicilian deputy, Ruggero Romano, suggested in a speech that the authorities should be more aware of 'the professional delators... who have sometimes used the police and the magistrates as weapons to strike at their personal enemies'. He said that the issue was particularly acute in the small towns in the interior of the island where partisan struggles had grown 'terrifyingly bitter': 'Slander can be an instrument of vendetta for the old displaced camarillas. Intolerant of the new order, they flood the province and the capital with denunciations and anonymous letters, sowing disquiet, mistrust, and suspicion of crime.'[43]

The situation would have been better if the fascist party in Sicily had provided strong moral leadership. Unfortunately feuding and inertia were hallmarks of many of the island's *fasci* in the 1930s. The Palermo *federale* from 1932 until the end of the decade was a young doctor called Ignazio Li Gotti. When he took over, the local party was described as 'existing only to recruit members'. In addition, the youth organisations 'languished', and *Dopolavoro* had degenerated at the provincial level into 'a series of clubs for card players', while in the city most members were said to join 'merely to get a reduction on cinema tickets'.[44] Seven years later, reports painted an even bleaker picture. The party suffered from a general lack of popular support in the province, and according to a number of commentators, routine administration was all that ever took place.[45] In some towns the *fascio* only opened on public holidays.

Much of the trouble stemmed from inadequate leadership; this in turn was a by-product of clientelism. Li Gotti was a protégé of the party secretary, Starace. He was generally regarded as having little authority and scant imagination, but Starace continued to support him.[46] One particular source of ill feeling was the local executive's veto on personal enemies joining the party.[47] Another cause of re-sentment was that Li Gotti became the puppet of some far from savoury characters. One was the vice-*federale*, Salvatore Villardo, who had been involved in several criminal proceedings. Another, Achille Corrao, had once been expelled from the party for wearing medals that he was not entitled to, and for forging the citation. He had used his contacts to secure various salaried posts for which he did little or nothing. Both these men appear to have enjoyed the backing of Starace.[48]

The fascist regime had attributed many of Sicily's problems to the corrupting effect of clientelism. It was hoped that the abolition of elections would end the favour enjoyed by criminals, and raise the tenor of public life. This did not happen. The competition for ad-vancement and status led to the formation of rival currents within the party. In provincial towns, the old factions vied, as earlier, for control of the local administration. Each group boasted a patron to whom it turned for support, and, as in the past, this could result in criminals securing immunity from prosecution, or in zealous and troublesome officials being posted elsewhere.

In the town of Caccamo in the early 1930s there were two factions, one of which controlled the party, the other the communal admin-istration. The *podestà*, Giuseppe Barbera, was a friend of the local *pretore*, who had great influence in Caccamo because he was a nep-hew of Salvatore Di Marzo, a deputy and former mayor of Palermo. The vice-*podestà* was one of the notorious Azzarello brothers (whom Mori had prosecuted); he was proud of having officials transferred 'simply because they had been seen, once or twice, in the company of his ...enemies'. Barbera and Azzarello used their political con-tacts to harry the opposition, who dominated the local party, and in the end Barbera secured himself the post of political secretary. His enemies immediately retaliated with anonymous letters to the au-thorities; but though Prefect Albini showed some sympathy with their cause, there was little to be done while Di Marzo still had influence and power.[49]

Another town where factional struggles persisted into the 1930s was Balestrate.[50] In 1922, the followers of Vincenzo Chimenti had won control of the local fascist party. Four years later, Mori dissolved the section, on the grounds that it had been infiltrated by the mafia, and Chimenti himself was arrested. His son took up the cudgels on behalf of his father, and in the autumn of 1928, Chimenti was acquitted for lack of evidence. After his release, Chimenti forced himself on the new *podestà*, who had been charged with rebuilding the *fascio*. His position was strengthened by his acquaintance with the Palermo *federale*, Roberto Paternostro; when the party in Balestrate was reconstituted, it was once again dominated by Chimenti's supporters.

The *podestà* of Balestrate, however, had no desire to be Chimenti's creature. He insisted that the new *fascio* contain members of the opposition group, led by Paolo Evola. This infuriated Chimenti, whose hatred of the rival faction was long-standing. Chimenti turned to Paternostro, and tried to persuade him to intervene, but Paternostro refused to become involved. In September 1930, by way of compensation, he managed to have his name put forward for the post of public security officer to the *podestà*. According to a police report, Chimenti hoped to use this position to destroy a number of his local enemies whom he had earlier asked the *carabinieri* to send to *confino* for their 'anti-fascist activities'. Chimenti's appointment, however, was vetoed by the prefect.

Early in 1931, Chimenti's protector, Roberto Paternostro, lost his position as *federale* and Evola's faction took the opportunity to counter-attack. In March, an inspector was sent to Balestrate to investigate the *fascio*. Chimenti's enemies succeeded in winning him over and the party section was dissolved. Chimenti blamed the *podestà* for not coming to his defence, and he publicly rebuked him, 'eyeing him in a grim and threatening manner, warning him to take care'. Early in April, the *podestà* announced the composition of the new *fascio*: it was dominated by Evola's supporters. Chimenti's followers could not contain their anger, and on 16 April they set fire to the headquarters of the *Dopolavoro* organisation. Among the charred remains of the building was a lithograph of Mori, its face disfigured with knife cuts.

Since, officially, the mafia no longer existed, crime continued beneath an umbrella of silence. Banditry and murder went unreported,[51] and as the 1934 scandal in the Palermo bureaucracy showed, the regime preferred to ignore corruption than cause a public scandal.[52] It is not surprising to learn from a party communiqué of 1932 that Sicilians working in Rome smiled at government claims that the mafia had been destroyed.[53] One particular sign that little had changed was the appalling state of municipal finances. Local taxes were exorbitant, and popular protests against them were common.[54] The condition of roads in the interior hardly improved in the 1930s, and a report of 1941 drew attention to the persistent overcrowding and poor facilities in elementary schools.[55] However, despite this apparent absence of expenditure, many local councils were heavily in debt. 'Almost all the towns in the province of Palermo', said a report in 1939, 'have severe deficits, and everywhere services are lacking.'[56]

Many of Sicily's problems in the 1930s were economic.[57] The world recession that began in 1929 hit the island hard. Quality goods, on which much of the region's wealth had traditionally depended, suffered heavily from the closure of export markets. In the period from the mid-1920s to 1939, grape and lemon production both dropped by nearly a third. A similar crisis affected olives, nuts, and other forms of fruit,[58] and though attempts were made to rationalise the sulphur industry, the general long-term decline persisted.[59] Almost the only commodity to do well in the 1930s was wheat. The Battle for Grain and government protection resulted in a 15% rise in the acreage under cereals between 1923 and 1939. In some places there were marked improvements in yields, and signs of greater mechanisation, but the progress was slight compared to the north of the country.[60] Furthermore, the attention given to wheat was an important reason for the decimation of Sicily's livestock in the 1930s.

The stagnation in the Sicilian economy during the 1930s was worsened by demographic pressure and inadequate governmental assistance. Prior to the Great War, emigration had offered an avenue of escape for the under-employed peasant, but the imposition of quotas (above all in America) put a stop to this. The population rose, and by 1936 the percentage of Sicilians in work had fallen by nearly 10% compared to fifteen years earlier.[61] Most important of all, perhaps, was the absence of overseas remittances to supplement meagre rural incomes. Government loans might have improved the situation, but the bulk of public money went to the north of the country where the regime was more worried about the possibility of organised opposition. By the eve of the Second World War, extreme poverty was endemic in the island. According to one observer in 1939, many families in the interior had nothing to live on but 'roots and herbs'.[62] When, in the same year, the Prince of Piedmont visited Palermo, crowds of desperate people broke through police cordons to deliver petitions.[63]

Some of the disruption in the interior stemmed from the continuance of the *latifondo* economy. Many of the smallholdings created after the war collapsed in the late 1920s and the *agrari* were apparently able to reclaim much of the land they had earlier been forced to sell.

Between 1930 and 1946 the percentage of the productive area covered by great estates rose from 28.2% to 34.1%.[64] To experts such as Giovanni Lorenzoni, this consolidation of the *latifondi* was distressing. When he visited the island in 1940, he found it little changed from a generation before.

> Everywhere there are fields of wheat (occasionally other cereals). They alternate with huge natural pastures and areas of fallow. Everything is cultivated in a remorselessly extensive manner. The eye travels for miles without seeing a house.... There are few passable roads and sometimes none at all. Goods have to be transported by animal, and at harvest time trains of mules or horses can be seen crossing the fields escorted by vigilant armed guards.[65]

Though the evidence is fragmentary, there is little reason to believe that the Sicilian countryside was less violent in the 1930s than it had been earlier. Landowners continued to be absentee;[66] and the pattern of leasing estates to *gabelloti* persisted, though sometimes in a disguised form. The pact of June 1927, which stipulated the abolition of intermediaries not directly involved in farming, was extended, by an agreement at Catania, to the whole of the island; but it seems that many *gabelloti* merely introduced share-cropping contracts which allowed them to claim a 'direct' stake in production. Alternatively, they could become 'stewards' or 'administrators' without changing their basic character.[67] However, it does seem that many more landowners than previously leased their estates in smaller lots, either directly to peasants or to intermediaries. This helped eliminate the worst excesses of parasitism.[68]

The condition of the rural middle class in the 1930s is hard to assess. With no political groups to represent the peasantry, the ruthlessness of the *gabelloti* and their dependents went unchronicled. At the same time, the big landowners were more secure than they had been immediately after the Great War. They enjoyed important positions at the local and national levels, and this protected them against the petty-bourgeois aspirations of much of the fascist party.[69] They were also in a strong economic position thanks to the tariff on wheat and the widespread practice of taking rent in kind which shielded them from the effects of inflation.[70] In these circumstances, the rural middle classes were unlikely to seem a threat, particularly as they could no longer use peasant disturbances as a stick to beat the landowners.

Almost the only interesting book on Sicily to be published in this period was a volume of essays edited by Arturo di Castelnuovo in 1934.[71] Many of its contributors simply toed the party line, but a few had the courage to suggest that fascism had done little or nothing for the island. Dr Antonino Cannone was particularly outspoken; so much so that the editor felt obliged to write a short preface in which he warned the reader about the author's 'somewhat exaggerated views'. The mafia, according to Cannone, had its roots deep in the past, 'and I doubt very much that it could have been destroyed by the energy of one prefect'. Furthermore, he said, it was an integral feature of the island's archaic social structure, and up to now 'very little or nothing has been done to free Sicily from the cancer of feudalism'. Change would only come about, he claimed, if the regime abandoned the upper and middle classes, and supported the mass of the Sicilian population. One of the best ways of liberating the peasantry would be to introduce reforms to create a fairer distribution of income, and destroy the 'cannibalistic character' of economic relationships.[72]

Cannone's views were too extreme to be heeded in 1934. A few years later, however, they were more acceptable. With the conquest of Abyssinia, Sicily acquired a new role as the 'centre of the Empire'. Mussolini visited the island in 1937 and told a local audience that he planned to make the region into one of the most fertile in the world.[73] Fascism was moving towards its final anti-bourgeois phase; this, combined perhaps with fears for Sicily's political loyalty (there had been indications of re-emergent separatist activity in the mid 1930s)[74] led to a decision in 1939 to break up the *latifondi*. It was now clear that all attempts to induce spontaneous land improvement had failed, and much of the blame had to attach to the inertia of the *agrari*.

In January 1940 a law was promulgated for 'the colonisation of the Sicilian *latifondo*'.[75] It provided for the construction of 20,000 farmhouses over an area of 500,000 hectares, and this, it was hoped, would lead to the fragmentation of property and more intensive agriculture. The new measures were to be carried out through private initiative (which would have given the landowners some protection); but the aim was to destroy the *latifondi*, and this was not something the *agrari* relished. Ironically, neither did the peasants. Reports suggested that they had no wish to abandon the security of the towns for the solitude and dangers of the interior. Even had there been time, it is unlikely that this ill-considered scheme would have met with success. As it was, the war intervened, and fascism's last attempt to change Sicilian society was shelved.

The Second World War

Sicily suffered enormously during the war, not least because it occupied a crucial position in the Mediterranean front. The difficulty of importing food meant that at times there was little to eat except oranges. Frustration mounted, and renewed concern about the island's loyalty led to the extraordinary decision in August 1941 to transfer all Sicilian-born officials to the mainland. Reports to the British Foreign Office in these months spoke of 'strong separatist tendencies'.[76] Sicilians, it was said, wore Union Jacks under the lapels of their coats, and eagerly awaited an Allied landing.[77] The strength of anti-Italian feeling was such, according to a communiqué in December 1941, 'that no Italian officer or official not speaking the Sicilian dialect can venture to leave his lodgings at night without running the risk of being stabbed in the back'.[78]

The breakdown of law and order in Sicily began to be attributed by British officials (who were unfamiliar with the island) to the mafia. A memorandum prepared for the Foreign Office in August 1942 said that the organisation was 'still active', despite the suppression in the 1920s; as evidence it quoted Count Sforza's claim that German soldiers were being 'picked off at the rate of almost one a day'.[79] Black-market activity could also be seen as an indication of the mafia's continued presence. In Italy, the censorship of the press ruled out any mention of the turmoil in Sicily, but the freer reporting that followed the Allied victory in the South led to the reappearance of the term 'mafia' in public discussions. The fact that this coincided with the American and British occupation gave rise to the belief that the mafia had been resuscitated from outside.

The idea that US Naval Intelligence had a policy to use the mafia in the invasion of Sicily must remain conjectural.[80] A number of Italo-American underworld figures certainly gave information to the Allies, but so did many Italian immigrants. What the authorities needed were the names of people who could be contacted by the Allied forces in Sicily, and men with criminal records were useful, as the prospect of an amnesty was likely to make them good collaborators. The intelligence officers working with the Americans seem to have had lists of men who had been deported back to Sicily.[81] However, the idea that the mafia was involved in the Allied conquest of the island resulted largely from an official enquiry of 1954. This took place in the wake of the Kefauver Commission on Organized Crime which had revived interest in the topic of the mafia in the United States after several decades of neglect.[82]

The US Naval Intelligence officers who landed with the Seventh Army at Gela and Licata appear from their subsequent testimony to have known little about the mafia. Almost anybody, it seems, who collaborated with the Allies counted as a *mafioso* in their eyes. 'The Mafia appealed tremendously to the British officers in Sicily', claimed one witness in 1954,

> because of its codes and centuries of chivalry....The mafia appealed similarly to American officers, especially the Italian speaking officers of Italian descent, who were impressed by the fact that

the *mafiosi*, far from coming on like disreputable gangsters, were Sicilians of immense pride and knowledge, ready to risk their lives to fight the enemy.[83]

Among other activities, '*mafiosi* bravely volunteered to serve in large numbers as "native guides" for Allied forces'.[84] When asked about the landings in Sardinia and Salerno, one intelligence officer claimed that he had contacted the local mafia here too, and it turned out, he said, to be as co-operative as in Sicily.[85]

In Sicily, the problem facing the Allies after occupation was the establishment of an administrative structure. The simplest solution, as so often in the past, was to turn to the local opposition faction in each town. In many cases this meant rehabilitating people who had been out of power since the 1920s, and among them were people who had fifteen years earlier been arrested by Mori. In the small town of Mussomeli, for example, Giuseppe Genco Russo (often spoken of as a leading mafia figure) took the initiative in July 1943, and declared publicly that there would be no resistance to the Allies. The Italian army commander was arrested, and the US forces entered the town without a shot being fired. A few days later Genco Russo was appointed mayor.[86]

Similar episodes must have been repeated throughout Sicily. The Allies were often grateful merely to find someone who would take charge; they had neither the time nor the information to discriminate. Lord Rennell, the head of the government of occupation, summed up the situation as follows:

The Sicilians of any standing, whatever their political views, who were ready to co-operate by work and responsibility, as opposed to advice and criticism, were singularly few. The majority of communes are rent by personal jealousies and feuds and found it difficult to agree in suggesting a name or names. With the people clamouring to be rid of a Fascist *Podestà*, many of my officers fell into the trap of selecting the most forthcoming self-advertiser, or following the advice of their self-appointed interpreters who had learned some English in the course of a stay in the USA. The result was not always happy. The choices in more than one instance fell on the local Mafia 'boss', or his shadow, who in one or two cases had graduated in an American gangster environment. All that could be said of some of these men was that they were as definitively anti-Fascist as they were undesirable from every other point of view. The difficulty in early days of an occupation for a foreign element to weigh up the value or danger of local characters must be clear to any one who has given the subject a moment's thought.[87]

Much attention has been focused in post-war years on the small town of Villalba. Contemporary reports gave it no prominence, nor did the US Naval Intelligence officers single it out in any way during the 1954 hearings. The interest in this community stems from the notoriety of Don Calogero Vizzini, who became mayor of Villalba after the arrival of the US forces. Vizzini was later to be referred to as 'the head of the mafia', and because of this, many extravagant claims have been made about his influence. A German sociologist recently stated that Vizzini and Genco Russo 'persuaded two-thirds of the Italian troops to desert' on the eve of the Allied invasion. He also (and even more absurdly) said that the ease of the US victory in the west of the island was due to the mafia's help, 'in contrast to what happened to the English, who encountered serious hindrance in eastern Sicily'.[88]

There is no reason to believe that Calogero Vizzini was an exceptional individual. He was probably rich, and locally very powerful. Much of his wealth had derived from his position as a *gabelloto*, and though his fortunes almost certainly waned under fascism, his skillful negotiation of the period between 1943 and 1948 ensured that he ended his days with influence and respect. One reason for his notoriety was an episode in 1944 when he ordered his followers to break up a Communist Party rally at Villalba by opening fire. More important, however, was the attention he received during the 1950s and 1960s from the writings of a local political adversary who branded him 'the head of the mafia'. The success of this author's works has ensured a lasting, if undeserved, fascination with Don Calò.[89]

The competition for power in Sicily after 1943 led to a great deal of violence. Class politics re-emerged, and once again there was a call for the division of the *latifondi*. Land laws were passed, and for the first time in over two thousand years, many of the great estates were partititoned. However, the post-war governments failed to meet the needs of the overpopulated countryside. Hundreds of thousands of Sicilian peasants moved to the cities in a desperate search for employment. Many of them went north, to work in the burgeoning factories of Turin and Milan. Those that stayed behind looked to Palermo – now the capital of an autonomous region – for secure jobs and advancement. Clientelism and corruption flourished here in the shadow of a stagnant economy.

By the mid-1950s, the countryside was no longer the principal battleground for status and wealth in Sicily. Those with ambition strove to secure a share of the large amounts of public money that were pouring into the regional capital from Rome. The competition was intense, and the individualism, mistrust, and assertiveness that had been hallmarks of the island's rural life for centuries were transferred to an urban setting. This led commentators to speak (as they had so often done) of a 'new mafia', which had taken over the cities with the methods of gangsterism. However, the nature of the Sicilian problem had not changed significantly. The mafia was referred to by politicians, magistrates, and journalists in similar terms to half a century earlier. As in the past, the idea of a criminal conspiracy served to mask a more complex political, social and cultural reality, and the traditional pattern of police operations continued in an effort to instil in the islanders 'the values of the state'.

NOTES

ACS   Archivio centrale dello stato, Rome.
ASP   Archivio dello stato, Pavia.
AS Palermo   Archivio dello stato, Palermo.
CG   Carteggio Giovanni Gentile.
CM   Carte Mori.
FO   Foreign Office papers.
GP   Gabinetto di Prefettura, Palermo.
OO   Opera Omnia di Benito Mussolini, ed. E. and D. Susmel, (Florence, 1951).
PRO   Public Record Office, London.
QP   Questura di Palermo, Atti di gabinetto (1920–43).

The following are used for the Archivio centrale dello stato:

CB   Carteggio Michele Bianchi (1923–5).
CF   Carte Farinacci.
GF   Ministero dell'interno, gabinetto Finzi, ordine pubblico (1922–4).
MRF   Mostra della rivoluzione fascista.
PS   Ministero dell'interno, direzione generale di pubblica sicurezza, divisione affari generali e riservati.
SPCR   Segreteria particolare del Duce, carteggio riservato.

Books and articles included in the bibliography are referred to in the notes by author (or editor) and year of publication of the edition for which page numbers are given.

Introduction

1 In what follows I have relied heavily on Albini 1971, in particular, pp. 191–256. His discussion of Cosa Nostra is especially interesting. For gangsterism in the inter-war years, Kefauver, and the Apalachin conclave of 1957, see Smith 1975, pp. 63ff, 121–42, 162–73. These two studies provide an excellent starting point for anyone who wishes to explore more fully the idea of the mafia in the United States. For the Hennessy episode in New Orleans, see below, pp. 43–7.

2 Gentile 1963, pp. 61, 68, 84.

3 Stajano 1986, p. 97.

4 The only general history of Sicily in English is the three volume work by M.I. Finley and D. Mack Smith: M.I. Finley, *Ancient Sicily to the Arab Conquest* (revised edition, London 1979); D. Mack Smith, *Medieval Sicily 800–1713* (London, 1968), and *Modern Sicily after 1713*. An abridged and revised version was published in 1986: M.I. Finley, D. Mack Smith, C.J.H. Duggan, *A History of Sicily*, (London, 1986).

PART I

Chapter 1

1 L. Sciascia (Sciascia 1964, p. 120) says the term may appear in a document of 1658 as a soubriquet for a witch. He is not, however, certain.

2 Pitré 1889, vol. II, pp. 289–90.

3 A useful survey of the various etymological suggestions is in Novacco 1959, pp. 206–212; cf. Novacco 1964, pp. 188–192.

4 Fiume 1984, p. 963. The first reference in a dictionary appears to be that of Traina (1868) where 'mafia' is defined as 'a neologism denoting any sign of bravado'.

5 *Giornale degli eruditi e dei curiosi*, 1 January 1884 (C. Lombroso); cf. Loschiavo 1962, p. 29.

6 A full discussion of the Vespers and Mazzini theories is to be found in Albini 1971. This work also contains an excellent general discussion of mafia etymologies. See also Hess 1984, p. 6; Bruno 1900, p. 132; Paton 1898, p. 359; Panzini 1935.

7 Novacco 1964, p. 190n.

8 *New York Times Magazine*, 4 March 1928. See below, p. 233.

9 *Panorama* (BBC), 1 April 1985.

10 Paton 1898, p. 359.

11 Bruno 1900, p. 132.

12 Pitré 1889, vol. II, p. 290.

13 *La Repubblica* (Rome), 4 April 1986. Buscetta said his opponents were no longer true *mafiosi*, which is why he felt entitled to denounce them. See also the remarks of Leonardo Vitale (1973) in Stajano 1986, p. 14.

14 The text of the play is reproduced (with an Italian translation) in Loschiavo 1962, pp. 211–359.

15 Novacco 1959, p. 208; cf. Mazzamuto 1964, p. 134.

16 Pitré 1889, vol. II, p. 291; Avellone and Morasca 1911, pp. 17–18; Pagano 1875, p. 40.

17 Pitré 1889, vol. II, p. 291; De Felice 1956, pp. 41–2.

18 Avellone and Morasca 1911, p. 41.

19 Alongi 1887, p. 73.

20 For example, Monnier 1863; De Castro 1862.

21 Lombroso 1889, vol. I, pp. 558–60; cf. ibid. vol. II, pp. 501–12. For the government's attitude, see Scirocco 1979, pp. 88–90.

22 For example, Merlino 1894, pp. 466–85; Griffiths 1901, vol. III, pp. 414–17.

23 Da Passano 1981, p. 118.

24 Ibid. p. 138.

25 For example, ibid. pp. 125, 156. Cf. Franchetti 1974. For a prisoner's view, see Brancaccio di Carpino 1901, pp. 101–203.

26 Report from the Procuratore Generale del Re (Palermo) to Min. Guardasigilli, 23 January 1868, in Scichilone 1952, pp. 215–18.

27 Lombroso 1879, p. 43.

28 Damiani 1881–6, vol. XIII, part 4, p. 421.

29 Ibid. p. 435.

30 Heckethorn 1897, vol. I, p. 277.

Chapter 2

1 Mack Smith 1968, vol. II, p. 410.

2 Report from Montezemolo to Presidente del Consiglio, 14 January 1861, in Scichilone 1952, pp. 67–8.

3 See, for example, several recent cartoons by Forattini in *La Repubblica*, e.g. 30 July 1985.

4 For example, Cutrera 1900, p. 26; Arcoleo 1898, p. 87.

5 Nicotri 1906, pp. 52–3.
6 *La Campana della Gancia* (Palermo), 5 March 1861, quoted in Renda 1984, vol. I, p. 185.
7 Virginio Rognoni to the Antimafia Commission, 11 November 1986 (see *La Repubblica*, 12 November 1986).
8 See, for example, Scichilone 1952, *passim*.
9 Speech by Presidente del Consiglio, 10 December 1863, quoted in Cerrito 1955, pp. 100–105.
10 Brancato 1964a, p. 17.
11 Falconcini 1863, pp. 49–50.
12 Renda 1984, vol. I, p. 196.
13 Minister of Interior to Prefect of Palermo, 22 June 1863, in Scichilone 1952, p. 150.
14 Cf. Pantano 1933, vol. I, pp. 150, 186.
15 Brancato 1964a, p. 18.
16 *Il Precursore* (Palermo), 5 September 1861, quoted in Brancato 1964a, pp. 19–20.
17 Cf. Da Passano 1981, p. 265 (Colombo); Pantano 1933, vol. I, pp. 109–17; Antinori 1877, pp. 19–20.
18 Renda 1984, vol. I, p. 206; D'Alessandro 1959, p. 88.
19 Cf. Alatri 1954, pp. 78–80; Romeo 1970, p. 344 and note.
20 Pantano 1933, vol. I, p. 154.
21 Ibid. p. 167.
22 Davis 1988, p. 84.
23 Pantano 1933, vol. I, pp. 168–9.
24 Anon. 1863, p. 212.
25 Anon. 1864, pp. ii–iii.
26 See, for example, Da Passano 1981, pp. 373–4 (Carderina); *Enciclopedia italiana* 1932–48, (Gualterio).
27 Pagano 1867, p. 58.
28 Gualterio to Giovanni Lanza, (mid)-April 1865, in Lanza 1936, vol. III, p. 203.
29 Gualterio to Giovanni Lanza, 25 April 1865, ibid. pp. 209–12.
30 See below, pp. 32–3, 42–3, 108–10, 112.
31 Cf. Pantano 1933, vol. I, pp. 229–231; Pagano 1867, pp. 99–100.
32 This is the general opinion of eyewitnesses. Cf. Da Passano 1981, pp. 98, 109, 121, 138, 143; *The Times*, 29 September 1866; Pagano 1867, pp. 122–3; Brancato 1966b, p. 526; Bua 1867. Pro-government accounts (such as those of G. Ciotti and V. Maggiorani) stress the unruliness of the rebels.
33 Ricasoli 1968 and 1970, vol. XXIII, Ricasoli to Cadorna, 25 September 1866; vol. XXIV, Ricasoli to Cadorna,

3 October 1866; Cadorna to Ricasoli, 4 October 1866; Ricasoli to Cadorna, 8 October 1866; Cadorna to Ricasoli, 16 October 1866.
34 Cadorna's report of 4 October 1866 is reproduced in Pagano 1867, pp. 239–43.
35 Cf. Ricasoli 1970, vol. XXIV, p. 42, Cugia to Ricasoli, October 1866.
36 *Gazzetta Ufficiale*, 12 October 1866.
37 Cf. Pantano 1933, vol. I, p. 239; Da Passano 1981, p. 103 (Cadorna).
38 Pantano 1933, vol. I, pp. 239–40.
39 Pagano 1867, pp. 239–43.
40 Da Passano 1981, p. 257 (Spallino); cf. pp. 127, 131, 134, 138, 260.
41 *Opinione* (Florence), 27 December 1866.
42 *The Times*, 11 October 1866. This seems to have been the first reference to the word in English.
43 *Opinione*, 7 October 1866.
44 Ganci 1966, pp. 412–3.
45 Da Passano 1981, pp. 117–8.
46 Ibid. for example, pp. 131, 153, 167, 175–6, 333.
47 Ibid. p. 158.
48 Ibid. p. 131.
49 Ibid. p. 175.
50 Cf. Maggiorani 1869/70, pp. 27–30, 194; Pagano 1867, p. 21; Tommasi Crudeli 1871, p. 24; anon. 1867, reproduced in Da Passano 1981, p. 507.
51 Cf. Cantù, 1872–7, vol. III, p. 555; Brancato 1964a, pp. 23–4; *Atti parlamentari, Camera dei Deputati, Discussioni*, 9 June 1875 (Cantelli).
52 Lombroso 1879, p. 21.
53 Alatri 1954, pp. 581–2; Marino 1964, p. 84.
54 Marino 1964, p. 77.
55 Report to Ministry of Grace and Justice (no date given), now in Russo 1964, pp. 42–3.
56 Marino 1964, p. 77; Renda 1984–7, vol. II, pp. 15–106 (particularly p. 95).
57 Cf. Procacci 1956, pp. 63–7; Marino 1964, pp. 115–17; Pagano 1875, p. 23.
58 Renda 1984–7, vol. II, pp. 41–2; Brancato 1964b, p. 39.
59 Renda 1984–7, vol. II, p. 47.
60 *The Times*, 21 June 1875.
61 Report from Prefect Berti, 30 June 1874, now in Russo 1964, pp. 21–4.
62 Renda 1984–7, vol. II, p. 55.
63 Report from Prefect Fortuzzi, 24 April 1875, in Russo 1964, pp. 24–7.
64 Report from Prefect Ramusino, 16 May 1874, in Russo 1964, pp. 16–20.
65 Cf. Renda 1984–7, vol. II, pp. 41–2; Pagano 1877, p. 23; *Atti parlamentari,*

Camera dei Deputati, Discussioni, 11 June 1875 (Cordova).

66 Minghetti to di Rudinì, 7 September 1874, in Minghetti 1978, vol. I, p. 356.

67 *Atti parlamentari, Camera dei Deputati, Discussioni*, 9 June 1875.

68 Ibid. 5 June 1875.

69 Ibid. 8 June 1875.

70 Ibid. 9 June 1875.

71 Cf. ibid. 8 June 1875 (Longo); 5 June 1875 (Paternostro); 11 June 1875 (Cordova).

72 Mori 1923, pp. 31–4.

73 Cf. PRO FO 45 261, British Ambassador in Rome to Foreign Secretary, 8 June 1875; *The Times*, 7 October 1874, 2 November 1874, 13 July 1875; 30 September 1876, etc.

74 *The Times*, 12 September 1878.

75 Paton 1898, p. 368.

76 Giordano 1964, pp. 75–6.

77 Capuana 1914, p. 90.

78 Cf. *Atti parlamentari, Camera dei Deputati, Discussioni*, 8 June 1875 (Castagnola).

79 Davis 1988, ch. 12; Niceforo 1898, passim; Niceforo 1901.

80 Lombroso 1889, vol. I, pp. 177–80, 229–34, 638–41.

81 Niceforo 1898.

82 Lombroso 1889, vol. I, pp. 85–6.

83 Ibid. p. 577.

84 Ibid. p. 565.

85 Ibid. p. 566. The Monte di Pietà theft was a sensational robbery in Palermo of 3 million lire. The trial in Milan in 1875 coincided with the great parliamentary debate on the mafia, and was an important factor in consolidating the idea of a criminal organisation in Sicily.

86 Ibid. pp. 566–7.

87 Costanza 1966, p. 436n.

88 Lombroso 1889, vol. I, p. 566.

89 Lombroso 1899, p. 260.

90 Niceforo 1898, pp. 297–99.

91 Davis 1988, p. 337.

92 See below, p. 238.

93 Colajanni 1900, p. 105; Cf. Corsi 1894, pp. 299–357; Bruno 1900, in particular pp. 51–5, 141–2; Di San Giuliano 1894, pp. 95–101; Alongi 1894, pp. 252–3.

94 Speech to Chamber of Deputies, 23 November 1899, in Russo 1964, pp. 471–87; cf. De Felice Giuffrida 1901, pp. 123–4; Bruno 1900, pp. 121–2; Bruccoleri 1913, pp. 49–50.

95 Corsi 1894, pp. 312–3.

96 Report from the *questore* of Palermo, 11 September 1893, quoted in Crispi 1924, p. 289.

97 *The Times*, 17 January 1894.

98 White Mario 1891b, p. 702; White Mario 1891a.

99 Two days after Hennessy's death, the Provenzanos gave a letter to the local *Times–Democrat* newspaper, and claimed it was evidence that the Matrangas were 'members of a branch of the Mafia, known as the Stoppaghiera' [sic]. The letter began with the sentence: 'You had better wake up and think of your outrage against justice if you don't want to be done up by the Mafia'. The authorship of this letter was never determined. (Cf. Albini 1971, pp. 162–3).

100 PRO FO 5 2114, report from British Consul in New Orleans, 26 March 1891.

101 White Mario 1891b, p. 703.

102 Ibid. p. 703.

103 Report from British Consul, 26 March 1891, *cit.*

104 Ibid.

105 Ibid.; cf. White Mario 1891b, p. 703.

106 Report from British Consul, 26 March 1891. The pretext for the display of patriotic fervour appears to have been the celebration of King Umberto's birthday; cf. Smith 1975, p. 35.

107 Desjardins 1891, p. 346; cf. White Mario 1891b, p. 702; anon. 1891, p. 341.

108 Newspaper cutting, 20 October 1890, forwarded by British Consul in New Orleans, in PRO FO 5 2114, report from British Consul, 26 March 1891, *cit.*

109 *New Orleans Times Democrat*, 6 May 1891 (in PRO FO 5 2114).

110 Stillman 1891a, p. 296.

111 Ibid.

112 Stillman 1891b, pp. 337–9. Alongi was in fact referring here to the Girgenti association known as the Fratellanza and not to the mafia as a whole. (Alongi 1887, p. 143.)

113 Report from British Consul, 26 March 1891, *cit.*

114 *The Times*, 5 February 1891.

115 Heckethorn 1897, vol. I, pp. 280–1.

116 PRO FO 45 800, Lord Currie to the Foreign Secretary, 11 December 1899.

117 The pitfalls of excessive zeal in the fight against organised crime have been most evident recently in Naples. The case of the television personality, Enzo Tortora, who was acquitted in 1986 after three years in prison, revealed the dangers of believing supergrass *camorristi* too readily.

118 *The Times*, 18 October 1901.

119 Ibid. 1 August 1902.

120 Ibid.
121 On the support for Palizzolo in Sicily, see Ganci 1980, pp. 66–9; Renda, 'Il processo Notarbartolo ovvero per una storia dell'idea di mafia', in Renda 1972, pp. 377–419; Raffiotta 1959, pp. 25–7.
122 Renda 1984–87, vol. II, pp. 249–51.
123 Capuana 1914, pp. 6–9, 13–15.
124 Ibid. pp. 35–6, 39–40.
125 Ibid. pp. 84–5.
126 Ibid. p. 86.
127 Avellone and Morasca 1911.
128 Ibid. p. 118.
129 Ibid. pp. 44–5.
130 Ibid. p. 62.
131 Ibid. p. 106.
132 Renda 1984–7, vol. II, p. 269.
133 Ibid. pp. 246–7; Ganci 1980, pp. 76–8.
134 Ibid. p. 79.
135 Gentile 1917.

Chapter 3

1 Franchetti 1974, p. 13.
2 Pantaleoni to Ricasoli, 10 October 1861, in Scichilone 1952, pp. 97–8.
3 Il Precursore (Palermo), 5 September 1861, quoted in Brancato 1964a, pp. 19–20. 4 April 1860 was the date of an attempted rising in Palermo. It was subsequently seen as marking the start of the revolutionary movement that led to unification.
4 Ulloa to Min. della Giustizia, 3 August 1838, in Marino 1964, p. 56.
5 Romeo 1970, p. 325.
6 Atti parlamentari, Camera dei Deputati, Discussioni, 10 June 1875.
7 Franchetti 1974, p. 12.
8 Pitré 1889, vol. II, pp. 294–301.
9 Hess 1984, pp. 147–50.
10 For example, Franchetti 1974, vol. I, p. 87; Atti parlamentari, Camera dei Deputati, Discussioni, 25 January 1877, (di Rudinì); Corsi 1894, pp. 323–4; Bruno 1900, pp. 156–7.
11 Lorenzoni 1910, vol. I, p. 678.
12 Damiani 1881–6, vol. XIII, part 4, p. 367.
13 Bonfadini 1876, p. 161.
14 Ibid.
15 For example, Da Passano 1981, pp. 153, 158, 337.
16 Giordano 1964, p. 74.
17 Russo 1964, p. 50.
18 Atti parlamentari, Camera dei Deputati, Discussioni, 8 June 1875 (Castagnola).
19 Franchetti 1974, p. 205.
20 For example, Bonfadini 1876, pp. 150–

3; Pagano 1867, p. 49; Antinori 1877, p. 123; Franchetti 1974, pp. 180–1.
21 Cf. Alongi 1894, p. 243.
22 Cf. Pagano 1875, pp. 28–34; Falconcini 1863, pp. 69–71; Franchetti 1974, pp. 50, 137.
23 Bruno 1900, p. 158; cf. Damiani 1881–6, vol. XIII, part 4, pp. 487–8.
24 Franchetti 1974, p. 13.
25 Ibid. pp. 13–14.
26 Ibid. p. 46.
27 Ibid. pp. 50–1; Bruno 1900, pp. 94–6.
28 See below, pp. 245–51.
29 For Medici's administration, see Alatri 1954, in particular ch. 6; for Malusardi, see Pagano 1877, pp. 32–9. Dalla Chiesa, like Mori, adopted a high profile. The opposition was accordingly ad hominem, as with the spate of killings in August 1982, known as the 'operazione Dalla Chiesa'. Malusardi endured a similar crime wave it seems; cf. Pagano 1877, p. 50.
30 Pagano 1877, p. 28.
31 Ibid. p. 57.
32 Cf. Atti parlamentari, Camera dei Deputati, Discussioni, 5 June 1875 (Paternostro); Bruno 1900, p. 187–8.
33 Franchetti 1974, p. 155; Alatri 1954, pp. 348–55; cf. Atti parlamentari, Camera dei Deputati, Discussioni, 23 November 1899 (De Felice Giuffrida).
34 For Tajani's speech, see Russo 1964, pp. 135–177.
35 For policing under the Bourbons, see Fiume 1984, pp. 109–142; Pagano 1875, pp. 19–28.
36 Franchetti 1974, p. 41.
37 Ibid. p. 42n.
38 Pagano 1867, pp. 61–62, 86–88; Bruno 1900, pp. 190–1; Atti parlamentari, Camera dei Deputati, Discussioni, 19 June 1875 (Cordova); Ibid. 11–12 June 1875 (Tajani).
39 Atti parlamentari, Camera dei Deputati, Discussioni, 11 June 1875 (Cordova); cf. Franchetti 1974, pp. 17, 41–2, 150–1; Bonfadini 1876, pp. 138–42; Pagano 1875, p. 29.
40 Agnetta 1892, p. 45.
41 On Dalla Chiesa, see Bocca, 'I Dalla Chiesa' in Arlacchi et al 1982, pp. 7–23; in particular, p. 18.
42 Cantelli to President of Chamber of Deputies, 18 January 1875, in Russo 1964, pp. 7–10.
43 Interdonato to Gualterio, 23 April 1865, in Lanza 1936, vol. III, pp. 221–2. Gualterio had wanted to know in what circumstances arrest warrants could be

dispensed with.

44 Gualterio to Lanza, 25 April 1865, ibid. vol. III, p. 209.

45 Cf. Gualterio to Lanza, 27 April 1865, ibid. pp. 234–5.

46 Gualterio to Lanza, 11 July 1865, ibid. p. 356.

47 Cf. Pagano 1877, p. 9; Franchetti 1974, pp. 101, 139; Tommasi Crudeli 1871, pp. 65–6.

48 Lestingi 1884, p. 458.

49 Lorenzoni 1910, vol. I, p. 704; cf. p. 677.

50 Ibid. pp. 691–2; Bruno 1900, p. 137; Alongi 1887, p. 58.

51 Bonfadini 1876, p. 120; Lorenzoni 1910, vol. I, p. 696.

52 For example, Fincati 1881, p. 135.

53 Lorenzoni 1910, vol. II, p. 510.

54 Falconcini 1863, pp. 110–111 (documenti).

55 Comparative statistics for 1873 are given in Russo 1964, p. 8.

56 See below, p. 124.

57 Bonfadini 1876, p. 131.

58 Ibid. p. 133; cf. Lorenzoni 1910, vol. I, p. 694.

59 S. Merlino 1894, p. 483.

60 Cf. Lorenzoni 1910, vol. I, p. 233; Fulco di Verdura 1976, p. 59.

61 Maggiorani 1869/70, pp. 14–22.

62 Dolci 1963, p. 246.

63 Paton 1898, p. 364.

64 Cf. Lorenzoni 1910, vol. I, p. 678; Bruno 1900, p. 137.

65 For example, Tommasi Crudeli 1871, pp. 65–6; Franchetti 1974, pp. 8–9, 101; Pagano 1875, p. 14.

66 Cf. Alongi 1887, p. 69.

67 Franchetti 1974, pp. 26, 34; cf. Corsi 1894, pp. 318–9.

68 Costanza 1964, p. 54.

69 Franchetti 1974, pp. 7–8.

70 Ibid. p. 101.

71 Montanelli 1955, p. 282.

72 Pantaleone 1966, preface by C. Levi, pp. 13–15.

73 Tommasi Crudeli 1871, pp. 65–6; Cutrera 1900, p. 36.

74 Gualterio to Lanza, 2 August 1865, in Lanza 1936, vol. III, p. 449.

75 Franchetti 1974, p. 52.

76 Ibid. p. 32; Alongi 1887, p. 89.

77 Franchetti 1974, p. 104.

78 Ibid. pp. 106–7.

79 Ibid. p. 101.

80 Ibid. pp. 132–4.

81 Cf. Brancato 1966a, p. 471.

82 Franchetti 1974, p. 224.

83 See below, pp. 234–6.

84 F.S. Merlino 1890, p. 164.

85 Bonfadini 1876, p. 119.

86 Franchetti 1974, p. 93.

87 Ibid. p. 38.

88 Ibid. p. 92.

89 Lombroso 1889, vol. I, p. 576.

90 Ibid. p. 576.

91 Alongi 1887, p. 42.

92 Ibid. p. 67.

93 Ibid. pp. 71–2, 111–6, 136–45.

94 Avellone and Morasca 1911, p. 52.

95 Cutrera 1900, p. 42.

96 Ibid. pp. 48–9, 82–7.

97 See below, p. 142.

98 Cf. Franchetti 1974, p. 17; Di San Giuliano 1894, p. 98.

99 See below, ch. 7.

100 Mosca, 'Che cosa è la mafia?' in Mosca 1980, p. 3.

101 Ibid. p. 10.

102 Ibid. pp. 11–12.

103 Ibid. p. 12.

104 Ibid. pp. 12, 15.

105 Cf. Lorenzoni 1910, vol. I, p. 696.

106 Mosca 1980, p. 3.

107 Ibid. p. 11.

108 See below, pp. 154–8.

109 Cf. Franchetti 1974, pp. 127–8.

110 See below, pp. 159–61.

111 Bonfadini 1876, pp. 103–4; Falconcini 1863, p. 240 (documenti); Alongi 1894, pp. 242–3.

112 Cf. Di San Giuliano 1894, pp. 114–5; Mercadante Carrara 1911, p. 47; Franchetti 1974, p. 39.

113 Alongi 1894, p. 243.

114 See, for example, L'Espresso, 20 February 1980 (C. Mariotti).

115 Cf. Bruccoleri 1913, p. 50, Bruno 1900, pp. 108–31; De Felice Giuffrida 1901, pp. 123–4.

116 For example, Appiani 1927, p. 19.

117 See below, chs. 8, 12.

118 Franchetti is continually wrestling with the problem of who to blame. Intellectual detachment gradually succumbs to anger at the ruling class; cf. Franchetti 1974, pp. 101–11; also the introduction by E. Cavalieri (1925), ibid. p. xxvii.

119 Cf. Lorenzoni 1910, vol. I, p. 234, vol. II, p. 837.

120 Mack Smith 1971, p. 191.

121 On the emergence and character of the gabelloti, see Romeo 1970, pp. 26–30; cf. Loncao 1900, pp. 78–88; Bruno 1900, p. 22.

122 Alongi 1887, p. 33.

123 Cf. Loncao 1900, pp. 85–8.

124 Cf. Franchetti 1974, pp. 81–3, 193–4;

Bonfadini 1876, pp. 99–100.

125 Loncao 1900, p. 89.

126 Fincati 1881, p. 125.

127 Brancato 1964b, pp. 41–2.

128 Gaetano Mondino to the Prefect of Palermo, December 1873, in Brancato 1964b, pp. 45–51.

129 Fincati 1881, pp. 125–6.

130 Sonnino 1974, p. 145; cf. ibid. pp. 140–5.

131 Lorenzoni 1910, vol. I, p. 234.

132 Cf. ibid. vol. II, p. 258.

133 For peasants and *gabelloti* collaborating against landowners, see Corsi 1894, pp. 339–40.

134 Cf. Blok 1974, pp. 124–6.

135 See below, pp. 155–6.

136 Cf. *La Repubblica* (Rome), 23 January 1986.

137 Cf. Hess 1984, pp. 100–101.

138 Cf. Alongi 1887, p. 69.

139 Villari 1972, pp. 92–94. However Villari also says that the *gabelloti* are 'often victims of the mafia, if they do not come to terms with it' (ibid. pp. 92–3).

140 Bonfadini 1876, p. 150 (paraphrasing Colonel Milon).

141 The question of complicity was as difficult for the *campieri* as for other groups: 'It cannot be ruled out that among the *campieri* there might be one or two who are of bad character, but in general these poor people are forced to behave as they do, that is by offering extensive help to criminals who in return guarantee the safety of the property that the *campieri* have in their custody. In this way estates are generally left undisturbed. However, it is not uncommon for a *campiere* to have to look after stolen cattle at his farmhouse, and even to give food and shelter to the rustlers themselves'. *Sicilia Agricola*, 27 January 1924.

142 Costanza 1964, pp. 55, 58.

143 Colajanni 1900, pp. 79–105.

144 Reprinted in Russo 1964, pp. 599–601.

145 Colajanni 1900, pp. 35–8.

146 For example, di Rudinì 1895, p. 150.

147 Cf. Lorenzoni 1910, vol. II, p. 258; Renda 1984–7, vol. II, pp. 272–3.

148 G. Barone, 'Ristrutturazione e crisi del blocco agrario. Dai Fasci siciliani al primo dopoguerra' in Barone *et al* 1977, pp. 34–50.

149 See below, pp. 107–10.

150 See below, pp. 100–2.

151 The following is taken from ACS PS, 1929, sez. la 5, Prefect of Messina to Minister of Interior, 27 September 1929, 1 October 1929. The file also contains a report of August 1928, saying that a prisoner in Bari had learnt of an imminent insurrection in Sicily which was to be organised by the mafia and led by Alfredo Cucco, who had received for this purpose 'a huge sum' from Baron Murgia. The revolt was to begin with the murder of Prefect Mori and the liberation, by ship, of prisoners on Sicilian islands. Additional funding was to come from Antonino Ortoleva. Mori told the Minister of Interior (9 October 1928) that these claims were 'simply absurd'. Apart from anything else, he said, Murgia and Ortoleva were both dead. There has never been a shortage of allegations of this kind, and they usually emanate from prisons. See, for example, Luciano Liggio's claims in 1986 that he helped avert a right-wing coup in the early 1970s involving the USA, the mafia, and Prince Junio Borghese. (*La Repubblica* (Rome), 16 April 1986, 24 May 1986). Buscetta endorsed the story (cf. *La Repubblica*, 17 August 1986). The connection between fantasy and truth in such cases is hard to determine.

152 The Ministry of the Interior appeared curiously uninquisitive about the affair.

153 The secret society of the *Beati Paoli* is alleged to have operated in the early eighteenth century. However, the only source for it is a brief article in the late eighteenth century *Opuscoli palermitani* of the Marquis of Villabianca. Popular fascination with the subject was reinforced early this century with the publication of Luigi Natoli's historical novel, *I Beati Paoli* (which first appeared in serial form in *Il Giornale di Sicilia* in 1909–10). Its success in Sicily, and particularly in Palermo, has been extraordinary. Cf. Linares 1886.

154 See below, p. 234.

155 Hess 1984, pp. 140–1.

156 Wolffsohn 1891, p. 694; cf. *The Times*, 21 May 1891, 25 May 1891.

157 Cf. Lombroso 1889, vol. I, pp. 287–323; De Blasio 1894a and 1894b; Merlino 1894, p. 481; Niceforo 1898, pp. 57–9.

158 *The Times*, 20 May 1891.

159 Ibid. 9 November 1891.

160 Heckethorn 1897, vol. I, pp. 275–6.

161 Lestingi 1884.

162 Hess 1984, pp. 140, 142.

163 Ibid. p. 140; cf. Cutrera 1900, pp. 138–9

164 Cf. Vaccaro 1899, p. 701.
165 Lestingi 1884, p. 454.
166 The idea that the mafia developed from a Mazzinian brotherhood was proposed by Vizzini 1880, pp. 67–72.
167 Lestingi 1884, p. 454. Exotic rituals and formulae were common features of nineteenth-century associations; cf. Hobsbawm 1959, pp. 150–74.
168 Lestingi 1884, p. 455; cf. Alongi 1887, pp. 140–1; Cutrera 1900, p. 119.
169 Stajano 1986, p. 43.
170 Alongi 1887, p. 140.
171 Hess 1984, p. 142.
172 Lestingi 1884, p. 455.
173 Alongi 1887, p. 142.
174 Lewis 1964, pp. 71–7.
175 Cf. 'Il processo alla mafia', supplement to *L'Espresso* (Rome), 9 February 1986, p. 14.
176 Enzo Tortora, one of Italy's leading television personalities, was accused of drug pushing and involvement in the *camorra*. He was held in prison for over three years, and the trial became a national *cause célèbre*. The evidence against him was furnished by a handful of supergrasses, who clearly hoped for an alleviation of their sentences in return for assisting the judiciary in its fight against the *camorra*. It took more than three years for the falsity of the prosecution case to be exposed. Tortora was released from prison on 15 September 1986.

PART II

Chapter 4

1 OO xix 1 (1 November 1922); cf. OO xxi 67–8 (16 September 1924).
2 OO xviii 347 (11 August 1922).
3 Giuriati 1981, pp. 197–8.
4 ACS SPCR b. 27, Mussolini to Giuriati, April 1925; cf. OO xxii 394 (26 November 1925), 397 (31 December 1925).
5 Cf. OO xxix 257 (31 March 1939); Santarelli 1967, vol. I, pp. 583, 588.
6 Bolzon 1927, p. 107.
7 Zanotti-Bianco 1964, p. xxii.
8 OO xviii 348 (11 August 1922).
9 Barone 1983, pp. 5–40.
10 Curcio 1925a, p. 285.
11 Bolzon 1927, p. 108.
12 Farinacci 1927, p. 70; cf. Farinacci 1937–39, vol. III, p. 301.
13 Bolzon 1927, pp. 117–21.
14 Ibid. p. 121.

15 Curcio 1925a, pp. 281, 285; cf. Curcio 1925b, pp. 310–14. See also, Bronzini 1929, pp. 385–7; Spampanato 1933, p. 178.
16 De Secly 1926, pp. 87, 93, 107, 116–20.
17 OO xxvi 321 (7 September 1934). See also Zingali 1933, vol. II, passim; Virnicchi 1935, passim.
18 ACS MRF b.Q (Palermo), Cucco to Segreteria dei Fasci, Milan, 6 December 1920; cf. Celentano 1934, pp. 6–7.
19 ACS MRF b.Q (Palermo), Cucco to Pasella, 13 January 1921.
20 Miccichè 1976, pp. 75, 97, 102, 113. See also, Marino 1976, pp. 225–36; Reece 1973, pp. 261–76; Chiurco 1929, vol. IV, pp. 340–3; Vetri 1976, pp. 62–3.
21 Cf. Casaccio 1935; Battaglia and Giurato 1923; De Antonellis 1977, pp. 209–11.
22 The murder of Orcel is usually ascribed today to the mafia. In 1942, G. Falzone said that the murder had been attributed to fascists, but that it was later found to be the result of jealousies among Orcel's colleagues. See, *Panorami di realizzazioni del fascismo*. vol. VI: *Il movimento delle squadre nell'Italia meridionale e insulare* (Rome, 1942), p. 163.
23 *La Regione*, 29 January 1922.
24 *Gazzetta Commerciale del Mezzogiorno*, 20 December 1922 (Avv. Mario Celentano).
25 *La Fiamma*, 11 March 1923, quoted in Filiberto Di Marco 1937, pp. 14–15.
26 ACS SPCR b.13, Tiby to Mussolini, 12 June 1929. For Gasti, see R. De Felice 1965, p. 462n.
27 ACS PS, 1923, b.94, report from Gasti, 18 April 1923; Licata 1959.
28 OO xxxviii p. 345 (28 May 1923).
29 ASP CM 21, memorial by Cucco, p. 9.
30 Cf. Romano 1964, pp. 21–2. For Cucco's later involvement with Sicily, see Cucco 1950; Cucco 1957.
31 ACS PS, 1924, b.66, report of conversation between Orlando and Acerbo, 27 February 1924.
32 ASP CM 21, memorial by Cucco, pp. 23–4. Gasti is cited as one of the witnesses. See also ACS PS, 1923, b.58, letter from Direttore Generale dell'Amministrazione Civile on Cuccia, 19 June 1923. Cuccia's statement in prison in Petacco 1978, pp. 97–100, dates from 7 May 1927, in other words after Cucco's fall. It should thus be treated cautiously.
33 Marino 1976, pp. 283–4; AS Palermo GP, b.69, report by the *Questore* of

Palermo, 15 March 1924.

34 ACS CB, b.2 fasc.20, letter (signature illegible) to Mussolini, 2 August 1923.

35 *Il Babbio*, 31 July 1923.

36 ACS PS, 1925, b.92, Prefect of Palermo to the Ministry of Interior, 23 June 1923, commenting on an anonymous letter against Cirincione sent to Mussolini.

37 ACS MRF, b.U (Sciacca), letter to the Direttorio of PNF, 20 (?) November 1922.

38 Ibid. reply from Starace, 28 November 1922.

39 ACS CB, b.2 fasc.15, report by Starace, 7 July 1923.

40 Filiberto Di Marco 1937, p. 88; Battaglia and Giurato 1923, p. 38.

41 Ragusa 1934, pp. 30, 41.

42 AS Palermo, Sottoprefettura di Cefalù, b.9, report from RR.CC (Cefalù), 7 March 1923.

43 Cf. ACS CB, b.2 fasc.15, report by Starace, 7 July 1923.

44 Lumbroso 1925, p. 65; Gaeta 1965, pp. 221–4.

45 Bianco 1923, p. 55.

46 AS Palermo GP b.478, reports on Gratteri (20 February 1924) and Castel-buono (5 February 1924); AS Palermo GP b.69, report from Sottoprefetto of Cefalù, 21 February 1924. See also, ibid. report from Sottoprefetto of Cefalù, 28 February 1924: 'The agreement, long hoped for, between the provincial exponents of fascism and the Servicemen, is to be welcomed. However, the disputes between these two groups will, in certain places, continue, not so much for political reasons, but rather for the purpose of maintaining power at the local level'. For further information on the Servicemen's movement see Barone 1984, pp. 203–44.

47 Marino 1976, pp. 307–8. For the 1924 elections in Palermo, see ACS PS, 1924, b.66; ACS PS, 1924, b.68 (Sicily in general); AS Palermo GP b.69 (Palermo), in particular the report by the *Questore*, 15 March 1924; Archivio Carnazzo fasc.52, b.Palermo, letter from Pietro Lanza di Scalea, 6 February 1924; *L'Ora*, in particular 9 April 1924 (for an optimistic appraisal); Lyttelton 1973, pp. 138–40, 146.

48 G. Barone, 'Ristrutturazione e crisi del blocco agrario', in Barone *et al* 1977a, p. 63; cf. Lupo 1981, pp. 25–8.

49 Barone *et al* 1977a, pp. 53–9; Lupo 1981, pp. 22–7.

50 Fulco di Verdura 1976. See also, Nicolosi 1979.

51 G. Barone, 'Guerra e sottosviluppo', in Barone *et al* 1977a, pp. 109–22; Lupo 1981, pp. 33–5.

52 Barone *et al* 1977a, p. 102.

53 Ibid. p. 105; cf. Serpieri 1930, p. 437.

54 Barone *et al* 1977a, p. 101.

55 Ibid. p. 99.

56 *Il Giornale di Sicilia*, 6 August 1917 (N. Colajanni).

57 Corselli 1931 (supplement), pp. 174–5; Barone *et al* 1977a, pp. 100–1.

58 Spanò 1978, p. 29.

59 Navarra Crimi 1925, pp. 96–100; *L'Avvenire di Sicilia*, 18 October 1925; Spanò 1978, pp. 29–32; AS Trapani, Gabinetto di Prefettura, Corrispondenza 1919–23, b.13, contains a number of reports on Battioni's activities in 1921.

60 Loschiavo 1962, p. 178; cf. Sansone and Ingrascì 1950, pp. 37–8; Falzone 1975, pp. 227–8; Novacco 1963, p. 278.

61 Mori 1923, p. 23.

62 *L'Espresso*, 7 December 1958 (M. Pantaleone); cf. *L'Ora*, 21 October 1958; Pantaleone 1966, p. 83.

63 *Il Giornale di Sicilia*, 1 March 1921 (N. Colajanni).

64 ACS Presidenza del Consiglio 1920, fasc.3, memorial, Cammarata, 20 November 1920; cf. Ruini 1946, p. 174; *Il Giornale di Sicilia*, 5 May 1922; ACS Presidenza del Consiglio, 1922, fasc.3, report from Dott. Aristide Giambelieri, May 1922.

65 Letter from A. Vacirca, February 1921, quoted in *Il Giornale di Sicilia*, 1 March 1921 (N. Colajanni). For the situation in Gangi in this period, see Monheim 1972.

66 Sereni 1946, p. 120.

67 Sirena 1927, in ASP CM 17.

68 Mori 1932, pp. 128–9.

69 AS Palermo GP, b.478, report on Collesano, 18 February 1924.

70 Ibid. report on Campofiorito.

71 Ibid. report on Bisacquino; cf. the open letter to Mussolini in *Sicilia Agricola*, 27 January 1924, requesting government action against criminals: 'Here everyone is calling everyone else '*mafioso*', but nobody *ever* knows what mafia means'.

72 AS Palermo GP, b.478, report on Corleone.

73 Associazione per Delinquere, Corleone, Processo, Verbali di Polizia, p. 13; ibid. Sentenza di Istruttoria, p. 36.

74 Mori 1932, p. 243; cf. p. 292.
75 ASP CM 16, Mori to Ministry of the Interior, 5 August 1926.
76 Mori 1932, p. 293.
77 Ibid. p. 293; cf. *Il Giornale d'Italia*, 10 December 1926; ACS PS, 1927, b.150, Mori to Ministry of the Interior, 24 January 1928.
78 Mori 1932, p. 85.
79 Ibid. p. 86.
80 Ibid. p. 84.
81 Ibid. p. 128; Romano 1964, p. 197; Sansone and Ingrascì 1950, pp. 37–8; Falcionelli 1936, p. 221; *Il Giornale di Sicilia*, 5 October 1925: 'Nel 1919–20 quello che era bolscevismo o pericolo rosso nel Continente in Sicilia era delinquenza e malavita'.
82 *Avvisatore*, 8 May 1924; *L'Ora*, 9 May 1924; Demarco *et al* 1969, p. 208.
83 Lupo 1981, pp. 58–60.
84 *L'Ora*, 9 July 1924 and 13 December 1924; *L'Avvenire di Sicilia*, 21 August 1924 and 25 January 1925; *Problemi siciliani*, October 1924; *Atti parlamentari, Senato, Discussioni*, 8 December 1924 (Libertini) and 8 December 1924 (Federzoni).
85 Quai d'Orsay, Archives, Italie 66, Consul of Palermo to Min. des Affaires Étrangères, 14 February 1925.
86 *Sicilia Nuova*, 2 May 1925.
87 Cucco, *Il mio rogo* (unpublished autobiography), ch. 1, pp. 12–13.
88 Ibid. ch. 1, pp. 13–14; ASP CM 21, memorial by Cucco, pp. 14–15; cf. *Avanti!*, 31 July 1925; *Sicilia Nuova*, 17 July 1925.
89 ASP CM 21, memorial by Cucco, p. 15.
90 Cf. Marino 1976, p. 316n; ACS PS, 1925, b.103, Benedetto Scelsi to Musolini, 20 July 1925; Archivio Carnazza, fasc.52, b.Palermo, Lanza di Scalea to Carnazza, 6 February 1924.
91 *La Fiamma*, 22 July 1925; cf. AS Palermo GP, b.329, Commissario Aggiunto di P. S. to *Questore*, 15 July 1925.
92 AS Palermo GP, b.329, reports of 13–15 July 1925.
93 SVIMEZ 1957, vol. II, pp. 2640–1, decree of 29 July 1925; Farinacci 1927, p. 199; *Sicilia Nuova*, 30 July 1925. See also AS Palermo GP, b.329 for pre-election tactics.
94 *L'Unità*, 1 August 1925; *Come il governo ha vinto a Palermo*, anonymous pamphlet, undated, in Archivio De Felice; *Avanti!*, 4 August 1925. See also *Il Corriere di Sicilia*, 30 July 1925 for other measures against the opposition.
95 Cucco, *Il mio rogo*, ch. 1, pp. 15–16.
96 *Il Giornale di Sicilia*, 20 June 1925; *Corriere Marittimo Siciliano*, 17 May 1925.
97 *Sicilia Nuova*, 28 July 1925. For fascism as heir to the Risorgimento, cf. Perez 1924, in AS Palermo GP, b.53 ('... most fascist of all was Giuseppe Garibaldi...')
98 *Sicilia Nuova*, 27 July 1925.
99 St Antony's Documents, Job 111, 030532, telegram from Mussolini to the Prefect of Messina, 18 July 1925.
100 *Sicilia Nuova*, 20 July 1925. See also Farinacci 1927, p. 198.
101 *Gazzetta di Messina e delle Calabrie*, 22 July 1925; cf. *Il Giornale di Sicilia*, 20 July 1925; *Il Corriere di Sicilia*, 21 July 1925. In Farinacci's defence, see *Sicilia Nuova*, 21 July 1925; *L'Eco della Sicilia e delle Calabrie*, 24 July 1925.
102 Marino 1976, p. 314. for the full text, *L'Ora*, 29 July 1925.
103 *Sicilia Nuova*, 29 July 1925; cf. Cucco, *Il mio rogo*, ch. 1, pp. 18–9.
104 Recalled by Bianca Cucco.
105 Cucco, *Il mio rogo*, ch. 1, p. 20; cf. *L'Ora*, 3 August 1925; *Sicilia Nuova*, 3 August 1925.
106 ACS PS, 1925, b.103, report from Ispettore Generale di P.S., 6 August 1925; AS Palermo GP, b.329, report from the *Questore*, 3 August 1925. The pamphlet, *Come il governo ha vinto*, speaks of '250 squadristi armati' ('250 armed *squadristi*'); cf. *Avanti!*, 4 August 1925; *Gazzetta di Messina e delle Calabrie*, 4 August 1925 (for the fascist patrols).
107 ACS PS, 1925, b.84, telegrams from Prefect Barbieri, 23 July 1925, 30 July 1925; ibid., reply from Ministry of Interior, 31 July 1925.
108 OO xxxix, 483 (4 August 1925).
109 Quai d'Orsay, Archives, Italie 66, telegram to Min. des Affaires Étrangères, 5 August 1925; cf. Schneider and Clough 1929, pp. 32–3.
110 *Corriere della Sera*, 6 August 1925 (quoting *Il Giornale d'Italia*); cf. *Avanti!*, 5 August 1925; *L'Eco della Sicilia e delle Calabrie*, 5 August 1925; Pignato 1925.
111 *Come il governo ha vinto....*
112 OO xxxix 483 (4 August 1925).
113 Cucco, *Il mio rogo*, appendix.
114 Volpe 1925, pp. 485, 494; cf. R. De Felice 1968, p. 123.
115 Cucco, *Il mio rogo*, ch. 2, p. 1; *Sicilia Nuova*, 21 August 1925; ASP CM 21, memorial by Cucco, p. 16. For the speech at Agrigento, OO xx, 264.

116 De Begnac 1950, p. 293.
117 Cucco, *Il mio rogo*, ch. 2, pp. 2–3; cf. ASP CM 21, memorial by Cucco, p. 16; *The Times* 7 February 1928, attributes Mori's appointment to Antonino Di Giorgio.

Chapter 5

1 Porto 1977, pp. 19–36; Petacco 1978, pp. 35–54; ASP CM 11, 12; cf. Mori 1932, p. 251.
2 Porto 1977, pp. 32–3.
3 Marino 1976, pp. 166–74.
4 Cf. ASP CM 1, request for a signed photograph from the king.
5 ASP CM 24.
6 ASP CM '*Relazioni, pubblicazioni, studi e discorsi (8)*'.
7 ASP CM 17.
8 Porto 1977, p. 37; ASP CM 39.
9 Salvatorelli and Mira 1956, pp. 137–8; ASP CM 41.
10 Porto 1977, p. 37; Petacco 1978, pp. 17–8.
11 Corner 1975, pp. 210–20; Veneruso, 1968, pp. 211, 336–8.
12 R. De Felice 1966, pp. 129n, 206; Petacco 1978, p. 19.
13 Balbo 1932, pp. 74–82.
14 Spanò 1978, p. 36.
15 Petacco 1978, p. 23.
16 Cf. Cucco, *Il mio rogo*, ch. 2, p. 6; *Atti parlamentari, Camera dei Deputati, Discussioni*, 19 November 1924 (Manaresi).
17 De Begnac 1950, p. 294.
18 Ferri 1928, p. 291.
19 Spanò 1978, p. 37.
20 ASP CM 9, Furolo to Mori, 23 August 1922.
21 ASP CM 1, Furolo to Mori, 30 March 1923.
22 ASP CM 1, Mori to Cav. Enrico Emanuele, 19 January 1923.
23 ASP CM 1, Signora Furolo to Signora Mori, 23 April 1923.
24 *Santa Riscossa*, 30 November 1924; cf. *L'Ora*, 11 November 1924.
25 *L'Ora*, 13 May 1924; ACS GF, b.13 (1924), typed report on the situation in Trapani, 9 May 1922 (for 1924); *Il Mezzogiorno d'Italia*, 20 September 1923 and 4 October 1923.
26 ACS CB, b.2 fasc.15, report by Starace, 7 July 1923: 'Cav. Pellegrino...is not up to the job. I will see to his liquidation.'
27 ACS CB, b.2 fasc.22, report by the Prefect of Trapani, 26 April 1923; ACS

GF, b.13 (1924), typed report on Trapani, 9 May 1922 (for 1924); ibid. typed defence by Pellegrino, 22 March 1924; cf. *La Valanga*, 16 August 1923; *Il Mezzogiorno d'Italia*, 20 September 1923.
28 Molè 1929, p. 128.
29 Ibid. pp. 128–9.
30 Prestianni 1931, pp. 12–3, and accompanying map, 'Comuni in cui è stata più intensa la formazione della piccola proprietà'; cf. Serpieri 1930, p. 492: 'Newly enriched leaseholders and speculators often carried out the work of intermediaries, buying the *latifondi* and then selling them in lots to the peasants' – referring in particular to the provinces of Palermo and Caltanissetta in this period.
31 *Il Giornale Fascista*, 24 December 1922; cf. *Il Corriere Italiano*, 5 May 1924.
32 'Il Solitario', *La malavita in Sicilia e l'azione fascista* (Palermo, 1923), pp. 14–5, 30. (Also serialised in *Il Giornale Fascista*, from 25 February 1923).
33 ASP CM 16, report to the Presidente del Consiglio, 7 June 1924, 'sulla situazione della pubblica sicurezza nella Sicilia occidentale'.
34 ACS PS, 1922, b.159, report from the Prefect of Trapani, 9 December 1922.
35 ASP CM 1, letter from Ing. Cav. Enrico Emanuele, 6 January 1923.
36 ASP CB, b.2 fasc.22, Seg. Politico, Alcamo, to Mussolini, 5 April 1923.
37 *Il Mezzogiorno d'Italia*, 20 September 1923; cf. Genovese 1963, pp. 127–8.
38 ASP GF, b.13 (1924), typed defence by Pellegrino, 22 March 1924.
39 *L'Ora*, 8 April 1924; cf. ACS PS, 1924, b.66, report on Trapani, 28 February 1924; ACS GF, b.13 (1924), report on Trapani, 9 May 1922 (for 1924).
40 Fondazione Gentile, CG, Giuseppe Gentile to Giovanni Gentile, 24 July 1925. For the support of the *agrari*, see *Il Risveglio Zootecnico*, particularly 1 November 1924, 1 May 1925, 1 June 1925; *Santa Riscossa*, November 1924–January 1925. For Mori's support of wine producers, see ACS PS, 1924, b.57 (Trapani).
41 Fondazione Gentile, CG, Gentile to Federzoni, 8 April 1925.
42 ASP CM 10, report to Mussolini (marked '*sospeso*'), 2 August 1927.
43 See below, pp. 186–7.
44 *Il Popolo*, 6 December 1924.
45 Cucco, *Il mio rogo*, ch. 2, p. 3.
46 Ibid. ch. 2, p. 3.

47 *The Times*, 7 February 1928; Caprì 1977, p. 39; cf. Cucco, *Il mio rogo*, ch. 2, p. 3.
48 Cucco, *Il mio rogo*, ch. 2, pp. 5–6.
49 *Sicilia Nuova*, 13 October 1925.
50 *Avvisatore*, 29 October 1925; cf. *L'Ora*, 23 October 1925; *Il Giornale di Sicilia*, 23 October 1925; *L'Avvenire di Sicilia*, 25 October 1925.
51 *Avvisatore*, 28 April 1924.
52 Ibid. 5 November 1925.
53 Cucco, *Il mio rogo*, ch. 3, pp. 7–8.
54 *Regime Fascista*, 20 March 1930.
55 *Sicilia Nuova*, 23 October 1925.
56 Ibid. 27 October 1925.
57 ASP CM 15. See also Petacco 1978, pp. 191–5.
58 *Sicilia Nuova*, 28 October 1925. In the weeks that followed Mori's arrival at Palermo, the local intransigents launched at least two new journalistic ventures: *Alalà* (from 12 December 1925) and *L'Independente* (from 27 December 1925).
59 Ibid. 29 October 1925. See also Filiberto Di Marco 1937, p. 39.
60 ASP CM 16, Mori to the Ministry of the Interior, 10 November 1925.
61 ASP CM 17, Mori to Mussolini, 1 July 1924; ASP CM 16, Mori to Mussolini, 7 June 1924; Mori 1932, pp. 240–2.
62 ASP CM 16, Mori to Ministry of the Interior, 10 November 1925.
63 *Sicilia Nuova*, 7 December 1925; *L'Ora*, 7 December 1925.
64 *Il Salso*, 19 December 1925.
65 *Il Giornale di Sicilia*, 22 December 1925; cf. *Sicilia Nuova*, 14 January 1926; *Il Giornale di Sicilia*, 15 January 1926.
66 Porto 1977, p. 61.
67 Mori 1932, pp. 276–81 (the date is incorrect).
68 *L'Ora*, 9 December 1925; *Sicilia Nuova*, 9 December 1925.
69 *Il Giornale d'Italia*, 30 November 1927. For Mori's provisions on city policing in October–November 1925, see *L'Ora*, 9 November 1925; *Il Giornale di Sicilia*, 9 November 1925; ACS PS, 1925, b.84, Mori to the Ministry of the Interior, 30 October 1925.

Chapter 6

1 Mori 1932, p. 14.
2 Ibid. p. 235.
3 ASP CM 16, Mori to the Ministry of the Interior, 5 August 1926; Mori 1923, p. 122.
4 ASP CM 16, Mori to the Ministry of the Interior, 5 August 1926.
5 Spanò 1978, p. 20. For the economic situation in Gangi in these years, and the determination of the landowners to maintain the integrity of their estates, see Monheim 1972.
6 Spanò 1978, pp. 20–1; *Il Giornale di Sicilia*, 14 November 1927, statement by Spanò; cf. *Il Giornale di Sicilia*, 18 February 1927, 30 September 1927, 1 October 1927; *L'Ora*, 16 February 1927.
7 *Il Giornale di Sicilia*, 1 May 1926.
8 AS Palermo GP, b.474, decree by Federzoni, 27 July 1924; *L'Ora*, 20 February 1925; *Il Magistrato dell'ordine*, June 1925, in ASP CM 17; *Atti parlamentari, Senato, Discussioni*, 8 December 1924 (Federzoni).
9 Spanò 1978, pp. 30, 39.
10 *Sicilia Nuova*, 7 December 1925; cf. *Sicilia Nuova*, 21 December 1925.
11 ASP CM 16, Mori to Mussolini, 7 June 1924; cf. ACS PS, 1925, b.84, telegram from Mori, 30 December 1925.
12 Spanò 1978, pp. 40–3. For a less plausible version of the meeting with Ferrarello, see *Corriere della Sera*, 26 February 1926.
13 ASP CM 16, Mori to the Ministry of the Interior, 5 August 1926; cf. Mori 1932 p. 316.
14 *Sicilia Nuova*, 4 January 1926.
15 Spanò 1978, p. 16; *Corriere della Sera*, 26 February 1926.
16 *Sicilia Nuova*, 4 January 1926; *Corriere della Sera*, 27 February 1926; *Il Giornale d'Italia*, 10 December 1926.
17 Mori 1932, p. 296.
18 Washburn Child 1929, in ASP CM 9.
19 Cf. ASP CM 16, report by De Feo on 'Ricovero famiglie latitanti', 7 February 1927; Chapman 1973, p. 8.
20 ASP CM 16, Mori to the Ministry of the Interior, 5 August 1926; cf. *L'Ora*, 16 February 1926; *Corriere della Sera*, 24 February 1926; *Piff Paff*, 9 January 1926.
21 *Il Giornale di Sicilia*, 20 November 1927, 22 November 1927; Spanò 1978, p. 39.
22 ASP CM 10, Sgadari to Mori, 31 January 1927.
23 Montanelli 1955, p. 284.
24 *Sicilia Nuova*, 7 January 1926; *L'Ora*, 7 January 1926.
25 *Sicilia Nuova*, 4 January 1926.
26 Cucco, *Il mio rogo*, ch. 2, p. 9.
27 *Sicilia Nuova*, 12 January 1926; *Corriere della Sera*, 27 February 1926.
28 *Sicilia Nuova*, 12 January 1926.

29 Cucco, *Il mio rogo*, ch. 2, pp. 8–10.
30 Ibid. ch. 2, pp. 12–15; Spanò 1978, p. 45; *Sicilia Nuova*, 12 January 1926; cf. Guercio 1938, p. 77.
31 ASP CM 16, Mori to the Ministry of the Interior, 5 August 1926; cf. *Corriere della Sera*, 27 February 1926.
32 ASP CM 16, Mori to the Ministry of the Interior, 5 August 1926.
33 Ibid.
34 Mori 1932, p. 26.
35 Ibid. p. 14; cf. Mori 1923, p. 74; *L'Ora*, 23 January 1928, speech by Mori at Palermo University.
36 Mori 1932, pp. 56–60, 68–74, 95–6; Mori 1923, pp. 10–13, 16.
37 Mori 1932, p. 79; Mori 1923, pp. 10, 17.
38 Mori 1932, p. 79; Mori 1923, p. 74; *Atti parlamentari, Senato, Discussioni*, 17 March 1930 (Mori).
39 Mori 1923, p. 60; Mori 1932, p. 80.
40 Mori 1932, p. 88; *Atti parlamentari, Senato, Discussioni*, 17 March 1930 (Mori).
41 Mori 1932, p. 89; Mori 1923, pp. 56–60.
42 Mori 1923, pp. 56–8.
43 Ibid. p. 59.
44 Ibid. p. 14; Mori 1932, p. 81.
45 Mori 1923, pp. 16–7.
46 Ibid. pp. 17–8.
47 Mori 1932, p. 85.
48 Ibid. p. 86.
49 Mori 1923, p. 19.
50 Mori 1932, p. 82.
51 ASP CM 16, Mori to the Ministry of the Interior, 5 August 1926.
52 Ibid.
53 Mori 1932, p. 32.
54 Cf. Romano 1964, p. 193.
55 *Il Popolo d'Italia*, 16 January 1926.
56 *Corriere della Sera*, 24–27 February 1926; cf. *La Civiltà cattolica*, 18 June, 1927, p. 503; *The Times*, 7 February 1928; *Il Secolo*, 24 February 1926.
57 *Il Tevere*, 27 February 1926.
58 Ibid.; cf. Lyttelton 1973, p. 400.
59 *Il Popolo d'Italia*, 16 January 1926, 5 February 1926.
60 Navarra Crimi 1925, p. 21.
61 *L'Ora*, 13 December 1924.
62 Lorenzoni 1923, p. 338. See also *Atti parlamentari, Senato, Discussioni*, 8 December 1924 (Federzoni); AS Palermo GP, b.474, long report on Sicilian crime (unsigned), 13 June 1923 (?); Frisella Vella 1928, p. 14.
63 *Il Martello*, 8 December 1923; cf. *L'Ora*, 17 January 1925; *L'Avvenire di Sicilia*, 25 January 1925; *Problemi siciliani*,

October 1924; *Sicilia Agricola*, 27 January 1924: 'Here everyone is calling everyone else *'mafioso'*, but nobody *ever* knows what mafia means. However, Excellency, we have here a greater problem, namely delinquency, which it is absolutely vital to eradicate if Sicily is to contribute to Italy what it should' (open letter to Mussolini).
64 *Il Corriere di Sicilia*, 12 November 1925.
65 *L'Ora*, 23 January 1928, speech at Palermo University. Mussolini himself made the same point to Yvon De Begnac, saying that he could never allow a 'republic' – the mafia – to exist within the state. (De Begnac 1950, p. 293.)
66 Appiani 1927, p. 18 (speech delivered 5 January 1927); cf. Mori 1932, p. 231; *The Times*, 20 January 1928.
67 Mignosi 1925.
68 Ferri 1928, p. 291.
69 Ibid. p. 295.
70 Ibid. p. 296. For further comments by Ferri on the mafia, see *L'Ora*, 8 May 1924; *Il Giornale di Sicilia*, 13 August 1928, speech by Ferri in defence of Giuseppe Troia; *La Prensa* (Buenos Aires), 1 July 1928, in Archivio Petacco, Rome.
71 De Begnac 1950, p. 294.

Chapter 7

1 Cf. *L'Ora*, 13 June 1924; *Avvisatore*, 5 November 1925; ASP CM 16, Mori to the Ministry of the Interior, 5 August 1926; Mori 1932, pp. 241–7.
2 *L'Ora*, 23 January 1928.
3 ASP CM 16, Mori to the Ministry of the Interior, 5 August 1926.
4 AS Palermo GP, b.474, Mori to the Prefect of Palermo, 11 January 1925; cf. ibid., Prefect of Palermo to the Ministry of the Interior, 19 September 1924.
5 *L'Ora*, 20 February 1925.
6 AS Palermo GP, b.474, *Questore* of Palermo to the Prefect, 1 May 1925.
7 ASP CM 16, Mori to the Ministry of the Interior, 5 August 1926.
8 Associazione per Delinquere, Corleone, Processo, Sentenza di Istruttoria, pp. 246–57; *Il Giornale di Sicilia*, 30 January 1929.
9 *Sicilia Nuova*, 16 June 1926.
10 Processo di Corleone, Sentenza di Istruttoria (31 July 1928), pp. 208–9.
11 Ibid. pp. 197–8.
12 Related by Michele Pantaleone.

13 Processo di Corleone, Verbali di Polizia (29 December 1926).

14 *Il Giornale di Sicilia*, 24 November 1928; Spanò 1978, pp. 49–57; Mori 1932, p. 310. See below, pp. 234–5.

15 *Il Giornale di Sicilia*, 24 November 1928; Spanò 1932, pp. 52–3.

16 Processo di Corleone, Sentenza di Istruttoria, p. 36 (Verbali di Polizia, 6 January 1927, 15 January 1927, 18 May 1927, 27 July 1927).

17 *Sicilia Nuova*, 30 January 1926.

18 ASP CM 16, Mori to the Ministry of the Interior, 5 August 1926; Mori 1932, pp. 315–6; cf. ASP CM 16, Mori to Presidente del Consiglio, 7 June 1924.

19 Processo di Corleone, Verbali di Polizia, p. 13.

20 Mori 1932, p. 316.

21 ASP CM 16, Mori to the Ministry of the Interior, 5 August 1926.

22 ASP CM 16, De Feo to Mori, 7 February 1927.

23 ASP CM 16, Mori to the Ministry of the Interior, 5 August 1926.

24 Ibid; cf. ASP CM 10, Mori to Suardo, 9 November 1927; ASP CM 10, Mori to the Ministry of the Interior, 11 October 1927; Mori 1932, pp. 259, 301.

25 ASP CM 10, Mori to Suardo, 9 November 1927.

26 Chapman 1973, pp. xiii, 8.

27 Ibid. pp. 7–8.

28 Ibid. p. 8.

29 Ibid. pp. 8–9.

30 Ibid. p. 232.

31 Ibid. p. 233.

32 Ibid. p. 232; cf. ibid. p. 156.

33 *Il Giornale di Sicilia*, 3 September 1926.

34 *L'Ora*, 24 February 1926.

35 Processo di Corleone, Sentenza di Istruttoria, p. 47.

36 Prestianni 1931, map of 'Comuni in cui è stata più intensa la formazione della piccola proprietà'; cf. ibid. p. 50.

37 L. Lumia, *Contadini e mafia nel primo dopoguerra* (unpublished typescript, Coll. J. Fentress, Rome), from which the following account is taken. See also, Sabetti 1984, pp. 126–133.

38 *Il Giornali di Sicilia*, 14 December 1928; cf. *L'Ora*, 21 October 1958.

39 Montanelli 1955, p. 283.

40 Cf. Serpieri 1930, p. 492. Serpieri says that the economic problems faced by many *latifondisti* in the war induced them, after 1918, to sell 'at freely negotiated prices rather than, as they feared, under duress and at imposed prices'.

41 In all, 174 were interrogated by the examining magistrate.

42 Processo di Corleone, Istruttoria, interrogation of Imputati, January 1927–March 1928.

43 Blok 1974, p. 185.

44 Ibid. pp. 168–71, 182.

45 Ibid. p. 186.

46 Mori 1932, p. 80.

47 Cf. Hess 1984, p. 77.

48 Pitré 1889, vol. II, pp. 289–99.

49 Mosca 1980, p. 7.

50 A report in *L'Ora*, 19 October 1920, spoke of 'the illustrious Councillor, Michelangelo Gennaro, tireless and devoted organiser of the local coalition against the socialists...who enjoys so much support in our town'.

51 Processo di Corleone, Verbali di Polizia, pp. 10, 13, 14. Corleone had apparently been subject to a particularly high murder rate during and after the war. A report in *L'Ora*, 7 April 1921, said that much of the town's population had been gripped by '*follia omicida*' (homicide mania), and that no one dared go out at night. It also said that more *Corleonesi* had been killed in the town during the war than at the front.

52 Processo di Corleone, Dibattimento (January 1930), p. 202.

53 Ibid. Denuncie (29 December 1926).

54 Ibid. Denuncie (29 December 1926).

55 Ibid. Dibattimento, p. 119.

56 Ibid. Istruttoria, Esame dei Testimoni.

57 Ibid. Dibattimento, p. 217 (Giovanni Palazzo).

58 Ibid. Dibattimento, p. 217.

59 Ibid. Dibattimento, p. 109.

60 Ibid. Dibattimento, p. 107.

61 Ibid. Dibattimento, p. 145.

62 Ibid. Dibattimento, pp. 61–2.

63 Ibid. Istruttoria, Testi.

64 Ibid. Denuncie (February–April 1927).

65 Ibid. Istruttoria, interrogation of Imputati.

66 ASP CM 16, Mori to the Ministry of the Interior, 5 August 1926.

67 Archivio Carnazza, fasc. 52, b. Palermo, di Scalea to Carnazza, 6 February 1924.

68 AS Palermo GP, b.478 report on Corleone.

69 AS Palermo, Sottoprefettura di Corleone, b.25, report to Mori, 20 August 1926.

70 Ibid. report to Mori, 10 December 1926.

71 Processo di Corleone, Sentenza di Istruttoria, pp. 36–7; ibid. Dibattimento, p. 107 (Liborio Anzalone).

72 ACS PS, 1928, b.171, telegrams from the Prefect of Caltanissetta, 15 December 1926, 16 December 1926; *Corriere d'Italia*, 10 May 1928.
73 Processo di Corleone, Verbali di Polizia, pp. 10–11.
74 Ibid. Dibattimento, p. 51.
75 Ibid. Dibattimento, p. 120.
76 Ibid. Verbali di Polizia, p. 13.
77 Ibid. Istruttoria, Testi, statements by Giuseppe Sarzano and Giuliano Angelo.
78 ASP CM 21, typed report to 'Eccellenza' (undated).

Chapter 8

1 OO xxxix 529 (13 October 1925); cf. Fornari 1971, p. 131.
2 *Atti parlamentari, Camera dei Deputati, Discussioni*, 12 December 1925; Fried 1963, pp. 186–7.
3 ASP CM 10, decree by Federzoni, 13 March 1926.
4 *Atti parlamentari, Senato, Discussioni*, 15 March 1926.
5 St Antony's Documents, Job 166, 049018/9; cf. R. De Felice, 1968, p. 192n.
6 *Atti parlamentari, Camera dei Deputati, Discussioni*, 1 May 1926.
7 Cucco, *Il mio rogo*, ch. 2, p. 17.
8 Filiberto Di Marco 1937, passim.
9 *Sicilia Nuova*, 7 January 1926.
10 *La Fiamma*, 31 January 1926.
11 Impastato 1926, pp. 6–9.
12 Cf. ASP CM 10, Sgadari to Mori, 31 January 1927.
13 ASP CM 21, memorial by Cucco, p. 18.
14 Ibid. p. 19.
15 Filiberto di Marco 1937, p. 59.
16 *La Fiamma*, 24 January 1926.
17 ASP CM 21, memorial by Cucco, p. 18.
18 Ibid. p. 19.
19 Ibid. p. 19.
20 ACS PS, 1925, b.84, Mori to the Ministry of the Interior, 30 October 1925.
21 ASP CM 21, memorial by Cucco, p. 19; ACS SPCR, b.39, appeal by Cucco to Grand Council, April 1927.
22 ACS SPCR, b.39, appeal by Cucco to Grand Council.
23 *Sicilia Fascista*, 14 March 1926; cf. ibid. 14 February 1926.
24 Ibid. 21 March 1926, 21 February 1926.
25 Ibid. 28 February 1926, 7 March 1926, 14 March 1926, 4 July 1926.

26 *La Provincia*, 2 August 1926.
27 ACS PS, 1926, b.107, Prefect of Caltanissetta to the Ministry of the Interior, 3 August 1926.
28 Ibid. 25 July 1926.
29 Ibid. 19 August 1926.
30 *Era Nova*, 23 October 1926.
31 ACS PS, 1926, b.107, Paolo Savoca to Farinacci, 31 January 1926.
32 Cucco, *Il mio rogo*, ch. 3, pp. 9–10.
33 Ibid. ch. 3, p. 11.
34 Ibid. ch. 3, p. 4.
35 *Il Giornale di Sicilia*, 18 October 1926.
36 Cf. *Avvisatore*, 5 November 1925.
37 Cucco, *Il mio rogo*, ch. 2, p. 30.
38 ACS CF, b.2., fasc.6c (1926), letter to Mussolini signed 'La Sicilia Fascista'. For other anonymous letters, see ACS SPCR, b.39.
39 ACS PS, 1926, b.109, Mori to the Ministry of the Interior, 13 August 1926, 16 August 1926; ACS SPCR, b.39, appeal by Cucco to Grand Council.
40 Cucco, *Il mio rogo*, ch. 2, pp. 24–30; *Sicilia Nuova*, 2 November 1926; ACS SPCR, b.39, appeal by Cucco to Grand Council.
41 Cucco, *Il mio rogo*, ch. 2, p. 28.
42 ASP CM 10, Mori to the Ministry of the Interior, 11 October 1927.
43 Cucco, *Il mio rogo*, ch. 2, p. 30.
44 Cucco later wrote of his Palermo followers: 'The rank and file fascists... were for so many years slandered and defamed as hooligans, criminals, and Heaven knows what'. (Cucco, *Il mio rogo*, ch. 2, pp. 29–30).
45 *Sicilia Nuova*, 8 June 1926.
46 Mori to Cucco, 22 October 1926, in 'Come l'ex Prefetto Mori giudicava Alfredo Cucco. Elemento della discolpa presentata per l'udienza del 4 aprile 1931, Corte di Assise ordinaria di Palermo'.
47 ASP CM 9, Cucco to Mori, 22 October 1926.
48 Petacco 1978, p. 127.
49 ASP CM 10, Sgadari to Mori, 31 January 1927.
50 ASP CM 9, Furolo to Mori, 30 September 1926.
51 Lyttelton 1973, p. 293; cf. *La Fiamma*, 12 December 1926.
52 Cucco, *Il mio rogo*, ch. 2, pp. 5–6; cf. Federzoni 1967, pp. 99–100.
53 OO xxii 467–70; cf. R. De Felice 1968 pp. 301–4.
54 AS Palermo, Sottoprefettura di Corleone, b.25, telegram from Mori, 3 December 1926.

55 Cucco, *Il mio rogo*, ch. 2, p. 32.
56 Ibid. ch. 2, pp. 33–4.
57 *Sentenza nel Procedimento Promosso dal Pubblico Ministero contro Cucco, Dr. Alfredo, 3/12/1927*, in ASP CM 21; cf. ACS SPCR, b.39, appeal by Cucco to Grand Council.
58 *Atti parlamentari, Camera dei Deputati, Discussioni*, 11 March 1925.
59 *Sentenza nel Procedimento. . .contro Cucco*, in ASP CM 21.
60 R. De Felice 1968, p. 187.
61 Ibid. p. 187; P. Morgan, 'Augusto Turati' in Cordova 1980, pp. 498–507.
62 ACS SPCR, b.28, report on Federazioni, 5 October 1926.
63 P.N.F. Foglio d'ordini, N.17, 17 December 1926.
64 Cucco, *Il mio rogo*, ch. 2, p. 33; ibid. ch. 3, pp. 1–2; cf. ASP CM 21, memorial by Cucco, p. 37.
65 Cucco, *Il mio rogo*, ch. 3, pp. 1–3; ACS SPCR, b.39, Cucco to Mussolini, 18 January 1927.
66 ACS PS, 1927, b.157, Cucco to Bocchini, 21 January 1927; ibid. Mori to Bocchini, 21 January 1927.
67 ACS SPCR, b.39, appeal by Cucco to Grand Council.
68 Ibid. anonymous letter from '*un Fascista*'.
69 Ibid. telegram from Mori, 20 February 1927.
70 Ibid. appeal by Cucco to Grand Council.
71 Ibid. card from Cucco to Mussolini (date illegible, but February/March 1927).
72 Ibid. appeal by Cucco to Grand Council.
73 Ibid. report from Mori, 24 February 1927.
74 Ibid. appeal by Cucco to Grand Council.
75 Trevelyan 1972, pp. 403–4 (diary entry for 23 January 1927).
76 ACS PS, 1927, telegram from Mori, 26 January 1927.
77 *Avvisatore*, 16 February 1927.
78 ACS SPCR, b.39, telegram from Mori, 2 March 1927; cf. *Il Tevere*, 2 March 1927.
79 ACS SPCR, b.39, appeal by Cucco to Grand Council (attached correspondence).
80 Ibid. Cucco to Mussolini, 20 April 1927.
81 ASP CM 15.
82 ASP CM 21, reports by Nicolosi.
83 ASP CM 10, Mori to Suardo, 9 November 1927.
84 ASP CM 16, Mori to Mussolini, 22 February 1927.
85 Archivio Petacco, letter to Mori (signature illegible), 29 May 1927.
86 ASP CM 10, Mori to the Ministry of the Interior, 11 October 1927.
87 *Il Giornale di Sicilia*, 22 January 1927.
88 *L'Ora*, 25 January 1927.
89 ASP CM 21, 'Appunti' on Mutilati and Palermo Fascism; ibid. 'Relazione della gestione federale dal maggio 1927 a dicembre 1928' (Belsito); ibid. typed report to 'Eccellenza' (undated).
90 ASP CM 21, typed report to 'Eccellenza' (undated); ACS SPCR, b.39, appeal by Cucco to Grand Council.
91 ASP CM 21, 'Appunti' on Mutilati and Palermo Fascism.
92 Ibid.
93 Cf. ASP CM 21, report by Pensovecchio to Melchiorri.
94 Archivio Petacco, letter to Mori (signature illegible), 29 May 1927.
95 ASP CM 21, report by Pensovecchio to Melchiorri; *Il Giornale di Sicilia*, 20 May 1927.
96 Cucco, *Il mio rogo*, ch. 3, p. 27.
97 ASP CM 50, Giuriati to Mori, 13 April 1927.
98 *Il Giornale di Sicilia*, 9 April 1927.
99 Ibid. 9 May 1927.
100 ASP CM 9, Restivo to Mori, 27 May 1927.
101 ASP CM 50, crime statistics, 20 February 1927.
102 *Atti parlamentari, Camera dei Deputati, Discussioni*, 26 May 1927.
103 ASP CM 21, 'Relazione della gestione federale. . .'.
104 Ibid.; *L'Ora*, 4 March 1929.
105 ASP CM 21, Relazionc della gestione federale. . . .
106 ASP PS, 1927, b.157, Salvatore Misuracca to Mussolini, 20 May 1927.
107 Ibid. Mori to the Ministry of the Interior, 30 July 1927.
108 ACS SPCR, b.39, appeal by Cucco to Grand Council.
109 ACS PS, 1927, b.157, copy of letter from Mariano Fazio forwarded to the Ministry of the Interior, 30 August 1927; cf. *Sicilia Zootecnica*, January 1927.
110 ASP CM 21, Cirincione to Di Giorgio, 5 January 1927. For Cirincione, see *Dizionario dei siciliani illustri* (Palermo, 1939), pp. 121–2.
111 AS Palermo QP, letter from Commissario di P.S., Bagheria, 21 May

1927; cf. ibid. letter from Commissario di P.S., Bagheria, 1 June 1927.

112 Ibid. report on 'Situazione politica di Bagheria' by Giuseppe Gotta, 20 September 1927.

113 ASP CM 21, typed report to 'Eccellenza' (undated).

114 ACS PS, 1927, b.157, Mori to the Ministry of the Interior, 6 June 1927.

115 ACS PS, 1927, b.158, Prefect Sallicano to the Ministry of the Interior, 5 February 1927.

116 Ibid. Prefect Sallicano to the Ministry of the Interior, 24 May 1927; cf. *Il Littorio*, 11 July 1927.

117 ASP CM 10, Mori to Suardo, 2 August 1927.

118 Ibid. Mori to Mussolini (marked 'sospeso'), 2 August 1927.

119 Ibid. Mori to Mussolini, 2 August 1927.

120 Ibid. statement by Domenico Coglitore, Commissario Capo di P.S., Palermo, 10 June 1927.

121 Ibid. Armato to Mori, July 1927.

122 *Il Littorio*, 10 August 1927; cf. ASP CM 21, report from Pensovecchio to Melchiorri.

123 ASP CM 19, Mussolini to Mori, 10 August 1927.

124 *Il Littorio*, 19 September 1927.

125 ASP CM 10, Mori to Suardo, 9 November 1927.

Chapter 9

1 *La Fiamma*, 11 March 1923.

2 Policastro 1929, p. 35.

3 Sirena 1927, p. 30.

4 ASP CM 17, poems in Mori's honour by F. Burgio, F. Agnello, G. Butice, etc; *Sicilia Nuova*, 4 January 1926; Giampietro 1925, p. 49.

5 *L'Impero*, 18 May 1926.

6 ASP CM 'Relazioni, pubblicazioni, studi e discorsi (8)', speech to Associazione Nazionale Insegnanti Fascisti, 6 June 1926.

7 *Atti parlamentari, Camera dei Deputati, Discussioni*, 26 May 1927.

8 *Sicilia Nuova*, 12 November 1925.

9 *Il Giornale d'Italia*, 12 November 1925.

10 *L'Avvenire di Sicilia*, 24 January 1926.

11 ASP CM 9, anonymous typed letter to Arnaldo Mussolini (at *Il Popolo d'Italia*); cf. *Piff Paff*, 13 February 1926.

12 *Corriere Marittimo Siciliano*, 14 February 1926.

13 *Sicilia Nuova*, 24 December 1926.

14 ASP CM 10, report from Mori to the Ministry of the Interior, 11 October 1927.

15 Cf. *Camera dei Deputati*, 1924–29, *Atti*, 27, 1698, conversion of decree of 27 October 1927 into law, 26 November 1927.

16 Archivio Petacco, Suardo to Mori, 27 September 1927.

17 ACS PS, 1928, b.174, Mori to the Ministry of the Interior, 27 July 1928.

18 ASP CM 21, report from Pensovecchio to Melchiorri.

19 ACS PS, 1928, b.174, Mori to the Ministry of the Interior, 27 July 1928.

20 SVIMEZ, *Legislazione per il Mezzogiorno 1861–1957*, vol. II, pp. 2676–9, decree of 6 May 1926.

21 PRO FO 371 18431 R1024, Dodds to Sir Eric Drummond, 1 February 1934.

22 Ibid. R1997, Sir Eric Drummond to Sir John Simon, 31 March 1934.

23 PRO FO 371 19549 R1015, Dodds to Sir Eric Drummond, 4 February 1935.

24 *Sicilia Nuova*, 18 May 1925.

25 *Sicilia Fascista*, 1 November 1925.

26 Ibid. 21 March 1926.

27 Blok 1974, p. 182.

28 Mori 1932, p. 351.

29 Ibid. p. 351.

30 Ibid. p. 352.

31 Ibid. pp. 282–90; cf. *Giornale dell'Isola*, 16 September 1928.

32 Mori 1932, p. 353.

33 Ibid. p. 354.

34 ASP CM 17, typed speech by Mori (undated).

35 Ibid. Filippo Agnello to Mori, 21 March 1927.

36 ASP CM 16, Atto di Gabella, ex-feudo Ciambra, 16 December 1926, Article 21. For poems praising Mori, see ASP CM 17.

37 ACS PS, 1926, b.107, Paolo Savoca to Farinacci, 31 January 1926.

38 ASP CM 16, report on 'Fondi e feudi dichiarati zone infette' (undated).

39 Ibid. list of estates with '*gabelloti mafiosi*' (undated).

40 ASP CM 17, typed speech by Mori (undated).

41 *Il Giornale di Sicilia*, 8 February 1927.

42 ACS PS, 1927, b.154, Mori to the Ministry of the Interior, 11 June 1927 (also for the text of the deliberation); cf. Porto 1977, p. 111.

43 Cf. *Battaglie Fasciste*, 9 July 1927; *L'Ora*, 25 July 1927; Salvioli 1927, pp. 8–9, and the reply in *Sicilia Agricola*, 31 October 1927 (Gerbino).

44 *Il Giornale di Sicilia*, 7 June 1928.
45 Ibid. 4 July 1928; cf. *Il Lavoro d'Italia agricola*, 8 July 1928.
46 Cf. Sereni 1968, pp. 158–65.
47 *Il Monitore Tecnico*, 31 March 1929; Prestianni 1929, p. 149.
48 Lorenzoni 1940, p. 12.
49 Sirena 1968, pp. 20–2, 28, 34.
50 *Il Giornale di Sicilia*, 26 March 1928; *L'Ora*, 27 February 1928; cf. *Il Giornale di Sicilia*, 27 February 1928; *L'Ora*, 31 May 1929; Spanò 1978, p. 38.
51 ASP CM 16, Mori to the Ministry of the Interior, 5 August 1926; Giampietro 1926; Appiani 1927, p. 20; *Il Popolo Toscano*, 24 November 1928.
52 Schmidt 1938, p. 133; Checco 1978, pp. 657–8, 675–6.
53 *Piff Paff*, 14 May 1927; cf. *Il Giornale di Sicilia*, 12 May 1927.
54 Salvemini 1936, p. 237.
55 Ibid. p. 244. In an article in *Sicilia Agricola*, 10 June 1928, Professor Gerbino admitted that many contracts were not being observed in Sicily, but said that the failing 'is also and especially on the part of the workers' ('*é anche e specialmente della parte dei lavoratori*').
56 Cucco said Ciardi always used 'that courtesy which should be used with employers' (*Sicilia Nuova*, 13 July 1926).
57 *Il Giornale di Sicilia*, 16 September 1928.
58 ASP CM 17, typed speech by Mori (undated).
59 Sirena 1927, p. 22.
60 Mori 1932, p. 242.
61 Ibid. p. 325; cf. *Sicilia Nuova*, 18 October 1926; ASP CM 16, for draft of speech.
62 Mori 1932, pp. 322–4.
63 ASP CM 17, two undated speeches to 'combattenti'; ibid. speech inaugurating Congresso dei Fasci e degli Enti Autarchi, February 1926; *Sicilia Nuova*, 12 January 1926.
64 Mori 1932, p. 320.
65 ASP CM 16, speech by Mori on eve of 1929 plebiscite elections, to 'Eccellenze, Signore, Signori'.
66 *L'Ora*, 13 May 1926; *Sicilia Nuova*, 13 May 1926; ASP CM 16, Mori to the Ministry of the Interior, 5 August 1926; Mori 1932, pp. 332–5.
67 *Sicilia Nuova*, 13 May 1926.
68 Mori 1932, p. 333.
69 *L'Ora*, 13 May 1926.
70 *Sicilia Nuova*, 13 May 1926.
71 ASP CM 16, Mori to Mussolini, 8 March 1927.
72 Falzone 1971, p. 36; cf. *Sicilia Zootecnica*, May 1928.
73 Mori 1932, pp. 339–40; ASP CM 16, speech to *guardiani*; *L'Ora*, 1 December 1927.
74 Mori 1932, p. 80; cf. *Atti parlamentari, Senato, Discussioni*, 17 March 1930 (Mori).
75 ASP CM 17, notes for speech to *squadroni* of San Cipirello and San Giuseppe Iato (undated).
76 ASP CM 16, Mori to the Ministry of the Interior, 5 August 1926.
77 *Il Giornale di Sicilia*, 30 May 1927.
78 Ibid.
79 ASP CM 17, typed speech by Mori (undated).
80 Lyttelton 1973, pp. 350–1.
81 Ibid. p. 351; Checco 1978, pp. 686–7; cf. Preti 1973, pp. 855–67.
82 Archivio Petacco, Suardo to Mori, 27 September 1927.
83 SVIMEZ 1957, vol. II, pp. 2625–34, 2640–41, 2655–6, 2676–9, decrees of 7 July 1925, 29 July 1925, 19 November 1925, 6 May 1926.
84 *Il Giornale di Sicilia*, 8 February 1927.
85 *L'Ora*, 31 December 1928.
86 Speech to Camera dei Deputati, in Serpieri 1932, pp. 162–3; cf. Tassinari 1938, p. 300.
87 Serpieri 1932, p. 213.
88 Policastro 1929, p. 10.
89 *Il Resto di Carlino*, 23 January 1929; *Il Messaggero*, 5 February 1929.
90 A. Bertolino, 'Divagazioni sul problema siciliano', in di Castelnuovo 1934, pp. 309, 311; cf. *Atti parlamentari, Senato, Discussioni*, 20 March 1931 (Libertini).
91 ASP CM 16, 'Notizie sull'attività del provveditorato dall'inizio della sua costituzione (Agosto 1925) al 15 Marzo 1929'.
92 Mazza 1937, p. 280 (issue of *La Phalange* dedicated to Sicily).
93 *L'Ora*, 31 December 1928.
94 Checco 1978, pp. 690–1; cf. Stampacchia 1978, p. 588.
95 Tassinari 1938, appendix, p. 79; cf. Lorenzoni 1940, p. 67.
96 Checco 1978, pp. 693–4.
97 ASP CM 10, Mori to the Ministry of the Interior 11 October 1927.
98 SVIMEZ 1954, p. 217; cf. F. Buffoni, 'Tendenze dell'agricoltura 1901–1961', in Sylos-Labini 1966, p. 274.
99 G. Francisci Gerbino, 'Il problema zootecnico in Sicilia', in di Castelnuovo 1934, p. 362; cf. Lupo 1981, pp. 73–7; Aguet 1926, *passim*; Bandini 1957, p. 117.
100 Mori 1932, pp. 346, 370 (and note).

101 ASP CM 17, figures from 'Ufficio anagrafe del bestiame in Sicilia, 1927'.
102 *Sicilia Zootecnica*, July 1928.
103 Mori 1932, p. 349.
104 Giampietro 1926.
105 Sirena 1927, pp. 1–2.
106 Mori 1932, p. 350; cf. ASP CM 17, figures for loans 1924–8.

Chapter 10

1 Franchetti 1974, p. 4.
2 Mori 1932, p. 40.
3 Ibid. pp. 46–7.
4 *Il Tevere*, 7 May 1932.
5 ASP CM 49, speech to I Congresso Regionale ANIF, 6 June 1926
6 ACS PS, 1926, b.90, telegram accompanying copy of *L'Ora*, 7 June 1926.
7 Mori 1932, p. 367; ASP CM 16, 'Bando di Concorso'.
8 Mori 1932, p. 368.
9 ASP CM 9, Antonietta S...(illegible) to Mori, 9 July 1929.
10 Chapman 1973, p. 27.
11 Mori 1932, p. 366.
12 Chapman 1973, p. 148.
13 Ibid. p. 10.
14 Fortunati 1941, p. 39.
15 Chapman 1973, p. 149.
16 Ibid. pp. 148–9.
17 ASP CM 17, Mori to the Ministry of the Interior, 11 October 1927.
18 Mori 1932, pp. 368–9; cf. *Sicilia Nuova*, 7 May 1925; *Il Giornale di Sicilia*, 23 December 1925, 26 July 1928.
19 *Il Giornale d'Italia*, 29 January 1929.
20 Giampietro 1930, p. 28.
21 ASP CM 17, figures for subsidies to families of '*detenuti poveri*'.
22 ASP CM 50, Mussolini to Mori, 30 March 1928; Mori 1932, p. 365; ACS PS, 1928, b.174, Mori to the Ministry of the Interior., 26 December 1928.
23 *L'Ora*, 26 December 1928; *Il Giornale di Sicilia*, 26 December 1928.
24 *L'Ora*, 31 December 1928.
25 *Il Giornale di Sicila*, 26 November 1928.
26 *L'Ora*, 13 October 1928.
27 ASP CM 10, Mori to the Ministry of the Interior, 11 October 1927.
28 ASP CM 10, Mori to the Ministry of Interior, 7 February 1927.
29 *Il Giornale di Sicilia*, 13 June 1927.
30 *Gazzetta del Popolo*, 8 May 1928.
31 ASP CM 'Relazioni, pubblicazioni, studi e discorsi (8)', speech to fascists of Termini Imerese.
32 Ibid. rough notes on Di Giorgio, Cucco, Giunta, Rocco, etc., in Mori's hand.

33 *L'Ora*, 25 December 1928.
34 ASP CM 'Relazioni pubblicazioni, studi e discorsi (8)', speech to Lega Nazionale Antiblasfema, 21 October 1928.
35 *Corriere delle Puglie*, 26 August 1922.
36 ASP CM 17, speech to *combattenti* (undated).
37 Ibid. another speech to *combattenti* (undated).
38 *L'Ora*, 23 January 1928.
39 ASP CM 17, speech inaugurating Congresso Provinciale dei Fasci e degli Enti Autarchi, February 1926.
40 Chapman 1973, p. 155.
41 ASP CM 16, speech to 'Cittadini' of Balestrate (undated).
42 *Sicilia Nuova*, 6 April 1926.
43 ASP CM 10, Archbishop Alessandro Lualdi to Mori, 4 February 1927 (forwarded to Rome with Mori's letter to the Ministry of the Interior, 7 February 1927, denying allegations of police violence).
44 Ibid. Archbishop Ernesto Filippo to Mori, 3 February 1927.
45 *Il Giornale di Sicilia*, 16 August 1927.
46 'La "rinascita siciliana" e la funzione sociale dell'autorità', *La Civiltà cattolica*, 18 June 1927, pp. 491–504.
47 ASP CM 'Relazioni, pubblicazioni, studi e discorsi (8)', speech to Lega Nazionale Antiblasfema, 21 October 1928 (introducing the meeting).
48 Ibid. speech to Lega Nazionale Antiblasfema, 21 October 1928.
49 ACS PS, 1924, b.57, Mori to the Ministry of the Interior, 29 October 1924.
50 *Il Giornale di Sicilia*, 10 September 1928.
51 Ibid. 1 May 1929 (Giuseppe Di Piazza); *L'Ora*, 11 January 1928 (Antonino Naselli and Santi Spena, who was sentenced to five years, and one of '*vigilanza speciale*').
52 ASP CM 10, Mori to the Ministry of the Interior, 11 October 1927.
53 PNF Foglio d'Ordini, N. 31, 6 July 1927.
54 ACS SPCR, b.29, distribution of *tessere* for *Fasci Maschili* up to 5 November 1927.
55 *L'Ora*, 4 March 1929.
56 Cf. De Grazia 1981, p. 119.
57 *L'Ora*, 4 March 1929. For further information about party and trade union membership in Sicily, see Renda 1984–7, vol. II, pp. 378–80; Miccichè 1976, pp. 210–12.
58 ASP, Sottoprefettura di Cefalù, b.9, membership of *fascio* at Gangi, 8 February 1926. No profession is recorded for the remaining twelve

members.

59 Ibid. membership of *fascio* at Isnello, 1925.
60 De Grazia 1981, p. 119.
61 Chapman 1973, p. 127.
62 Ibid. pp. 9, 20, 48, 155.
63 *Il Giornale di Sicilia*, 19 September 1927.
64 Ibid. 31 October 1927.
65 Cf. Di Mino 1933, pp. 93–127; Chapman 1973, pp. 248–51.
66 Ciarlantini 1933, p. 110.
67 Giudice 1971, p. 405.
68 Sciascia 1975, p. 37.
69 Chapman 1973, p. 155.
70 Ibid. p. 249.
71 Ciarlantini 1933, p. 110.
72 ASP CM 17, notes for speech to *squadroni* of San Cipirello and San Giuseppe Iato.
73 Mori 1932, p. 39.
74 ASP CM 'Relazioni, pubblicazioni, studi e discorsi (8)', speech to Palermo *federazione*, June/July 1929.
75 *Il Giornale di Sicilia*, 4 May 1926.
76 Chapman 1973, p. 227.

Chapter 11

1 Mori 1923, p. 92
2 Ibid. p. 121.
3 Ibid. pp. 92–3.
4 ASP CM 16, Mori to the Ministry of the Interior, 5 August 1926; see above p. 142.
5 ASP CM 16, Mori to the Ministry of the Interior, 5 August 1926.
6 Ibid.
7 This can only be a rough estimate based on the average size of *retate* in 1926. Ferri (1928, p. 293) gives 5,000 'arrested and imprisoned' in Palermo province up to the spring of 1928, with 'the same number and more' for the rest of Sicily. This tallies with the figure of 11,000 for Sicily given to Di Giorgio by Mussolini also in the spring of 1928 (Caprì 1977, p. 43). Such figures are probably conservative and obviously exclude those arrested as hostages. Prefect Sallicano of Trapani said in the summer of 1927 that Mori had 'on his conscience the weight of 13,000 arrested men' (ASP CM 10, Armato to Mori, July 1927).
8 ASP CM 16, Mori to the Ministry of the Interior, 5 Aug. 1926.
9 Ibid.
10 Giampietro 1925, p. 49.
11 Ibid. p. 34. For Mori's copy, ASP CM Omaggi 1925–29.
12 Giampietro 1925, p. 47.
13 Loschiavo 1972, pp. 26–7.
14 ACS PS, 1929, sez. 2a, b.40, Prefect Albini to the Ministry of the Interior, 19 July 1929.
15 Archivio Petacco, Giampietro to Mori, 1 October 1929.
16 ASP CM 16, Mori to the Ministry of the Interior, 5 August 1926.
17 ACS PS, 1927, b.128, Mori to the Ministry of the Interior, 13 January 1927.
18 Loschiavo 1972, p. 29.
19 Cucco, *Il mio rogo*, ch. 3, pp. 9–10.
20 Processo di Corleone, Istruttoria, Testi.
21 Ibid.
22 Ibid. Sentenza di Istruttoria, p. 194.
23 Ibid. Dibattimento, p. 107.
24 Loschiavo 1962, pp.117–8.
25 Archivio Petacco, Giovanni Guarino Amella to Mori, 20 July 1929.
26 *The Times*, 20 January 1928, 7 February 1928, 4 May 1929.
27 Medlicott 1928, p. 233, Graham to Chamberlain, 1 August 1928. Graham's informant appears to have been Antonino Di Giorgio, who was a personal friend. Baron Sgadari is referred to by the ambassador as 'the directing brain of the whole organisation' (p. 233).
28 PRO FO 371 14414 C1115, memorandum by McClure, 7 February 1930.
29 Trevelyan 1972, pp. 413–4.
30 *Il Giornale di Sicilia*, 18 February 1927, 29 September 1927, 30 September 1927, 1 October 1927; *L'Ora*, 1 October 1927, 2 October 1927, 4 October 1927, 5 October 1927.
31 *L'Ora*, 16 February 1926; cf. *Sicilia Nuova*, 27 February 1926; *Il Giornale di Sicilia*, 18 February 1927.
32 *Corriere della Sera*, 25 February 1926; *Il Giornale di Sicilia*, 4 October 1927; *The Times*, 20 January 1928; *Daily Mirror*, 13 February 1928.
33 *L'Ora*, 5 October 1927; *Il Giornale di Sicilia*, 4 October 1927.
34 *Il Giornale di Sicilia*, 4 October 1927, 6 October 1927.
35 Ibid. 4 November 1927.
36 *L'Ora*, 5 October 1927, 8 October 1927, 11 October 1927.
37 *Il Giornale di Sicilia*, 11 October 1927.
38 Ibid. 15 October 1927.
39 Ibid. 10 October 1927.
40 Ibid. 14 November 1927.
41 Ibid. 10 October 1927.
42 Ibid. 11 October 1927.

43 Ibid. 8 October 1927.
44 Ibid. 10 October 1927.
45 Ibid. 10 October 1927.
46 See Ortoleva trial, in *Il Giornale di Sicilia*, August 1928–May 1929, in particular 15 November 1928.
47 *Il Giornale di Sicilia*, 4 November 1927.
48 OO xl, 526 (30 November 1927).
49 Ibid. xli 6 (10 January 1928).
50 *Il Giornale di Sicilia*, 4 November 1927.
51 Ibid. 5 December 1927.
52 Ibid. 18 November 1927.
53 Ibid. 29 October 1927.
54 Ibid. 22 November 1927, 1 December 1927.
55 Ibid. 20 November 1927.
56 Ibid. 19 December 1927.
57 Ibid. 11 January 1928.
58 Ibid. 11 January 1928.
59 *La Stampa*, 13 January 1928.
60 *La Tribuna*, 13 January 1928.
61 *Il Popolo d'Italia*, 13 January 1928.
62 *The Times*, 20 January 1928.
63 Ibid.
64 *Daily Herald*, 12 January 1928.
65 *New York Times Magazine*, 4 March 1928.
66 *The Observer*, 22 January 1928.
67 *L'Interprete*, March 1928.
68 ACS PS, 1928, b.164, request by Mori for police reinforcements for trial at Termini, 11 July 1928.
69 *Il Giornale di Sicilia*, 1 May 1929.
70 Ibid. 24 November 1928.
71 Mori 1932, p. 310.
72 *Il Giornale di Sicilia*, 24 November 1928.
73 Ibid. 24 November 1928.
74 Ibid. 24 November 1928.
75 Berardelli 1929.
76 *Il Giornale di Sicilia*, 26 November 1928.
77 Lorenzoni 1940, pp. 49–50.
78 *Il Giornale di Sicilia*, 3 September 1928.
79 ASP CM 50, report by Spanò, 'riservatissima', 3 April 1928, on 'Processo Ortoleva e C.i'.
80 *Il Giornale di Sicilia*, 13 November 1928, 24 November 1928.
81 Piana dei Colli (243), Circondario di Termini Imerese (240), Roccella (174), Mistretta (161), Madonie (154), Bisacquino (153). The Bagheria trial, which began 18 October 1929, had 260 defendants. Some of the accused stood trial for more than one criminal association.
82 Giampietro 1929, p. 9.
83 Ferri 1928, pp. 291–6.
84 Manci 1928, pp. 389–408.
85 Ibid. p. 390.
86 Puglia 1930, pp. 149–50.
87 Ibid. p. 150.
88 Ibid. pp. 150–1.
89 Processo di Corleone, Sentenza di Istruttoria, pp. 257–63.
90 ASP CM 16, Mori to the Ministry of the Interior, 5 August 1926.
91 ASP CM 10, Mori to Suardo, 9 November 1927.
92 ASP CM 21, report by Nicolosi, 18 March 1928; cf. ASP CM 10, Ministry of the Interior to Mori, 1 February 1927.
93 ASP CM 10, Mori to the Ministry of the Interior, 7 February 1927.
94 Ibid. letters from L. Malaguti (4 February 1927) and E. Filippo (3 February 1927), attached to Mori's letter to the Ministry of the Interior, 7 February 1927.
95 Ibid. report of eleven alleged instances of maltreatment by the police, with parallel versions by the police (supplied by the *questura*), attached to Mori's letter to the Ministry of the Interior, 7 February 1927.
96 Sciascia 1975, p. 33.
97 Pantaleone 1966, p. 49; Lewis 1964, p. 62.
98 Cf. Lewis 1964, p. 58.
99 ASP CM 10, two circulars dated 21 May 1926 and 28 June 1926, to Questore, Sottoprefetti, Comandi CC.RR. (Palermo), Funzionari Capi Nucleo Servizio Interprovinciale P.S.
100 Puglia 1930, pp. 452–7.
101 Ibid.
102 De Bella 1933, p. 61.
103 Ibid. p. 66.
104 Di Blasi 1930, p. 227 (n.10).
105 Ibid. pp. 227–8 (n.11).
106 G.G. Loschiavo, 'Il reato di associazione per delinquere nelle province siciliane' (1933), now in Loschiavo 1962, p. 132.
107 Ibid. p. 137, and n.
108 Ibid. p. 145n.
109 Ibid. pp. 147–8.
110 Ibid. p. 149.
111 Ibid. p. 149.
112 Ibid. p. 149.

Chapter 12

1 Cf. G. De Stefani, 'Profilo biografico', in Di Giorgio 1978, pp. XXI-LXIV; *Dizionario dei siciliani illustri*, pp. 182–3; Rochat 1967, p. 521.
2 Caprì 1977, p. 41.

3 Ibid. pp. 42–3.
4 Ibid. pp. 43–8, Di Giorgio to Mussolini, 19 March 1928, with 'nota annessa'. What follows is a resumé.
5 Trevelyan 1972, p. 408 (diary entry for 15 April 1928).
6 Caprì 1977, p. 49.
7 Cf. ASP CM 50, Mori to Under-Secretary of Interior, 7 May 1927.
8 ASP CM 50, Mussolini to Mori, 30 March 1928.
9 ASP CM 5, Questore Crimi to Mori, 25 September 1927; Spanò 1978, p. 61.
10 ASP CM 15.
11 ASP CM 50, report from Mori to Mussolini accompanying Spanò's report on 'Processo Ortoleva', 7 April 1928.
12 Ibid. Mori to Mussolini, 7 April 1928, and accompanying documents.
13 Ibid. report by Spanò on 'Processo Ortoleva', 3 April 1928.
14 Archivio Petacco, Mori's copy of Spanò's report with marginal notes.
15 Caprì 1977, pp. 49–50.
16 Trevelyan 1972, p. 408 (diary entry for 2 May 1928). For the Marchioness De Seta, see ACS SPCR, b.100.
17 Caprì 1977, p. 49.
18 Ibid. p. 50.
19 Ibid. pp. 50–1.
20 Trevelyan 1972, Tina Whitaker's diary, p. 44 (entry for April 1928). The version in Trevelyan p. 410, omits a sentence between 'slapped Mori's face' and 'the lies are innumerable'. The original, though incredulous in tone, does not imply any firm refutation.
21 ASP CM, 'Relazioni, pubblicazioni, studi e discorsi (8)', rough notes on Di Giorgio, Cucco, Giunta, Rocco, etc, in Mori's hand.
22 Caprì 1977, p. 42.
23 Ibid. p. 45.
24 Il Giornale di Sicilia, 15 May 1928; ASP CM 17, for draft of speech.
25 ASP CM 15.
26 ASP CM 'Relazioni, pubblicazioni, studi e discorsi (8)', rough notes on Di Giorgio, etc.
27 Il Giornale di Sicilia, 15 May 1928.
28 ASP CM 10, Mori to Suardo, 9 November 1927.
29 Ibid. Mori to the Ministry of the Interior, 25 January 1928; ibid. reply from Capo Gabinetto, the Ministry of the Interior, 8 February 1928.
30 Il Popolo d'Italia, 23 February 1928.
31 ASP CM 50, Mussolini to Mori, 30 March 1928.
32 Atti parlamentari, Senato, Discussioni, 30 May 1928.
33 Il Giornale di Sicilia, 3 May 1928.
34 Trevelyan 1972, Tina Whitaker's diary (entry for 2 May 1928).
35 Il Giornale di Sicilia, 5 May 1928.
36 Ibid. 16 May 1928; L'Ora, 16 May 1928.
37 Il Giornale di Sicilia, 26 November 1928.
38 L'Ora, 8 October 1928.
39 Ibid. 13 October 1928.
40 For example, L'Avvento Fascista, 9 July 1928.
41 Ibid.
42 Corriere Marittimo Siciliano, 22 July 1928.
43 Il Giornale di Sicilia, 11 February 1928; Washburn Child 1929, in ASP CM 9.
44 L'Impero, 18 May 1926.
45 Il Giornale d'Italia, 16 December 1928.
46 Il Resto di Carlino, 23 January 1929.
47 Il Messaggero, 5 February 1929.
48 ASP CM 38, Comendador con Placa de la Orden del Merito Civil, 27 July 1928.
49 ASP CM 9, Margherita Sarfatti to Mori, 27 December 1928.
50 Piff Paff, 29 December 1928.
51 ASP CM 'Relazioni, pubblicazioni, studi e discorsi (8)', speech by Mori, 28 February 1929.
52 ASP CM 17, speech by Mori, 5 March 1929.
53 Il Giornale di Sicilia, 22 March 1929.
54 Chapman 1973, pp. 155–6.
55 Ibid. p. 156.
56 ASP CM 50, Nicolosi to Mori, 7 May 1928.
57 ASP CM 21, Nicolosi to Mori, 16 April 1928.
58 Ibid. Nicolosi to Mori, 14 June 1928.
59 Ibid. Nicolosi to Mori, 17 April 1928.
60 Ibid. Nicolosi to Mori, 13 July 1928.
61 Ibid. Nicolosi to Mori, 20 July 1928.
62 Ibid. Nicolosi to Mori, 13 December 1928.
63 Ibid. Nicolosi to Mori, 4 January 1929.
64 Ibid. Nicolosi to Mori, 20 January 1929.
65 Ibid. Nicolosi to Mori, 2 February 1929.
66 Ibid. Cucco to Franco Ciarlantini, 11 February 1929.
67 Ibid. Nicolosi to Mori, 26 February 1929.
68 Ibid. Nicolosi to Mori, 1 March 1929.
69 Corriere Marittimo Siciliano, 21 April 1929.
70 ACS PS, 1922, b.141, telegram from the Prefect of Palermo, 30 June 1922.
71 ASP CM 21, Nicolosi to Mori, 6 May

1929.

72 ASP CM 2, Mussolini to Mori, 23 June 1929.

73 ASP CM 9, Mussolini to Mori, 24 June 1929.

74 ASP CM 2, Mori to Mussolini, 7 July 1929.

75 Jung had already tried to intervene with Mussolini on 20 June, along with the Duke of Belsito, Pottino di Capuano, Di Marzo, and Ercole, at the time when rumours first began to circulate in Rome of Mori's impending retirement. (See ACS SPCR, b.86, Guido Jung to Mussolini, 20 June 1929.)

76 ASP CM 2, Guido Jung to Mori, 19 July 1929.

Epilogue

1 Archivio Petacco, Giampietro to Mori, 6 August 1929.

2 ASP CM 9, Archbishop of Monreale to Mori, 29 November 1929.

3 ASP CM 2, Capo Gabinetto, the Ministry of the Interior to Mori, 2 July 1929; Mori's reply, 3 July 1929.

4 Ibid.; cf. ASP CM 2, Vincenzo Valerio to Mori, 3 August 1929.

5 *Atti parlamentari, Senato, Discussioni,* 17 March 1930; cf. *Atti parlamentari, Camera dei Deputati, Discussioni,* 6 March 1930 (Arpinati).

6 Cf. *Corriere della Sera,* 7 May 1932.

7 *Il Tevere,* 7 May 1932.

8 ASP CM 8, Granfiglio to Mori, 9 May 1932. The book sold 1,340 copies in Italy up to June 1933.

9 Starace invited Mori to desist. Cf. ASP CM 12, De Vecchi to Mori, 22 April 1933; and Mori's reply, 25 April 1933.

10 The Bodley Head (Putnam & Co.), Orlo Williams to Huntington, 3 February 1932.

11 *Time and Tide,* 8 April 1933; cf. *Times Literary Supplement,* 23 March 1933. One of the more perceptive reviews was by R. Warner in the *Egyptian Gazette,* 18 May 1933.

12 ASP CM 12, Mori to Mondadori, 2 April 1933.

13 ASP CM 24, draft of short story; ASP CM 'Relazioni, pubblicazioni, studi e discorsi (8)', draft of poem. The poem is probably from earlier in his career.

14 Archivio Petacco, accusation of '*disfattismo*', January 1941.

15 *Il Giornale d'Italia,* 5 June 1931.

16 ACS SPCR, b.39, report (unsigned), Rome, 13 April 1931.

17 Ibid. Cucco to Mussolini, 27 May 1932.

18 Ibid. Cucco to Federzoni, 23 October 1932.

19 Ibid. Federzoni to Mussolini, 24 October 1932.

20 Cf. Deakin 1962, p. 324.

21 ACS SPCR, b.39, report of May 1942 (quoting Starace to Mussolini's secretary, 9 August 1938).

22 ACS, PNF Senatori e Consiglieri Nazionali, Gray to Farnesi, 18 December 1942.

23 Cf. Deakin 1962, p. 324.

24 Cf. Archivio Petacco, profile of Cucco by Aurelio Bruno. The piazza is on the ring-road to the west of the city.

25 For details of Albini's career, see Cannistraro 1982.

26 ACS SPCR, b.25, anonymous letters to Mussolini, November 1929, December 1929, March 1931, etc.

27 Ibid.

28 *Il Giornale di Sicilia,* 20 August 1929.

29 ACS SPCR, b.25, anonymous letter to Mussolini, December 1929.

30 ACS PS, 1929, sez. 2a, b.32, Albini to the Ministry of the Interior, 16 August 1929.

31 ACS PNF Sit. politica ed economica delle provincie, 12 (Palermo), Marziali to Mussolini, 5 Dec 1934; ibid. 6 January 1934.

32 Archivio Petacco, Agnello to Mori, 27 June 1932.

33 Archivio Petacco, Avv. Comm. Giuseppe Sciarrino to Mori, 26 December 1931.

34 Laudani and Travagliante 1984, p. 127.

35 ACS PNF Sit. politica ed economica delle provincie, 12 (Palermo), report of 20 July 1938.

36 Laudani and Travagliante 1984 p. 121; ACS PNF Sit. politica ed economica delle provincie, 12 (Palermo), report of 5 July 1934.

37 ACS PS, 1930–1, sez. II, b.56, report from Albini, 21 April 1930.

38 ACS, PNF Sit. politica ed economica delle provincie, 12 (Palermo), report on Palermo, 13 December 1939.

39 Giordano 1964, p. 86.

40 Bartolini 1934. For the continuance of 'mafia crimes' in the 1930s, see also Renda 1984–87, vol. II, p. 386.

41 ASP CM 9, Vincenzo Messeri to Mori, 20 April 1930.

42 ASP CM 9, ?Giudice (illegible) to

43 *Atti parlamentari, Camera dei Deputati, Discussioni*, 9 April 1932 (Romano).

44 ACS PNF Sit. politica ed economica delle provincie, 12 (Palermo), report of July 1932.

45 Ibid. reports of 13 December 1939, 16 December 1939 (Agostino Rubino), etc.

46 Cf. ibid. reports of 10 April 1934, 16 December 1939.

47 Ibid. report of February 1935.

48 Ibid. report of 13 December 1939.

49 ACS PS 1930–1, sez. II, b.56, Albini to the Ministry of the Interior, 29 November 1930.

50 For what follows see ACS PS, 1930–1, sez. II, b.69, report by Maresciallo Capo RR.CC. on the fire in the Sezione del fascio, Balestrate, 24 April 1931.

51 British Foreign Office reports spoke of the dangers of travelling in the interior of the island. See, for example, FO 371 19549 R6321, Drummond to Hoare, 17 October 1935.

52 See above, pp. 192–3.

53 Tannenbaum 1973, p. 75.

54 See, for example, the various reports on demonstrations in ACS PS, 1930–31, sez. II, b.56, and PS 1932, sez. II, b.49.

55 Fortunati 1941, pp. 38–9.

56 ACS PNF Sit. politica ed economica delle provincie, 12 (Palermo), report of 13 December 1939. For the persistent disarray in the Palermo administration, see for example, ibid. Li Gotti to Starace, 12 April 1939.

57 There are several excellent studies of the Sicilian economy in the 1930s. See in particular Lupo 1981; Checco 1983.

58 SVIMEZ 1954, p. 498.

59 Lupo 1981, pp. 128–42, 171–2.

60 Cf. SVIMEZ 1954, pp. 196, 211, 217.

61 Barone *et al* 1977, p. 508.

62 ACS PNF Sit. politica ed economica delle provincie, 12 (Palermo), report of 13 December 1939.

63 Ibid. report by G. Belelli, 26 May 1939.

64 Barone *et al* 1977, p. 510; cf. Checco, 'Le campagne siciliane nella crisi degli anni Trenta', in Checco 1983, pp. 27–34.

65 Lorenzoni 1940, p. 9.

66 Cf. Ibid. p. 12. Gaetani Macrì 1938, p. 4, refers to 'a few *latifondi*' ('*qualche latifondo*') farmed directly by the owner.

67 See above pp. 197–8; cf. P. Orteca, 'Produzione e fattori della produzione nelle campagne', in Checco 1983, pp. 86–91.

68 Gaetani Macrì 1938, p. 4.

69 The Duke of Belsito, Ettore Pottino di Capuano and Ugo di Paternò were all returned to parliament in 1934. The Prince of Spadafora was *podestà* of Palermo in the early 1930s. For other indications of the continuing power of the *agrari*, see Barone *et al* 1977, p. 517. See also Renda 1984–87, pp. 275–77.

70 Gaetani Macrì 1938, p. 4.

71 Di Castelnuovo 1934.

72 Dott. Pipitone Cannone, 'Aspetti inesplorati del problema siciliano', in di Castelnuovo 1934, pp. 625–87.

73 Mack Smith 1968, vol. II, p. 520.

74 A number of the reports in ACS PNF Sit. politica ed economica delle provincie, 12 (Palermo) contain warnings about growing hostility to the regime, particularly in the later 1930s. The British Foreign Office catalogue for 1935 refers to a report on a 'movement by 2,000 Sicilians to make Sicily an independent republic'. The report is now missing.

75 For a recent appraisal, see Stampacchia 1978, pp. 586–610.

76 FO371 29930 R9810, report from the Greek Minister, 10 November 1941; cf. FO 371 30093 R8824, report from Admiral Kelly, 28 September 1941.

77 FO 371 29931 R10578, report from Prof. Stranski, December 1941.

78 Ibid.

79 FO 371 33220 R6784, memorandum prepared by Political Warfare Executive, August 1942.

80 The case for collaboration is given in Campbell 1977. The idea that 'Lucky' Luciano gave invaluable assistance is not substantiated. He had been in prison since 1936, and there is nothing to suggest that he did more than provide information. Unlike Vito Genovese he was not allowed to accompany the allied troops to Sicily. Campbell in fact says: 'Just how useful [Naval Intelligence's] maps and files were in mounting the invasion of Sicily must remain a matter of conjecture' (p. 142). Genovese clearly convinced the authorities that he might be useful, and was given some form of liaison position in Nola. He does not appear to have been regarded in any sense as special; cf. Renda 1984–87, vol. III, p. 96.

81 Cf. Campbell 1977, p. 176.

82 Cf. Smith 1975, pp. 62–89.

83 Campbell 1977, pp. 181–2.

84 Ibid. p. 180.

85 Ibid. p. 184.
86 Gaja 1962, pp. 116–7.
87 Harris 1957, p. 63.
88 W. Raith, epilogue to Hess 1984, p. 256.
89 Michele Pantaleone's opposition to Don Calò seems to date from the war years, when the two men found themselves in opposing parties in Villalba. One interpretation of Pantaleone's writings is that they are the continuation of a political and personal battle by other means. His best known book, *Mafia e politica, 1943–1962* (Pantaleone 1962), revolves to a large extent around Don Calò. It was translated into English in 1966.

SELECT BIBLIOGRAPHY

Manuscript sources

The principal documentary source for the second part of this book is the personal archive of Cesare Mori. His papers were given to the historian and journalist, Arrigo Petacco, by an elderly relative of the prefect, some ten years ago. Signor Petacco presented them to the Archivio di Stato, Pavia, where they are now kept. When I consulted them in 1981, they were still uncatalogued, and were contained in fifty stiff but decaying cardboard folders. I asked the archivists to number each file in pencil as I used it; and this is the numeration I have used in this book. Since then, the Ministry of the Interior has forbidden access to the most interesting of the papers on the grounds that they contain material 'of a personal nature'. It is to be hoped that this regrettable decision will soon be reversed. Several important documents (chiefly those quoted in his book, *Il prefetto di ferro*) were retained by Signor Petacco (as he was fully entitled to do). I have referred to them under the heading 'Archivio Petacco'.

Mori was an instinctive hoarder, and preserved everything from gas bills to press cuttings. He made no attempt, it seems, to vet his papers. Chance, rather than design, probably accounts for any filtering that has taken place. However, much of what transpired during Mori's operation is likely to have remained unrecorded. The petty intrigues that constituted so much of political life in Sicily can often only be guessed at. Friendships and clienteles are also all too frequently elusive. The historian of Sicily is particularly ill-served when it comes to 'public opinion'. In the first place, the great majority of people were illiterate, and lacked the means and channels whereby they could voice their feelings. Secondly, common sense taught that it was usually better to be silent than to speak. This was particularly true when it came to the issue of the mafia: a careless word might cost a person his livelihood or even his life.

The Archivio Centrale dello Stato at Rome contained much that was useful. The files for the Ministry of the Interior (*Direzione Generale di Pubblica Sicurezza*) were particularly important. I consulted nearly a hundred for the years 1920 to 1932, with the emphasis, naturally, on the period 1924 to 1929. I also looked at about a dozen files from the *Carteggio Riservato del Duce*. The *Carteggio Michele Bianchi* had much that was interesting on the situation in Sicily down to 1923. The same applied to the series *Gabinetto*

Finzi, Ordine Pubblico (1922–24). The *Carte Farinacci,* though uncatalogued, yielded a few items of interest. As far as Sicilian fascism was concerned, the period prior to the March on Rome was fairly well served by the files of the *Mostra della Rivoluzione Fascista.* The years subsequent to 1922 were not well documented, certainly for Palermo. *PNF, Situazione Politica ed Economica delle Provincie* had several enlightening reports on Palermo for the 1930s. By contrast, *PNF, Segreteria Amministrativa Federazioni Provinciali* was prosaic, and for the most part unrevealing. Some items of interest were to be found in the file *PNF, Federazioni Provinciali di Catania, Palermo, Siracusa (1923 –43).*

I had considerable difficulty in gaining access to archival material in Sicily. A year of letter-writing and lobbying passed before I received permission to consult documents in the Archivio di Stato, Palermo. However, the waiting proved worthwhile. There was much of value on provincial fascism in the series *Questura di Palermo, Atti di Gabinetto 1920–43.* Many of the files on individual fascist sections were withheld from me, on the grounds that they had information relating to specific crimes. My feeling is that the process of censorship was arbitrary and largely a token gesture, as many of the files I did consult also had material on criminal activity. The *Gabinetto Prefettura* series was restricted to the years down to 1925. More profitable for the period of Mori's campaign were the files for the *Sottoprefetture* of Termini Imerese, Corleone, and Cefalù.

The archives at Trapani were badly damaged in the last war, and what remains is in great disarray. I found only one file from the *Prefettura* that was in any way pertinent. The Agrigento archives suffered from relative inaccessibility. They had moved several times in recent years and nobody knew where they were. In the end I found them at the back of a very luxurious sweet factory a few miles from the centre of the town. I was assured that nothing of relevance survived from the 1920s, and the inventories I saw bore this out. The same applied at Caltanissetta. I made no attempt to consult state archives in the east of the island, thought at Catania I had access to the privately owned Archivio Carnazza, and found several letters that had a bearing on the research.

At Palermo, Orietta Sorgi allowed me to see a complete set of photocopies of the Corleone criminal association, 1926–30. These had been obtained, in exceptional circumstances, with the help of her father, Avv. Antonino Sorgi. The Cucco family gave me the typescript of Alfredo's unpublished autobiography and allowed me to photocopy it. This work deals almost entirely with the decade down to the early 1930s, and in particular with the author's judicial rehabilitation. It was written shortly after the war, and is about 150 pages in length. Though originally intended as a book, the author came to the conclusion that it was of insufficient general interest to merit publication. I accepted help from the Cucco family on the strict understanding that it was unconditional.

The Fondazione Gentile in the Via Nomentana at Rome has a rich and well-catalogued collection of letters written by and to the philosopher. Those that related to the political situation in Trapani while Mori was prefect there were extremely helpful. Professor Renzo De Felice let me photocopy an interesting pamphlet in his possession on the Palermo elections of 1925. Signora Argentieri, Luigi Federzoni's daughter, allowed me to browse through some of her father's papers. Very little seems to have remained from his time as Minister of the Interior. I found nothing that referred to Mori or indeed to Sicily. Rosita Lanza di Scalea showed me a number of interesting items relating to her father, Giuseppe, and her uncle, Pietro, and Raleigh Trevelyan gave me transcripts of hitherto unpublished sections of Tina Whitaker's diary.

In England, the Foreign Office papers at Kew proved disappointing for Sicily in the 1920s. A number of potentially interesting items relating to Mori's campaign were listed in the inventory, but they had not been preserved. The only relevant contemporary document was Ambassador Graham's lengthy report on Italy, of 1928, which contained some stringent comments on Sicily. However, the early 1930s were richer, with a series of papers dealing with corruption in the Palermo administration in 1934. The French Foreign office archives in Paris were as disappointing as their English counterparts. Nothing at all on Sicily had been preserved for the period of Mori's stay at Palermo. The St Antony's Documents at Oxford furnished the text of an important letter from Federzoni and a telegram from Mussolini.

AGNETTA, F., 1892, *Brevi osservazioni sulla pubblica sicurezza in Sicilia e sui mezzi più acconci di instaurarla* (Rome).

AGUET, J., 1926, *Come conseguire nel Mezzogiorno la vittoria del grano, creare cambi e capitali* (Rome).

ALATRI, P., 1954, *Lotte politiche in Sicilia sotto il governo della Destra (1866–74)* (Turin).

ALBINI, J.L., 1971, *The American Mafia. Genesis of a Legend* (New York).

ALONGI, G., 1887, *La maffia nei suoi fattori e nelle sue manifestazioni. Studio sulle classi pericolose della Sicilia* (Turin).

———, 1894, 'Le condizioni economiche e sociali della Sicilia', Archivio di psichiatria, scienze penali ed antropologia criminale (Turin), vol. xv, pp. 229–55.

ANON., 1867, *Il Foro alla Commissione d'inchiesta* (Palermo).

ANON., 1863, *Results of Victor Emanuel's Rule. By an Eye-Witness* (London).

ANON., 1864, *The State of Sicily. From the Official Reports of the Debates in the Parliament of Turin* (London).

ANON., 1891, 'Wild justice at New Orleans', *The Saturday Review* (London), 21 March 1891, pp. 341–2.

ANTINORI, G., 1877, *La Sicilia. Quistioni economiche, amministrative e politiche* (Palermo).

APPIANI, G., 1927, 'La giustizia nel nuovo stato', *Gerarchia* (Milan), January 1927, pp. 17–31.

ARCOLEO, G., 1898, *Palerme et la civilisation en Sicile* (Paris).

ARLACCHI, P. et al, 1982, *Morte di un generale. L'assassinio di Carlo Alberto Dalla Chiesa, la mafia, la droga, il potere politico* (Milan).

AVELLONE, G.B., and MORASCA, S., 1911, *Mafia* (Rome).

BALBO, I., 1932, *Diario 1922* (Milan).

BANDINI, M., 1957, *Cento anni di storia agraria italiana* (Rome).

BARONE, G., 1983, 'Politica economica e istituzioni. Il Ministero dei Lavori pubblici, 1922–1925', *Italia contemporanea* (Milan), September 1983, pp. 5–40.

_____, 1984, 'Statalismo e riformismo: l'Opera Nazionale Combattenti (1917–1923)', *Studi storici* (Rome), January-March 1984, pp. 203–44.

_____, LUPO, S., PALIDDA, R., and SAIJA, M., 1977a, *Potere e società in Sicilia nella crisi dello stato liberale* (Catania).

_____, LUPO, S., SAIJA, M., and VITTORIO, A., 1977b, 'La Sicilia negli anni Trenta: appunti di ricerca', *Archivio storico per la Sicilia orientale* (Catania), fasc. 3, pp. 507–23.

BARTOLINI, C., 1934, *Corte d'appello di Palermo. Inaugurazione dell'anno giudiziario XIII dell'E.F.* (Palermo).

BATTAGLIA, T., and GIURATO, T., 1923, *Tre anni di battaglie 1919–1922* (Ragusa).

BERARDELLI, A., 1929, *Contro la mafia e per la giustizia* (Rome).

BIANCO, A., 1923, *Il fascismo in Sicilia* (Catania).

BLOK, A., 1974, *The Mafia of a Sicilian Village 1860–1960. A Study of Violent Peasant Entrepreneurs* (Oxford).

BOLZON, P., 1927, *Nel solco della vittoria* (Milan).

BONFADINI, R., 1876, *Relazione della giunta per l'inchiesta sulle condizioni della Sicilia del 1876* (Rome).

BRANCACCIO DI CARPINO, F., 1901, *Tre mesi nella Vicaria di Palermo nel 1860*, 2nd edition (Naples).

BRANCATO, F., 1964a, 'Genesi e psicologia della mafia', *Nuovi quaderni del Meridione* (Palermo), January–March 1964, pp. 5–26.

_____, 1964b 'La mafia, l'Internazionale socialista e una diagnosi inedita', *Nuovi quaderni del Meridione* (Palermo), January–March 1964, pp. 37–51.

_____, 1966a, 'Il Marchese di Rudinì, Francesco Bonafede e la rivolta del 1866', *Nuovi quaderni del Meridione* (Palermo), October–December 1966, pp. 460–91.

_____, 1966b, 'La rivolta palermitana del 1866 nella critica storica', *Nuovi quaderni del Meridione* (Palermo), October–December 1966, pp. 525–55.

BRONZINI, G., 1929, 'Il problema del Mezzogiorno nella concezione fascista', *Vita nova* (Bologna), May 1929, pp. 385–7.

BRUCCOLERI, G., 1913, *La Sicilia di oggi. Appunti economici* (Rome).

BRUNO, C., 1900, *La Sicilia e la mafia* (Rome).

BUA, G.F., 1867, *Palermo. Governanti e governati prima e dopo il tumulto di settembre* (Palermo).

CAMPBELL, R., 1977, *The Luciano Project. The Secret Wartime Collaboration of the Mafia and the U.S. Navy* (New York).

CANNISTRARO, P.V. (ed.), 1982, *Historical Dictionary of Fascist Italy* (Westport).

CANTÙ, C., 1872–77, *Della indipendenza italiana. Cronistoria*, 3 vols, (Turin).

CAPRÌ, G., 1977, 'Di Giorgio e Mori ai ferri corti', *L'Osservatore politico letterario* (Milan), January 1977, pp. 38–55.

CAPUANA, L., 1914, 'La Sicilia e il brigantaggio', reprinted in L. Capuana, *Isola del sole* (Catania).

CASACCIO, V., 1935, *Frammenti di azione fascista in terra iblea* (San Remo).

CELENTANO, M., 1934, *Relazione sull'attività del fascio palermitano di combattimento dalla costituzione al 30 aprile 1922* (Palermo).

CERRITO, G. (ed.), 1955, *La Sicilia dal 1860 al 1870. Antologia di documenti* (Messina).

CHAPMAN, C.G., 1973, *Milocca. A Sicilian Village* (London).

CHECCO, A., 1978, 'Le campagne siciliane degli anni Venti', *Archivio storico per la Sicilia orientale* (Catania), fasc. 2–3, 1978, pp. 645–703.

————, (ed.), 1983, *Banca e latifondo nella Sicilia degli anni Trenta* (Naples).

CHIURCO, G., 1929, *Storia della rivoluzione fascista 1919–1922*, 5 vols. (Florence).

CIARLANTINI, F., 1933, *Mussolini immaginario* (Milan).

CIOTTI, G., 1866, *I casi di Palermo. Cenni storici sugli avvenimenti di settembre 1866* (Palermo).

La Civiltà cattolica (Rome), 18 June 1927, pp. 491–504 ('La "rinascita siciliana" e la funzione sociale dell'autorità', n.a.).

COLAJANNI, N., 1900, *Nel regno della mafia. Dai Borboni ai Sabaudi* (Rome).

Come il governo ha vinto a Palermo, anonymous pamphlet (undated, but August – September 1925), in Archivio De Felice, Rome.

CORDOVA, F. (ed.), 1980, *Uomini e volti del fascismo* (Rome).

CORNER, P., 1975, *Fascism in Ferrara, 1915–1925* (Oxford).

CORSELLI, R., 1931, 'La Sicilia nella Grande Guerra', *Rassegna storica del Risorgimento* (Rome), January–March 1931, Supplement (XVIII Congresso sociale di Palermo, 7–9 May 1930), pp. 164–76.

CORSI, C., 1894, *Sicilia*, (Turin–Florence).

COSTANZA, S., 1964, 'Una inchiesta poco nota sulla mafia', *Nuovi quaderni del Meridione* (Palermo), January-March 1964, pp. 52–8.

————, 1966, 'La rivolta contro i "Cutrara" a Castellammare del Golfo (1862)', *Nuovi quaderni del Meridione* (Palermo), October–December 1966, pp. 1–20.

CRISPI, F., 1924, *Politica interna. Diario e documenti* (ed. T. Palamenghi-Crispi), (Milan).

CUCCO, A., *Il mio rogo* (unpublished autobiography).

————, 1950, *Non volevamo perdere* (Rocca San Casciano).

————, 1957, *Questo deprecato decennio* (Palermo).

CURCIO, G., 'Il Mezzogiorno e la nuova politica nazionale', *Critica fascista* (Rome), 1 August 1925a, pp. 281–5, 15 August 1925b, pp. 310–14.

CUTRERA, A., 1900a, *La Mafia ed i Mafiosi. Origini e manifestazioni* (Palermo).

_____, 1900b, *La Mala Vita di Palermo. Contributo di sociologia criminale*, 2nd edition (Palermo).

D'ALESSANDRO, E., 1959, *Brigantaggio e mafia in Sicilia* (Messina–Florence).

DAMIANI, A., 1881–6, *Relazione sulla prima circoscrizione*, in *Atti della giunta per la inchiesta agraria e sulle condizioni della classe agricola*, vol. XIII (Rome).

DA PASSANO, M. (ed.), 1981, *I moti di Palermo del 1866. Verbali della commissione parlamentare di inchiesta* (Camera dei Deputati, Rome).

DAVIS, J., 1988, *Conflict and Control. Law and Order in Nineteenth-Century Italy* (London).

DEAKIN, F.W., 1962, *The Brutal Friendship. Mussolini, Hitler and the Fall of Italian Fascism* (London).

DE ANTONELLIS, G., 1977, *Il Sud durante il fascismo* (Manduria).

DE BEGNAC, Y., 1950, *Palazzo Venezia. Storia di un regime* (Rome).

DE BELLA, V., 1933, *Il reato di associazione a delinquere* (Turin).

DE BLASIO, A., 1894a, 'Il tatuaggio dei camorristi e delle prostitute di Napoli', *Archivio di psichiatria, scienze penali ed antropologia criminale* (Turin), vol. xv (1894), pp. 185–204.

_____, 1894b 'Ulteriori ricerche intorno al tatuaggio dei camorristi napoletani', *Archivio di psichiatria, scienze penali ed antropologia criminale* (Turin), vol. xv (1894), pp. 510–29.

DE CASTRO, G., 1862, *Il mondo segreto* (Milan).

DE FELICE, F., 1956, *Storia del teatro siciliano* (Catania).

DE FELICE, R., 1965, *Mussolini il rivoluzionario* (Turin).

_____, 1966, *Mussolini il fascista (i)* (Turin).

_____, 1968, *Mussolini il fascista (ii)* (Turin).

DE FELICE GIUFFRIDA, G., 1901, *La questione sociale in Sicilia* (Rome).

DE GRAZIA, V., 1981, *The Culture of Consent. Mass Organization of Leisure in Fascist Italy* (Cambridge).

DEMARCO, D., BRANCATO, F., LAURO, P. and LA DUCA, R., 1969, *Centocinquanta anni della camera di commercio di Palermo, 1819–1969* (Palermo).

DE SECLY, L., 1926, *La conquista regia. Il Mezzogiorno e il fascismo* (Trani).

DESJARDINS, A., 1891, 'Le droit des gens et la loi de lynch aux États-Unis', *Revue des deux mondes* (Paris), 15 May 1891, pp. 321–55.

DI BLASI, F.U., 1930, 'Il reato di associazione per delinquere nel codice vigente e nel progetto del nuovo codice penale', *Giurisprudenza italiana* (Turin), November 1930, pp. 225–30.

DI CASTELNUOVO A. (ed.), 1934, *La Sicilia. Affermazioni e orientamenti* (Rome).

DI GIORGIO, A., 1978, *Ricordi della Grande Guerra (1915–1918)* (Fondazione G. Whitaker, Palermo).

DI MINO, C., 1933, 'L'Italia di Mussolini cantata dal popolo siciliano', *La Sicilia nel Risorgimento italiano* (Palermo), July–December 1933, pp. 93 –127.

DI RUDINÌ, A., 1895, 'Terre incolte e latifondi', *Giornale degli economisti* (Bologna), February 1895, pp. 141–231.

DI SAN GIULIANO, A., 1894, *Le condizioni presenti della Sicilia. Studii e proposte* (Milan).

Dizionario dei siciliani illustri, 1939 (Palermo).

Documents on British Foreign Policy 1919–1939 – *see* Medlicott *et al.* 1973.

DOLCI, D., 1963, *Waste. An Eyewitness Report on some Aspects of Waste in Western Sicily* (Translated by R. Munroe) (London).

Enciclopedia italiana, 1932–48 (Rome).

FALCIONELLI, A., 1936, *Les sociétés secrètes italiennes* (Paris).

FALCONCINI, E., 1863, *Cinque mesi di prefettura in Sicilia* (Florence).

FALZONE, G., 1971, 'Cesare Mori, prefetto contadino', *L'Osservatore politico letterario* (Milan), June 1971, pp. 31–6.

———, 1975, *Storia della mafia* (Milan).

FARINACCI, R., 1927, *Un periodo aureo del Partito nazionale fascista* (ed. R. Bacchetta) (Foligno).

———, 1937–39, *Storia della rivoluzione fascista*, 3 vols. (Cremona).

FEDERZONI, L., 1967, *Italia di ieri per la storia di domani* (Milan).

FERRI, E., 1978, 'La lotta contro la mafia in Sicilia', *La Scuola positiva* (Milan), July–August 1928, pp. 289–96.

FILIBERTO DI MARCO, G., 1937, *Clima di una impresa storica. Come il Duce ed il fascismo hanno creato la nuova coscienza della Sicilia* (Palermo).

FINCATI, E., 1881, *Un anno in Sicilia, 1877–78. Ricordi di un bersagliere* (Rome).

FIUME, G., 1984a, *Le bande armate in Sicilia (1819–1849). Violenza e organizzazione del potere* (Annali della Facoltà di lettere e filosofia dell'università di Palermo).

———, 1984b, 'Mafia, società e potere nella Sicilia contemporanea', *Storia contemporanea* (Bologna), October 1984, pp. 963–70.

FORNARI, H.D., 1971, *Mussolini's Gadfly. Roberto Farinacci* (Nashville).

FORTUNATI, P., 1941, *Aspetti sociali dell'assalto al latifondo* (Rome).

FRANCHETTI 1974, *see* Franchetti and Sonnino, vol I.

FRANCHETTI, L. and SONNINO, S., 1974, *Inchiesta in Sicilia* (first published in 1877 as *La Sicilia nel 1876*, 2 vols. (Florence)); new edition with 1925 preface by E. Cavalieri, vol. I, *Condizioni politiche e amministrative*, vol. II, *I contadini* (Florence).

FRIED, R.C., 1963, *The Italian Prefects. A Study in Administrative Politics* (New Haven).

FRISELLA VELLA, G., 1928, *Temi e problemi sulla cosidetta questione meridionale* (Palermo).

FULCO DI VERDURA, 1976, *The Happy Summer Days. A Sicilian Childhood* (London).

GAETA, F., 1965, *Nazionalismo italiano* (Naples).

GAETANI MACRÌ, V., 1938, 'Il latifondo siciliano', *Problemi mediterranei* (Palermo), November–December 1938, pp. 334–53.

GAJA, F., 1962, *L'esercito della lupara. Baroni e banditi siciliani nella guerriglia contro l'Italia* (Milan).

GANCI, S.M., 1966, 'La rivolta palermitana del settembre 1866', *Nuovi quaderni del Meridione* (Palermo), October–December 1966, pp. 381–418.

———, 1980, *La Sicilia contemporanea* (Naples–Palermo).

GENOVESE, A., 1964, *Paceco. Un comune agricolo della Sicilia occidentale. 1860–1923* (Trapani).

GENTILE, G., 1917, *Il tramonto della cultura siciliana* (Bologna).

GENTILE, N., 1963, *Vita di capomafia* (Rome).

GIAMPIETRO, L., 1925, *Relazione statistica dei lavori compiuti ne l'anno giudiziario 1925 nel distretto de la corte d'appello di Palermo*.

———, 1926, *Relazione statistica dei lavori compiuti ne l'anno giudiziario 1926 nel distretto de la corte d'appello di Palermo*.

———, 1929, *Relazione statistica dei lavori compiuti nell'anno giudiziario 1929 nel distretto della corte d'appello di Palermo*.

———, 1930, *Relazione statistica dei lavori compiuti nell'anno giudiziario 1930 nel distretto della corte d'appello di Palermo*.

GIORDANO, A., 1964, 'La mafia nelle relazioni inaugurali degli anni giudiziari dall'Unità ad oggi', *Nuovi quaderni del Meridione* (Palermo), January–March 1964, pp. 72–90.

Giornale degli eruditi e dei curiosi (Padua), 1 January 1884

GIUDICE, G., 1971, *Benito Mussolini* (Turin).

GIURIATI, G., 1981, *La parabola di Mussolini nei ricordi di un gerarca* (ed. E. Gentile) (Rome).

GRIFFITHS, A., 1901, *Mysteries of Police and Crime. A General Survey of Wrongdoing and its Pursuit*, special edition, 3 vols. (London).

GUERCIO, F.M., 1938, *Sicily* (London).

HARRIS, C.R.S., 1957, *Allied Military Administration of Italy, 1943–1945* (London).

HECKETHORN, C.W., 1897, *The Secret Societies of all Ages and Countries*, new edition, 2 vols. (London).

HESS, H., 1984, *Mafia*, new edition, with an epilogue by W. Raith (Bari).

HOBSBAWM, E.J., 1959, *Primitive Rebels. Studies in Archaic Forms of Social Movement in the 19th and 20th Centuries* (Manchester).

IMPASTATO, R., 1926, *Il fascismo in Sicilia* (Palermo).

LANZA, G., 1936, *Le carte di Giovanni Lanza*, (ed. De Vecchi di Val Cismon), vol. III (1865), (R. deputazione subalpina di storia patria, Turin).

LAUDANI, S., and TRAVAGLIANTE, P., 1984, 'Palermo e Catania: dinamica demografica e trasformazioni urbane (1880–1940)', *Storia urbana* (Milan), April–June 1984, pp. 99–131.

LESTINGI, G., 1884, 'L'associazione della Fratellanza nella provincia di Girgenti', *Archivio di psichiatria, scienze penali ed antropologia criminale* (Turin), vol. v (1884), pp. 452–63.

LEWIS, N., 1964, *The Honoured Society. The Mafia Conspiracy Observed* (London).

LICATA, B., 1959, 'Le Madonie dall'Unificazione all'Autonomia', *Sicilia al lavoro* (Palermo), July–August 1959, pp. 8–67.

LINARES, V., 1886, *Racconti popolari* (Palermo).

LOMBROSO, C., 1879, *Sull'incremento del delitto in Italia e sui mezzi per arrestarlo* (Turin).

––––––, 1889, *L'uomo delinquente in rapporto all'antropologia, alla giurisprudenza ed alle discipline carcerarie*, 4th edition, 2 vols. (Turin).

––––––, 1899, *Le crime. Causes et remèdes* (Paris).

LONCAO, E., 1900, *Il lavoro e le classi rurali in Sicilia durante e dopo il feudalismo* (Palermo).

LORENZONI, G., 1910, *Inchiesta parlamentare sulle condizioni dei contadini nelle provincie meridionali e nella Sicilia*, (vol. vi of the Faina report), 2 vols. (Rome).

LORENZONI, G., 1923, 'Latifundia in Sicily and their possible transformation', *International Review of Agricultural Economics* (Rome), July–September 1923, pp. 316–49.

LORENZONI, G., 1940, *Trasformazione e colonizzazione del latifondo siciliano* (Florence).

LOSCHIAVO, G.G., 1962, *100 anni di mafia* (Rome).

––––––, 1972 'Il terribile Giampietro', *Gli Oratori del giorno* (Rome), September–October 1972, pp. 25–30.

LUMBROSO, G., 1925, *La crisi del fascismo* (Florence).

LUMIA, L., *Contadini e mafia nel primo dopoguerra* (unpublished typescript, coll. James Fentress, Rome).

LUPO, S., 1981, *Blocco agrario e crisi in Sicilia tra le due guerre* (Naples).

LYTTELTON, A., 1973, *The Seizure of Power. Fascism in Italy 1919–1929* (London).

MACK SMITH, D., 1968, *A History of Sicily. Medieval and Modern Sicily*, 2 vols., (vol. i, *Medieval Sicily, 800–1713*; vol. ii, *Modern Sicily after 1713*) (London).

––––––, 1971, *Victor Emanuel, Cavour and the Risorgimento* (Oxford).

MAGGIORANI, V., 1869/70, *Il sollevamento della plebe di Palermo e del circondario nel settembre 1866*, 3rd edition (Palermo).

Il Magistrato dell'ordine, June 1925, in ASP CM 17.

MANCI, F., 1929, 'Il problema della delinquenza in Sicilia', *La Scuola positiva* (Milan), September–October 1928, pp. 389–408.

MARINO, G.C., 1964, *L'opposizione mafiosa (1870–1882). Baroni e mafia contro lo stato liberale* (Palermo).

––––––, 1976, *Partiti e lotta di classe in Sicilia da Orlando a Mussolini* (Bari).

MAZZA, A., 1937, 'Le Duce et la Sicile', *La Phalange* (Paris), 15 September –15 December 1937, pp. 280–3.

MAZZAMUTO, P., 1964, 'La mafia nella letteratura', *Nuovi quaderni del Meridione* (Palermo), January–March 1964, pp. 127–68.

MEDLICOTT, W., DAKIN, D., and LAMBERT, M., (ed.), 1973, *Documents on British Foreign Policy 1919–1939*, series 1a, vol. v (1928), (London).

MERCADANTE CARRARA, T., 1911, *La delinquenza in Sicilia nelle sue forme più gravi o specifiche* (Palermo).

MERLINO, F.S., 1890, *L'Italie telle qu'elle est*, 2nd edition, (Paris).

MERLINO, S., 1894, 'Camorra, maffia and brigandage', *Political Science Quarterly* (New York), September 1894, pp. 466–85.

MICCICHÈ, G., 1976, *Dopoguerra e fascismo in Sicilia 1919–1927* (Rome).

MIGNOSI, P., 1925, 'La mafia', *La Rivoluzione liberale* (Turin), 25 October 1925, pp. 153–4.

MINGHETTI, M., 1978, *Copialettere, 1873–1876* (ed. M. Cuccoli), 2 vols. (Rome).

MOLÈ, G., 1929, *Studio-inchiesta sui latifondi siciliani* (Rome).

MONHEIM, R., 1972, 'La città rurale nella struttura dell'insediamento della Sicilia centrale', *Annali del Mezzogiorno* (Catania), vol. xii, 1972, pp. 195–303.

MONNIER, M., 1863, *La Camorra. Mystères de Naples* (Paris).

MONTANELLI, I., 1955, *Pantheon minore. Incontri* (Milan).

MORI, C., 1923, *Tra le zagare oltre la foschia* (Florence).

——, 1932, *Con la mafia ai ferri corti* (Milan). English edition, (translated by O. Williams), *The Last Struggle with the Mafia* (London, 1933).

MOSCA, G., 1980, *Uomini e cose di Sicilia* (ed. V. Frosini), (Palermo).

NAVARRA CRIMI, G., 1925, *Problemi dell'economia siciliana* (Turin–Genoa).

NICEFORO, A., 1898, *Italia barbara contemporanea* (Milan).

——, 1901, *Italiani del Nord e italiani del Sud* (Turin).

NICOLOSI, P., 1979, *Palermo fin de siècle* (Milan).

NICOTRI, G., 1906, *Rivoluzioni e rivolte in Sicilia. Studio di psicologia sociale* (Palermo).

NOVACCO, D., 1959, 'Considerazioni sulla fortuna del termine "mafia" ', *Belfagor* (Florence), vol. xiv, 1959, pp. 206–12

——, 1963, *Inchiesta sulla mafia* (Milan).

——, 1964, 'Bibliografia della mafia', *Nuovi quaderni del Meridione* (Palermo), January–March 1964.

PAGANO, G., 1867, *Sette giorni d'insurrezione a Palermo. Cause, fatti, rimedi* (Palermo).

——, 1875, *Le presenti condizioni della Sicilia e i mezzi per migliorarle* (Florence).

——, 1877, *La Sicilia nel 1876–77* (Palermo).

Panorami di realizzazioni del fascismo, vol. VI: *Il movimento delle squadre nell'Italia meridionale e insulare* (Rome, 1942).

PANTALEONE, M., 1962, *Mafia e politica, 1943–1962*, with a preface by C. Levi (Turin); English edition, *The Mafia and Politics* (London, 1966).

PANTANO, E., 1933, *Memorie. Dai rintocchi della Gancia a quelli di S. Giusto*, vol. I (1860–70) (Bologna).

PANZINI, A., 1935, *Dizionario moderno delle parole che non si trovano negli altri dizionari*, 7th edition, (Milan).

Foglio d'ordini 1926, 1927, (occasional publication of the Partito Nazionale Fascista).

PATON, W.A., 1898, *Picturesque Sicily* (London).

PEREZ, M.se., *Francesco Perez e la rivoluzione fascista. (Omaggio al Duce, maggio 1924)*, in AS Palermo GP, b.53.

PETACCO, A., 1978, *Il prefetto di ferro. Cesare Mori e la Mafia*, new edition (Milan).

PIGNATO, L., 1925, 'Dopo Palermo', *La Rivoluzione liberale* (Turin), 30 August 1925, p. 122.

PITRÉ, G., 1889, *Usi e costumi, credenze e pregiudizi del popolo siciliano*, 4 vols. (Palermo).

POLICASTRO, G., 1929, *Mussolini e la Sicilia* (Mantua).

PORTO, S., 1977, *Mafia e fascismo. L'azione del prefetto Mori in Sicilia 1925–1929* (Palermo).

PRESTIANNI, N., 1929, 'I patti agari in Sicilia', *Il Monitore tecnice* (Rome), 31 March 1929, p. 149.

————, 1931, *Inchiesta sulla piccola proprietà coltivatrice formatasi nel dopoguerra* (Rome).

PRETI, D., 1973, 'La politica agraria del fascismo: note introduttive', *Studi storici* (Rome), October–December 1973, pp. 802–69.

PROCACCI, G., 1956, *Le elezioni del 1874 e l'opposizione meridionale* (Milan).

PUGLIA, G.M., 1930a, 'Il carcere preventivo', *La Scuola positiva* (Milan), March–April 1930, pp. 149–52.

————, 1930b, 'Il mafioso non è un associato per delinquere', *La Scuola positiva* (Milan), October–November 1930, pp. 452–7.

RAFFIOTTA, G., 1959, *La Sicilia nel primo ventennio del secolo XX* (vol. III of *Storia della Sicilia post-unificazione*, 3 vols., Bologna – Palermo, 1956–9) (Palermo).

RAGUSA, P., 1934, *Lo squadrismo palermitano* (Palermo).

REECE, J.E., 1973, 'Fascism, the Mafia, and the emergence of Sicilian separatism (1919–43)', *Journal of Modern History* (Chicago), June 1973, pp. 261–76.

RENDA, F., 1972, *Socialisti e cattolici in Sicilia 1900–1904. Le lotte agrarie* (Caltanissetta – Rome).

————, 1984–87, *Storia della Sicilia dal 1860 al 1970*, 3 vols: vol. I, *I caratteri originari e gli anni della unificazione italiana*; vol. II, *Dalla caduta della Destra al fascismo*; vol. III. *Dall'occupazione militare alleata al centro-sinistra* (Palermo).

RICASOLI, B., 1968 and 1970, *Carteggi di Bettino Ricasoli*, vols. 23, 24 (ed. S. Camerani and G. Arfè) (Istituto storico italiano per l'età moderna e contemporanea, Rome).

ROCHAT, G., 1967, *L'esercito italiano da Vittorio Veneto a Mussolini (1919–1925)* (Bari).

ROMANO, S.F., 1964, *Storia della mafia*, 2nd edition (Milan).

ROMEO, R., 1970, *Il Risorgimento in Sicilia*, new edition (Bari).

RUINI, C., 1946, *Le vicende del latifondo siciliano* (Florence).

RUSSO N. (ed.), 1968, *Antologia della mafia* (Palermo).

SABETTI, F., 1984, *Political Authority in a Sicilian Village* (New Brunswick).

SALVATORELLI, L., and MIRA, G., 1956, *Storia d'Italia nel periodo fascista* (Turin).

SALVEMINI, G., 1936, *Under the Axe of Fascism* (London).

SALVIOLI, G., 1927, 'Gabelloti e latifondo in Sicilia', *Echi e commenti* (Rome), 5 September 1927, pp. 8–9.

SANSONE, V., and INGRASCÌ, G., 1950, *Sei anni di banditismo in Sicilia* (Milan).

SANTARELLI, E., 1967, *Storia del movimento e del regime fascista*, 2 vols. (Rome).

SCHMIDT, C.T., 1938, *The Plough and the Sword. Labor, Land, and Property in Fascist Italy* (New York)

SCHNEIDER, H., and CLOUGH, S., 1929, *Making Fascists* (Chicago).

SCIASCIA, L., 1964, 'Appunti su mafia e letteratura', *Nuovi quaderni del Meridione* (Palermo), January–March 1964, pp. 118–26.

———, 1975, *Le parocchie di Regalpetra*, new edition (Bari).

SCICHILONE, G., (ed.), 1952, *Documenti sulle condizioni della Sicilia dal 1860 al 1870* (Rome).

SCIROCCO, A., 1979, *Il Mezzogiorno nell'Italia unita (1861–65)* (Naples).

SERENI, E., 1946, *La questione agraria nella rinascita nazionale italiana* (Rome).

———, 1968, *Il capitalismo nelle campagne, 1860–1900*, new edition (Turin).

SERPIERI, A., 1930, *La Guerra e le classi rurali italiane* (Bari).

———, 1932, *La legge sulla bonifica integrale nel secondo anno di applicazione* (Rome).

SIRENA, S., 1927, *L'agricoltura passata e presente attraverso le leggi del governo nazionale e l'opera di Cesare Mori* (unpublished typescript, 23 May 1927, in ASP CM 17).

SMITH, D.C., 1975, *The Mafia Mystique* (London).

'IL SOLITARIO', 1923, *La malavita in Sicilia e l'azione fascista* (Palermo).

SONNINO 1974, *see* Franchetti and Sonnino, vol. II.

SPAMPANATO, B., 1933, *Idee e baionette* (Naples).

SPANÒ, A., 1978, *Faccia a faccia con la mafia* (Milan).

STAJANO, C. (ed.), 1986, *Mafia. L'atto d'accusa dei giudici di Palermo* (Rome).

STAMPACCHIA, M., 1978, 'Sull "assalto" al latifondo siciliano', *Rivista di storia contemporanea* (Turin), October 1978, pp. 586–610.

STILLMAN, W.J. ('X'), 1891a, 'The mafia', *The Nation* (New York), 9 April 1891, p. 296.

———, 1891b, 'The maffia once more', *The Nation* (New York), 23 April 1891, pp. 337–9.

SVIMEZ (Associazione per lo sviluppo dell'industria nel Mezzogiorno), 1954, *Statistiche sul Mezzogiorno d'Italia 1861–1953* (Rome).

———, 1957, *Legislazione per il Mezzogiorno 1861–1957*, 2 vols. (Rome).

SYLOS-LABINI, P., (ed.), 1966, *Problemi dell'economia siciliana* (Milan).

TANNENBAUM, E.R., 1973, *Fascism in Italy. Society and Culture 1922–1945* (London).

TASSINARI, G., 1938, *La bonifica integrale nel decennale della Legge Mussolini* (Rome).

TOMMASI CRUDELI, C., 1871, *La Sicilia nel 1871* (Florence).

TREVELYAN, R., 1972, *Princes under the Volcano* (London).

VACCARO, A., 1899, 'La mafia', *Rivista d'Italia* (Rome), vol. III, 1899, pp. 686–704.

VENERUSO, D., 1975, *La vigilia del fascismo. Il primo ministero Facta nella crisi dello stato liberale in Italia*, 3rd edition (Bologna).

VETRI, G., 1976, 'Le origini del fascismo in Sicilia', *Nuovi quaderni del Meridione* (Palermo), January–March 1976, pp. 33–81.

VILLARI, P., 1972, *Le lettere meridionali ed altri scritti sulla questione sociale in Italia* (ed. L. Chiti) (Turin).

VIRNICCHI, P., 1935, *L'evoluzione della coscienza politica del popolo meridionale*, 2nd edition (Naples).

VIZZINI, A., 1880, *La mafia* (Rome).

VOLPE, G., 1925, 'Ripensando al congresso fascista', *Gerarchia* (Milan), August 1925, pp. 483–95.

WASHBURN CHILD, R., 1929, 'How Mussolini smashed the Mafia', Sunday supplement to *La Nación* (Buenos Aires), 24 February 1929.

WHITE MARIO, J., 1891a, 'Maffia, Camorra, brigandage – alias crime', *The Nation* (New York), 16 April 1891, pp. 314–15.

———, 1891b, 'Italy and the United States', *The Nineteenth Century* (London), May 1891, pp. 701–18.

WOLFFSOHN, L., 1891, 'Italian secret societies', *The Contemporary Review* (London), May 1891, pp. 691–6.

ZANOTTI-BIANCO, U., 1964, *Meridione e meridionalisti* (Rome).

ZINGALI, G., 1933, *Liberalismo e fascismo nel Mezzogiorno d'Italia*, vol. I, 1860–1922; vol. II, 1923–1932 (Milan).

The following newspapers were consulted for Part II:

Alalà (Palermo), 1925

Avanti! (Milan), 1924–26

L'Avvenire di Sicilia (Palermo), 1924–27

Avvisatore (Palermo), 1923–27

Il Babbio (Palermo), 1921–24

Baluardo (Trapani), 1924

Battaglie Fasciste (Caltanissetta), 1926–28

Corriere della Sera (Milan), 1925–27

Il Corriere di Sicilia (Catania), 1925–27

Il Corriere Marittimo Siciliano (Palermo), 1924–29

Daily Herald (London), 1926–28

Daily Mail (London), 1928

La Difesa (Palermo), 1920–23

L'Eco della Sicilia e delle Calabrie (Messina), 1925–26

Era Nova (Caltanissetta), 1926

La Fiamma (Palermo), 1923–27

La Fiamma Nazionale (Palermo), 1920–24

Fiamma Nera (Alcamo), 1923

Gazzetta Commerciale ed Agricola del Mezzogiorno (Palermo), 1924–27

Gazzetta di Messina e delle Calabrie (Messina), 1925–26

Il Giornale di Sicilia (Palermo), 1924–29

Il Giornale Fascista (Trapani), 1922–23

L'Idea Ennese (Castrogiovanni), 1927

L'Idea Nazionale (Rome), 1923

L'Indipendente (Palermo), 1925–26

Il Littorio (Trapani), 1925–29

Il Martello (Palermo), 1923

Il Massello (Marsala), 1923–24

Il Mezzogiorno (Palermo), 1920–23

Il Mezzogiorno d'Italia (Palermo), 1923

Notiziario Canicattinese (Canicattì), 1927

The Observer (London), 1925–28

L'Ora (Palermo), 1924–29

L'Osservatore Romano (Rome), 1926–28

Piff Paff (Palermo), 1924–29

Il Popolo di Sicilia (Palermo), 1920–23

Il Popolo d'Italia (Milan), 1925–29

La Provincia (Caltanissetta), 1926–28

Regime Fascista (Cremona), 1930

La Regione (Palermo), 1921–22

Il Rinnovamento (Mazara), 1924–25

Il Risveglio Zootecnico (Trapani), 1924–26

Il Salso (Caltanissetta), 1925–26

Santa Riscossa (Alcamo), 1924–25

Sicilia Agricola (Palermo), 1924; new series, 1927–30

Sicilia Fascista (Caltanissetta), 1923–26

Sicilia Nuova (Palermo), 1925–7

Sicilia Zootecnica (Palermo), 1927–30

La Stampa (Turin), 1926–28

Sunday Times (London), 1926–28

Il Tevere (Rome), 1925–27

The Times (London), 1925–29

La Tribuna (Rome), 1926–28

La Vanga (Trapani), 1923

La Vedetta Fascista (Trapani), 1923–24

La Vittoria (Palermo), 1923–24

Il Vomere (Marsala), 1924–25

INDEX

188–9, 208, 222, 241
powers of in Sicily, 165, 168
mistrust of in fascist party, 123–4, 128
relations with local fascists, 127, 166,
  172–2
relations with Cucco, 128, 130, 165–6,
  168, 170–2, 175
and destruction of Cucco, 77, 112, 174–7,
  179, 255–6
relations with government, 143, 165, 179,
  181–2, 187, 248, 250–1, 254
support from Federzoni, 165, 167, 174
relations with landowners, 121, 127,
  177–8, 195, 252, 258
relations with peasantry, 126, 138, 139,
  152, 153, 208–9, 212, 221, 252
popularity of his campaign, 137, 138, 143,
  152, 212, 221, 247
opposition to his campaign, 139, 171, 179,
  186–7
and destruction of Di Giorgio, 248–50,
  252, 255
ordinances of, 131, 194–5
rhetoric of, 122, 214, 216
visits of to provincial towns, 212, 216–17,
  252–3; Pls. 14, 15
and purge of Palermo bureaucracy, 189–92
and promotion of agriculture, 142, 252
and liberation of latifondi, 194–6, 199
and promotion of work ethic, 189, 202,
  215
and propaganda and education, 142,
  200–2, 209–11, 214–5
and defence of private property, 189,
  200–2
as executor of fascist policies, 212–14
and 1929 plebiscite, 254–5
withdrawal from Palermo, 257–8, 265
as a writer, 122–3, 259–60
later career of, 258–60
criticisms of his campaign, 225–6, 238–9,
  240, 246–8
foreign perceptions of his campaign, 225,
  232–3, 253, 260
Mosca, Gaetano, 73–4, 158
Mosca, Gaspare, 17
Musotto, Francesco, 105
Mussolini, Arnaldo, 190, 251
Mussolini, Benito, 85, 95, 96, 99, 101, 114,
  116, 117, 118–19, 130, 144, 179, 212,
  214, 220–1, 230, 245, 261
views on mafia, 119, 146, 182, 230
visits to Sicily (1923, 1924, 1937), 112, 119,
  124, 220, 270; Pls. 6, 7
relations with Mori, 77, 123, 137, 179,
  181–2, 187, 248, 250, 257

Naples, 64
Nasi, Nunzio, 51, 127

Nationalists, 50, 104, 105, 181
Navarra Crimi, Gaetano, 144
Newman, John, 20
New Orleans, 43–6
newspapers, during Mori's campaign,
  128–30, 147, 178, 180, 221, 228, 230,
  232, 253
New York, 4
Niceforo, Alfredo, 41
Nicotri, Gaspare, 22
Nitti, (Fausto) Francesco, 86
Nitti, Francesco Saverio, 103, 177
nobility, see latifondisti
Normans, 8
Notarbartolo, Emanuele, Marquis, 43, 47
Notarbartolo, Leopoldo, 47

omertà, 31, 40, 46, 54, 55–7, 61, 64, 67, 69,
  132, 139–40, 215, 241
Opera Nazionale per i Combattenti, see
  Servicemen's Association
oranges, see fruit
Orcel, Giovanni, 100, 282
Orlando, Vittorio Emanuele, 114, 117, 158
Ortoleva, Antonino, 150, 234–5, 237, 249
Oviglio, Aldo, 123

Palazzo Adriano, 154, 155
Palermo, 8, 55, 168, 204, 264
  administration of during fascist period,
    189–91, 192–3, 264
Palizzolo, Raffaele, 47–8, 51
Pantaleoni, Diomede, 53
Partito Siciliano, 51
Pascazio, Nicola, 180
Pasquale, 32
Pasqualino Vassallo, Rosario, 116
Paternostro, Paolo, 35
Paternostro, Roberto, 171, 256–7, 267
patriotism, local, see sicilianismo
peasants, 10, 11, 37, 64, 67, 78, 81, 82, 107,
  194, 199, 202, 210–11, 215, 219–20,
  221, 264, 270, 273
  and land occupations, 85, 97, 194
  attitudes to Mori's campaign, 198–9, 212,
    221, 247
  relations with landowners, 9, 79, 83,
    210–11
Pellegrino, Giuseppe, 124, 127
Petacco, Arrigo, 172–3
Phalaris, 7
Phillips, Percival, 253
Piana dei Colli, 149, 224
Piana dei Greci (Piana degli Albanesi), 102;
  Pl. 14
Pica Law, 24
Piedmont, Piedmontese, 9, 12, 22
Pinna, Felice, 60
Pisanelli Commission (1867), 30, 56